Cottage to Crèche
Family Change in Ireland

Finola Kennedy

IPA
INSTITUTE OF PUBLIC
ADMINISTRATION

First published 2001
Institute of Public Administration
57–61 Lansdowne Road
Dublin 4
Ireland

ISBN   1 902448 58 8
          1 902448 62 6

British Library Cataloguing-in-Publication Data
A catalogue record for this book is available from the British Library.

Cover design by Creative Inputs
Typeset in 10/12.5 Times Roman by Carole Lynch, Dublin
Printed by Future Print

In memory of
Nora Stack and Frank Flanagan

Contents

Preface

Throughout most of the twentieth century, Irish family patterns were distinctive, and provided a major exception to generally prevailing European patterns. The Irish had late ages at marriage combined with enormous rates of spinsterhood and very low levels of births outside marriage. Yet at the same time Irish women had large families because little birth control was used within marriage, and few married Irish women participated in the labour force. The Irish Constitution even proclaimed that homemaking was a natural activity for women.

During a span of a mere few decades starting mainly during the third quarter of the twentieth century, Irish family life has undergone a remarkable transformation. Ireland is no longer an exception to European family patterns, and it is merely at the high end of a more or less continuous variation in fertility among members of the European Community. Irish fertility rates have joined other European nations at below replacement levels, and births to unmarried mothers now comprise 30 per cent of all Irish births. About 40 per cent of married women are working, and an increasing number are the main, and sometimes sole, economic provider for their children. Divorce rates have been picking up since divorce was legalised by the referendum of 1995, and appear to be still growing.

Finola Kennedy documents these changes in Irish family patterns as she returns to this fascinating subject in her new book. But she does much more than describe what happened. She shows how changes in Irish families resulted from developments in the economy, new government policies, and changing moral and other values. In my judgement, she correctly puts greatest emphasis on the economic changes.

Farmers in traditional agriculture benefit greatly from having children who can help with farm chores, and as late as 1950, about 40 per cent of all Irish families were on farms. But by the end of the century, less than 10 per cent of the population worked in agriculture. Work opportunities of urban women are typically in shops or factories, and hence are less compatible with the childcare requirements of large families than is working on farms.

Moreover, urban employment is much more remunerative to educated individuals, so parents who are concerned about their children's future tend to shift away from having many uneducated children toward having fewer, more educated, children. It is also difficult for elderly parents and grown children to share the cramped quarters in towns and cities, so urban older men and women are more likely to live separately from their children than are the rural elderly.

Kennedy also documents how the Irish government responded to these economic developments. Although the Irish Constitution introduced in 1937 proclaimed that the place of women was in the home, various governments during the rest of the century recognised the profound changes occurring in family patterns. For example, laws that required children to support their elderly parents were replaced by more generous programmes of government-financed old age support.

Overturning a law passed in 1935, the sale of contraceptives became legal, despite the Church's continuing opposition. Allowances to help defray the cost of rearing children were introduced in the 1940s, and these were expanded in subsequent decades. Public support to unmarried mothers began in the 1970s, which helped encourage the rapid growth in the number of children born to single mothers during the 1980s and 1990s.

Income tax reforms in the 1980s reduced the taxes of married women by using tax rates appropriate to their own lower earnings instead of rates applicable to higher family earnings that included the earnings of husbands. The government managed in 1995 to obtain a slight majority on a referendum to approve the legalisation of divorce, despite the vocal opposition of the Catholic Church.

This defeat for the Church is one of the most dramatic indications of its declining influence over the behaviour of most Irish men and women, including those who consider themselves quite devout. Over 90 per cent of the Irish continue to report that they are Catholic, but their behaviour clearly shows that they break with the Church on many issues related to the family. Their low fertility rates are achieved through extensive use of contraceptives, despite the Church's opposition to all mechanical methods of birth control. Their high out-of-wedlock birth rate contradicts Church teaching that marriage is the only legitimate basis for reproduction. And a majority supported legalising divorce in the face of the Church's opposition.

Even religious women began to rely on contraception because changes in the economy reduced the advantages of large families. Increasing employment opportunities for women raised their financial independence, and hence stimulated their interest in divorce when their marriages were failing. Despite the conflict induced in many men and women by the differences between their behaviour and church doctrine, most persons attended mass and definitely continued to believe that they are Catholics.

The struggle between economic incentives and religious beliefs probably slowed down the Irish adjustment to changes that affected preferred family arrangements. However, one does not have to be an 'economic determinist' to recognise that economic incentives ultimately won this struggle, as it has won similar struggles elsewhere in the world. Indeed not only is the decline in Irish fertility remarkable, but so too is that the lowest fertility rates anywhere are found in Catholic nations such as Spain, Italy and Portugal, whereas a half century ago Catholic nations generally had considerably higher fertility rates than Protestant ones.

These and other developments are detailed in this valuable study of the evolution, indeed revolution, in Irish family life that took place during the twentieth century. Changes in family patterns are discussed carefully, and they are linked to developments in the economy, public policies, and religious beliefs. I benefited greatly from reading this study, and I am confident that others will too, be they economist, sociologist, or anyone else who might be intrigued by the fascinating changes in Ireland during the past 100 years.

Gary S. Becker
University of Chicago

Acknowledgements

Without the expertise and generosity of many people, I would not have written this book. Words of encouragement from Gary Becker were very important to me. At times when I asked myself if the book was worth the effort, the fact that he thought it worthwhile, found time to read the manuscript and to write a *Preface*, was sustaining.

Some years ago, when Paddy Lynch asked me if I had any work in hands, I told him about a project on family change. From that moment he persisted with enquiries and assistance until I had finished. My debt to Paddy goes back to my student days at UCD and extends beyond economics, as it does to Bishop James Kavanagh who also commented on an earlier draft. Seán Cromien, Tony Fahey, Charles Lysaght, Margaret MacCurtain, Aidan Punch and Brendan Walsh read drafts, or substantial parts of drafts. Each one made suggestions over a range of topics.

In assembling material for the book a number of librarians and archivists were exceptionally helpful. In particular I would like to thank Mary Prendergast very specially and those who work, or have worked, with her in the IPA: Mary Guckian, Joanne Grimes, Marie Kilcullen, Renuka Page and Trudi Pirkl; Fergus O'Donoghue, SJ and Mary Cunningham in the Jesuit Library in Milltown, Eithne Meldon in UCD, Elizabeth Gleeson in Trinity College, as well as librarians in the National Library and the Gilbert Library. Archivists Helen Hewson, David Sheehy, Orna Somerville and Thomas Quinlan were all most helpful.

When the book was well under way I decided that I should try to talk to certain political figures in relation to policies significant to the story of family change. I confined myself to those who had retired from active politics. Those I approached all generously agreed to give their time. They were Dr Patrick Hillery, former President of Ireland and first Commissioner of the European Union for Social Affairs; and former Taoisigh: Liam Cosgrave, Garret FitzGerald and Charles Haughey. Through his father, W.T. Cosgrave, Liam Cosgrave reaches back to the establishment of the State, while the father-in-law of Charles Haughey, Seán Lemass, was in the first Fianna Fáil Government in 1932 and later, Taoiseach.

Lucy Cantwell, Jack Jones, Ita Healy, Gerard Hogan, SC, James McPolin, SJ, Donal Nevin, Máire and Conor Cruise O'Brien, Séamus Ó Cinnéide, Matt Russell and T.K. Whitaker all gave time to discuss different aspects of the study. The enthusiasm of Margaret Ó hÓgartaigh who came to me in relation to work of her own, and ended by exhorting me to press on with my work, was infectious.

The following helped either with material, ideas or comment: Deirdre Carroll, Catherine Conway, Mary Cullen, Maura Dempsey, Margaret Dromey, Lindsay Earner, Harry Ferguson, John FitzGerald, the late Michael Fogarty, Peter Gaffey, Robbie Gilligan, Catherine Haslett, Seán Healy, SMA, Mary Heanue, the late Maurice Hearne, John Horgan, Mary Horkan, Franz-Xaver Kaufmann, Adrian Kelly, Rev Donal Kelly, Simon Lang, Tony McCashin, Brian Nolan, Senator David Norris, Cormac Ó Gráda, Brian Ó Raghallaigh, Eoin O'Sullivan, Joseph Robins, Hans-Joachim Schulze, Elaine Soffe, Klaus Peter Strohmeier and Gerry Whyte. To these and to many civil servants in the Central Statistics Office, the Revenue Commissioners, the Departments of Social, Community and Family Affairs and in several other Government Departments, I offer my thanks.

Noel Barber, SJ, Editor of *Studies*, was most helpful regarding related work on the contribution of Edward Cahill, SJ, to the Constitution, as well as work on the Carrigan Report.

Tony McNamara and his publishing team, Eleanor Ashe in particular, merit special thanks for a job well done. I am grateful to Helen Litton for help in preparing the index.

Special thanks are also due to the late Anne Dunne. Like my family, her help extended far beyond this book. My sister, Deirdre, and my late sister, Peggy, helped me in one way or another for as long as I can remember. Kieran read an earlier draft and once I received his *imprimatur*, I began to believe that the finishing post was in reach, if not in sight. In addition to explaining the mysteries of computers to me, Michael produced the graphs. His expertise, calm and patience were invaluable. Kieran F.'s advice to keep writing short pieces, but to keep writing, Lucy's experience in the publishing world, the support of Ruth and Susan, the buoyant optimism of Frank who spoke confidently about 'the book', long before I thought in such concrete terms myself, transformed what might have been just hard work into enjoyment. My hope now is that readers also may find something of enjoyment in the book.

1 May 2001

Chronology

1903   *Irish Land Act*
1908   *Old Age Pensions Act*
1910   Founding of the Irish Countrywomen's Association (ICA, called United
       Irishwomen, until 1934)
1924   National Council of Women of Ireland (NCWI) founded
1935   Widows' and Orphans' Pensions
1935   Joint Committee of Women's Societies and Social Workers (JCWSSW)
1935   *Criminal Law Amendment Act*
1936   *Conditions of Employment Act*
1937   The Constitution
1941   Founding of the Irish Housewives' Association (IHA)
1944   Children's Allowances
1951   Mother and Child Crisis
1952   *Adoption Act*
1961   Opening of Radio Telefís Éireann
1965   *Succession Act*
1968   *Humanae Vitae*
1972   Report of the Commission on the Status of Women
1972   Council for the Status of Women (CSW) founded
1973   Entry to EEC
1973   Unmarried Mothers' Allowance
1977   *Employment Equality Act*
1979   *Family Planning Act*
1980   Murphy Case – Taxation of Families
1983   Abortion Referendum
1986   First Divorce Referendum
1989   *Judicial Separation and Family Law Reform Act*
1993   Report of the Second Commission on the Status of Women
1995   Second Divorce Referendum
1998   Report of the Commission on the Family

1

Introduction

Context and theme

For much of the twentieth century family patterns in Ireland differed from those in other European countries. Analysis based on marriage, birth and fertility rates, at intervals across the century, could lead to the conclusion that the Irish experience was unique. A contention of this book is that while, in many respects, family change in Ireland constitutes a special case, it has followed a path similar to other European countries. A commonly held belief is that the Roman Catholic Church, through its social and moral teaching, has been a dominant influence on family behaviour patterns in Ireland. In this book it is argued that, while Church thinking and teaching have indeed been significant, economic influences tended to dominate.

The story of family change in Ireland is both unique, and at the same time, similar to that of many other countries. Throughout the developed world there has been a movement towards a plurality of family forms, accompanied by a decline in fertility, in turn linked to economic and cultural modernisation (Van de Kaa, 1987). Emphasis has been placed on the uniqueness of Irish family patterns in the past (Commission on Emigration, 1954; Coleman, 1992; Fahey/FitzGerald, 1997). In this context, timing is crucial. To the extent that demographic variables portray family change, Ireland was a late starter, especially by contrast with her closest neighbour, Great Britain. At the time of Irish Independence in 1922, Britain was the most industrialised country in Europe, while Ireland was predominantly an agrarian society, in which the small farm provided the economic base for a majority of families. The tendency to view Irish demography as unique is part of the wider emphasis on 'exceptionalism' as a fundamental of Irish history. One example which captures this general idea neatly is the opening sentence of John Ardagh's book, *Ireland and the Irish*: 'Ireland has always been a special case' (Ardagh, 1995: 1).

In a passage critical of some of her fellow historians, Mary Daly calls for a balanced interpretation: 'By definition, the history of every nation is unique; however, while being aware of this truism, it remains important not to lose sight of the extent to which developments in different societies follow similar paths' (Daly, 1997: 103). In an article published in 1992, David Coleman wrote, 'The demography of Ireland has been unique in Europe since the nineteenth century' (Coleman, 1992). He went on to say that convergence with the rest of Europe was taking place quite rapidly. In 1997, in a study entitled *The Welfare Implications of Demographic Change,* Tony Fahey and John FitzGerald also stated that the Irish experience was unique (Fahey/FitzGerald, 1997).

The interpretation of demographic changes in twentieth-century Ireland which is adopted in this book is in sympathy with the approach adopted by Timothy Guinnane in his study of Irish demography in the period from the Famine to the Great War (Guinnane, 1997). Guinnane fits features of Irish demography into a more general framework, rather than relying on the 'uniqueness' interpretation. He also sets out Ireland's demographic experience in a broader European context. Every country has its own demographic peculiarities. In mid-Victorian England, for example, almost one-third of women aged 20-44 years had to remain spinsters because of a higher death rate for males, especially in infancy, and the fact that the available reservoir of men had been depleted due to wars and migration to the colonies (Fox Harding, 1996:48). For the first half of the century Irish patterns of marriage, births and labour force participation were out of line with the rest of Western Europe. On closer inspection, and with the benefit of a longer time horizon, it emerges that the pace and timing of modernisation in Ireland differed, but the pathway travelled was similar. Until the 1960s, Irish patterns might be described as conservative; on the other hand from around 1980, the pace of modernisation was more rapid than elsewhere, so that changes in demographic indicators which occurred in Ireland within a decade, occurred over a longer time-span elsewhere.

By the 1930s the industrialised world had reached the last stages of the demographic transition that began around the 1870s, from high birth rates and high death rates to a pattern of low birth and low death rates. In a comparative study of European demographic trends, Van de Kaa shows that by 1985, fertility rates in Europe were below the replacement level of 2.1 births per woman in every country except Ireland, Albania, Malta, Poland and Turkey, having declined steadily from a post-war peak of 2.5 in most countries. Ten years later fertility rates in Ireland had fallen below replacement level:

> The decline to low fertility in the 1930s during Europe's first demographic transition was propelled by a concern for family and offspring. Behind the second transition is a dramatic shift in norms toward progressiveness and individualism, which is moving Europeans away from marriage and parenthood. Cohabitation and out-of-wedlock fertility are increasingly acceptable; having a child is more and more a deliberate choice made to achieve greater self-fulfilment (Van de Kaa, 1987: foreword).

The Irish marriage rate remained well below the average for Western Europe until the years prior to 1980. The catastrophe of the Famine one hundred and fifty years earlier left a deep imprint on the Irish psyche. Because children then followed marriage in plentiful numbers, marriage could bring starvation; it was a case of, 'Marry if you can afford to do so.' It was not until the economic upswing of the 1960s that marriage became both possible and popular on a scale comparable to other European countries. By 1980 the Irish marriage rate was above the European average (based on eight European countries), but had fallen below it once more by 1990 and remained below it in 1997 (Table A.1.2). The birth rate, while well below that in Italy and the Netherlands, was actually above the average in the decade 1926-35, notwithstanding the lower than average marriage rate.[1] Given a low level of births outside marriage, this implies higher than average fertility of marriage. As the birth rate fell in Europe during the 1970s, it remained high in Ireland, so that in 1980 the birth rate in Ireland was just 22, compared with an average of 13.6 for a group of eight European countries. The birth rate tapered off to 13.5 in 1995, but rose again to 14.2 in 1997, leaving Ireland clearly at the top of the scale (Table A.1.3).

The characteristics which marked family life until the 1960s and 1970s – low marriage rates combined with high fertility of those who did marry, together with a high incidence of permanent bachelorhood and spinsterhood – were the chief factors that led to the characterisation of Irish demography as unique (Commission on Emigration, 1954; Coleman, 1992). When the dramatic changes that have occurred in Irish family patterns since the late 1970s are viewed alongside the 'unique' patterns of the rest of the century, an alternative interpretation – that of the 'late starter' – emerges. According to this view Ireland fits in at the lower end of the scale of the general pattern of demographic transformation associated with economic development. Thus the pattern, which was spearheaded by the Nordic countries, in particular Sweden, was followed by Ireland at a later date, but at a very rapid pace once change started. A comprehensive explanation seeks to combine the two elements of 'uniqueness' and 'late starter'. This suggests that while general trends undoubtedly exist, national cultural-specific factors are also very important. This more complex interpretation may be illustrated by an example from four different countries in the 1980s. In a study of ten European countries between 1980 and 1990, Ireland and Sweden were the two with the highest total fertility rates, while Italy and West Germany had the lowest rates (Kaufmann *et al* (eds), 1997). However, with regard to patterns of family life, Ireland was closest to Italy, while Italy differed markedly from West Germany. These findings illustrate strong cross-national variations, related to a range of factors that include culture, ideology and policy. Thus it cannot be assumed that Sweden, for example, provides a picture of Ireland's demographic future (Kaufmann *et al*, 1997).

An illustration of the importance of the culture-specific context is provided by a policy measure: the timing of the introduction of the prohibition against contraceptives and the subsequent removal of that prohibition (see Chapters 7 and 9). Legal prohibition against contraceptives was introduced at a relatively late date in Ireland compared with France, Belgium and Italy, but earlier than in Germany and Spain, while the prohibition was removed latest in Ireland, one year after it was removed in Spain (Table A.1.4). Ireland, while not the first country to make contraceptives illegal, was the last to legalise their use. A study by Francis Castles of the Australian National University suggests that cross-national variation in the relationship between modernisation and fertility in the 1970s 'was hugely influenced by the differential adoption of modern contraceptive practices'; fertility in Ireland, Portugal and Spain was 'elevated by the fact that they were in the rearguard of modern contraceptive use' (Castles, 1998:17).

Two important reasons why Ireland was a 'late starter' may be located in the later onset of economic development and the gradual slackening in the influence on behaviour of the major cultural matrix – the Catholic Church. Economic development, accompanied by a shift away from agriculture, led to a weakening of the economic imperatives that bound together family members, often at considerable cost to individuals. Economic development provided greater occupational opportunities and lifestyle choices for individual men and women, while greatly extended educational opportunities meant that children could achieve levels of education far above those of their parents. At the same time economic prosperity meant that the state, via welfare payments and other schemes, could replace certain activities of families. Thus the state, in endeavouring to support family members, modified the overall economic responsibilities of the family. These economic and policy elements were associated with major changes in values.

In the most recent census, 1991, during which a question concerning religious affiliation was posed, 91.6 per cent of the population was Catholic. This compares with 92.6 per cent at the first census of the State in 1926. Nonetheless, a range of indicators, including births outside marriage and the increased use of contraception, show a behavioural drift from the tenets of the Catholic Church. In less prosperous times a value system based on traditional Catholic tenets was a given fact of Irish life, informing legislation, government policies and behaviour. This has changed, and the change has been reflected in legislation, policy and behaviour. Two broad strands of Catholic teaching have been of special significance. These are the *social teaching* which laid stress on the family as the basic unit group of society, on the entitlement of the family breadwinner to a living wage to support his wife and dependants, and for the family to provide as far as possible for its own requirements in accordance with the principle of subsidiarity; and the *moral teaching*, the term more often used in relation to sexual behaviour.

At the mid-point of the twentieth century Alexander Humphreys, an American professor of sociology who was also a Jesuit priest, studied the process of urbanisation of the family in Dublin between 1949 and 1951. He could then confidently, and correctly, conclude that the transformation observed in the family life of the 'New Dubliners', that is those who lived in the city but who had at least one country-born parent, was mainly the result of organisational changes due to economic factors, rather than the effect of any profound ideological shift:

The Irish religious conception of the purposes of human existence; the premium it places on religious, particularly sacramental activity; the tempered importance it attaches to business activity as a result; the strong code of sexual morality bearing on pre-marital relations; and the mode of family limitation and the manner of dealing with irreconcilable conflicts between spouses – all these ideological elements clearly affect its organisation and distinguish the typical Irish urban family from typical urban families in societies where different ideological values prevail (Humphreys, 1966: 227).

The opening of Ireland to the wider world via the media gradually introduced a secular value system. The media, including newspapers, cinema, radio and television, provided an alternative pulpit to the Church whose tenets came to be viewed as less relevant to family life, and at times in conflict with the interests of individual family members. The impact of the Second Vatican Council, together with the increase in educational opportunities from the late 1960s, encouraged people to think for themselves. When *Humanae Vitae* was published in 1968, it was greeted with open challenge, rather than docile and automatic acceptance. The Women's Movement in Ireland, and the evident determination of women to limit their childbearing, coincided with the development of the economy and an increased range of employment possibilities for women. Economic development brought new options and new choices.

To understand family change, it is necessary to understand the change in roles and behaviour of individuals – men, women and children – within the family. How was their behaviour shaped and reshaped by economic forces, by policies and by values in such a way that the collective unit, 'the family', was transformed? In analysing demographic changes in Ireland in the late nineteenth and early twentieth centuries, Guinnane, drawing on the work of Becker, views demographic patterns as '… the outcome of individual behaviors motivated by Irish men and women's efforts to make their way in the world' (Guinnane, 1997: 16-18). Aggregate demographic patterns reflect the decisions of individuals. The economic, the policy and the values elements are three arches on which the family edifice is based. Because of the dominance of agriculture in the Irish economy until after 1960, choices open to men and women for at least the first half of the century were heavily influenced by the pattern of agriculture. Family farms were maintained intact through a combination of high celibacy rates, high emigration rates and high fertility amongst those who did marry, thus ensuring a pool of family labour to work on the farm. The desire to expand the family holding was great. In 1996, Tom Clinton, leader of the Irish Farmers' Association stated, 'The basic ambition of any farmer is to leave a bigger and better farm on the day he dies than on the day he inherited. There are many who would put their farm before their family' (*The Irish Times*, 17 August, 1996).

The tradition that the farm must be maintained regardless of the cost to individual family members was deeply embedded and, for the small farmer, was grounded in economic reality. A strict sexual code was necessitated by economic facts. The preferences of individuals could be subordinated to economic considerations through the dowry system and the control that parents exercised over the marriages of their children. As historian Seán Connolly remarks, 'Rural societies in which the family unit is central to the working of the land can rarely afford to allow their members to conduct their personal lives in such a free and easy manner' (Connolly, 1985: 95). The demise of the small family farm, finally sealed by the transformation of Irish agriculture following entry into the EEC in 1973, was the catalyst leading to the modernisation of family patterns since the 1970s.

Land, family and Church form a trinity which dominated much of Irish life at least until the 1960s. The move from the land, and the severing of the links that bound families to the land in a manner essential to their survival, was accompanied by a weakening of Church influence on the behaviour of the people. As long as widespread celibacy, combined with high fertility of those marriages that did take place, was essential to economic survival, these practices persisted. When both the economic structure changed, and the possibility to decouple sexual activity from procreation was made possible by the availability of contraceptives, Irish family patterns were transformed. In addition, a greatly expanded social welfare system, including allowances for lone parents, removed the economic penalties of extra-marital parenthood, while the advent of legal abortion in Britain following the *Abortion Act*, 1967, contributed to a silencing of Church criticism of extra-marital births, because henceforth such criticism might be interpreted as encouraging women to choose abortion.

A tendency which may be regarded as peculiarly Irish might be described as the 'Pierrepoint syndrome', that is the tendency to solve awkward problems by recourse to Britain. When capital punishment existed in Ireland, ordinary hangings, as distinct from military executions, were carried out by the English hangman, Albert Pierrepoint, who travelled to Ireland for the purpose. We did not have our own Irish hangman. Likewise until the late 1990s we did not have divorce or legal abortion in Ireland, yet many Irish people obtained foreign divorces; and 93,000 abortions, the equivalent of almost twice the total births in 1998, were obtained by Irish women in the UK between 1973 and 1998. We live in a wider world and this was the case even in the days when it was much less obvious because international communications and travel were more limited. Ideas on the role of women have changed radically. The idea that de Valera and the Catholic hierarchy, in particular the Catholic Archbishop of Dublin, Dr John Charles McQuaid, were, as a result of their study of Catholic teaching, largely responsible for the notion that a woman's place was in the home, and that they embedded this idea in the Irish Constitution in 1937, is not the whole truth. While, as we shall see, the role of Catholic social teaching was of paramount importance in the formulation of the Constitution, and in particular in the formulation of the Articles referring to the home and family, similar ideas were widely held outside Ireland. One of the most memorable statements regarding the role of women in the home is found in the Beveridge Report published in 1942. Beveridge says, 'In the next thirty years housewives as mothers have vital work to do in ensuring the adequate continuance of the British race and of British ideals in the world' (Beveridge, 1942: 53).

World War II brought an upsurge in the participation of women in the workforce all over Europe. After the War came the baby boom, followed in turn by a decline in fertility, a drift from marriage and a pluralisation of family forms. Ireland marched to the same drum, but at her own pace and in her own style. It is precisely because Irish patterns were out of step, and then converged, yet retained their own distinctiveness, that the Irish case is so interesting. Nobel laureate Gary Becker has pointed out that, 'It is well-known in the social sciences that the underlying causes of changes are usually most easily seen from behaviour that deviates far from the norm' (Becker, 1989: xv). Thus an examination of family change in Ireland provides more than a case study; it provides an insight into the factors driving family change in general. The objective of this book is to chart the path of family change in Ireland over the twentieth century, and to try to understand and interpret that change. No sweeping claims are made for the interpretation offered. In the future other interpretations and other data may be presented; that is how understanding proceeds. In that sense the book is no more than a contribution to continuing work in progress in a particular field of research. Historians including Connell (1950), Fitzpatrick (1990), Guinnane (1997), Mokyr (1985) and Ó Gráda (1994) continue to engage in scholarly debate concerning the reasons for Irish demographic and family patterns in the nineteenth century. Consensus has yet to arrive. With consensus absent from interpretations of the nineteenth century it is hardly likely to be reached more rapidly or more easily for the twentieth. What is put forward here by one economist in relation to twentieth-century family patterns will, hopefully, serve to provide grist for some future revisionist mill. In working towards its objective the book forms a narrative which recreates many elements of the family over the past century and situates the family in Ireland at the start of the twenty-first century in the context of that past. Attention is first directed to the concept of 'family' itself.

Concept of family

'Family' may be one of the most commonly used words in everyday language, but there is no single common understanding of the term. The concept has evolved from a broad notion of a household under a common head, to that of a nuclear family based on lifelong marriage, to a wide diversity of family forms, including solo parent families, and families that have been reconstituted following the breakdown of an earlier family. Two elements are central to understanding the family in twentieth-century Ireland – dependency and marriage. In times past and well into the twentieth century the family was widely understood as a group of dependants: wife, children, some relatives, servants, belonging to the household of the male head – the master/husband/father (Davidoff, 1992: 71). The Irish language version of the 1937 Constitution which, in the case of dispute, is the definitive version, reflects this very point. In the Irish text, the Family is 'An Teaghlach'; the home is also 'an teaghlach'; while mothers are 'máithreacha clainne', 'an clann' being used in this instance for family. The Irish word 'an teaghlach' makes the household coterminous with the Family.[2] This broad view of the family was endorsed in Catholic social teaching in the era in which the Constitution was drafted. In his book *The Framework of a Christian State*, published in 1932, Rev Edward Cahill, SJ, who had been appointed Professor of Ecclesiastical History and Social Science at Milltown Park in 1924, was a friend of de Valera's, and would have an influence on the shaping of the Constitution (Kennedy, 1998), wrote:

> The family in its wider significance means an assemblage of individuals, dwelling in the same house under a common superior or head, and united by ties founded on the natural law. In this sense, the family is a composite society, which may be composed, at least potentially, in all or any of three ways – the union, namely, of husband and wife, of parents and children and of master and servants (Cahill, 1932: 320).

Cahill proceeds to say that the foundation of the family is the union of husband and wife, and, as a consequence of this union, the duties and rights of parents and children. He argues that the relations of the head of the family with others in the household such as servants, while on a different plane, 'are also founded on the natural law' (Cahill, *ibid*: 320). Cahill further distinguishes labourers or workpeople from servants 'in that the latter live in the master's house, forming part of the family, and apply their whole labour to the service of the master; while labourers do not form portion of the master's family, but contract to perform certain specified services in return for definite remuneration' (Cahill, *ibid*: 378-79). That this broader view of the family persisted well into the twentieth century and was not just endorsed, but advanced as natural law, by a leading Catholic thinker, sets down a clear marker at the outset that 'the Family' is a complex phenomenon.

The linking of the family with the household contains within itself another link, that of the family with dependency. The concept of dependency originates with the notion of the duty of one person to support one or more other persons. One of the areas in which Adam Smith believed the law should lay specific obligations on people related to the family: 'The laws of all civilised nations oblige parents to maintain their children, and children to maintain their parents' (Smith, 1969: 159). In Britain until the repeal of the Poor Law in 1948, a large number of extended family members, including brothers and sisters, were deemed responsible for supporting each other. Since then 'the range of relatives liable to maintain a person who would otherwise be dependent on the state has been much narrower: spouses, cohabitees and parents of dependent children' (Fox Harding, 1996: 107).

A special feature of the first census of the Saorstát in 1926 was an enquiry into child dependency. Each married man, widower and widow was required to state the number of living sons, daughters, step-sons and step-daughters under 16 years of age, whether residing as members of the household or elsewhere. Dependency is central to the social welfare system and in relation to means-tested payments it can be of crucial importance in determining eligibility for payments. Thus a man or a woman may be disqualified from receiving a payment on the grounds that the income of a wife, husband or cohabitee is above the prescribed limit. The *Public Assistance Act*, 1939 represented the taking of ownership by the Irish government of the old Poor Law principles and procedures as updated by the *Local Government (Temporary Provisions) Act*, 1923 (Ó Cinnéide, 1969: 305). Introducing the Second Stage of the Public Assistance Bill, 1939, the Parliamentary Secretary (Minister for State) to Minister for Local Government and Public Health, Dr Francis C. (Conn) Ward, said that, 'The Bill contains very little that is new in principle' (*PDDE,* 76, 519). The Act contained a section dealing with liability to maintain relations which included the following:

(a) every legitimate person shall be liable to maintain his or her father and mother;
(b) every illegitimate person shall be liable to maintain his or her mother;
(c) every man shall be liable to maintain such of his legitimate children as are for the time being under the age of sixteen years;
(d) every woman shall be liable to maintain such of her children, whether legitimate or illegitimate, as are for the time being under the age of sixteen years;
(e) every married man shall be liable to maintain his wife and shall also be liable to maintain every child, whether legitimate or illegitimate, of his wife who was born before her marriage to him and is for the time being under the age of sixteen years;
(f) every married woman shall be liable to maintain her husband.

In 1975, liability to maintain dependants became more limited, as the obligation of children to maintain parents was dropped. The *Social Welfare (Supplementary Welfare Allowances) Act*, 1975 set down the following obligations regarding maintenance liability:

(a) every man shall be liable to maintain such of his legitimate children as are under the age of sixteen years;
(b) every woman shall be liable to maintain such of her children as are under the age of sixteen years;

(c) every married man shall be liable to maintain his wife and any child of his wife, who was born before her marriage to him and is under the age of sixteen years; and

(d) every married woman shall be liable to maintain her husband.

Following the *Status of Children Act*, 1987, which in effect abolished the concept of illegitimacy (see Chapter 9), a man's liability for the maintenance of his children was extended to include any child of his, whether born to him in or out of wedlock (*Social Welfare Act*, 1989, Section 12). For social welfare purposes the age limit for child dependency was raised to 18 years, or to 21 years if the child is in full-time education. The definition of adult dependency was further revised in 1985 (*Social Welfare (No. 2), Act*), subsequent to the Equality Directive of the European Community in 1979, so that henceforth for social welfare purposes a spouse is regarded as a dependant only if he or she is wholly or mainly maintained by the other party. An assumption of liability for mutual support exists between cohabitees as well as married couples.

The close linking of the term 'family' with 'household' existed in census tabulations from the nineteenth century. An early example occurred in the private census of Mr Dobbs in 1732 which was based on 'Hearth-money collectors' and showed that there was 'an average of six souls to a house' (Census 1901, *General Report*). The 1901 census was the first census to employ *Forms of Family Return,* to be filled by the Head of the Family, instead of having the particulars entered by the enumerator from *viva voce* inquiry. The census was taken on the night of 31 March 1901 and the instructions stated that no persons absent on that night were to be entered on the Form of Family Return except those, not enumerated elsewhere, who might be out at work or travelling during that night and who would return home on 1 April. Subject to that proviso regarding those absent, the name of the Head of the Family was to be written first; 'then the names of his Wife, Children, and other Relatives; then those of Visitors, Boarders, Servants, &c.' (Census, 1901, *General Report*: 600).

In a paper entitled 'The Family in Irish Census of Population Statistics', read to the Statistical and Social Inquiry Society of Ireland in 1954, Dr R.C. Geary, Director of the Central Statistics Office, maintained that the term 'family' as used for census purposes was a misnomer and that it would be better to use the term 'household' and reserve the term 'family' for a group related by blood or marriage. It is interesting, particularly in the light of Cahill's definition, that according to the census, a family is defined as 'any person or group of persons living in a single household ... and included in a separate census return as being in separate premises or part of premises' (Geary, 1954/55: 3). Geary objected that the census private family did not necessarily connote a group related by blood or marriage. Domestic servants and other employees who lived in the household, as well as temporary visitors, were included in the family, while on the other hand the family did not include members who might have been temporarily absent on the census night, e.g. as seasonal workers in Britain or children at boarding schools (Geary, *ibid*: 3). Geary proceeded to analyse a sample of over 6,000 families drawn from the 1951 census for which 'family' was defined as a group of persons residing in the same household related by blood or marriage. He then classified families by number and age of dependants and other features. Geary's outstanding finding was the 'revelation of the fact that the "simple family" of parents or guardians and children under 15 is so untypical. It contains only 28 per cent of the families and 36 per cent of the population'.

The 1979 census was the first Irish census in which the population was classified by number and type of family unit. The family unit was defined as (i) a man and his wife, or (ii) a man and his wife together with one or more single children, of any age, or (iii) one parent together with one or more single children, of any age. In the 1979 census the family unit was implicitly extended to include a couple who, although not married, cohabit, with or without children. In that year cohabitation was negligible.

Figure 1.1: Family units in private households, 1996

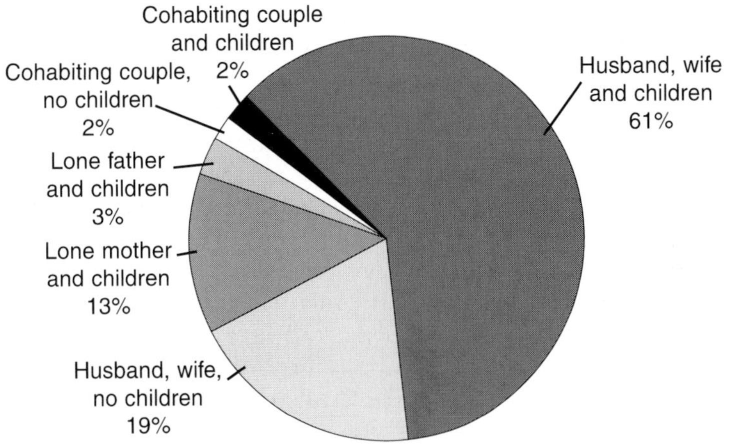

Source: Census of Population, 1996

In 1996 there were over 1.1 million private households in Ireland, of which 807,000 comprised family units. The total number of households in the State changed little in the forty years from 1926 to 1966, but almost doubled in the thirty years from 1966 to 1996. In 1996 a husband and wife, or couple, with children, comprised 39 per cent of total households, while one-person households accounted for 22 per cent of the total. The share of one-person households has grown steadily from one in twelve in 1926 to more than one in five in 1996 (Table A.1.5), while the proportion of those aged 65 years and over living alone has more than doubled in the past thirty years, from 11 per cent in 1966 to 26 per cent in 1996, indicating a long-run increase in the share of those who live outside families. In 1996, 30 per cent of women and 20 per cent of men aged 65 years and over, lived alone (Figure 1.2, Table A.1.6).

The growth in one-person and two-person households reflects declining fertility and increasing household formation (Punch and Finneran, 2000:21). A married couple with children comprised 61 per cent of family units, while the lone parent (widowed, divorced, unmarried) with children, accounted for 16 per cent of family units in 1996. Four per cent of family units were cohabiting couples, with or without children (Figure 1.1 and Commission on the Family, 1998). Eighty-two per cent of children lived in family units comprising husband, wife and children, while 17 per cent of children lived with a mother or a father.

Figure 1.2: Per cent persons aged 65 years and over living alone, 1966-96

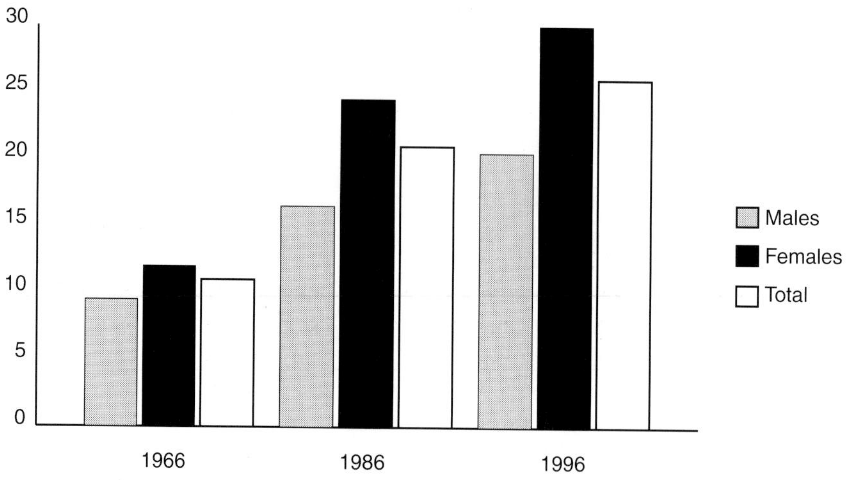

Source: Censuses of Population (various)

Although not essential to the census definition, and not coterminous with dependency, the element of the family which was most clearly defined by social and legal custom, throughout the greater part of the century, and which straddled class and economic differences, was that the basis of the family was marriage. Children born out of wedlock were illegitimate, without inheritance rights. The fact that the family was founded on marriage was clearly signalled in the Constitution where it is stated that 'The State pledges itself to guard with special care the institution of marriage, on which the Family is founded, and to protect it against attack' (Art. 41.3.1°), and until 1995, 'No law shall be enacted providing for the grant of a dissolution of marriage' (Art. 41.3.2°). The introduction of divorce in 1995 would alter this, but long before 1995, a series of changes in the law on illegitimacy, and in the social welfare code, signalled a broadening of the term 'family'. By the 1990s the changes in family patterns, as well as legal changes, including the introduction of divorce, were such that both the Review Group on the Constitution and the Joint-Oireachtas Committee on the Constitution recommended a widening of the definition of the family in the Constitution in order to reflect more closely the reality of everyday life.

The family is in part a legal construct. Those who hold a 'natural law' view of the family as expressed in the 1937 Constitution will not be in sympathy with this. The move towards divorce is part of the shift from the 'natural' to the 'legal' family model (Fox Harding, 1996: 56). This in turn is yielding to a legal-economic model. Dewar, an expert on English family law, makes the following comment:

> There is now less emphasis on the exclusivity of the legal status of marriage and evidence of a move towards constructing status-like relationships around new organising concepts. The primary aim, it was argued, is to construct a set of legal-economic relations among family members that are clearly demarcated from, and thereby reduce the financial burden on, the state. In this process, the legal concept of marriage is logically, and is *de facto* becoming, redundant (Dewar, 1992: 71).

Dewar stresses that it is parenthood rather than marriage which is significant regarding the rights and responsibilities of family members, with the focus shifting from the rights of parents to the rights of the child (Dewar, *ibid*: 109).

For many years the United Nations followed a definition based on 'the conjugal family concept', as established in 1978 and revised in 1987. This definition was implemented by Eurostat in gathering family data. According to recommendations of the UN Statistical/Economic Commission for Europe Conference of European Statisticians, in 1987, '... a family nucleus comprises a married couple without children or a married couple with one or more never-married children of any age or one parent with one or more never-married children. ... The term "married couple" is to include consensual unions' (Hantrais and Letablier, 1996: 131-2).

In its recommendations for the 2000 Censuses the UN has extended the definition of family to include lone parent families:

> A *family nucleus* is defined in the narrow sense as two or more persons within a private or institutional household who are related as husband and wife, as cohabiting partners, or as parent and child. Thus a family comprises a couple without children, or a couple with one or more children, or a lone parent with one or more children (United Nations, 1998:43).[3]

In the discussions held by the UN prior to drawing up the recommendations for the 2000 Censuses, representatives of some Eastern European countries wished to extend the definition of the family to include grandparents, reflecting situations where children were cared for by grandparents in the absence of parents who had to leave the family home and home country for work purposes.[4]

Sources and plan

The sources used in this study include statistical data, archival material, a wide range of published material, including research papers and reports, as well as biographical and autobiographical writings, and personal interviews. Interviews, including those with former Taoisigh Liam Cosgrave, Charles Haughey and Garret FitzGerald and the first European Commissioner for Social Affairs and former President of Ireland, Patrick Hillery, provide insights into aspects of policy formation regarding the family.

A number of studies stand out as landmarks in the field of family research in Ireland. The first of these is the anthropological study of farm families, *Family and Community in Ireland* (1940), undertaken by the American anthropologists Arensberg and Kimball in the 1930s. Their study revealed a family structure that was founded on a rigid gender-based division of labour and a patriarchal authority structure. Over three decades later, Hannan and Katsiaouni attempted to explain change over time in farm families (1977). Their study was entitled *Traditional Families? From Culturally Prescribed to Negotiated Roles in Farm Families*. They employed a linear model of family change underpinned by traditional and modern family farms. The study, which analysed 'interaction patterns and interpersonal relationships existing within a sample of 408 Irish farm families', focused on three basic elements of family interaction: (i) the division of labour in sex roles, (ii) decision-making patterns, and (iii) social-emotional patterns within the family. Five years after World War II, another American sociologist, Humphreys, commenced an intensive sample survey of families in Dublin across the different social classes. His findings were published in 1966 under the title *New Dubliners*. This study has not hitherto received the recognition which it merits; it is of considerable significance as a unique study of the urban family at the time. Humphreys' central conclusion, valid at the time, was that the transformation observed in the family of the 'New Dubliners' was mainly the result of an adjustment on the level of organisation rather than the effect of any profound ideological shift. The heart of the changes in the family related to the ways in which it gained its livelihood due to economic and occupational organisation. The dominant Catholic ideology of the family appeared intact and the family remained devoutly Catholic.

A different genre of investigation is provided by Commissions of Enquiry. There are two clear landmarks in this area. The first is provided by the *Reports* of The Commission on Emigration and other Population Problems (1954), a substantial part of which deals with marriage, births, fertility and family size. A member of the Commission, Roy Geary, delivered the pioneering paper, referred to earlier. A second report that merits 'landmark' status is the *Report of the Commission on the Status of Women,* published in 1972. This study was of unique importance in paving the way for many changes in Irish lifestyles, changes that were to have a direct influence on the evolution of family patterns. The Commission was established in 1970 to examine and report on the status of women in Irish society, to make recommendations on the steps necessary to ensure the participation of women on equal terms and conditions with men in the political, social, cultural and economic life of the country and to indicate the implications generally, including the estimated cost, of such recommendations. The Chairman of the Commission was Dr Thekla Beere, a former Secretary of the Department of Transport and Power. Until 1995, when Margaret Hayes was appointed Secretary of the Department of Tourism and Trade, Dr Beere was the only woman ever to have been head of a Government Department in Ireland.

Twenty years after the First Commission, a Second Commission on the Status of Women was established by the Taoiseach, Charles Haughey, under the chairmanship of Miss Justice Mella Carroll. Its terms of reference were virtually identical with those of the First Commission, with the significant addition that the Second Commission was requested 'to pay special attention to the needs of women in the home'. Early in 1996 the Minister for Social Welfare, Proinsias de Rossa, established a Commission on the Family chaired by Dr Michael Dunne. It issued an *Interim Report* late that year and in August 1998 the final Report was published which set forth a broad agenda for family policy over the coming years. During the past two decades there has been a definite increase in the quantity of material published relating to the family. Evidence of this is clear from the flow of work emanating from the National Economic and Social Council (NESC), The Economic and Social Research Institute (ESRI), the Universities, including the Family Studies Unit in the Department of Social Science at University College Dublin, as well as the Conference of Religious of Ireland (CORI, formerly known as the Conference of Major Religious Superiors).[5] The slowly mounting volume of research on family matters indicates the steady growth in importance of the topic. Among this research four areas have been dominant, and though these areas are distinct, they also overlap. They relate to: family formation and fission, including demographic issues; family policy; women and work; and dysfunction within families.[6]

The chapters of this book are organised on a thematic basis and within each chapter chronological order is followed to the extent possible and appropriate. Following this introductory chapter, Chapter 2 covers trends in the main indicators of family life, and changes within families. Chapter 3 deals with changes in living standards and changing ways of earning a living. Its focus is mainly on economic factors. It examines the shift in the economic base of the family from a predominantly agricultural and rural setting in which the requirements of the small family farm were dominant to a breadwinner father pattern in a predominantly urban setting. This in turn is yielding, on the one hand, to a more egalitarian pattern in which the central economic focus is not so much on gender roles of breadwinner and homemaker, but rather on the combining of income earning with caring for dependent family members; and on the other hand, to an increase in solo parenting, often dependent on state payments to sustain existence.

Marshall described economics as the study of man in 'the ordinary business of life'. How people provide for their economic needs and how they care for their dependants are issues central to human existence, and central to family life. Changes in the workplace and in working conditions have had a major impact on family. There has been a huge increase in the numbers dependent on a wage from an employer, including the state, for a living. Work at home, on the farm, or at one's own craft, for example, as a shoemaker, a shirtmaker, or a blacksmith, has been gradually displaced. Yet at the dawn of the twenty-first century a return to homeworking is occurring as a result of the information technology revolution, while labour-intensive organic farming is a small, but growing, segment of agriculture. Conditions of employment including hours of work, pay and time off work, and in particular, the introduction of equal terms for women in regard to equal work, have all had an impact on family living conditions.

Chapter 4 deals with the changing role of men and women, while Chapter 5, 'Catalysts for Change', highlights some of the most influential factors in creating family change, including the role of women's organisations, the impact of EEC entry and the influence of the media. Chapter 6 deals with changes in the role and status of children. The next two chapters, 7 and 8, deal with the influence of Church thought and teaching on behaviour patterns and its influence on, and interaction with, policy. The 'Church' refers to the Roman Catholic Church, as the declared Church of over 90 per cent of the population throughout the century. The shift from acceptance of church authority on a range of issues pertaining to the family, such as cohabitation, extra-marital sex and the use of contraception, to a situation in which individuals follow what they perceive to be their own interests, is examined. It is argued that the notion of a rigid clerical/lay divide is an oversimplification. Chapter 9 presents the main landmarks in government policy towards the family. Changes in policy tended to be of two kinds – those directed towards redistributing resources towards families, such as children's allowances, and those that changed the rules within which families operated, such as the Succession Law.

At the start of the twentieth century Catholic social thought laid great emphasis on the entitlement of the worker to a living wage to support himself and his dependants. The guideline for policy makers was to provide help, or 'subsidium', for the family; to supplement, not to supplant. As state policy developed and associated public expenditure programmes expanded, the state began to assume functions which previously had been fulfilled, or left unfulfilled, by family members. Changes in the law regarding marriage, for example, the legal age of marriage, separation and divorce, ownership and inheritance of property, legitimacy, as well as the extension of social welfare services in the form of children's allowances, allowances for lone parents, and a wide range of other supports, all have relevance to family change. Also included in the sphere of state policy are the mechanisms whereby the fruits of major scientific and technological developments which impinge on the family, for example in regard to immunisation programmes for children, have been incorporated into the health services. These have contributed to the spectacular decline in infant and maternal mortality rates. The development of oral and other contraceptives as well as the legalisation of abortion in the UK, and to a limited extent in Ireland, following the X case, have had a big influence on family behaviour in Ireland. Early in the century the development of homogenised milk for babies and the shift away from breast-feeding represent important, if frequently over-looked, elements of change in the family sphere. At the start of a new century questions surrounding fertility treatments, human embryology, cloning and surrogacy, are set to feature on the agenda in the coming years.

In the concluding chapter, entitled 'Three Arches', the links between economic and policy factors, as they affect family patterns, are examined in relation to changing values. The general hypothesis suggested is that change in family patterns is 'people driven'. As economic factors change, new opportunities lead to a transformation in the interests of individuals, and behaviour changes accordingly. Government and politicians in general reflect what the people want in family matters. Once economic factors become sufficiently strong, they can dominate tradition and Church teaching, and while cultural background and history can slow down response to these forces, they do not in the long run tend to override them.

Appendix 1

Table A. 1.1: Family units in private households, 1996

Family type	Units	Per cent	Children	Per cent
Husband, wife, no children	155,000	19	-	
Cohabiting couple, no children	19,000	2	-	
Husband, wife and children	492,000	61	1,206,000	82
Cohabiting couple and children	13,000	2	23,000	2
Lone mother and children	108,000	13	203,000	14
Lone father and children	21,000	3	38,000	3
Total family units	807,000	100	1,470,000	100

Source: Census 1996, Vol. 3

Table A. 1.2: Marriage rate, selected European countries, 1930-97 (per 1000)

	1930-35	1936-45	1946-51	1980	1990	1995	1997
Denmark	8.6	9.2	9.2	5.2	6.1	6.6	6.5
France	7.6	6.5	9.3	6.2	5.1	6.6	4.8
Italy	6.9	6.7	8.3	5.7	5.6	4.9	4.7
Netherlands	7.3	7.7	9.3	6.4	6.4	5.3	5.5
Sweden	7.3	9.4	8.3	4.5	4.7	3.8	3.7
Switzerland	7.8	7.9	8.3	5.7	6.9	5.8	5.5
UK (a)	8.1	9.0	8.7	7.4	6.5	5.5	5.4
Ireland(b)	4.7	5.4	5.5	6.4	5.1	4.3	4.3
Average	7.3	7.7	8.4	5.9	5.8	5.1	5.1

Source: Commission on Emigration, 1954; Council of Europe, 1999
(a) England & Wales for 1930-35, 1936-45, 1946-51
(b) 26 Counties

Table A. 1.3: Birth rate, selected European countries, 1926-97 (per 1000)

	1926-35	1936-45	1946-51	1980	1990	1995	1997
Denmark	18.6	19.7	20.2	11.2	12.3	11.3	12.8
France	17.5	15.1	20.8	14.9	13.5	12.5	12.4
Italy	25.3	21.5	20.9	11.3	9.8	9.1	9.2
Netherlands	22.2	21.3	25.3	12.8	13.2	12.3	12.4
Sweden	15.0	16.8	17.7	11.7	14.5	11.7	10.2
Switzerland	17.0	17.0	18.7	11.7	12.5	11.7	11.0
UK (a)	15.8	15.3	17.6	13.4	13.9	12.5	12.3
Ireland (b)	19.8	20.4	22.0	21.8	14.7	13.5	14.2
Average	18.9	18.4	20.4	13.6	13.1	11.8	11.8

Source: Commission on Emigration, 1954; Council of Europe, 1999
(a) England & Wales for 1926-35, 1936-45, 1946-51
(b) 26 Counties

Table A. 1.4: Legal prohibition on, and access to contraception, selected European countries, twentieth century

Country	Prohibition Year	Access Year
France	1920	1967, 1974
Belgium	1923	1973
Italy	1926	1971
Ireland	1935	1979
Germany	1941	1968
Spain	1941	1978
UK	1930 (limited access)	1930 (limited) 1949/1967 (general)

Source: Gauthier, 1996: 31

Table A.1.5: Share of one-person households in total households, 1926-96 (%)

Year	Total households	One-person households
	Number	Per cent
1926	622,670	8.3
1946	662,654	10.4
1966	687,304	12.9
1986	976,304	18.5
1996	1,127,318	21.5

Source: Censuses of Population, various

Table A.1.6: Persons aged 65 years and over living alone, 1966-96 (%)

Year	Males	Females	Total
	Per cent	Per cent	Per cent
1966	9.7	11.9	10.8
1986	16.6	24.7	21.2
1996	20.3	30.0	25.8

Source: Censuses of Population, various

2

Dimensions of Family Life

The principal dimensions of family life include birth, fertility, infant and maternal mortality, marriage and widowhood. In this chapter these and other dimensions of family life, and their linkages, are examined. At the start of the twentieth century less than one in three men in the prime age group 25-34 was married, compared with two in three who were married in that age group by 1980. When marriages occurred, children were numerous, although many children died before their first birthday, reflecting widespread poverty and the underdeveloped state of health services. The low marriage rate in the early decades was closely related to economic opportunities that varied markedly between rural and urban areas. Emigration has for generations interacted closely with family life in Ireland; it siphoned off those children who could not find jobs at home, or opportunities to marry. Since the 1970s marriage has fallen out of fashion. It is a striking fact that in the twenty years from 1975 to 1995, the probability of female marriage declined by one-third from 90 per cent to 60 per cent (Punch, 1999). However, in the 1990s there has been a marked increase in the marriage rate of women aged 30-34 years (FitzGerald, 2001). By the end of the twentieth century, the marriage rate had dropped back to the same level as at the beginning of the century, while the birth rate was 25 per cent lower. The lower marriage rate was dictated more by lifestyle choice than by economic necessity as the economic boom of the 1990s witnessed a surplus of immigrants over emigrants. The decline in marriage at a time of unprecedented growth does not mean, however, that economic factors have not played a role. Rather, rapid growth has contributed to a change in the context of marriage due both to increased employment opportunities and the demands of the workplace.

From the 1950s to the 1980s legal adoption provided a mechanism for absorbing non-marital children into traditional families. In the 1990s abortions have increased rapidly, indicating changing choices and changing values. All these changes, and more, are occurring in a context of altered living arrangements with an increase in dual-earner households. Early in the century a high proportion of households was headed by a lone parent, generally a widow or widower; by the end of the century, the most frequent head in a lone parent household was a solo mother.

21

Marriage

Compulsory registration of marriage was introduced in Ireland in 1864, within two decades of the Famine. In that year just over 20,000 marriages were registered compared with 16,800 in 1998, over one hundred and thirty years later. Since 1864 the lowest number of marriages recorded was 13,029 in 1932, while the highest number was 22,833 in 1974. The trend in the number of marriages was downwards until the 1930s; it picked up with World War II, fell again in the 1950s, then climbed in the 1960s to a peak in 1974. From 1974 the annual number of marriages fell, to under 16,000 in 1995. It rose again to nearly 17,000 in 1998. The marriage rate varied from a low of 3.6 in 1880, to a rate almost twice as high, 7.4, in 1973. The marriage rate then fell steadily to 4.4 in 1993, increasing to 4.5 in 1998 (Table A.2.1).

The marriage rate relates to the total population and therefore conceals as well as reveals. Like any national measure, the average conceals regional and county differences, some of which are due to variations in the proportion of the population in the marriageable age groups. One fact that averages conceal is the extent to which the low marriage rate was a rural phenomenon, although this feature is itself related to the age-distribution of the population, reflecting the relatively greater number of elderly in rural areas. To give just two examples of the range in the marriage rate: in 1910-12 the marriage rate varied from 3.8 in Clare to 8.6 in Limerick, while in 1945-47 rates varied from 3.9 in Laois to 11.3 in Limerick City (Commission on Emigration, 1954: 307). Daly (1986:119), drawing on evidence of a number of researchers, including Walsh (1970: 153-4), shows the complexity of the situation in the immediate post-Famine decades:

> Marriages in the decades after the famine took place at an earlier age and with greater frequency in Connaught than in more prosperous parts of the country. In consequence the birth rate was considerably higher. This discrepancy even applied between east and west Cork with the poorer west recording a much higher natural increase in population in the 1850s and 1860s. The marriage rate in the west does not begin to drop until the 1870s and it is not until the early twentieth century that Connaught no longer records the highest marriage rate in Ireland (Daly, 1986: 119).

Walsh (1970a) addresses the extent to which regional variations in marriage patterns in the 1960s reflected the imbalance in the sex ratio. He found that the low marriage rate in rural areas reflected the fact that out-migration of young women from rural areas made it difficult for males to obtain a partner. The mechanisms at work were complex; women's 'outside options' were raised by education, while men remained attached to the land. The predominantly rural distribution of the population throughout the first half of the century constrained marriage opportunities, '... as Ireland's population has been predominantly agricultural, the deterioration of the marriage pattern, which the famine set in motion with a severe initial impetus, has been largely a rural phenomenon' (Commission on Emigration: 79-80).

From the 1860s until the 1960s when alternative forms of employment started to become available within travelling distance, the opportunity for marriage in rural areas depended on access to land. The Land Purchase Acts of the late nineteenth century effectively prevented the subdivision of holdings, and as there were few forms of employment in rural areas other than on the land, a pattern of late marriages and celibacy emerged. Serjeant Sullivan, who had an extensive practice at both the Irish Bar and the English Bar, and is probably best know in Ireland for his defence of Roger Casement, has emphasised how the law enforced the prohibition on subdivision by avoiding all transactions in breach of it (Sullivan, 1952:141). The rural influence spread to the urban areas:

> Given the strength of family ties and the extension of rural ways of life into the towns, the same pattern became discernible even in urban life. Thus, the society that emerged from the later decades of the nineteenth century was largely based on the refusal to many of its members of the opportunity to found a home and family (Meenan, 1970: 336).

The Census Commissioners of 1871 firmly believed that the low marriage rate and associated high fertility rate was explicable in terms of a lack of material development, saying, 'The Irish beyond all dispute are a nation whose individuals will marry when they can, and be celibates only when they must' (Census 1871, *General Report*: 54). In an analysis of the marriage rate between 1865 and 1925, Meenan shows how after the period 1879-88, when the rate averaged under 4 per cent, it rose steadily with improved economic conditions until 1919-20 when it began to decline, bearing out the description of 'the marriage rate as the barometer of a country's prosperity' (Meenan, 1933:20).

Walsh has emphasised the links between social class and both age at marriage and likelihood of eventual marriage as an indicator of the importance of economic factors in influencing marriage patterns. He shows the striking contrast between the marriage patterns of 'farm labourers' and 'farmers' who were born around the turn of the century. Farm labourers born around 1900 had the lowest marriage rate of any social class, with about half still unmarried by 1950. The next lowest marriage rates were among small farmers and unskilled urban workers. Higher proportions eventually married among larger farmers, managers, professional and other skilled workers, while 'the proportion of male labourers (agricultural and non-agricultural), who never married was about *four times* the corresponding proportion among professionals and employers' (Walsh, 1995: 5). According to the Emigration Commission, 88 per cent of agricultural labourers, 'living-in', in 1951, remained single in the age group 65-74 (Commission on Emigration, 1954: 73).

With the significant exception of the period since the mid-1980s, changes in the marriage rate in Ireland corresponded fairly well with changes in the level of economic activity. Based on trends in a number of countries over long periods, Becker concludes that, 'For centuries marriages, births and other family behaviour have been known to respond to fluctuations in aggregate output and prices' (Becker, 1988: 6). In Ireland, marriage rates were at their lowest during the 1930s, a period of widespread depression, aggravated by the Economic War with Britain. After World War II the marriage rate revived in comparison with the 1920s and 1930s. The development of large housing estates on the perimeter of cities, especially the local authority housing expansion which started in Dublin in the 1930s, and continued after the War until the severe cutbacks in 1956-58, facilitated the move from rural areas, and provided shelter for the growing number of urban families. The marriage rate continued to rise with the economic growth of the 1960s. It is possible that the surge in marriages in the late 1960s and early 1970s reduced the pool of people presenting for marriage at a later date. A number of factors contributed to the fall in the marriage rate in the 1970s, including the first oil crisis, rising unemployment, and lack of availability of mortgages. Postponement of marriage was reflected in the increase in the average age of brides which rose from 24.8 years in 1970 to 27.8 years in 1995.

There was a slight pick-up in the marriage rate and a rise in the absolute number of marriages in the spurt of economic expansion following the General Election in 1977. However, this soon petered out. Changes in the 1970s, which included the removal of barriers to the employment of married women, and the availability of contraceptives, helped to forge a change in attitudes towards marriage. In the 1980s marriage lost popularity; there was a sharp fall in marital births while births outside marriage soared. With an increase in marriage breakdown and the introduction of legal provision firstly, for marriage separation in 1989, and then in 1995, for divorce, the family based on life-long marriage was no longer the exclusive model of family life. Notwithstanding record-breaking economic growth in the early 1990s, the marriage rate continued to fall until small increases were recorded in 1994 and 1998. Between 1992 and 1996, the marriage rate for women in the 30-34 years age group rose significantly which suggests that a postponement factor may be at work (FitzGerald, 2001).

Table 2.1: Ever-married men and women, 1901-96 (%)

Year	Men			Women		
	25-34	35-44	15 & over	25-34	35-44	15 & over
1901	28	62	43	47	72	51
1926	28	55	42	47	70	57
1951	33	60	47	54	72	57
1961	42	64	52	63	77	61
1971	58	71	54	74	82	64
1981	66	81	57	78	89	66
1991	56	82	56	68	88	65
1996	45	80	55	58	86	63

Source: Censuses of Population, various

The rise in the popularity of marriage between 1901 and 1981 is shown by the rise in the share of ever-married men and women from 43 to 57 per cent and from 51 to 65 per cent respectively. The change is particularly striking for men aged 25-34 years in the period 1951-81, when the proportion doubled, rising from 33 to 66 per cent; while there was a jump of one-third from 60 per cent to 81 per cent for the age group 35-44 years. The upward trend has been reversed since 1981.

Figure 2.1: Per cent single in 25-34 age group, 1901-96

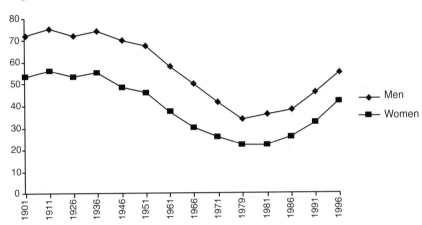

Source: Censuses of Population (various)

Between 1981 and 1991 there has been a sharp drop of one-sixth in the proportion aged 25-34 years who were married, with the share falling back to 56 per cent. In 1901 less than half of all women aged 25-34 years had married; by 1951 slightly more than half those aged 25-34 years had married. Thirty years later in 1981 the proportion married in this age group had risen to over three-quarters, but dropped back to two-thirds in 1991 (Table 2.1 and Fig 2.1). Until the late 1950s men on average remained single until at least 30 years of age. In 1957-60 the average age of men at marriage was over 31 years, having been just over 33 years in 1945-46 and almost 35 years in 1925-26. Average age for men at marriage dropped to under 27 years – the lowest since Independence – in the 1970s. Since then it has climbed upwards and was 29 years at the start of the 1990s. Since 1980 there has been a marked fall in the proportion of younger women who are married. Between 1983 and 1990 the proportion who were married aged 20-24 years fell from 24.6 per cent to 14.5 per cent, falling further to 8.4 per cent in 1994, while for the age group 25-29 years the decline was from 67 per cent in 1983, to 58 per cent in 1990, to 52 per cent in 1994 (Kennedy and McCormack, 1997; Labour Force Surveys). Across the decade of the 1980s average age at marriage for women rose by two years from 24.5 to 26.6 years. Thus the trend towards younger marriages, which was very marked in the 1960s and carried over into the 1970s, was reversed after 1980. Younger cohorts of Irish women are at least postponing marriage; for how long, or to what extent permanently, remains to be seen. The legal minimum age for marriage has risen over the twentieth century. The legal minimum age of marriage for both men and women has been 18 years since the *Family Law Act,* 1986. Thirty years ago, in 1972, the legal minimum age of marriage for girls was raised from 14 to 16 years. In the years 1957-59, for example, four girls aged 14 years married, while sixty girls and one boy aged 15 years married.

Judgements vary on the extent to which the strong Catholic ethos affected behaviour and possibly rendered harsh economic realities more bearable. The *Majority Report* of the Emigration Commission is dismissive of the influence of the Catholic ethos, but the author of a *Minority Report,* James Meenan, argues the opposite. The Emigration Commission maintained that no convincing evidence was put before the Commission to support the contention that '… the indissolubility of marriage and, in the absence of contraception, the fear of large families, deter many from marriage altogether and others until a relatively advanced age' (Commission on Emigration, 1954, para 166: 80). On the contrary, the Commission pointed to the fact that other Catholic countries had higher marriage rates while the marriage rate in Northern Ireland, with only a third of the population Catholic, was also low. No facts, however, were given by the Commission regarding the relative economic development of the other Catholic countries or of Northern Ireland. By contrast, Meenan had no doubt as to the influence of the Catholic ethos, saying that the '… low marriage rate should be recognised for what it is, the form of birth control adopted by a practising Catholic people' (Meenan, 1970: 337). Meenan's view was in sympathy with that of Carr-Saunders who, following a discussion of declining birth rates in Western Europe in the 1930s, concluded that the growth of contraceptives was the immediate cause of the declining birth rate, except in Ireland, where the effective cause was the postponement of marriage; in an evocation of the 'special case', he says, 'Ireland is an exception to most rules' (Carr-Saunders, 1936).

If economic forces which frustrated marriage hopes were made bearable by religious values which supported chastity and self-restraint, such values were reflected in the respect shown towards vocations to the celibate priesthood and religious life. Vocations to the priesthood and for religious orders were abundant during the first half of the twentieth century in Ireland. Walsh is in no doubt that the Catholic Church played a role by providing a degree of social control that helped to enforce the restraint associated with late marriage and celibacy: 'The Catholic Church played an important role – the efforts of priests and nuns to ensure that the growing caution with respect to marriage did not become an occasion for extra-marital sex have become legendary' (Walsh, 1995: 10). The legalisation of contraceptives in 1979 meant that the link between marriage and sexual activity was weakened. The introduction of the *Unmarried Mother's Allowance* in 1973 helped to reduce the stigma associated with illegitimacy, a stigma which was strong in Irish culture, particularly in rural areas, and which led to secrecy, concealment and suffering for women and children. One way of dealing with extra-marital pregnancy was the 'shot-gun' marriage. While it happened in every social class, the following refers to the labouring class:

> Frequently enough to make it a common source of parental concern, girls find themselves in the classic trouble. When this happens, the labourers report that people usually blame the girl for such a turn of events. In any case, both the family of the girl and the family of the boy move to secure the quick marriage of the couple (Humphreys, 1966: 204).

Emigration

In the past forty years the population in the Republic has increased by over one-third from its lowest recorded level of 2.8 million in 1961 to 3.7 million in 1996, the highest level since 1881. In addition to basic demographic variables, net migration has been a key factor in population change. Marriage patterns have been linked to emigration which has been a feature of Irish life for generations, even centuries. At the start of the twentieth century, net emigration, although substantially lower than in the closing years of the nineteenth century, averaged well over 20,000 per annum. If the unique year of 1921-22 is excluded, a year in which 88,000 left Ireland, associated with British withdrawal, emigration fell until the end of World War II; in the Depression years of the early 1930s, there was net immigration. When Fianna Fáil came to power in 1932 they supported a shift away from mixed farming for export, favoured by the Cumann na nGaedheal Government, towards tillage and a policy of self-sufficiency, supported by protectionism, with the objective of maintaining more families on the land. It was argued that only tillage could spare the young from emigration. The *Capuchin Annual* 1931 contained a short story by Frank Gallagher, editor of the Fianna Fáil newspaper, the *Irish Press*, entitled 'The Big Fields', which captures the family argument in favour of tillage:

> The moral of this fiction was that only tillage could spare the youth from emigration. John and Mary O'Donnell had seven children, the eldest being Seán. His ability to remain at home depended on the success of a crop of wheat and oats. As the crop grows, Gallagher has it speak to us. 'Seán is to stay, to stay, to stay', the oats whispered to the wheat. 'Seán need not go, not go, not go,' the wheat whispered to the oats (Murphy and Rouse, 1999:13).

The upswing in emigration in the 1950s led to a questioning of the capacity for Irish self-government for it had long been argued by nationalist opinion that

Ireland could sustain a much greater population, if left to manage her own affairs. Looking back it is easy to see why emigration rose in the 1950s. Pent-up demand to emigrate existed from the war years. With post-war reconstruction taking place in Britain, jobs became available there in building and construction which coincided with the outflow of agricultural workers from the Irish countryside. In the 1950s most emigrants came from agricultural occupations or else were unemployed or unskilled (Commission on Emigration, 1954: para 272). In the booming economy in the 1990s immigration exceeded emigration, reversing a long-term trend. In the year to April 1999 there were 47,500 immigrants compared with 29,000 emigrants, resulting in net immigration of 18,500.

Emigrants have been predominantly young, single persons, a fact regarded as peculiarly damaging by Professor Oldham who wrote in 1914 that

> An emigration by individuals is very much more injurious to a country than an emigration of families. ... The economic units are unchanged, but each is depleted and its efficiency is reduced. Thus there has been, in Ireland, a perpetuated survival of the unfittest, a steady debasement of the human currency – very similar to Gresham's Law, by which bad money continually tends to displace good money in circulation (Quoted in Meenan, 1970: 346).

Figure 2.2: Net migration (inward less outward), inter-censal periods, 1901-96

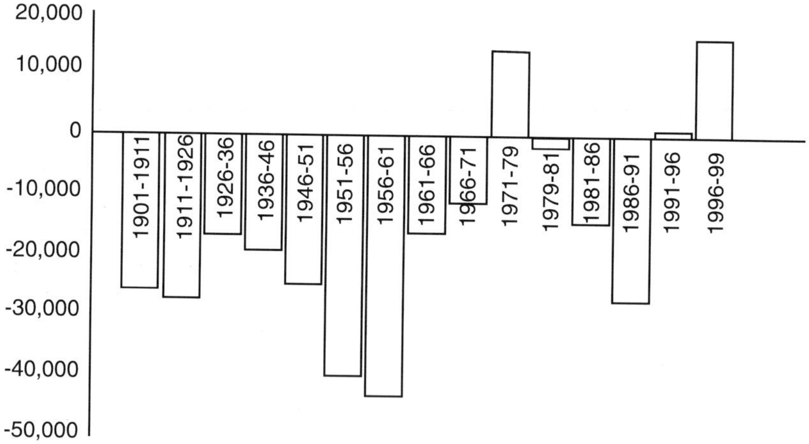

Source: Censuses of Population (various)

Between 1891-1921 two-thirds of all emigrants were aged 20-24 years. Between 1924-39 over 60 per cent of males and over 70 per cent of females were aged under 24 years, a proportion repeated in the late 1950s. In 1999 the age profile of emigrants was younger than that of immigrants. The majority of emigrants (53 per cent) were aged 15-24 years, while 45 per cent of immigrants were 25-44 years. With the possible exception of the years immediately following the Famine, there has been comparatively little emigration of families, reversing a trend that has been characteristic of the emigration of other peoples (Meenan, *ibid*: 208). In the 1970s there was substantial net immigration, including the return of many families formed by individuals who had emigrated in earlier years. In the 1980s net emigration resumed once more but in the 1990s the pattern has been reversed once again, with net immigration. A special feature in the early 1990s was the substantial immigration of women while there was net emigration of men. In 1999 13 per cent of people who live in Ireland were born outside, or have lived outside Ireland, and a total of 170,000 persons have one migrant parent (Punch, 1999).

It is possible to distinguish between cyclical and structural causes of emigration. Cyclical causes relate to poor employment prospects in Ireland relative to prospects abroad, as occurred in the 1950s and the 1980s, while structural causes are long run and relate to the economic and social structure of the country. The structural causes are, in important respects, family-related causes, including farm family structure and marriage opportunities for women. Writing in 1929 on 'Why Girls Leave Ireland', Signe Toksvig, the Danish writer, and wife of the Irish writer Francis Hackett, blamed the severe attitude of the clergy, in turn related to the poverty of families too big to sustain (Pihl, 1999: 450-51). In large families living on small farms, only one son could expect to inherit the farm and in turn establish a family of his own on the holding. His siblings moved to towns and cities in Ireland and abroad in search of their livelihoods. This created conditions for the emigration of members of each succeeding generation and only came to an end with the demise of the small family farm, a process that was completed with the consolidation of holdings following Irish entry to the EEC. In 1951, over half of the women in the age group 15-44 who lived in rural areas were unmarried. With the exception of war time, until the 1950s, the number of women emigrants exceeded the number of men in each decade. The Commission on Emigration considered, but rejected, the possibility of introducing marriage loans and grants in order to encourage marriage. They argued instead that measures to improve the general level of economic and social development would lead to an improved marriage rate (Kennedy, Giblin and McHugh, 1988:151).

Because emigration has been concentrated in the young active age groups, and because of the high birth rate until the early 1980s, Ireland has had, for most of the century, a lower share of its population in the active age groups than other European countries. Therefore for much of the century, there was a high and rising level of age dependency. In 1966, while the population was similar to that in 1936, the numbers in the active age groups had declined by about 11 per cent, while the numbers in the dependent age groups had risen by almost the same amount (Kennedy, *et al*: 146-7). This pattern changed dramatically in the 1990s when the dependency ratio fell sharply, not only as a result of a change in age structure, but also because of the increased labour force participation of women, and falling unemployment.

Birth and fertility

Total births fell fairly steadily from the 1870s until the 'baby boom' during World War II (Table A.2.2 and Figure 2.3). The level rose sharply throughout the 1940s from 57,000 in 1940 to 69,000 in 1949 due to a number of factors. Firstly, there was a reduction in emigration when war broke out. Secondly, a marked concentration of the increase in registered births occurred in a single year, 1942. This was probably due to the stemming of emigration in that year, a particularly unpleasant war year in Britain. The introduction of work permits contributed to a curbing of emigration, while the introduction of food rationing probably increased the accuracy of registration of births. The introduction of children's allowances for the third and each subsequent child in 1944 also provided an incentive to register births.

The number of births in 1981 – 72,000 – was close to the level eighty years earlier, in 1901. Births rose to a twentieth-century peak of 74,000 in 1980 and then fell continuously by more than one-third to below 48,000 in 1994. Since then births increased by 5,000 to 53,000 in 1998. It is difficult to interpret the recent increase in births; age-specific fertility of women in the age groups 20-24 and 25-29 fell in the 1990s, while age-specific fertility for the age groups 30-34 and 35-39 increased, reflecting a postponement factor. Some of the increase may be due to the return of former migrants as well as the inflow of foreign nationals.

The increase in births outside marriage has been very striking, rising from 1,600 in 1921 to over 15,000 in 1998, or from 2 per cent to 28 per cent of total births. Births outside marriage in Ireland are now higher than the EU average (Heanue, 2000: 30-31). In 1998 four out of every five births outside marriage were to women under 25 years. The decline in births within marriage has been equally striking, almost halving between 1980 and 1995, from 70,700 to 37,700. In 1996 births *within* marriage increased for the first time in nearly twenty years. The overall drop in births is linked to the decrease in family size. In 1955 twenty-one per cent of births were first births. In 1998 first births accounted for 40 per cent (21,000 out of 53,000) of births (Punch, 1999). In 1955 thirty-one per cent of births were fifth births compared with only 5 per cent in 1998. In 1962 there were 2,000 births to mothers with 10 children and over, compared with 55 such births in 1998 (Heanue, *ibid* :32).

Figure 2.3: Birth rate and share of non-marital births, 1901-98

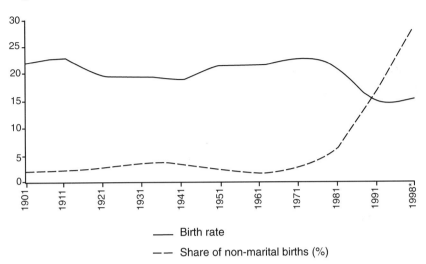

Source: Central Statistics Office; *1991-98 is a seven-year interval

An increase in permanent childlessness is becoming evident, as has already occurred in continental countries and in the United Kingdom. In the UK the likelihood of childlessness has increased steadily over the past 50 years. Only 10 per cent of women born in 1945 did not have a child, whereas it is estimated that 17 per cent of women born in 1955 and 21 per cent of those born in 1965 will remain childless (Fox Harding, 1996: 27-8). In Germany it is estimated that of women now entering their child-bearing years, 25 per cent will remain childless.

Ninety per cent of all births are to women aged 20-39. The age-specific fertility rate for 20-24 year old women began to decline in 1970 while for women aged 25-29 years the decline began in 1965. The fall in fertility is marked in the age group 25-29. In 1971 one-quarter in that age group gave birth compared with one-tenth in 1996 (Heanue, 2000: 30). In both groups the decline has begun to taper off while the long-term decline in the age-specific fertility rate of women aged 30-34 and 35-39 was halted in 1994 and since then has moved upwards (Table 2.2). The total fertility rate (TFR) declined from 4.03 in 1965 to 2.08 in 1989, the first year in which fertility fell below replacement level. The TFR fell further to 1.85 in 1995. Since then it increased to 1.93 in 1998.

Table 2.2: Age-specific fertility rate and total fertility rate, 1960-98 (Live births per 1,000 females at specified ages)

Year	15-19	20-24	25-29	30-34	35-39	40-45	45-49	TFR
1960	8.8	102.9	209.6	213.1	156.3	56.0	4.2	3.76
1965	14.0	125.1	236.1	218.9	150.3	57.6	4.2	4.03
1970	16.3	145.5	228.7	201.9	131.9	45.3	3.7	2.87
1975	22.8	138.6	216.1	162.2	100.1	36.8	2.6	3.40
1980	23.0	125.4	202.3	165.7	97.4	29.6	2.3	3.23
1985	16.6	87.2	158.6	138.4	75.2	21.6	1.5	2.50
1990	16.8	63.3	137.6	126.2	63.1	15.4	1.1	2.12
1995	15.1	50.3	106.7	123.5	60.3	13.1	0.8	1.85
1998	18.6	50.6	99.8	133.9	69.8	13.4	0.6	1.93

Source: Central Statistics Office

Although total fertility halved between 1970 and 1997, Ireland still has the highest rate in the EU. An indication of the impact of the decrease in fertility rates between the mid-1960s and the mid-1990s can be obtained by calculating the number of births that would have occurred in 1996 if the age-specific fertility rates of 1965 applied. On this basis births in 1996 would have been more than double what they actually were, i.e. 107,000 births as against actual births of 50,000.

Maternal mortality

In 1994 Ireland had the lowest rate of maternal mortality in the world following a steady improvement over several decades (Figures 2.4, 2.5; Tables A.2.3, A.2.4). In 1921 the maternal mortality rate, that is deaths per 100,000 registered births from puerperal conditions and diseases of pregnancy and childbirth, was 481, or 4.8 per 1,000, equivalent to the death of a mother for every 200 births. The actual number of maternal deaths that year was 293. Maternal mortality rates were higher in rural than in urban areas. In 1929 the rates for the rural districts in Laois, Kilkenny, and Leitrim were, respectively, 7.8, 6.9 and 7.1 per 1,000 births (LGD, 1929-30: 33). The causes of maternal deaths varied. Of 104 deaths recorded mid-way through the century in 1948, 32 were due to haemorrhage at childbirth, 20 to toxaemia of pregnancy, while puerperal infection was responsible for 18 deaths.

The Emigration Commission described the absolute number of deaths as small from a population perspective, noting that the annual 'average number of such deaths for 1941-50 was only 139' (Commission on Emigration, 1954: 113).

But the average annual number of 139 deaths means that during the 1940s a total of almost 1,400 such deaths took place, an appalling number by the standards of fifty years later. The seemingly dismissive observation of the Emigration Commission must be seen as emanating from a culture where high maternal mortality was a fact of everyday life. In 1941 the number of deaths had been 182, and in 1931 the number had been 246. From the 1950s the use of penicillin and other drugs dramatically reduced maternal mortality in childbirth. The maternal mortality rate has dropped steadily over the past four decades to the present level of three in 100,000 in 1996.

Figure 2.4: Trends in maternal mortality, selected countries, 1950-54 to 1990-94 (average annual deaths per 100,000 births)

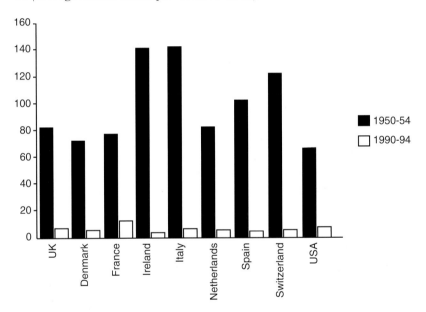

Source: World Health Statistics (WHO) and OECD

The decline in maternal mortality has contributed to a marked increase in the expectation of life. In 1900 the expectation of life at birth for men and women was just over fifty years compared with 73.6 years for men and over 79.2 years for women in 2000. In the mid-1920s, the average age at marriage for a man was just under 35 years and the average age for a woman was just under 30 years (Census, 1926). In 1990 the average age at marriage for a man was 30 years and for a woman 28.1 years. As a consequence of high mortality and late age at marriage the number of orphans was high. At the 1926 Census the number of children under 15 years with father dead (58,000) was greater than the number with mother dead (48,000) because of the older ages of fathers and because at the same age men have a higher death rate than women (Census 1926, *General Report*: 87). However, 44 per 1,000 children in the 26 Counties had mother dead but father alive, compared with 25 per 1,000 in England and Wales, reflecting a relatively high mortality rate for mothers in the 26 Counties.

Figure 2.5: Maternal mortality rates (per 100,000 births), and maternal deaths 1921-91

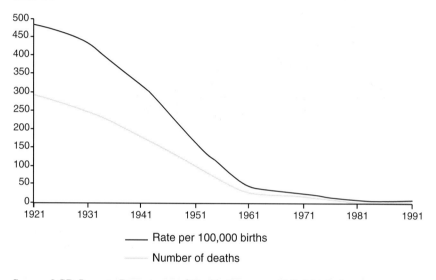

Source: LGD *Reports*, Department of Health *Reports* and Vital Statistics

Infant mortality

Substantial numbers of children do not survive their first birthday. The infant mortality rate refers to deaths of live-born infants under one year per 1,000 live births. The neonatal mortality rate refers to the deaths of live-born infants under four weeks per 1,000 live births, while the perinatal mortality rate, which was first measured in Ireland in 1957, is a measure of foetal deaths at or over 28 weeks gestation plus deaths of live-born infants under one week, per 1,000 live and still births. The neonatal rate is a component of the infant mortality rate. In 1995 stillbirths were registered in Ireland for the first time under the *Stillbirths Registration Act,* 1994. A stillbirth is defined as weighing 500 grams or more or at a gestation age of 24 weeks or more. This is a broader definition than the definition which was used for late foetal deaths until then. Prior to the 1994 Act a late foetal death was a death at or over 28 weeks. In 1995 there were 330 stillbirths compared with 311 deaths of infants under one year.

Figure 2.6: Average annual deaths of infants under 1 year by decade since 1871

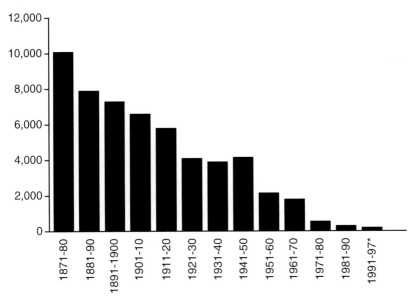

Source: Central Statistics Office; *1991-97 is a six-year interval

The infant mortality rate fell from 99 to 6 per 1,000 live births between 1900 and 1995 (Figure 2.6, Table A.2.5). The absolute number of deaths brings home the magnitude of infant mortality more starkly than the rate. In the first decade of the century, 6,500 children under one year died on average each year, compared with 550 in the 1980s. In 1926 infant mortality was as high as 170 per 1,000 in one North City area of Dublin, where the standard of housing was very poor with two-thirds of the people in the area living in housing with two or more persons per room (Census 1926, *General Report*: 70). Infant mortality fell steadily until the 1950s when it fell more sharply. In 1949 there were 3,415 deaths of infants under one year. By 1955 the number had fallen to 2,264 and to 2,027 by 1957. Relatively, the decline has been greatest in the death rate over four weeks and under one year as the share of neonatal deaths in the infant mortality rate has risen from less than one-third in the 1920s to over one-half in the 1980s. In 1986 the infant mortality rate was 8.7 and the neonatal rate was 4.8 compared with rates of 69 and 26 respectively in 1931. The perinatal rate was higher again at 13.6, or 879 deaths in 1986, but this rate also had fallen from 36.1, or approximately 2,000 deaths, in 1961.

In a paper first published in 1955, Dr James Deeny, Chief Medical Adviser in the Department of Health, tells the story of the decline in perinatal mortality in Ireland. He discusses the prevalent causes of the deaths, stressing the crucial importance of prematurity with its largely social causes at the time. He argues that perinatal mortality should be high on the medical agenda, especially in a 'Christian country':

> It is particularly apt in a Christian country such as ours that we should study this problem of perinatal mortality. The prevention of antenatal death or stillbirth of a viable foetus is in true agreement with the Christian belief that the human soul and human personality have the same existence in intra-uterine as in extra-uterine life (Deeny, 1995: 116).

In 1951 infant deaths exceeded deaths from tuberculosis – which were 2,107 – by almost 800. However, TB deaths declined much more rapidly so that in 1955 infant mortality (2,264) exceeded TB deaths (889) by nearly 1,400 and only 17 infant deaths were due to tuberculosis. Five causes accounted for two-thirds of the infant deaths in that year. These were congenital malformations (387), immaturity (370), pneumonia (325), birth injuries (217) and postnatal asphyxia (184).

In contrast to maternal mortality, which was highest in rural areas, infant mortality was highest in the County Boroughs, i.e. the city areas. In 1929 when the infant mortality rate for Ireland was 70 per 1,000, the rate for the County Borough of Limerick was 116.7, while for Waterford, Dublin and Cork the rates were 100.3, 106.2 and 85.2 respectively. The highest infant mortality was found among poor tenement dwellers. According to the Dublin Civic Survey Report, 1925, the infant mortality rate in Dublin City was 116 per 1,000, five times higher than the rate in certain suburbs. About 20 per cent of *all* deaths in Dublin in the 1920s occurred among infants under one year and nearly all of these among the poor. An article in the *Irish Press* in 1936 describes

> ... the slaughter of the innocents in these germ-soaked dens and rookeries. ... The hereditary tenements waif's chances of survival to manhood or womanhood are so slight ... the little ones, flecked with a beauty of their own, which gives a deeper tinge of pathos to their unhappy plight, die like flowers in a blight when they are stricken by disease which is always laying in wait for them (Kearns, 1994: 14).

A major element in the 'slaughter of the innocents' from the mid-1930s to the early 1940s was the series of enteritis epidemics in which as many as 1,000 babies died each year, the majority in Dublin. Deeny undertook pioneering research which established the contagious nature of the disease. He found that the Rotunda Hospital at the time was a focus of infection and that hospital outpatient departments where sick children were assembled together led to the spread of the disease; by contrast Deeny found that the Coombe Lying-in Hospital did not have enteritis:

> There they stuck to the old-fashioned idea of putting the babies in the same beds with the mothers. This seemed to have two effects. One was that, not only had the babies

the protection of the colostrum in the breast milk, but as their gastro-intestinal canals were invaded by bacteria in the normal way after birth these bacteria came from the mother and in some way, then unknown, conferred a degree of the mother's immune mechanism on the child (Deeny, 1995: 57).

The epidemic was successfully brought to an end in Dublin with the provision of a special 100-bed hospital, St Clare's, which provided for the isolation of infected children, a round-the-clock resuscitation service, as well as the disinfection of the dwelling in which the child lived. An accompanying measure was careful monitoring of the standard of milk given to poor families.

Infant mortality rates varied markedly according to whether the child was legitimate or illegitimate, possibly related to the poorer social and economic conditions of unmarried mothers, as well as the relative state of their health. In 1930 one out of every four illegitimate children died in the first year of life; their mortality rate was more than four times greater than that of children of married parents. In 1930 the death rate of illegitimate children in the Irish Free State, 251 per 1,000 births, was twice the rate in Northern Ireland, 140 per 1,000, and nearly three times the rate in England and Wales, 105 per 1,000 births. The overall infant mortality rate continued to decline during the 1930s, improving most rapidly in the urban areas. By contrast with the fall in the overall infant mortality rate, the rate for illegitimate children actually *rose* in the early 1930s. In 1934 a total of 2,030 children were born out of wedlock. One year later 538, or more than one in four, were dead. The Department of Local Government and Public Health Report 1934-37, observed: 'This mortality rate is out of all proportion to the corresponding rate in respect of legitimate infants and calls for investigation as to its causes and as to what measures should be taken to effect a reduction in this abnormal mortality' (LGD, 1934-37: 97).

Infant mortality rose somewhat in 1937 and the Medical Officer of the Maternity and Child Welfare Scheme in Dublin County Borough blamed special factors: 'A succession of strikes during the year and consequent distress, bad housing, and infection ... no doubt all played a part ...' The Medical Superintendent Officer of Health in Cork County Borough reported that, apart from prematurity, the two main factors in infant mortality were diarrhoea and broncho-pneumonia. He blamed 'improper feeding' for the increased number of deaths from diarrhoea:

The enormous preponderance of deaths of artificially-fed babies leads to the conclusion that this is the main factor which determines the death of infants from this condition. Of the 45 deaths from gastro-enteritis in infants under one year, no less than 42 were artificially-fed babies (LGD, 1934-37: 55).

In the 1950s the Commission on Emigration highlighted the high mortality rate for illegitimate children. Adverting to the fact that deaths of illegitimate children were not always recorded as such, the Commission raised the possibility of infanticide, but dismissed its importance, while admitting to a lack of information:

> While the general infant mortality rate for the Twenty-Six Counties in 1950 was 46, the legitimate rate was 45 and the illegitimate rate was 78. Full registration of deaths of illegitimate children would, no doubt, increase the disparity, a fact which is confirmed by a sample investigation made by us of the infant mortality rate in institutions which provide specially for the care of illegitimate infants. While adequate information is lacking as to the extent of infanticide we believe that its incidence is not sufficiently significant to require comment from us (Commission on Emigration, 1954: 112).

Court records show that convictions for infanticide occurred. At the start of the twentieth century a significant number of homicide victims were babies (Lysaght, 1998:148). Infanticide was highlighted by historian and archivist Catriona Crowe, in the RTÉ Documentary 'Hoodwinked', screened in April 1997. In the same year, Nicola Lafferty, a graduate in Film at the Dún Laoghaire College of Art and Design (DLCAD), directed a short documentary film dealing with infanticide – 'They Went Away in Silence'. The synopsis of the film stated:

> For many years in Ireland a single woman's pregnancy was enough to isolate her from any help or support. Some women feared their fate so much that they concealed their pregnancy until it reached full term. Many risked their lives delivering babies by themselves in secrecy. It's fair to assume that many of the babies were so well hidden that they were never found (DLCAD, IFC Showcase 1997, Programme).

During World War II, or 'the Emergency', as it was known in Ireland, access to Britain became more restricted, and it seems that more single pregnant women remained in Ireland. In 1949 the *Infanticide Act* was passed, whereby a special ground of temporary insanity was introduced as a means of reducing charges of murder to that of manslaughter. In that year there were five recorded cases of infanticide (Redmond and Heanue, 2000: 59). Infanticide was a reality regardless of the absence of comprehensive statistics. In 1919, the link between infanticide, illegitimacy and deprivation was remarked upon by Countess Markievicz, the first woman elected as a Member of Parliament, although she never took her seat, in an article which discussed the social conditions that drive women into crime and which was based on her own experience of jail in Aylesbury:

> I worked with a gang of murderesses in Aylesbury. Some were bad, but the most were foolish working girls who had got into trouble and had killed their little babies because life with them was impossible: because they had no way of earning a living, nowhere to go and nothing to eat (Quoted in R.M. Fox, 1935: 29).

Speaking in the Senate in 1935 on Section 17 of the Criminal Law Amendment

Bill which banned the sale or importation of contraceptives, Oliver St John Gogarty described infanticide as 'the dreadful alternative facing the unfortunate poor'. The question of infanticide was raised in the Dáil by another doctor, Deputy Rowlette, on several occasions, but the issue was not discussed (Clancy, 1989: 214-15).

Abortion

Abortion was a term rarely mentioned in public in Ireland until the 1980s. Mention of abortion in one of the haunting novels of Paul Smith depicting Dublin tenement life in the 1920s contributed to the banning of his books by the censor. In *The Countrywoman*, the young, unmarried, Queenie Mullen confides in Mrs Baines that she is pregnant. She recounts:

> 'I went to see Mrs Ennis. ... But she won't do anything. I'm too far gone, she says.' Then suddenly she gasped out in an uneven, incoherent plea what she had come to Mrs Baines for. 'But she gave me the address of a nurse in Wexford Street who'll do it. For five quid down and another five quid when it's over' (Smith, 1975: 167).

On one occasion in the 1950s, the subject of abortion captured the headlines. This occurred when a woman died following a clandestine abortion carried out by a Nurse Cadden in premises in Hume Street in Dublin. The woman apparently bled to death in the street outside the premises after a botched abortion. Nurse Cadden was portrayed in contemporary reports as the personification of evil. All changed utterly in the 1980s when politicians of the main political Parties were successfully lobbied to introduce a 'pro-life' amendment to the Constitution. Among those who did not support the idea of holding a referendum were the members of the Executive Council of the Irish Congress of Trade Unions (ICTU) who believed that 'such an amendment is unnecessary and ... it would be unwise and undesirable to proceed with it'. They believed that the matter should be dealt with by legislation (ICTU, 1983: 300). Prior to the amendment to the Constitution in 1983, 'the unlawful procurement of a miscarriage', or abortion, was prohibited under *The Offences Against the Person Act*, 1861, an Act which remains in force (Constitution Review Group, 1996). Following a referendum in 1983 the Constitution was amended to include the following in Article 40.3.3°:

> The State acknowledges the right to life of the unborn and, with due regard to the equal right to life of the mother, guarantees in its laws to respect, and, as far as practicable, by its laws to defend and vindicate that right.

In 1992, following a further referendum, additions were made to Article 40.3.3° to include the right to travel and the right to information. The Article was amended accordingly:

This subsection shall not limit freedom to travel between the State and another State.

This subsection shall not limit freedom to obtain or make available, in the State, subject to such conditions as may be laid down by law, information relating to services lawfully available in another State.

These additions became necessary following the 'X case'. In 1992, in *The Attorney General v. X* (1992) 1 IR 1, the Attorney General sought an injunction under the 'right to life' provision of the Constitution to prevent a suicidal teenager, who was pregnant following sexual abuse, from travelling to England for an abortion. The granting of the injunction was followed by a swift appeal to the Supreme Court. In a majority judgment the Supreme Court determined that the injunction preventing the girl from travelling should be lifted on the grounds that her own life was in danger from her threatened suicide which resulted from her pregnant state. Following the judgment, amendments to the Constitution permitting travel and information were passed by referendum, but a third proposed amendment, regarding the substantive issue of abortion, was defeated. The proposed amendment which was rejected was as follows:

It shall be unlawful to terminate the life of an unborn unless such termination is necessary to save the life, as distinct from the health, of the mother where there is an illness or disorder of the mother giving rise to a real and substantial risk to her life, not being a risk of self-destruction (Constitution Review Group, 1996: 274).

This proposed amendment was rejected by a two-to-one majority, apparently by a coalition of those who were opposed to abortion on any grounds, as well as those who thought the proposal was too restrictive. The current position is that abortion is legal in Ireland on the terms given under the Supreme Court judgment. During the nine years that have elapsed since the 1992 judgment there has been no legislation either to give effect to, or to limit, the judgment.

Following the enactment of the *Abortion Act*, 1967 in England, the Office of National Statistics (ONS), formerly the Office of Population Census and Surveys (OPCS) in London, has since 1968 published statistics regarding the place of residence of women who have had abortions carried out in England and Wales. These data show that a growing number of women with addresses in Ireland have undergone abortions in England and Wales. More detailed information is available from a survey carried out by the Health Research Board in the 1980s, while a study led by Evelyn Mahon of Trinity College, Dublin, was published in 1998. Mahon's study shows that social and economic pressures weigh heavily on women who have abortions. Since the introduction of the Act the number of abortions on women normally resident in the Republic grew from zero to over 6,000 in 1999. Data for 1994 show that just 77 per cent of abortions were in relation to single women, 15 per cent in relation to married women and 8 per cent in relation to widowed, separated and divorced women. In 1997, 882 or 15.4 per cent of abortions were carried out on women under 20 years. Over 70 per cent of abortions were carried out on women aged 20-34 years. Single women outnumber married and widowed/divorced/ separated women, in all age categories under 35. At ages over 35, married women outnumber single women by 2:1. An analysis of class factors showed that the highest termination rates were in the 'other non-manual' category, and the second highest in the 'professional managerial class'.

The issue of abortion has not gone away. In 1999 a Green Paper was published by a Group established under the aegis of the Department of Health and Children, setting out alternative constitutional and legal options. These options were reviewed by the Oireachtas Committee on the Constitution chaired by Brian Lenihan, TD. The Committee published an exhaustive report of approximately 700 pages in November 2000, but failed to reach consensus on the way forward (The All-Party Oireachtas Committee, 2000). The Committee suggested three possible approaches. Firstly, to leave the legal position unchanged. Secondly, to introduce legislation that will protect medical intervention to safeguard the life of the mother, within the existing constitutional framework. Thirdly, to legislate to protect best medical practice while providing for a prohibition on abortion, and consequently accommodate such legislation by referendum to amend the Constitution. There was general agreement among the Committee members on the need to support a plan to reduce the number of crisis pregnancies (*The Irish Times*, 16 November 2000). The matter rests in the hands of the Government.

Adoption

Legal adoption was introduced into Ireland with the passing of the *Adoption Act*, 1952, which provided for the establishment of the Adoption Board, An Bórd Uchtála, with powers to make adoption orders. Prior to 1952 informal adoption, as well as fosterage, existed on a limited scale with adoptions being arranged through private adoption societies, usually affiliated to the Catholic Church. The *Adoption Act*, 1952, together with further Acts of 1964, 1974, 1976 and 1988, comprise the law governing adoption in Ireland. Since the passing of the 1952 Act, 40,000 adoption orders have been made, an average of 1,000 per year, with the annual number varying from a high point of almost 1,500 in 1967, to less than 500 in 1997.

One of the consequences of the Great War was to increase the number of orphans and the number of illegitimate births, and this in turn helped to create a climate favourable to legal adoption, which was introduced in the UK in 1929. In Ireland the Joint Committee of Women's Societies and Social Workers took up the issue in the late 1930s. Not everyone favoured adoption, especially in rural areas where succession to land was involved (Whyte, 1980: 187). Early in 1948 an organisation to campaign for legal adoption in Ireland was founded. Examination of the issue had been undertaken by Fianna Fáil Minister for Justice, Gerry Boland, in 1944-45, and by Fine Gael Minister for Justice, Seán MacEoin, in 1948-51. MacEoin decided not to proceed with legislation because the Attorney

General had expressed doubts as to the constitutionality of an adoption law, while the minister himself harboured doubts as to the correctness of a natural parent surrendering her rights over her child forever. In light of subsequent events and the frequent desire of children who have been adopted, as well as the wishes of many natural parents to make contact with their children subsequent to adoption, the concerns of MacEoin were prescient. He maintained that to deprive a natural mother of all rights over her child was unjust and unchristian: 'No law could be framed that would compel a mother to waive for all time her rights to her child. Such a law would be against charity and against the common law of justice' (*The Irish Times*, 8 February 1951, quoted in Whyte, *ibid*: 188).

The concerns of the Attorney General were also reasonable although in the event when the constitutionality of the *Adoption Act*, 1952 was tested in the courts in the Nicolau case in 1966, the Act was found not to breach the Constitution. Nicolau was a Greek Cypriot who had an illegitimate child by an Irish girl. He wished to marry the girl and keep the child, but she gave the child up for adoption. Nicolau argued that the Adoption Act infringed his constitutional rights. The courts, however, ruled that the family in the Constitution is the family based on marriage and that the rights of the natural father accordingly receive no protection.

In the 1940s the Archbishop of Dublin, Dr McQuaid, was consulted by the Government on religious issues relating to adoption. In 1950 a sub-committee of the Catholic hierarchy was set up under the chairmanship of Dr McQuaid to consider the matter. When Gerry Boland once again became Minister for Justice in 1951, agreement had been reached on religious safeguards. The formula set out by the sub-committee stated:

> Legal adoption, if it be restricted within certain limits and protected by certain safeguards, is consonant with Catholic teaching. A child's right in respect of faith and morals must be protected by such safeguards as will assure his adoption by persons who profess and practise the religion of the child and who are of good moral character (Quoted in Cooney, 1996).

The way was opened for the *Adoption Act*, 1952, which provided for the adoption of children born out of wedlock and for children both of whose parents were dead. The Act contained a condition which required that adopting parents 'were of the same religion as the child and his parents or, if the child is illegitimate, his mother'. In effect the measure prevented couples in a marriage where spouses were of different religions from adopting a child. Subsequently, following a High Court case, this element of the Act was found to be unconstitutional in that it discriminated against Protestants. A new Adoption Act in 1974 repealed the religious clause in the 1952 Act.

An important feature of the 1952 Act was the ban on the payment of money for the purposes of the adoption of a child. Under the informal adoption system which operated prior to the Act a form of adoption 'trade' had been permitted whereby adopting parents made unspecified, variable and private donations to the adoption societies which facilitated the provision of babies for adoption. There was no popular or organised outcry against these payments, rather the view at the time tended to be that children were lucky to find a way out of their unenviable circumstances to prosperous homes, frequently in America. It is believed that some prominent obstetricians co-operated with the process, not, however, for any financial reward, rather because of their belief that the process was in the best interests of all concerned. It may be recalled that in the 1940s and 1950s Mother and Baby Homes, in which unmarried pregnant women often took refuge until such time as their babies could be put up for adoption, were very poorly funded; capitation grants paid by the Dublin Board of Assistance and other local authorities were as small as £2 per week.

A discovery by Catriona Crowe in 1996 brought to light the secret stories of nearly 2,000 Irish babies who had been sent to America for adoption between 1948 and 1961. Crowe came across a file from the Irish embassy in Washington which contained personal records for about twenty children, their birth mothers and adoptive parents. This in turn led to the discovery of 1,500 restricted files from the Department of Foreign Affairs, each one relating to an Irish baby sent to America for adoption. A further 400 files were subsequently found in the Department of Foreign Affairs where all the files had been processed because passports were required for the babies. Each file contained one key document – a letter of surrender by the mother of the baby. The mother declared that the baby was born to her 'out of wedlock', that she was relinquishing 'full claim forever' to her child and surrendering the child to the person in charge of the orphanage or adoption agency, generally a nun or a priest. The letter continued, 'I further undertake never to attempt to see, interfere with or make any claim to the said child at any further time.' The letter was signed in the presence of a notary (McKay, 1996).

The files also contained baptismal and marriage certificates of the adoptive parents, as well as references concerning the suitability of the adopters from a priest and from a 'Catholic Charities Home Study and Recommendation' body. Certain conditions regarding education and child-rearing were attached. The adoptive parents were to undertake to give the child a Catholic education and 'if the wife is at present employed, she must submit a statement from her employer that she will resign from her employment if a child is placed with her'. The Adoption Board was not involved in the American adoptions. These were carried out through voluntary adoption societies, which existed prior to the establishment of the Board. When the files on the American adoptions came to light, Sister Gabriel of Saint Patrick's Guild, one of the main adoption societies in the country, said that her society had placed about 400 children in the United States. Sister Gabriel said that false names were sometimes given on birth certificates because the mothers wanted their anonymity guaranteed (*The Irish Times*, 6 March, 1996).

Illegitimacy was central to adoption. Adoption was largely a method of providing homes with a father and a mother for illegitimate children while at the same time meeting the needs of, in general, but not exclusively, infertile couples. Between 1952 and 1988 children born within marriage could only be adopted if both their father and their mother were dead. This meant that a number of children who were in institutional care, because, for example, a surviving parent was unable to look after them, would have no option but to remain in institutional care. In May 1988, the then Minister for Health, Dr Rory O'Hanlon, brought an Adoption Bill before the Dáil, according to which provision was made for the adoption of legitimate children under certain circumstances. For a legitimate child to be adopted the High Court would have to be satisfied that the parents had failed for physical or moral reasons for at least a year before the adoption application could be made. The Court would also have to be satisfied that it was likely that the parents would continue to fail to care for their child (children) until the child (children) reached 18 years. In June 1988 the President, Dr Hillery, having consulted the Council of State, referred the Bill to the Supreme Court to test its constitutionality. The constitutionality of the Bill was confirmed by the Supreme Court and the way was then opened for the adoption of certain children born within marriage who had a living parent or parents.

Until the *Adoption Act*, 1988, apart from a very small number of legitimate orphans who had survived both parents, adoption in Ireland was limited to illegitimate children. At the high point of adoption in 1967 when just 1,500 adoption orders were made, the number of orders was almost identical with the number of illegitimate births in that year. In 1973 when the allowance was introduced for an unmarried mother who kept her child, the number of adoptions was over 1,400, not very different from the 1967 level. Gradually the number of adoption orders began to decline and, significantly, of the adoption orders made, the share of orders made in respect of family adoptions rose dramatically. Family adoptions refer to adoptions made by birth mothers and their husbands, and by other relatives including grandparents, brothers, sisters, uncles and aunts. In the last ten years the total number of adoption orders made fell from 715 in 1987 to 422 in 1997. In 1987, one quarter of adoptions were family adoptions; by 1995 just two-thirds of adoptions were family adoptions and over 90 per cent of those were by birth mothers and their husbands.

Notwithstanding amending Acts, adoption procedures remain rooted in the 1952 Act and the nature of the adoption system derives from the attitudes and customs of the 1950s. Central to these attitudes was the sanctity and supremacy of the marriage-based family, which was both a constitutional cornerstone of society and a sacrament of the Catholic Church. Giving birth to a child outside marriage stemmed from a sin in the eyes of the Church and was a social offence meriting punitive social treatment that included social denial. The social offence factor was widely accepted outside Catholic circles and outside Ireland at the time. The entire procedure from pregnancy to birth and frequently to adoption was shrouded in secrecy. Under the law as it remains to the present an adopted person does not have the right to his or her original birth certificate, a practice shaped by attitudes when adoption was introduced, reflecting a determination to ensure confidentiality and anonymity. However, in practice, more and more access is being granted to those who seek access to records. The initial problem that the adopted person must overcome is that of delay. Adoption societies have long waiting lists for information and the process can take up to two years. If the birth parent does not want contact there is not much that can be done by the adoption society. Every case goes to the Adoption Board which, following a Supreme Court decision that each case must be decided on its own merits, has been entrusted with the final determination of whether or not to grant the original birth certificate.

Widows, widowers and elderly

In 1926 widows outnumbered widowers by more than two to one; the ratio rose to almost four to one in 1991. A number of reasons help to explain the relatively larger number of widows, including the longer expectation of life of women than men, the fact that men are, on average, older at the time of marriage, often markedly so in the past (Walsh, 1972) and the higher remarriage rate of men. With regard to remarriage, in 1900 for example, nearly 2,000 widowers remarried in that year, but less than 1,000 widows remarried (Census of Population, 1901, *General Report*). In 1926, in the age range 30-54 years, there were 31,422 widows compared with 13,191 widowers, a ratio of nearly 2.5:1. The high incidence of widowhood contributed to a high incidence of orphanhood. At 14 years of age over 8 per cent of children in the 26 Counties in 1926, had father alive but mother dead, as compared with 4.4 per cent in England and Wales (Census 1926, *General Report*: 86). The total number of widows in 1926 amounted to 135,000 and of these, 55,000, or more than 40 per cent were gainfully employed. By 1996 there were 147,000 widows and 37,000 widowers, a ratio of just 4:1. Just 10 per cent of widows were at work in 1996. Farming was by far the biggest occupation for widows in 1926, accounting for 65 per cent of those who were gainfully occupied. When shopkeepers, publicans and other proprietorial occupations were included, 86 per cent of widows could be described as being involved in 'family businesses'. In 1951 farming accounted for 64 per cent of the gainfully occupied widows, almost identical with the share in 1926, while in 1991, farming still accounted for 31 per cent of gainfully occupied widows.

The identity of widows often remained closely linked with that of their deceased husbands. Hilda Tweedy, founder of the Irish Housewives' Association (IHA), makes the following observation on the position of widows in political life in the 1940s in the context of the candidature of Hanna Sheehy Skeffington as an Independent candidate for the Dáil in the 1943 General Election:

At that time the women TDs were usually widows, put there by political parties on the death of their husbands to secure the seat on a sympathy vote. Little was heard from them, or of them. We called them the 'silent sisters', but perhaps that was a hasty judgement. They probably proved their worth on the various committees then deemed suitable for women, but their work was not reported (Tweedy, 1992: 22).

Table 2.3: Widows and widowers, 1926-96

	1926	1996
Widows	135,000	147,000
Widowers	59,210	37,000
Widows gainfully occupied	56,604	13,280*
Widows per 100 widowers	228	398
Gainfully occupied as per cent all widows	40	10*
Gainfully occupied widows in farming as per cent all gainfully occupied widows	65	31*

Source: Censuses 1926, 1991 and 1996
* 1991 Census

A high incidence of lone parent families in earlier generations resulted from the frequent incidence of widowhood. In 1911 widows outnumbered married women by age 65-69; in 1926 widows were almost as numerous as married women aged 65-69 while in 1951 widows outnumbered married women by age 70-74. In the UK 'the proportion of women potentially lone mothers through either widowhood or marital breakdown was very similar in 1861 (8.1 per cent) and 1981 (8.9 per cent)' (Fox Harding, 1996: 64).

In the hundred years between 1841-1941, when the total population of the 26 Counties fell by about 3.5 million, there was an increase of 117,000 in the number of persons aged 65 years and over. In the sixty years from 1936-96 the number of persons aged 65 years and over increased from 287,000 to 410,00, an increase of more than 220,000. Between 1996 and 2031 the numbers aged 65 years and over are projected to double to 800,000. The very old population, i.e. those aged 80 years and over is projected to increase from its 1996 level of 90,000 to over 200,000 in 2031 (CSO population projections). The proportion of the total population aged 65 and over has grown steadily from 6.5 per cent of the population in 1901, to 9.7 per cent of the population in 1936, to over 11 per cent in 1996. The proportion is projected to rise to between 18-21 per cent by 2031. According to current mortality patterns, just over 90 per cent of British women are expected to reach their sixtieth birthday; a century ago only 46 per cent did so. Over three-quarters of men are expected to reach their sixty-fifth birthday, compared with only 40 per cent a century ago. This has major implications for the provision of pensions and for the care of the elderly because when state retirement pensions were introduced, the majority of people did not survive to retirement age. Nowadays survival to retirement age is likely and people have many more years of life after retirement.

A feature of economic development is an increase in both the share of the elderly in the population and the share of the elderly who live alone (Table A.1.6). The number of multigenerational households has declined steadily. In the small farm economy until the 1950s it was commonplace for a couple to share accommodation with one or more in-law. This pattern persisted in urban areas also, as Humphreys describes in the case of the Dunn family in Dublin:

> It is possible, and perhaps likely, that at least one of the three younger children will not marry until John and Joan die but will remain with them in their old age, for their sense of filial piety and its obligations is strong. It is even more likely that if all should marry before their parents' death, whoever of the parents survives the other will be taken into the household of one of the children (Humphreys, 1966: 133).

Living arrangements

Aggregate demographic indicators, such as marriage and birth rates, provide an overview of changing family trends. Further information can be obtained from examining 'forms of life' in households, or *Lebensformen*, as defined by Zapf and others (Kaufmann *et al*, 1997: 4). The 'forms of life' typology combines the following variables: marital status and labour force participation of household members, number of generations in the household, and numbers of children. Labour force participation of the adult household members represents the main connection between the family and the world outside. A survey carried out by the ESRI in 1987 has made it possible to examine household composition and 'life forms' in Ireland. The survey covered 3,500 households in which there were 4,200 women aged 20 years and over. The focus here is directed on the household composition and the 'life forms' of two age cohorts of women, 25-29 and 45-54 years, in 1987. The first cohort represents women in the early phase of family formation, when a balance between employment outside the home and family work within the home has to be achieved. The second cohort represents women once again balancing work within and outside the home, at a time when children are reaching independence (Kennedy and McCormack, 1997). Three main variables were used for classification purposes: marital status, number of children and some basic characteristics of the relationships of people in the households, for example, whether a multigenerational household existed. From a total of twelve household composition categories, the five most popular categories accounted for over 80 per cent of all women. These categories are: (1) married, living with husband with two or more children, (2) married, no children, on own with husband, (3) single, no children in household with parents, (4) married, one child, with husband, and (5) widowed, separated, divorced with others in household.

Households with two or more children, with both parents present, comprise just under 30 per cent of households in which women aged 25-29 years are present, and just over 30 per cent of households in which women aged 45-54 years are present. For 25-29 year olds, the most popular household options are marriage with one or two children (41 per cent), single and still living at home (28 per cent), and single living with other/s (12 per cent). For those aged 45-54, over 80 per cent are married, living with their husbands with one, two or more children, or no children.

'Lifestyle' was classified using a number of variables that included marital status, children and employment status of the woman and her spouse. Six 'lifestyle' arrangements accounted for 57 per cent of all women aged 20 years and over in 1987. These were the conventional nuclear family arrangement – married, with conventional wife-mother-homemaker/husband-provider roles, and at least two children at home (15.4 per cent); married, one child, wife at home, husband working or not working (7.3 per cent); single, no children, living at home, working or not working (17.7 per cent); and the general older 'empty-nest' arrangement (16.8 per cent). Over 17 per cent of both 25-29 and 45-54 year olds are in the category married, breadwinner husband, and more than two children (Table A.2.6). Twenty-one per cent of 25-29 year olds are single with no children, at work and living at home. Almost one in five of the 45-54 year olds are in the 'empty-nest' category. For 25-29 year olds the category single, no children, living in non-family households accounts for 11 per cent; while single, not at work and living at home accounts for over 8 per cent. Over half of the 45-54 year olds are in conventional, wife in home duties, husband working, situations, with 14 per cent having no children, 20 per cent having one child and 18 per cent having two or more children. Very few of this age cohort, about 10 per cent at most, are in 'dual-career' households. The newer lifestyle, dual-earner households (categories 7 and 12 in Table A.2.6), together with two categories in the residual, account for 9 per cent of all women and 18 per cent of all women aged 25-29. Such new-style households are much more characteristic of better-educated people, particularly of better-educated young people (Kennedy and McCormack, 1997: 216-18).

Appendix 2

Table A.2.1: Average annual number of marriages and marriage rate per decade since 1864

Decade	Average annual number	Average annual rate per 1,000
1864-70	21,150	5.1
1871-80	18,014	4.5
1881-90	14,692	4.0
1891-1900	14,805	4.5
1901-10	15,325	4.8
1911-20	15,785	5.1
1921-30	14,245	4.8
1931-40	14,359	4.9
1941-50	16,585	5.6
1951-60	15,742	5.4
1961-70	17,430	6.0
1971-80	21,562	6.8
1981-90	18,888	5.4
1991-95	16,345	4.6
1996	16,255	4.5
1997	15,631	4.3
1998	16,783	4.5

Source: Central Statistics Office

Table A.2.2: Average annual number of births and birth rate per decade since 1864

Decade	Total number	Non-marital number	Total per 1,000	Non-marital as % of total
1864-70	106,926	2,584	25.8	2.4
1871-80	104,379	1,705	26.3	1.6
1881-90	83,762	1,575	22.9	1.9
1891-1900	73,995	1,468	22.0	2.0
1901-10	71,380	1,468	22.5	2.1
1911-20	66,507	1,595	21.5	2.4
1921-30	60,406	1,706	20.2	2.8
1931-40	57,105	1,893	19.3	3.3
1941-50	65,011	2,285	21.9	3.5
1951-60	61,700	1,220	21.2	2.0
1961-70	62,400	1,385	21.7	2.2
1971-80	69,400	2,633	21.8	3.8
1981-90	61,628	5,644	17.6	9.2
1991-95	50,044	9,656	14.1	19.3

Source: Central Statistics Office

Table A.2.3: Trends in maternal mortality, selected countries, 1950-54 to 1990-94 (average annual deaths per 100,000 births)

Country	1950-54	1985-89	1990-1994
U.K.	81.7	6.9	7.2
Denmark	72.7	5.3	4.8
France	78.6	10.1	11.2
Ireland	141.1	4.2	4.1
Italy	142.4	6.1	5.8
Netherlands	82.9	7.0	5.0
Spain	102.2	4.7	4.1
Switzerland	122.8	6.4	4.3
USA	67.5	7.6	7.9

Source: World Health Statistics (WHO) and OECD

Table A.2.4: Maternal mortality rates, 1921-96 (per 100,000 births)

Year	Rate	Number of deaths
1921	481.0	293
1931	431.0	246
1941	321.0	182
1951	164.0	103
1961	45.0	27
1971	22.5	15
1981	4.2	3
1991	3.8	2
1996	5.6	3

Source: LGD Reports, Department of Health Reports, and Vital Statistics, various

Table A.2.5: Average annual deaths of infants under 1 year and infant mortality rate by decade since 1864 (per 1,000 births)

Period	Average annual number	Rate per 1,000
1864-70	10,222	96
1871-80	10,104	97
1881-90	7,795	93
1891-1900	7,357	99
1901-10	6,522	91
1911-20	5,591	84
1921-30	4,222	70
1931-40	3,907	68
1941-50	4,278	66
1951-60	2,258	37
1961-70	1,553	25
1971-80	1,110	16
1981-90	569	9.2
1991-97	318	6.3

Source: Central Statistics Office. Prior to 1994 data refer to the year of occurrence; since 1994 data refer to year of registration

Table A.2.6: 'Lifestyle' characteristics of women aged 25-29 and 45-54 in 1987(%)

Lifestyles	Age 25-29	Age 45-54	Age 20+
1 Married, > 2 children, home duties, husband working	17.4	17.6	15.4
2 Single, no children, at work, living at home	20.9	0.4	10.6
3 Married, no children, home duties, husband not working	-	4.5	9.8
4 Married, 1 child, home duties, husband working/ not working	5.4	20.2	7.3
5 Single, not at work, living at home	8.4	1.8	7.1
6 Married, no children, home duties, husband working	0.7	13.5	7.0
7 Married, 1 or > 1 child, husband and wife working	7.6	6.3	5.6
8 Widowed/separated/divorced, with/without children	2.4	5.7	5.5
9 Married > 1 child, wife not working, husband not working	7.4	7.3	5.4
10 Single, no children, working, non-family household	10.6	1.3	4.6
11 Single, no children, not working, living on own	2.0	1.4	3.4
12 Married, no children, both working	7.9	3.5	3.3
13 Residual	8.3	16.6	15.8
Total per cent	100	100	100
Total number	407	716	4,173

Source: ESRI (1987)

3

Living Standards and Earning a Living

The economic basis for family formation and support covers a wide spectrum, from the family farm or business to a state pension for widows and an allowance for lone parents. The range also includes the male breadwinner and the dual-earner couple. Language itself captures the essence in the phrases 'to earn a living', to be 'a breadwinner', or 'Saothar a bhaint amach'. Over the century, living standards, both absolute and relative, have altered significantly. The improvement in absolute standards is uncontested, notwithstanding some reassessment of measurement tools, while changes in relativities pose complex technical issues. This chapter sets out to give a broad picture of the changes in absolute living standards as well as some idea of changes in relative standards, partly by highlighting class differences. The relative importance of the chief sectors of the economy – agriculture, industry and services – is examined. For several decades the small farm, or 'family homestead', was of special importance. As the services sector expanded and more women sought to combine motherhood and livelihood, the economic basis of many families was transformed. Dual earner families have increased in number in recent years. At the same time there has been a marked growth in families dependent on social welfare payments for their sustenance.

Living standards

The indices of economic growth – GNP or GDP per capita – did not exist at the start of the twentieth century. Estimates for GNP were first made in Ireland for the year 1926 by T.J. Kiernan and George Duncan and estimates for earlier years were constructed retrospectively (Kennedy, Giblin and McHugh, 1988). Until the 1960s, public debate was more likely to focus on 'the state of the country' rather than 'the state of the economy'. With the increase in living standards since the 1960s it is easy to forget that from the mid-1920s to the mid-1940s real wages scarcely rose at all (Ó Gráda, 1998). The share of total household expenditure that is devoted to the most basic necessity of life – food – gives some idea of living standards. At the time of the first Household Budget Inquiry in 1926 over half of the weighting in household expenditure was for food; fifty years ago in 1947, not much less than half, 46 per cent, was for food. Since then the share has halved, falling to 23 per cent in 1996. This shift gives some indication of the improvement in average living standards but it does not tell us of the extremes of poverty or wealth. The standard of living in Ireland cannot be understood without reference to emigration. Between 1926 and 1960 real national income increased by 40-50 per cent, an unfavourable rate when compared with the rest of Europe (O'Brien, 1962: 22), but income per head increased more rapidly because population fell. Between 1926-60 a quarter of a million workers left agriculture and many of them emigrated. In the thirty years between 1929 and 1960 real output in agriculture increased by only 14 per cent. The standard of those who remained rose largely because of the decline in the numbers engaged in agriculture.

An extensive literature exists regarding Irish economic growth during the twentieth century (Kennedy, Gibling and McHugh, 1988; Lee, 1989; Ó Gráda, 1997). Using traditional measures of growth, GDP and GNP, the conventional interpretation has been that Irish economic performance was relatively poor until the emergence of the 'tiger economy' in the 1990s. However, on the basis of the more inclusive, Human Development Index of the United Nations (HDI), devised by the Pakistani economist Mahbub ul Haq, longer-term Irish performance has been more impressive. The HDI is a composite index of GDP/person, life expectancy and educational attainments, i.e. income, longevity and knowledge. Although remaining lowest ranked of six countries (Table 3.1), Ireland closed the gap to a remarkable degree between 1913 and 1992. The emergence of the HDI is a recognition

> ... that conventional measurements of real GDP/person or real wages may be inadequate as an estimate of changes in living standards and that more attention needs to be paid both to aspects of well-being that are not determined by the purchasing power of private incomes and to the quality of life (Crafts, 1997: 299).

Since 1913 the welfare gap, as depicted by the HDI, has narrowed for the seven countries shown in Table 3.1. The rank order for Ireland has remained unchanged while the UK has been displaced from pole position by France. In 1913 the gap between Ireland and the UK was 0.167; in 1992 the gap had closed to 0.001, while the gap between Ireland and France was 0.015.

Participation in education, one of the components of the HDI, is closely associated with rising living standards. In the 1920s about 80 per cent of the population left school after the primary level. In the late 1990s about 80 per cent left school with the leaving certificate. The *Investment in Education* Report, (OECD, 1965), followed by the introduction of free secondary education in 1967, helped to shape the education system and Irish society for the remainder of the century. The major spurt in post-primary participation that followed the Report was preceded by a slow and steady rise in second level participation from the 1920s, with an upward tilt occurring in the middle 1950s (Minister for Education, 1963). In 1946, 24 per cent of those aged 14-19 years were at school or students. The share had risen to 41 per cent in 1966 before the introduction of free secondary education. For those born in the 1930s, about two-thirds left school after the primary level and less than 10 per cent went on to third level. For those born in the 1960s, less than 10 per cent left after primary level, with 60 per cent attending post-primary level and about 25 per cent going on to third level. For those born in the late 1970s who left school in 1995, 80 per cent had a leaving certificate and around 50 per cent were going on to some form of third level education (Fahey, FitzGerald, Maître, 1998).

Table 3.1: Human Development Index, selected European countries, 1913-92

Country	1913	1992
Belgium	0.621 (4)	0.925 (2)
Denmark	0.677 (2)	0.920 (4)
France	0.611 (5)	0.930 (1)
Germany	0.632 (3)	0.921 (3)
Ireland	0.563 (6)	0.915 (6)
UK	0.730 (1)	0.916 (5)

Source: Crafts, 1997: 310-11

A major programme of slum clearance and local authority house-building began in the 1930s, tapered off during World War II, and recommenced in the early post-war years. The result was an enormous improvement in housing standards. In 1946 less than one-third of households had more than four rooms; by 1991 the proportion was 70 per cent. In 1991, 80 per cent of homes were owner-occupied compared with 53 per cent in 1946. In 1946, 400,000 households or 60 per cent of the total lacked a piped water supply. By 1991, the number had fallen to 13,000. In 1946 sanitary facilities were limited. Between 1946 and 1991 the number of households with flush toilets grew from 255,000 to over 970,000 (Punch and Finneran, 2000: 21-2).

Technological progress has been a major factor in rising living standards. In Edwardian days horses, bicycles, trams, trains and boats provided the means of transport. Homes were lit by candle-light and oil lamps, while the lamplighter was a common sight in city streets as gas provided the means of public lighting. Cooking and heating depended on turf fires, ranges and stoves. From the 1930s to the 1950s, electricity became widely available. In the 1930s wirelesses were still luxury items and in the countryside on Sunday afternoons neighbours would gather together in whichever house had a wireless to listen to the transmissions from Croke Park. The number of radio licences increased steadily until the war years when batteries became scarce, but demand rose rapidly after the war. In 1952-55 the CSO conducted a listenership survey. It showed very high levels of listenership, especially for the news at 1.30 pm (Redmond and Heanue, 2000: 56). Buses and private motor cars increased in number and aeroplane travel began to develop. In 1936 there were 14 private motor cars per 1,000 population; this rose to 100 in 1966 and to 300 in 1996 (Ó Gráda, 1998).

Refrigerators transformed shopping patterns, making weekly, rather than daily shopping a possibility, and leading to a proliferation of supermarkets. Supermarkets replaced the corner stores that had been supplemented by daily deliveries to households of bread, milk, and sometimes meat and other groceries. Labour saving devices, including vacuum cleaners, washing machines, and later, dishwashers, were replacing domestic workers and reducing the workload of housewives. Disposable nappies and TV dinners were still a little into the future. As the new century dawns, however, the increase in households in which both partners are in the workforce may lead once more to a growth in employment of domestic workers as cleaners and child carers. The twentieth century opened with the arrival of the Kodak camera; it closed with the computer and the Internet. In between have come radio, cinema, aeroplanes, television, antibiotics, contraceptives and organ transplants, as well as the Russian Sputnik and the American man on the moon.

One indicator of economic change, one that tells a simple and striking story, is that which shows the change in the purchasing power of the pound. George O'Brien, former Professor of Political Economy and National Economics at University College Dublin, once remarked that the change in the value of money was the biggest change to have occurred in his lifetime. O'Brien who was born in the 1892, died on New Year's Eve, 1973, when the purchasing power of the pound (£) was more than five times its current value. Since 1914, with the exception of the period 1922-35, the purchasing power of the pound has fallen steadily. The purchasing power of £1 in 1998 is equivalent to about 2p in 1935. Many of those who worked in the 1920s and 1930s did not receive wages in cash; they were part of the pool of family labour on the land. In industry wages were, for the most part, very small.

A consistent trend in household patterns has been the decline in the number of domestic servants. At the 1911 census there were over 135,000 indoor servants, predominantly female, in the whole of Ireland (32 Counties). In 1926, in the 26 Counties, there were 88,000 domestic servants, of whom less than 3,000 were men; by 1951, the total had dropped to 60,000. In 1991 there were less than 5,000 domestic servants, of whom less than 300 were men. According to sociologist Patricia O'Connor, the implications of the decline in domestic servants for the lifestyles of married women have not been recognised (O'Connor, 1998: 112).

Ability to afford servants is an indicator of living standards. In 1911 it was estimated that an income of about £150 per year was required to afford a domestic servant (Hearn, 1993: 5). In her study of domestic service in Dublin in the late nineteenth and early twentieth century, Mona Hearn describes the situation of one man with approximately the required income:

A typical example was C.L. Doyle who was a sorting clerk in the GPO in 1911. He lived with his wife and two sons in a small house, 157 St Helen's Terrace, Clonliffe Road. He was forty-eight years of age and was earning approximately £146 a year. He and his wife kept a boarder which gave him a higher income and he was able to employ a young girl aged eighteen from County Meath (Hearn, *ibid*: 5).

The higher the social class, the more servants were employed. Hearn describes how some higher professional families employed six or seven staff:

> Mr Justice John Ross, then a High Court judge, who lived with his wife and grown-up daughter at 66 Fitzwilliam Square in 1911, had six servants: a butler, footman, cook, two housemaids and a chauffeur. Sir Charles Cameron, who in 1911 was medical superintendent officer of health and held other public health positions for which he was paid £1,000 a year, lived at 51 Pembroke Road, and employed four servants (Hearn, *ibid*: 7).

In the same era Lady Fingall employed a staff of thirteen:

> The staff at Killeen in those days – and I dare say it was always an inadequate one – consisted of twelve servants in addition to my own maid. The housekeeper, butler, footman and three housemaids saw to the house. There were the two lamp and fire boys; in the vast kitchen a cook with a kitchen-maid under her, and, as well, a laundrymaid and a dairymaid (Hinkson, 1995: 116).

In the early 1930s, it was regarded as normal for civil servants to employ at least a 'maidservant'. In the context of an examination of civil service pay and the cost of living, the Civil Service Federation pointed out how the outlay of the civil servant's household differed from that of the working-class household. The former included travelling expenses, life insurance, restaurant meals, medical expenses, books and maidservants. 'At least one maidservant was normally employed in the former and the period of dependency of the children was more extended than in a working-class family' (Sweeney, 1990: 55).

Class differences

At the start of the twentieth century the factors that most differentiated families were economic and class factors. Family life was very different for the poor slum dwellers, the working class, the growing bourgeoisie in the towns and cities, as it was different also for the farm labourers, the small tenant farmers, the larger farm proprietors and the substantial landed gentry in the rural areas. Class distinction was rife in rural Ireland, and farming people would seldom mix with servants. The distinction between farmers with a reasonable standard of living and the rural poor – those with potato patches, or landless labourers – stretched back for centuries. In the judgement of historian Art Cosgrove, 'The widest social gap in rural Ireland was that between the farmer and the landless labourer, and marriage rarely, if ever, bridged that gap' (Cosgrove, 1985: 3). Folklorist Caoimhín Ó Danachair is even more emphatic, saying that marriage could never take place between the farmer's child and the labourer because 'The landless labourer was the untouchable of Irish rural society' (Ó Danachair, 1985:101). Liam O'Donnell tells us that if a farmer's son married a servant girl 'it had to be a runaway marriage as they were blacklisted by the boy's family. When a thing like that happened it was a crime and they'd be whispering and talking about it for weeks' (O'Donnell, 1997: 87).

The family life of Lady Fingall at the turn of the century could not have been more different from that of the dwellers in O'Casey's tenements, while the family life of the servant girl or boy was a world apart from that of his or her farmer master, especially if the farmer were wealthy. Eighty years after the Famine death from starvation was not unknown. In 1927 a mother and two of her five children died of starvation in Adrigole in the Beara peninsula in Cork. Her husband died a day or so afterwards. The tragedy was immortalised in a novel by Peadar O'Donnell (Fanning, 1983: 71). Absolute poverty persisted for decades after Independence. At a meeting of the Welfare Section of St John's Ambulance Brigade in November 1941, Sir John Lumsden described how two poor Dublin mothers owned one pair of shoes between them, and wore them in turn to attend the welfare dining room of the Brigade to avail themselves of dinners, at a time when the *Herald Boot Fund* was providing boots for poor children. During the previous year over 70,000 dinners had been served to an average of 235 Dublin mothers (Russell Scrapbook, press cutting). At the same meeting, Dr Ninian Falkiner, Master of the Rotunda hospital, said that in his hospital and its district they had attended 5,000 mothers in the previous year, 1,000 of whom were suffering from malnutrition. He said, 'Malnutrition was an unpleasant word, and was sometimes a substitute for a more unpleasant one, semi-starvation' (Russell Scrapbook, press cutting).

In 1943 a series of articles entitled 'Other People's Incomes' appeared in *The Bell*, a monthly journal established by Sean O'Faolain in 1940, which dealt with social as well as literary matters, and reflected 'a bit of Life itself' (O'Faolain, 1940:5). 'From how to live on £200 a year as a single parent in a country cottage, to the more elegant lifestyle of a young solicitor family of five earning £850 per annum, the series recorded the spending habits and the aspirations of different economic classes' (Kirwin, 1989:103). At an income of £100 per annum a family was in severe poverty with 'no fruit, no vegetables, no cheese, no eggs', and must rely on the charity of the St Vincent de Paul Society. An article about the £400 'average' family concluded that the family required £462 to maintain its modest lifestyle. The series concluded that it would not be prudent for any man to marry in the cities unless he had an income of between £400-£425 per annum. *The Bell* hoped that the legislators would take note of the conditions in which people were struggling to live.

The work of Farmar and Kearns provide a stark contrast between the family life of the middle class and that of the poor (Farmar, 1995; Kearns, 1994). Farmar's study refers chiefly to middle class lives. He examines what he terms 'ordinary lives' at three points in the twentieth century – 1907, 1932, and 1963. In dealing with the first benchmark date of 1907, Farmar draws on Todd Andrews' autobiography, *Dublin Made Me*. In that book Andrews provides a comprehensive class rundown of the world in which he grew up:

> The top of the Catholic heap – in terms of worldly goods and social status – were the medical specialists, fashionable dentists, solicitors, wholesale tea and wine merchants, owners of large drapery stores and a very few owners or directors of large business firms. ... At the bottom of the heap were the have-nots of the city, consisting of labourers, dockers, coal heavers, messenger boys and domestic servants (Farmar, 1995: 13).

Andrews highlights features of family life that are frequently overlooked, for example how mothers were often involved in earning the family living, even though they might not be recorded in the official statistics. In his own family, his mother ran a dairy and provision shop in an era when a proliferation of small local grocery shops existed. In the case of most of these shops, except those run by widows, the ownership would, most likely, be registered in the name of the man of the house.

In 1907, in Dublin, the wages of unskilled labourers were generally less than £1 a week, and often as low as 15s: 'With this level of earnings a working man, even though sober and with a small family, found it virtually impossible to provide adequately for his family. ... The constant items of a working-class diet were bread, usually without butter, and well stewed tea with sugar' (Farmar, 1995: 19).

The income distribution range was wide, with top barristers, doctors and administrators earning between £2,000-£5,000, equivalent to £100,000-£250,000 in today's money. Middle-class respectability required an income of £250 a year (Farmar, *ibid*: 25). A book published in 1903 by Mary Halliday addressed the question of *Marriage on £200 a Year*. Middle class men rarely earned enough to support a wife and family before their thirties. Only the rich could afford to buy their own homes. In Edwardian Dublin, and for many years afterwards, the majority of people rented their homes. Farmar tells us that two semi-detached houses in Lr Beechwood Avenue in Ranelagh were available to rent at £42 per annum in 1907. An identical house sold for £285,000 in 1998. In a century-long house-price survey, *The Irish Times* cites another Ranelagh house, one in Cherryfield Avenue, which sold for £210 in 1910 and achieved £300,000 in 1999. Samuel Beckett's home, Cooldrinagh in Foxrock, cost £1,500 to build in 1905, and was estimated to be worth approximately £3 million in 1999 (Morgan: 1999). Early in the century the horse and carriage was widely used for transport, with dray horses pulling delivery carts for milk, bread and coal. Before sliced pans and bottled milk, the breadman and the milkman left whole pans, and measured milk in tin jugs early in the morning. In 1907 when bicycles were widely used, a good bike could be had for £5, while a four-seater motor car cost £300 (Farmar, *ibid*: 32).

In 1932 traditional family roles were strong, although Farmar argues that attitudes to sex, marriage and other aspects of behaviour were being challenged. With a sure touch for the signs of snobbery, he notes the great respect for 'appearances'. Dress, including clerical dress, gives the wearer a certain image and prominence. Likewise eating habits reflect a way of life. The sophisticated city dwellers dine in the evening, while the provincial cousins partake of high tea. Public respectability was no less important in the 1960s when a cynical respondent to a survey is quoted as saying, 'There is nothing like attending at mass with your wife and kids, making sure to be seen of course, to help the business' (Farmar, *ibid*: 154).

By 1932 the average industrial wage was £126 per annum, or less than £3 per week. An executive officer in the civil service started at £144, a national school teacher at £140, and a bank clerk at £100 per year. Probationer nurses started at £10-£12 per year, living in, having themselves first paid training fees to the hospitals. The renting of housing continued to predominate – three-quarters of civil servants rented – but house purchase was becoming more common (Farmar, *ibid*: 96). A three-reception room, six-bedroom house in Rathgar cost £1,400, while a four-bedroom house in Drumcondra cost £835. In 1939 a new house on Mount Merrion Avenue cost £1,500. The same house sold in 1998 for over £500,000. Domestics servants, including maids, cooks, nannies and gardeners were still commonplace among the middle classes.

In 1963 the average industrial wage was £541. The Taoiseach, Seán Lemass, earned £4,000, similar to the Secretary of the Department of Finance, Dr T.K. Whitaker, while the Director General of RTÉ, Kevin McCourt, earned £5,000. A comparison between pay in 1963, 1932 and 1907 shows striking changes both in real incomes and in relativities. The cost of living in 1963 was about three times its level in 1932, while the average industrial wage had risen more than four times, indicating a real increase in living standards of 25 per cent. For top level civil servants the increase in money income, not counting occupational children's allowances, over the thirty years had been 225 per cent, indicating a narrowing in the range between higher and lower levels of the income distribution. In 1907 the ratio between top civil servants and skilled labourers was 25:1; in 1932 it was 12:1; by 1963 this had narrowed to 6.5:1 (Farmar, *ibid*: 172). In 1996 the ratio between the pay of the average industrial worker in manufacturing industry and the standard grade Departmental Secretary was 5.5:1, while it was 6:1 between the average industrial worker and the Secretary of the Department of Finance. These are very crude indicators of relative pay movements and must be interpreted with extreme care. They take no account of taxation and the after tax position, but it is probably safe to conclude that the gap between the pay of workers and top civil servants was greater in the 1930s than in the 1960s. By the 1960s both house purchase and house prices were on the increase. A five-bedroom, three-reception room house in Rathgar now sold for £6,000.

Kearns's chronicle of the extraordinary deprivation of tenement life in Dublin during the early decades of the twentieth century contrasts sharply with the 'ordinary lives' of the middle classes. Despite extreme poverty the remarkable resilience of the tenement dwellers shines through. In the words of one elderly former tenement dweller, 'We were all one family, all close. We all helped one another' (Kearns, *ibid*: 5). But invisible walls, stronger than any visible ones, existed between the tenement dwellers and the rest of society. Jimmy McLoughlin, who grew up in the worst slums in Marlborough Place in Dublin, testified, 'Actually, I think my house was the nearest tenement to Nelson's Pillar, so we were near a better area. But we never played on O'Connell Street … it wasn't *our* world' (Kearns, *ibid*: 16). That so many people survived was due to a great extent to the calibre of the womenfolk: 'One of the most powerful and recurrent themes emerging from the oral narratives in this book – from both men and women – is that of the indispensable, often "saintly", role of mothers and grannies in holding the very fabric of tenement family life together' (Kearns, *ibid*: 23).

A priest who worked among the tenement dwellers, Father Michael Reidy, agreed that the mothers and grannies were the mainstay of the community:

> … the mothers, they were heroines because there was a lot of problems with men and alcoholism, and the thirties was a time of depression. … They had tremendous resilience and spirit, strength of character. And grannies were tremendous people because of the maturity and wisdom which was beyond what the others had and they had a very steadying influence on the family (Kearns, *ibid*: 49).

McNabb found a comparable importance attaching to rural women, when he concluded, '… it is generally held that the standing of individual families in the community is due to the work and influence of the mother. "A good mother is everything"' (McNabb, 1964: 199).

Kearns describes how, during the first three decades of the century, one small tenement room was home for nearly one-third of Dubliners. Large numbers of families shared a single lavatory. Water had to be carried in pails, often up several flights of stairs, and heated on a fire. Women managed the family finances, and when men were unemployed, often provided the finances as well. They found work in small local factories, making shirts, sacks and even rosary beads, or as charwomen or street-traders. Some walked miles 'out into the country' from city tenements to help pick potatoes and other vegetables for farmers in Crumlin and Tallaght. In those years, Crumlin itself was a farm. The grinding hardship and suffering of the tenement families was made bearable, even transformed, by the Catholic faith of the people, particularly of the womenfolk. Each home had a Sacred Heart lamp which 'kept flickering hope barely alive' (Kearns, *ibid*: 43).

Tenement doors were left unlocked and, in the words of Gárda Paddy Casey, the tenement dwellers 'had a code of honour among themselves and were extremely religious'. During the days and years of the Great Depression and the Economic War in the 1930s the Labour movement in Ireland was weak and communism made no inroads in the Dublin slums. A conservative movement known as the *Christian Front* led by Deputy Patrick Belton, an Independent TD, was thriving at the time. If the pub drew the men, the Church provided the only social life for women outside the home. There was great respect for the clergy and a strict sexual code was enforced through the confessional. Men's 'marital rights' were upheld by the clergy, contributing to multiple pregnancy for married women at a time of high infant and maternal mortality. Pregnancy outside marriage was considered a disgrace. Generally such an event was concealed; the girl was sent away to a home run by nuns where she would do domestic work until after confinement when the baby would be placed in an orphanage, in the days prior to legal adoption. A pioneering break with this bleak pattern was provided by the lay-run Regina Coeli hostel, on Dublin's northside, which opened in 1930. It opened its doors to down-and-out women. But the first persons to present themselves for admission to the Regina Coeli hostel were an unwed mother and her child. Thus began the then radical trend of unwed mothers keeping their babies and rearing them in small community groups within the framework of the Regina Coeli hostel.

Kearns describes how romances blossomed among the tenement dwellers and how weddings were always major events in the community. Apart from the wedding cake there was usually ham, corned beef, cabbage, potatoes and jelly at the wedding breakfasts which took place after mass in Francis Street Church in the south inner city (Kearns, *ibid*: 47). The couple then set up home in a tenement room of their own. Moving up the social scale, weddings were much more grand affairs. A picture of a wedding cake, which incidentally symbolised much of contemporary values, appeared in *Model Housekeeping*, a popular women's magazine, in November 1934. It was the wedding cake of Mr Frank Aiken, Mr de Valera's right-hand man. The report that accompanied the picture was as follows:

> Mr Frank Aiken's Wedding Cake, made in Dundalk, his own constituency, weighed 110 lbs, stood 5 ft high and was artistically decorated with celtic interlacing in green and orange. Swords and crossguns, tiny green clad soldiers and musical instruments (in compliment to both bride and bridegroom) were some of the interesting features (*Model Housekeeping*, 1934).

Mick McCarthy, born into a newly independent Ireland that was rent by the bitterness of civil war politics, grew up in rural Kerry. His autobiography, *Early*

Days, provides a representative insight into family life in a small country town at that time. He describes how he heard of the arrival of his new baby sister. Having stayed at his uncle's for a few days, his father came to collect him, and told him, 'I nearly forgot to tell you … we bought a new baby while you were away' (McCarthy, 1990: 24-5). This procedure was later confirmed by his mother who explained, 'The woman who brought Peg had to stay here until she got used to us' (*ibid*: 25).

McCarthy informs us about women's work in those days through the experience of his mother, grandmother and neighbours. Mick's grandmother was a dressmaker while his mother collected the laundry for St Michael's College, where his father was a gardener. A neighbour, Mary Finucane, mended sacks for Latchford's Mill. 'I've spent a lifetime mending them things for Latchford's Mill. Slavery, slavery,' she said. McCarthy gives us a glimpse into the start of his own working life. He left school at fourteen and got a job with Mr McMahon, a builder, at 15 shillings a week. It was the early 1930s after de Valera's election and the Fianna Fáil building programme was underway. McCarthy worked tiling houses: 'Of one thing I am quite certain: No wind, cyclone or hurricane will ever move the tiles from numbers 1 and 2 O'Connell's Avenue, Listowel. People further down the scheme should not feel so secure: as time went on a trusted tile fastener was not so rigidly supervised' (*ibid*: 83-4). He also tells us, 'Gran's house occupied the exact spot where the goal posts used to be' (*ibid*: 84). It is all a very far cry from the world of *Family* depicted by Roddy Doyle in the 1990s. Roddy Doyle's version has unemployment, crime and battered wives.

Earning a living

Since 1926 the labour force participation rate of men has fallen steadily from 88 in 1926 to 74 in 1996, while the participation rate for women has risen from 32 in 1926 to 38.5 in 1996. In the case of single, married and widowed males, and single and widowed females, the rate has declined. The sole category in which the participation rate has risen has been that of married females. Almost the entire increase in the participation rate of married females has taken place since 1970, with the rate rising from 7.5 in 1971 to 37 in 1996 (Table A.3.2).

Since 1926 the shares of both married men and married women in the workforce have risen from 40 to 61 per cent for men, and from 7 to 51 per cent in the case of women. In the forty-five years between 1926 and 1971 the married female share doubled; it then more than doubled in the decade 1971-81. In 1996 the married female share exceeded the single female share for the first time (Figures 3.1, 3.2).

The increase in the share of married persons in the labour force has been accompanied by a decline in the share of single persons and by a very marked decline in the share of widows and widowers. The decline in the share of widowed persons, from 16 per cent to 2 per cent over the past seventy years is partly explained by the shift away from agricultural occupations. The introduction of widows' pensions, both contributory and non-contributory, in 1935, has also had an effect on the labour force participation of widows.

Figure 3.1: Share of male labour force by marital status, 1926-96

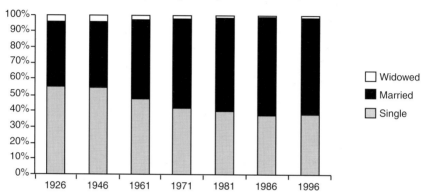

Source: Census of Population (various); Labour Force Surveys, 1986, 1996

For every ten people at work in 1926 slightly more than five were in agriculture, while just over three were in services and over one in industry. By 1996 for every ten persons at work, six were in services, almost three in industry, and slightly over one in agriculture (Table A.3.3). The 1971 census was the first to show that industry provided more employment than agriculture. Ireland today has a predominantly service-based economy. Since 1991 women have been entering the workforce at twice the rate of men. Between 1991 and 1996 the workforce increased by 150,000 of which 102, 000 were women (Census 1996).

Figure 3.2: Share of female labour force by marital status, 1926-1996

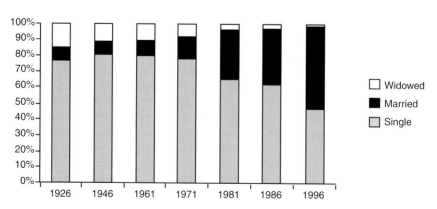

Source: Census of Population (various); Labour Force Surveys, 1986, 1996

Family homesteads

Data from the 1926 Census illustrate the striking difference between the place of agriculture in the economy of the 26 Counties compared with its place in the economies of its neighbours in Northern Ireland, Scotland, England and Wales. When the Free State was established the industrial wing of the 32 Counties remained north of the Border. In the words of Professor George O'Brien, 'It was as if Scotland had obtained self-government with Glasgow and the Clyde left out' (O'Brien, 1962: 11). Over half of those gainfully occupied in the Saorstát in 1926 were in Agriculture, while less than 10 per cent were so occupied in England and Wales in 1921, a proportion not reached in Ireland until the 1990s. In Scotland the proportion was also less than 10 per cent while in Northern Ireland it was just 25 per cent. What John Mitchel said in the middle of the nineteenth century, 'Land in Ireland is life', held true for another hundred years.

In the 1937 Constitution a section of Article 45, 'Directive Principles of Social Policy', says that the state shall, in particular, direct its policy towards securing, among other goals, 'That there may be established on the land in economic security as many families as in the circumstances shall be practicable'. In a letter written in 1935, Joseph Connolly, Minister for Lands, set out the policy of the de Valera government in regard to the establishment of small family farms that would be economically viable:

> Our main policy in dividing the land is to give economic farms to the allottees. The danger of giving smaller holdings on the '3 acres and a cow' basis is that we will only be repeating and continuing the evil of congestion. It will be remembered that on the breaking up of land into 20 acre farms or thereabouts there will be few opportunities for the employment of labourers in the old sense. The farms will be mostly worked as family units (Connolly, 1935).

The work of the Land Commission was central to the process of dividing up the land among the Irish farming community (Fahey, 1998a). When the tenant farmers became peasant proprietors, living standards remained frugal. In the 1930s de Valera's government could offer little by way of material improvements in rural life. The drive for rural electrification had yet to gather force. It was not until after World War II that milking machines, washing machines, and 'plugged-in' radio came to rural Ireland (Ó Tuathaigh, 1998). Instead of material improvement de Valera offered the farming community greater hardship as a result of the Economic War with Britain. Consequences regarding land use followed de Valera's policies, as historian Gearóid Ó Tuathaigh remarks:

> Fianna Fáil's ardent protectionism envisaged self-sufficiency in food, but it also had more explicitly social aims in its agricultural policy, seeking as it did to settle as many farm families as possible in reasonable comfort on the land. In practical terms, this

meant a renewed effort at further land distribution and a drive towards increased tillage and more balanced land use (Ó Tuathaigh, 1998: 43).

De Valera was not unaware of the need for industrial progress. However, in a speech in 1935, when proposing the Vote of Thanks to the Auditor of the Literary and Historical Society at University College Dublin, who in his Address had identified the provision of capital as the real problem, de Valera declared that it was the social side of the work of industrial restoration that was the most difficult and perplexing. Referring to the objectives of his Party and government, he said:

> They wanted every Irish citizen to regard his neighbour as his brother, one in race and language, a member of the one family. They tried to get the people voluntarily to make sacrifices, to think in terms of the community as a whole; on that was going to be based the only satisfactory solution of the problem of industrial restoration in a manner that would be permanent (de Valera, 1935).

Robert O'Connor describes how the system of vocational education, put in place following the *Vocational Education Act*, 1930, was directed towards keeping people on the land. O'Connor began his first teaching job in Ballaghaderreen vocational school in Co. Roscommon in September 1940. According to O'Connor:

> The official philosophy of vocational education in rural areas in those early days was based on keeping as many young people as possible on the land. This philosophy was enshrined in the Constitution and was pursued rigorously by the Department of Education. Boys were to be taught rural science and woodwork to make them better farmers; girls were to be taught domestic economy and some rural science to make them good farmers' wives (O'Connor, nd: 3: 2).

Young people pursued education in an effort to escape from the miserable economic conditions in rural Ireland. O'Connor tells how the official philosophy of vocational education, which aimed to keep rural youth on the small farms, was at variance with the ideas of the pupils who came to the schools:

> They came for one purpose only, to get an off-farm job. There was no future in being a farmer or a farmer's wife unless you had a very large farm. It was patently obvious that small farmers had very low incomes and that no amount of technical education could give them a living comparable with skilled industrial or commercial workers.
>
> The boys came to school specifically to learn woodwork and become carpenters. They tolerated the other subjects for the sole purpose of getting the woodwork instruction. The girls gave domestic science a very low rating. They saw no future in it. They wanted to do shorthand, typing and commercial subjects so as to get office jobs (O'Connor, *ibid*: 3, 1-2).

As a young man, de Valera himself had tenaciously pursued educational opportunity, the only route out of rural Ireland apart from emigration. When he found himself in Blackrock College in Dublin, he was thrilled to be out of rural Ireland (Farragher, 1984).

While the reality of rural life included hardship, deprivation and curtailment of individual freedom, life on the small family farm began to be idealised in such a way that it was made acceptable, indeed rhetorically transformed. In 1937, the writer Shane Leslie, in a reference to rural life in Ireland in the nineteenth century, spoke of a time when 'strange to say, people could be equally poor and happy' (Leslie, 1937: xviii). He warned that 'Ireland relinquishing her old ways in the farm and on the roadside will lose something that no new constitutions can possibly give her' (Leslie, *ibid*). There were dissenting voices. Alice Curtayne remarked that those who spoke and wrote about the ideal rural world were men who did not depend on the land themselves: 'The romantic and sentimental lovers of the land are beyond classification. They have one thing positively in common. None of them derive their livelihood from the land. Few of them even live on it …' (Quoted in Ferriter, 1995: 3).

Sociological evidence was beginning to emerge regarding rural realities. Arensberg and Kimball (1940) highlighted the hardships and frustrations associated with agricultural life. The smaller the farm the greater the labour intensity. In 1926 there were five times as many persons working on farms of 15-30 acres and three and a half times as many on farms of 30-50 acres, as on farms over 200 acres. Furthermore family labour accounted for 89 per cent of the total workforce on farms of 1-15 acres, compared with 24 per cent at the other end of the scale on farms over 200 acres.

Elderly parents were reluctant to pass on their small farm to the heir; there were too many stories in circulation of parents who signed over their farm and were treated badly by their son and daughter-in-law; some, according to reports, 'were treated as slaves and others almost left to starve' (McNabb, *ibid*: 226). Marriage was not simply a contract between individuals; it was a property transaction that involved the rights of other members of the family and particularly the father's authority and right to dispose of his property. When the farm was eventually passed on to the chosen heir it was necessary to find some dowry or fortune for sisters and possibly small sums for other family members. Serjeant Sullivan had no doubt as to the priority of property in a marriage. 'Upon a marriage, as we have seen, a farm and stock passed in exchange for a fortune. This *was* the marriage; the boy and girl and the ceremony were circumstances' (Sullivan, 1952: 144). Arensberg and Kimball did not doubt that there was a darker side to the marriage system necessitated by the family farm economy. They quote the observation of a contemporary solicitor which serves as a caution against idealising the past. He describes the marriage and match-making system as 'pernicious': 'You'll go out to a small-holding and see several able-bodied men and women waiting around doing nothing. They are waiting for the eldest son to get married and for their share of the fortune that the wife brings in' (Arensberg and Kimball, 1940: 112).

Matches were made and dowries paid as the demands of the land required. Patrick Kavanagh describes the marriage of a young girl to a much older farmer in the 1930s: 'In normal times in a normal country her husband wouldn't get a young girl like her even if he had fifty acres of land. But in South Monaghan marriages were becoming a rare event' (Kavanagh, 1971: 161). The exigencies of the family farm continued to dictate marriage patterns:

> In order to ensure the continuation of the family holding, the man will look for someone who has the requisite qualifications in money and social standing and, if she is agreeable, they will get their families to make a match. It is not, of course, a purely materialistic arrangement (McNabb, *ibid*: 220).

There were those who, like Fr Murphy, a priest working in rural Ireland in the 1950s, continued to attribute to urban development a bad influence on society and who emphasised the value of a rural environment in fostering family life: 'On the social plane, the family, the primary unit and basis of society, is degraded by the unfavourable conditions of urban environment. ... Divorce, birth control, contempt for family life are destroying the foundations of western civilisation' (Murphy, 1952: 30).

But economic and social forces proceeded to undermine the viability of the small family farm. By the time the Commission on Emigration reported in 1954 there was an awareness of the need to provide jobs outside agriculture if emigration was to be stemmed. A critical change in the relationship between the farmer and the farm worker came about as a result of legislation regarding pay and hours of work in 1939. As a result of this many farmers claimed that they could not afford to hire workers. Some became more dependent on family labour. By demanding improved wages and working conditions the farm worker struck at the foundations of the rural social structure – the traditional role and position of farmers. This proved a defining influence for change, in time leading to the gradual disappearance of the farm working class as an integral part of the rural social structure. Furthermore, farm workers who migrated to urban centres either within Ireland or abroad, by making unfavourable comparisons, relayed their new found freedom, back 'into the heart of the farm family and initiated the decay of family loyalty' (McNabb, *ibid*: 245). For why should family members endure conditions of life which were no longer acceptable to farm workers?

Women were also in search of change. Girls with farming backgrounds tended to remain longer at school than boys; also their education stressed greater refinement than that received by boys and so they were quicker to seek more intimate and personal relationships in marriage. De Valera's 'comely maidens' were heading towards the bright lights and a metamorphosis. In the late 1940s,

Humphreys had pointed out that the increasing opportunities for women were already having an impact

> ... because it tends impersonally to select the competent individual, the corporation in Dublin has opened up jobs and occupational careers for women on a hitherto unprecedented scale, and employment and promotional policies that are still discriminatory against women stem less from any internal principle of organisation within the corporation than from the requirements of outside groups, and especially the family (Humphreys, 1966: 31).

The massive rural exodus of the 1950s to cities, including Dublin, London, Manchester, Liverpool, Birmingham and New York, smashed the myth of farm families experiencing the undiluted joys of a simple rural life. By 1961, when the Irish population fell to its lowest ever recorded level of 2.8 million, and the flow from agriculture continued unstemmed, it was clear that an Ireland of small family farms was not viable. People were not prepared to accept the standard of living that such a 'way of life' could offer. However, as late as 1963, when the *Second Programme for Economic Expansion* was published, it was stated in the *Programme* that, while the economic ideal for agriculture was to increase efficient production, 'The social ideal is to obtain the increased economic production from the maximum number of family farms' (*SPEE,* 1963: 21). In the way that old ideas reappear in new forms, the social objective of stabilising or increasing rural population within the framework of regionalisation re-emerged in the context of EU Structural Funds in the 1990s.

Following Irish entry into the EEC in 1973, Irish agriculture was transformed as aid was directed in favour of larger farms and larger producers. The number of farmers continued to decline while the average size of holdings increased. It is conceivable that at some future date changed patterns of farm practice, for instance more organic methods of production, could lead to a resurgence of small farms, even small family farms. If this were to happen, such family farms of the future might echo back to a vanished world. Already there have been calls to try and reinstate the old ways. Father Harry Bohan, well known for his work in promoting rural development, has argued that Church, Farm and Family are all linked in a natural bond that has been ruptured at great risk to society. Bohan writes:

> Sir, Your reports of December 16th on two surveys – Catholics and the teaching of the Church, and the changing structure of Irish farming – are closely interconnected. Both indicate a fall off from the Church, and from farming. Christian morality has become seriously detached from the central mechanisms of Irish society, and Christianity has become marginalised in the public life of modern Ireland.
>
> ... For centuries, the basic component of Irish and indeed European agriculture has been the family farm. It was the foundation or the 'groundedness' of our society.

Certainly, it was a source of a lot of conflict but it was rooted in the nature of its place, harmonious, personally tested by generations of farmers and certified by the results of their husbandry (Bohan, 1996).

The business world and the urban world were looked on as less wholesome and less 'Irish' by traditionalists, yet families also played a considerable part in the development of business life in Ireland. The great Guinness Brewery began as a family firm, accounting for the bulk of industrial output in the early years of the State. Other businesses that started as family enterprises and became household names include Jacob's, W.D. and H.O. Wills, Carrolls, and in the retail area, Dunnes Stores, or smaller specialist chains like Boylan's Shoes and Kenny's Shoes, Shaw's (Clothing and Drapery) and Doyle Hotels in the service sector.

The occupations and employment of women

For sixty years from 1926 to 1986 there was scarcely any change in the share of women in the labour force – 32 per cent in 1926 compared with 31 per cent in 1986.

Table 3.2: Females in the labour force and not in the labour force, 1926–96 (%)

	1926	1946	1961	1971	1981	1986	1996
Labour-force	32.1	31.0	28.9	27.3	29.7	30.9	38.5
Not labour-force	67.9	69.0	71.1	72.7	70.3	69.1	61.5
Of which:							
Home duties	51.4	54.5	60.1	60.2	54.9	53.4	40.9
At school/students		3.9	5.7	8.6	8.5	9.8	13.0
Others	[16.4]	10.6	5.3	3.9	6.8	5.9	7.7

Source: Census data, 1926-81, aged 14 years and over; 1981, aged 15 years and over; Labour Force Surveys 1986 and 1996, aged 15 years and over. For 1926 the total 'At School/Students' together with 'Others' is 16.4 per cent.

Accordingly, the share of those not in the labour force was also static – 68 per cent in 1926 and 69 per cent in 1986. The composition of those not in the work force showed that the proportion engaged in home duties hardly changed, while the rise in the proportion who were at school, or students, was offset by a decline in the residual category. Marked changes have occurred in the past few years. In 1991 the share of women in home duties dipped below 50 per cent for the first time; falling to 41 per cent in 1996 (Table 3.2). Over the past decade the number of working mothers has increased rapidly, almost doubling between 1987 and 1997 when it reached 235,000 (Treacy and O'Connell, 2000:111).

Figure 3.3: Females at work in agriculture, industry and services, 1951-96

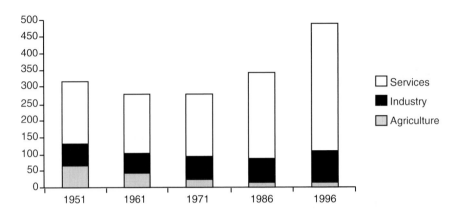

Source: Census of Population (various), Labour Force Surveys, 1986, 1996

Over the years women have had some surprising occupations. Roy Geary tells us that when the results of the 1926 Census were published banner headlines in the evening newspapers pointed to the 'one female chimney sweep' (Geary, 1954/55). By far the most striking aspect of where women work is the fact that over three-quarters of women at work are in services, if not uniquely traditional ones. The share of women in industry, 19 per cent in 1996, is slightly less than in 1926, while their share in agriculture has declined from 21 per cent to 3 per cent (Figure 3.3, Table A.3.4).

The increased participation of wives and mothers in the labour force in the years since World War II may tend to overlook the productive work done by earlier generations of women:

Prior to industrialisation women had done economically productive work in farms, trades and households; and in the early nineteenth century they had worked in, *inter alia*, factories and mines, though for lower wages. ... The move to exclude women from the workplace developed from the struggle of working-class men for a 'family wage' that would enable them to support a wife and children, as middle-class men already did; this struggle was in part successful, certainly for the more skilled and affluent working class (Fox Harding, 1996:2).

At the end of the nineteenth century married women at home were 'often taking in laundry or lodgers, or cleaning, or doing other unrecorded part-time work. The presence of the wife in the home, financially maintained by her husband, became part of the notion of working-class identity, respectability and success' (Fox Harding, *ibid*: 3). An illustration of women's farm work, doubtless unrecorded in census data, is given by writer Liam O'Donnell who describes how women prepared the seed potatoes for sowing, while women and children were employed for thinning turnips, mangolds and sugar beet:

> Before the planting of potatoes there was the task of getting the seed ready. This entailed the cutting of the *sceallâin*. The small seed potatoes were passed on as suitable for planting but the big ones were split into two or three parts according to size. This work was mainly done by women (O'Donnell, 1997: 114).

Another seasonal occupation for women was plucking turkeys. O'Donnell tells us that in the run-up to Christmas, 'The women plucked all day long helped by their children when they came from school and at night their menfolk would give a hand' (O'Donnell, *ibid*: 176). Describing the traditional farm family, Ó Danachair tells how a woman never dug with a spade or cut turf, while a man might mend clothes, but never knit, although some Scottish shepherds did. A man would never get involved with the fowl. The hens, geese and turkeys were all looked after by the women. 'Even small boys should not be asked to feed the hens or go to the neighbours for a sitting of eggs. To ask a boy to do this was a deadly insult' (Ó Danachair, 1962: 188).

The manner of recording the work of women, in particular of married women, is significant if a true picture of women's contribution to economic production is to be obtained. For example, Kennedy *et al* tell us that in the mid-nineteenth century, there were almost 700,000 recorded textile workers in the whole of Ireland compared with a little more than 90,000 in 1907. They also tell us that the great majority of linen workers were women (Kennedy *et al*, 1988: 9-10). Allowing for the undoubted decline of the textile industry, the extent to which historical statistics accurately reflect the economic contribution of women is open to question. Admittedly without presenting statistics, Ó Danachair claims that '... almost up to the end of the nineteenth century any woman with time to spare could earn money by spinning – whence our word "spinster" for an unmarried woman' (Ó Danachair, 1985: 109-10). The changing practices of census enumerators has resulted in some categories of women being classified as 'occupied' at one census, but not at another (Daly, 1997a: 8).

According to economic historian Joanna Bourke, between the closing decade of the nineteenth century and the outbreak of the Great War Irish women bade 'farewell to labour in the fields and in other men's homes, [and] they enlisted for full-time work in the unpaid domestic sphere':

> In 1901 only 430,000 women in Ireland were employed, compared with 641,000 twenty years earlier. Single women performed housework, free of charge, for fathers, brothers, and uncles. Or they emigrated. Married women nursed their children and strove to improve the standard of services that they provided to their family, while widowed women competed with their children's spouses in the production of domestic goods. Female labour came to be dominated by housework (Bourke, 1993: 1). [1]

How can the astonishing change be explained between the 1871 census when there were 362,000 'Wives of Specified Occupations' returned in the 32 Counties, and the 1926 census in the 26 Counties when there were just 23,895 married women returned as 'gainfully occupied'? Is it possible that some of the decline was due to the changes in census classification which were introduced in 1871 and implemented in succeeding censuses? At the time of the 1861 census the Irish Commissioners had devised a system that allocated an occupational category to every individual. Married women and widows who had 'specified' occupations other than domestic duties were counted in that occupation, for example as dressmakers. Married women and widows who had no 'specified' occupations were placed in the domestic class, engaged in home duties, and as 'wives not otherwise described', or 'widows not otherwise described'. For the census of 1871 the Irish Commissioners received instructions from England to transfer wives, who until then had been included in the domestic class as engaged in home duties, into the 'indefinite and non-productive' class and to transfer wives *with* specified occupations out of the occupational categories in which they were included, into the domestic class. For the 1871 census the Commissioners produced a Table giving the specified occupations of all wives, thus providing a detailed breakdown of the occupations of married women outside domestic duties. It is likely that the instructions from London took some time to implement fully and so the full impact of the changes may not have shown up for a couple of censuses.

The background to these changes is as follows. As early as the 1841 census the Irish Commissioners devised a classification of occupations, comprising nine categories or orders. In 1861 the number of orders was increased from nine to thirteen. Wives who had a specified occupation, for example dressmaking, were counted as such and included under the appropriate order, in this case, clothing. According to the 1871 census, 47 per cent of married women and just over 60 per cent of widows had specified occupations. By the time of the 1926 census, the first of the Free State, 40 per cent of widows, and only 8 per cent of wives, were returned as 'gainfully occupied'. What happened?

The Irish Commissioners were clearly proud of the system they had devised for the 1841 census, regarding it as well suited to Irish conditions. When the Instructions were issued for the 1871 census it was like dropping the proverbial bombshell. The Irish Commissioners were instructed to apply the English system of Occupation Tables. The English system was divided into 6 classes, 18 orders and 80 sub-orders. The Irish Commissioners observed, 'The division into class, order and sub-order would be admirable as regards convenience if the classes did not in many instances confuse their boundaries, and if the orders always ranged properly under their respective classes. This, we are compelled to observe, is not the fact, or so much as an approximation to the fact' (Census 1871, *General Report*: 71).

The six classes under which the people of Ireland, England and Scotland were tabulated for the first time in 1871 were: 1. The Professional, 2. The Domestic,

3. The Commercial, 4. The Agricultural, 5. The Industrial and 6. The Indefinite and Non-productive. Let the Irish Commissioners speak for themselves regarding the implications for wives of the imposition of the English system:

> Deferring simply to the will of the Government, and conforming strictly to the English methods as set out in the Book of Instructions compiled for the tabulators in the English Census Office, we referred for instance all wives of specified occupations to Order IV of the Domestic class, although nothing, as it occurred to our judgment, could be more erroneous in principle than such a classification. A wife of specified occupation may be a milliner or dressmaker, a draper, a governess or schoolmistress, bookbinder, or a seamstress. In all these capacities – and we have enumerated but a few at random – she belongs, unless as governess or schoolmistress, to what would be called the Industrial class, while the governess and schoolmistress, or music or drawing mistress, would belong to the Professional class. The Domestic class, however, under the scheme in hand, abstracts, at a clean sweep, every wife of a professional or industrial calling from the class to which she is naturally referable, and transfers her to a class which represents in great part not so much a calling as a relation (Census 1871, *General Report*: 65).

In compliance with instructions received from London, the Irish Commissioners, obediently, if reluctantly, transferred 362,000 'wives of specified occupations' into the Domestic class, while wives within the Domestic class were transferred to 'persons of no specified occupation'. The obliteration of 'wives of specified occupations' from an occupational classification was copper-fastened in the 1881 census in which it was stated that wives of specified occupations were not to be separately tabulated, but referred to 'the particular headings under which their calling naturally ranged' (Census 1881, *General Report*: 20). The Commissioners pointed to the near impossibility of making comparisons between censuses due to classification changes. Alterations 'render it almost impossible to institute accurate comparisons between the results obtained in 1871 and 1881' (Census 1881, *General Report*: 19).

One effect of the differences between the classification in 1871 and in 1881 was that 'of causing an apparently large increase in the number of persons of no specified occupations' (Census 1881, *General Report*: 20). For example, farmers' daughters and grand-daughters who were tabulated separately and included under the agricultural class in 1871 were listed as persons of 'no specified occupation' in 1881. A further significant change with regard to wives came in the 1891 census when 140,000 wives who had been included as 'Others engaged in Service' were transferred to the non-productive class as described in the 1891 *Report:*

> In 1881 there were tabulated under the heading of 'Others engaged in Service' 139,092 females, almost all of whom – being cases of wives, and other near relatives

of the heads of families, returned as 'housekeepers' – have on this occasion been placed in Order 24, the 'Indefinite and Non-productive class' (Census 1891, *General Report*: 23).

It is possible to see the sorts of activities engaged in by 'wives of specified occupations' in 1871 thanks to the special Table published by the Commissioners in that year. There were, for example, 55 wives in the Civil Service, 205 midwives, 1 author, 29 actresses, 1,146 teachers, 5,883 general domestic servants, 31 pawnbrokers, 3,174 unspecified dealers, 5,858 shopkeepers (Branch unspecified) and over 13,000 seamstresses. By far the largest number, over 250,000, were agriculturists, generally graziers' wives, who presumably helped in the work of their husbands. A similar picture is found in England where in 1881 the Census excluded women's household work from the category of productive work and from then on housewives were classified as unoccupied. Before these classificatory changes were introduced, the economic activity rate for both men and women had been recorded at close to 100 per cent. Subsequent to the changes only 42 per cent of women were classified as economically productive (Lewis, 1984).

The gradual disappearance of wives from recorded occupations, notwithstanding the high unrecorded occupational involvement of women, should be borne in mind when contemplating the very low level of recorded workforce participation by married women in Ireland, until the share began to rise in the 1970s to its present level of nearly 40 per cent, bringing about a decline in reliance on a sole male breadwinner. By 1996 men were sole breadwinners in less than 40 per cent of couples; over 30 per cent are dual earner families, while one quarter have no earner due to unemployment or a single parent situation where the parent is dependent on a state welfare payment. In the case of 31,500 couples or 4 per cent of total couples, the woman is the sole earner (Table 3.3). Men are increasingly falling into one of three categories – traditional breadwinner, more prevalent in the older age groups; part breadwinner, part carer, where men do not carry the exclusive income earning burden, and where they share far more in the child care and domestic activities of the family; and those men who either have no children or, if they have children play little part in their care, either financially or emotionally. This latter group, 'men without children', are attracting the attention of analysts; Akerlof attributes the rise in crime, and other social pathologies, in the United States, to the decline in the marriage rate amongst young men and the reduction in their domestic responsibilities. In apocalyptic vein, he compares what has been happening to the family in America in this century with the Great Famine in Ireland in the last century (Akerlof, 1998).

Table 3.3: Couples classified by work-status of partners, 1986–96

Work-status	1986 000s	1986 Per cent	1996 000s	1996 Per cent
Both at work	108	16	227	32
Man only at work	355	53	277	39
Woman only at work	22	3	32	4
Neither at work	128	27	174	25
Total	667	100	710	100

Source: Labour Force Survey, 1996

A growing divide: social welfare families and dual earner families

Economic prosperity has brought with it an increasing divide between those families who depend on social welfare payments for a living and those with two earners. Studies show that where one partner in a couple is dependent on social welfare, the likelihood increases that the other is also dependent on social welfare. It is estimated that 15 per cent of families live in poverty, with up to one-third on a relatively low income (O'Connor, 1998: 11). In 1995 there were 840,000 recipients of a weekly social welfare payment. When adult and child dependants are taken into account 1.5 million persons, or 41 per cent of the total population, benefited from a weekly social welfare payment. Fifty years ago, in 1950, there were 330,000 recipients of social welfare payments; recipients and dependants amounted to 21 per cent of the population. A core assumption upon which the Welfare State was constructed was the centrality of a breadwinner male with dependent wife and children (Pedersen, 1995). Since 1980 that core assumption has been altered by changing realities of family life, with three-quarters of the increase in numbers of social welfare recipients accounted for by unemployment assistance, lone parents and deserted wives. The growth in unemployment in the 1980s undermined the breadwinner role while changing lifestyles reduced the scope for that role.

The labour force participation rate of married women which has risen sharply in the past two decades, gives some indication of the trend in dual income households, although it must be interpreted with caution, bearing in mind the *caveat* attached to the statistical measurement of married women in the labour force. Between 1986 and 1996 the share of couples in which both partners were at work rose from 16 to 32 per cent (Table 3.3). A *sine qua non* of the increase in dual income earning families has been the removal of discriminatory barriers against the participation of married women in the workforce, notably the bar against the employment of married women as teachers in national schools and in the public sector, as well as in important areas of the private sector, including banking. It is probably fair to say that the removal of the bar came partly in response to a shortage of teachers and partly in response to arguments concerning employment opportunities for women and their effects on family formation as outlined in the *Reports* of the Commission on Emigration. Reflecting the contemporary ethos, the Commission deplored the possibility that economic necessity might force a woman out of her home to take up employment. However, the Commission remarked, in a practical way, that if a woman could continue in employment after marriage, the extra income might facilitate earlier marriage, and provide a greater sense of security to couples embarking on marriage: 'If, therefore, it were the custom here for women to remain in employment after marriage, it is probable that marriage rates would improve' (Commission on Emigration, 1954: 81).

Table 3.4: Distribution of income-tax payers by marital status, 1977/78-1996/97 (%)

Year	Single		Married		Widowers	Widows	Total
	Males	Females	2 Earner	1 Earner			
1977/78							
PAYE	26.4	26.0	9.3	34.4	1.2	2.6	100
All	26.6	24.0	9.8	34.9	1.3	3.3	100
1987/88							
PAYE	27.1	26.2	9.6	31.8	1.3	4.0	100
All	26.5	23.4	8.8	35.7	1.4	4.1	100
1996/97							
PAYE	31.0	30.0	14.0	20.0	1.0	4.0	100
All	30.0	26.0	15.0	24.0	1.0	4.0	100

Source: Reports of the Revenue Commissioners

The distribution of income taxpayers by marital status reflects the growth in dual earner couples. Between 1977 and 1997 there was a significant change in the distribution of PAYE taxpayers, reflecting a sharp fall in the share of the 'traditional' married units with one earner, from over one-third of the total in 1977/78 to one-fifth in 1996/97, with most of the fall occurring since 1987/88 (Table 3.4). The trend has been broadly similar in the case of all personal income taxpayers, although as might be expected, the fall has not been as marked because non-PAYE taxpayers include the farming community. The fall in the share of all married units, one and two earner units, was from 45 per cent to just 39 per cent between 1977/78 and 1996/9, notwithstanding the marked increase in the share of married units with two earners from 9.8 per cent to 15.0 per cent, with almost all of the increase in the share occurring since 1987/88.

Changes in the system of taxation of married couples subsequent to the Murphy case in 1980 have facilitated the growth in dual earner married couples, or at any rate reduced the tax disincentives that existed prior to the Murphy judgment. The nub of the Murphy case, which is dealt with more fully in Chapter 9, was that for tax purposes the incomes of husband and wife were added together and taxed as a single income. The result was that the joint income of a married couple was subject to higher tax as it reached higher tax bands more quickly than the same total income if earned by two single people. In his High Court decision, Mr Justice Hamilton held that Section 192 of the *Income Tax Act*, 1967, which obliged a husband and wife to pay more tax on their combined salaries than they would if they were single, was unconstitutional. In the 1980 Budget the benefits of the Court decision were extended to all married couples by the then Minister for Finance, George Colley, by granting to married couples double the personal allowance of a single person, whether or not both husband and wife were in paid employment. In a controversial change introduced in Budget 2000, and continued in Budget 2001, Finance Minister Charlie McCreevy moved towards individualisation of the tax code by favouring couples with two incomes and rowing back on the manner in which Colley had implemented the Murphy judgment. The Minister contended that the change would encourage more married women to return to the workforce.

Appendix 3

Table A.3.1: Shares of male and female labour force by marital status, 1926-96 (%)

Year	Male			Female			Total Female
	Single	Married	Widowed	Single	Married	Widowed	Married & Widowed
1926	55.4	39.9	4.7	76.9	7.0	16.1	23.1
1946	55.4	40.7	4.0	80.4	6.8	12.9	19.7
1961	47.0	50.1	2.9	80.0	8.5	11.5	20.0
1971	42.2	55.7	2.1	77.7	13.6	8.7	22.3
1981	39.6	59.2	1.2	65.3	30.2	4.5	34.7
1986	37.3	61.6	1.0	62.0	34.1	3.9	38.0
1996	38.0	61.0	1.0	46.9	50.9	2.2	53.1

Source: Census of Population *Reports*, various; Labour Force Surveys, 1986, 1996

Table A.3.2: Male and female labour force participation rates by marital status, 1926-96

Year	Single		Married		Widowed		Total	
	Male	Female	Male	Female	Male	Female	Male	Female
1926	84.6	51.0	94.3	5.7	76.0	41.1	87.7	32.1
1946	86.2	54.0	92.2	5.0	65.8	32.9	87.4	31.0
1961	77.5	59.3	90.8	5.2	51.7	26.2	82.4	28.9
1971	70.9	59.8	89.9	7.5	45.0	19.3	79.2	27.3
1981	69.9	56.4	84.4	16.7	29.6	11.4	76.4	29.7
1986	65.6	54.1	82.7	21.3	23.4	8.5	73.6	30.9
1996	59.9	49.1	79.3	37.3	22.5	8.1	69.1	38.5

Source: Census of Population *Reports*, various; Labour Force Surveys, 1986, 1996

Table A.3.3: Numbers at work in agriculture, industry and services, 1926-96

Year	Agriculture	Industry	Services	Total	Unemployed	Labour Force
	000s	000s	000s	000s	000s	000s
1926	653	162	406	1,220	79	1,300
1946	568	225	432	1,225	64	1,289
1971	272	320	457	1,049	61	1,110
1981	196	363	587	1,146	126	1,272
1986	168	301	606	1,075	227	1,302
1996	136	351	798	1,285	190	1,475

Source: Kennedy, Giblin and McHugh, 1988: 143, Table 7.2 and Labour Force Survey, 1996

Table A.3.4: Females at work in agriculture, industry and services, 1951-96

	1951		1961		1971		1986		1996	
	000s	%	000s	%	000s	%	000s	%	000s	%
Agiculture	67.6	21.5	42.1	15.1	25.5	9.2	14.5	4.3	14.7	3.0
Industry	61.7	19.6	61.6	22.2	68.1	24.5	71.6	21.1	92.6	18.9
Services	185.6	58.9	174.3	62.7	184.0	66.4	253.4	74.6	380.8	78.0
Total	314.9	100.0	278.0	100.0	278.3	100.0	339.5	100.0	488.1	100.0

Source: Census of Population 1951-1971, aged 14 years and over; Labour Force Surveys, 1986, 1996, aged 15 years and over

4

Family Roles: Men and Women

The perspective of de Valera's Constitution of 1937, defining the role of a woman as primarily within the domestic sphere, has yielded gradually to one that emphasises a woman's role in the workforce. Here, discussion of 'a woman's place' is approached in two stages. Firstly, starting with the Constitution of 1937, the extent to which the home is viewed as the exclusive sphere of a woman and the degree to which she has a role in the public arena and the work place are considered. Secondly, two components of woman's role within the home – 'housewife' and mother – are examined. The decoupling of the exclusive link between marriage and motherhood has coincided with a change in attitude to marriage *per se*. Associated with the possibility of greater economic independence via the workplace, the relative economic attractiveness of marriage for women has declined (Kiernan, 1992). From being viewed as the ultimate goal of a majority of women, marriage has come to be viewed as an option. Increased emphasis on the parenting and partnership roles of men together with the increase in career opportunities for women has facilitated the shift from a male breadwinner pattern of family towards a broader sharing of paid work and domestic tasks. The establishment of the rights of certain groups of men, including homosexual men and men who fathered children outside marriage, has required judgments from the European Court of Human Rights.

'A woman's place is …'

Women are mentioned in two Articles of the Constitution; in Article 41 the references are to 'woman' and 'mothers', while in Article 45 the reference is to 'women'. Article 41.2.1° and Article 41.2.2° state:

> 2.1° In particular, the State recognises that by her life within the home, woman gives to the State a support without which the common good cannot be achieved.
> 2.2° The State shall, therefore, endeavour to ensure that mothers shall not be obliged by economic necessity to engage in labour to the neglect of their duties in the home.[1]

Article 45.4.2° states:

> 4.2° The State shall endeavour to ensure that the strength and health of workers, men and women, and the tender age of children shall not be abused and that citizens shall

not be forced by economic necessity to enter avocations unsuited to their sex, age or strength.

The Constitution of 1937 has come to be viewed as the legislative symbol of the separate sphere of the home as the arena of a woman's life. It has been argued by Maryann Valiulis of Trinity College, that a particular identity was constructed for women by the political and ecclesiastical leaders early in the twentieth century:

> Any description of the ideal Irish catholic woman of the 1920s and 1930s must begin in that bastion of domesticity, the home. Overwhelmingly, political and ecclesiastical leaders in the Irish Free State constructed an identity for Irish women – solely in domestic terms: women were mothers, women were wives (Valiulis, 1995: 169).

Valiulis would, however, agree that the ideas of Irish leaders regarding the role of women were part of a general movement of European conservatism. Concern for encouraging women to remain in the home arose from the fall in the number of births during the 1930s in many European countries, including Ireland and Britain. Throughout the 1930s policies, forged by strong political ideologies, were put in place in a wide range of countries to encourage women to stay in the home and to rear more children (Harriss, 1992: 113). The fact that a broad consensus existed at the time of the Constitution regarding women's place in the home, and that it was not purely a reflection of Roman Catholic or conservative political views, was to be found in *The Irish Times* which, according to one writer, 'is owned and edited by members of the former Ascendancy and often expresses disagreement with ideas and values that are traditionally Catholic' (Humphreys, 1966: 231). In the same year as the Constitution was passed, *The Irish Times,* on its Leader page, expressed criticism of working wives or of marriages based on the 'fifty-fifty' principle, where husbands and wives were joint earners:

> It is one of the great tragedies of today that marriage on the old-fashioned basis becomes increasingly difficult, and that far too often the choice lies between this 'fifty-fifty' marriage and no marriage at all. Too often, however, the 'fifty-fifty' system prevails where there is no justification for it. Hundreds of married women, whose husbands already draw adequate salaries, hold jobs in Dublin today, thereby closing them against unmarried women, and often against men who are in dire need of work. Such cases, we think, demand investigation, not only on the score of justice, but also on the ground that a dangerous view of the marriage state is being inculcated. Some day, please Heaven! the nation will be so organised that work will be available for every man, so that he may marry and assume the burdens of a home, and for every woman until she embarks upon her proper profession – which is marriage. In that more prosperous nation there will be no question of the woman who 'will not allow marriage to interfere with her career' (*The Irish Times*, 22 February, 1937).

Many in the Trade Union Movement endorsed the view that a woman's place was in the home. One of the most prominent trade unionists, and founding President of the Irish Labour History Society, John Swift, held those views all his life. According to his son, John P. Swift, '… Swift held extremely traditional views on the role of women in society, believing, for instance, that a woman's primary function should be that of wife and mother in the home' (Swift, 1991: 198-9). Likewise, the legendary Union leader John Conroy held that 'women should be at home' (Heron, 1993: 50). Sheila Conroy recalls a seminar in Cork in the mid-1970s where the trade unionist and academic Charles McCarthy spoke about the end of the marriage bar, and the typical reaction came from a man in the audience who shouted, 'Over my dead body will my wife go to work' (Heron, *ibid*: 141). Anne Riordan, the first general manager of Microsoft Ireland in 1991, encountered trade union opposition to her employment as a married woman in the 1960s. While management were happy to continue her employment following her marriage '… it was the union that resisted because they feared women were taking "breadwinners' jobs"' (Lyons, 2000).

The implication that the proper sphere of women's activity was the home, and that women should be limited to that sphere, was at the root of much of the criticism of the references to women in the Constitution and sparked a campaign against the draft Constitution which contained the phrase, 'the inadequate strength of women'. The campaign, mainly from middle-class women, was led by the National University Women Graduates' Association, the Irish Women Workers' Union, the Standing Committee on Legislation Affecting Women, and the Joint Committee of Women's Societies and Social Workers representing more than a dozen women's groups (*Irish Press*, 11 May, 1937). Speaking in the Dáil during the debates on the Constitution, de Valera defended himself against the criticisms of women's organisations, arguing at length that the object of the references to women in the draft Constitution was protective:

> With regard to women, they are mentioned in two Articles. But why are they mentioned? They are mentioned to give the protection which, I think, is necessary as part of our social programme, and I am prepared to go with that programme before the country. … Is there any woman who is a mother who will say that it is right that when her husband is idle or otherwise when she has the care of her children that she should be forced by economic necessity – she is not forced by law and is not prevented by law from doing these things – and by our social system to go and earn what is necessary to maintain the household? (*PDDE*, Vol. 67, Col. 67, 11 May 1937).

De Valera further claimed – and the claim was made at a time when legislative measures *did* in fact prevent the employment of married women as national teachers and in the civil service – 'There is no suggestion that women should be stopped from entering into avocations for which they have aptitude or will or desire' (*PDDE*, Vol. 67, Col. 71, 11 May, 1937). De Valera tried to rebut the suggestion that he wanted to keep women in the kitchen. He said that such an idea may have originated with his rejection of the offer of Cumann na mBan to enter the army in 1916:

> That may be the beginning of all my trouble. I am not saying for a moment that they may not fight as well as men. That was not the question I said I had to decide, but I said I did not want them. ... I also indicated that we would have to take some of the men out of the firing line for the purpose of cooking food and that sort of thing. Perhaps that is the origin of the suggestion that I wanted to put women in the kitchen (*PDDE*, Vol. 67, Col. 462- 463, 13 May 1937).

Three weeks later de Valera emphasised that, in his view, when the Constitution spoke of woman's life in the home, it was dealing with only one aspect of her life:

> My mind was running rather upon whether there was some possible suggestion that 'by her life within the home' it should necessarily be spent within the home. There is no suggestion of that in the clause as it stands. If I were disposed to amend it at all, it would be to try to make it certain that nobody was going reasonably to read into it by the words 'by her life within the home' that there was some suggestion that woman's life was to be confined absolutely within the home. I am only dealing with one aspect of woman's life (*PDDE*, Vol. 67, Col. 1880, 4 June 1937).

Speaking in the debate on 12 May 1937, Deputy Mrs Concannon referred to the objections of the Women Graduates' Association and other women's groups, quoting from the account in the *Irish Press* on the previous day, 'The omission of the principle of equal rights and equal opportunities, enunciated in the proclamation of the republic in 1916 and confirmed in Article 3 of the Constitution of Saorstát Éireann, was deplored as sinister and retrogressive' (*PDDE*, 1937: 67, 242, 12 May).

Mrs Concannon contrasted the 'unequivocal declaration from the President that there is nothing in the Constitution which detracts from the rights which women possess in this country' with the reservations of the women's organisations 'backed by the opinions of two very authoritative lawyers, Deputy Lavery and Deputy Costello'. In view of any possible ambiguity, she welcomed the President's assurance that he would look into the matter again (*ibid*, Col. 242). Deputy Concannon herself agreed with the idea that women should be protected from unsuitable work, including night work. In support of her view she read into the Dáil record a newspaper account of the Post Office Workers' Conference at which women telephonists stated emphatically that they would not agree to night work. Mrs Concannon said:

The extract reads as follows:

'Miss D.A. Pearce, of London, said that under no conditions at all would they work until half-past eight, let alone any other time at night, and her statement was loudly cheered; complaint was made of the effect on telephonists' nerves of the special buzzer used for emergency calls. Miss Doris Curnow, of London, said the girls felt that the red warning light was sufficient without a buzzer as loud as a siren. In one or two London exchanges girls had been carried out with hysteria owing to the sounding of the buzzer when they were working at high pressure.'

That shows that the nervous system of women needs to be specially protected, and I think that Article 45, which gives them a constitutional right to that protection, should not be interfered with (*PDDE*, 1937: 67, 246, 12 May 1937).

De Valera met delegations from the Joint Committee and the Women Graduates' Association and agreed to consider their concerns. A campaign that provided evidence of a considerable level of organisation on the part of middle-class, professional women, was organised to lobby TDs and to get women's groups at home and abroad to take up the issue. According to Travers, 'The women's campaign against the provisions of the Constitution achieved a modest success in persuading the normally unyielding de Valera to drop the reference to the "inadequate strength of women"' (Travers, 1995: 193). Among those who roundly criticised the sections regarding women in the Constitution, in private, though not in public, was Margaret MacEntee, wife of de Valera's cabinet colleague Seán MacEntee. According to her daughter, the poet Máire Cruise O'Brien (Máire Mhac an tSaoi), her mother thought the Constitution deliberately aimed at keeping women in their place: 'On women's issues, she had no confidence in male politicians – ever. She had been the main breadwinner. My father had been in and out of jail. *Her* money kept the household going.' [2]

Máire Mhac an tSaoi makes the striking observation that Fianna Fáil politicians of the civil war generation frequently had to *rely* on earning wives. She recalls that, as a young boy, her brother Séamus had said that he would not like to be a politician, 'because it would be too cruel to his wife and little children'. To the children of that generation, including herself, the idea of a mother in the home was appealing. Her mother worked very hard and the family did not see that much of her; she was out of the house from 9 am to 9 pm. Although they had very little money, they had two maids to look after the household. Like so many working mothers before and since, Mrs MacEntee used to slip home for a few moments at lunch hour, when possible, in order to see her daughter. Máire says that, unlike her mother, she herself agrees with the notion of a woman's place in the home. She thinks that it is wrong that a mother should be under any compulsion to work. However, in her view, Article 41 was never implemented, as women in the home have not been adequately supported in practice. She recalls that when she became engaged, she invited her mother to her home for lunch. She had gone to some trouble to prepare the lunch, and she was devastated by her mother's reaction, 'Your grandmother and I did not work all our lives for you to end up in the kitchen.' Yet her mother never regarded her career as her primary function but as a means of 'keeping a roof over our heads'.

Brian Walsh, a former member of the Supreme Court, rejected the view that Article 41 implied that 'a woman's place is in the home':

> ... such a claim completely misreads the constitution. ... In the Article, the state acknowledges that, by her life within the home, woman gives the state the support without which the common good cannot be achieved. That is a statement of fact. ... It does not in any way exclude from that acknowledgement the woman who works outside the home and who also runs a home. Article 41 goes on to say that the state shall therefore endeavour to ensure that mothers should not be obliged by economic necessity to engage in labour to the neglect of their duties in the home. Astonishingly, this protective guarantee has never been invoked in any litigation (Walsh, 1988: 98).

Anthony Coughlan, lecturer in social policy in Trinity College, concurs with Walsh:

> Women possess all the personal and civil rights guaranteed by the constitution, quite apart from this Article. To recognise the special importance of women's role in the home – the principal sphere of altruism, non-reciprocal and non-cash exchange – is not to denigrate women's work elsewhere (Coughlan, 1988: 153).

Walsh further observes that the guarantee regarding economic necessity refers only to mothers and not to women generally, and only to women who are *obliged* by economic necessity to neglect their duties in the home. He concludes, 'In so far as the Article may be said to be discriminatory, it might be claimed that there is discrimination against men because there is no expressed acknowledgement of the benefits to the community that flow from a man's or a father's duties within the home' (Walsh, *ibid*: 98). The former Social Affairs Commissioner of the European Community, President of Ireland, and holder of key portfolios as a Fianna Fáil minister, Dr Patrick Hillery, takes a guarded view as to the actual economic benefits that women derived from the Constitution. He believes that it would be a great constitution which did indeed compensate women if they devoted their lives to caring for their families. However, when one looks, for example, at the position with regard to pension provision for women who care full-time for their families, it is clear that they are not rewarded in practice:

> If a man has a pension and his wife dies, he continues on that pension, but if the man dies, his wife gets half the pension. A philosophy of keeping women in the home and then at the end of it she is not going to be paid for keeping the home – she is going to get half-paid for keeping the home.[3]

Some progress was made by Dr Michael Woods when Minister for Social Welfare towards recognising work done by homemakers for pension purposes. Under the Homemakers' Scheme introduced in April 1994 both men and women who take some years out of the workforce for the purpose of caring for young children at home can have those years counted for pension purposes. The *Family Acts* 1995 and 1996 give a wife an interest in her husband's pension assets, which can be realised in the event of a judicial separation. Generally, the wife would have an interest in that portion of the pension which was built up during the marriage. In the event of a judicial separation, the courts will issue a pension adjustment, which splits the pension plan assets between the spouses. These measures were introduced in the context of the divorce referendum in 1995. However, Dr Hillery's point remains valid.

Insight into opposite points of view on the role of women a few years prior to the enactment of the Constitution may be found in a debate between Helena Moloney and Alice Curtayne published in *Model Housekeeping,* a contemporary women's magazine, in the late summer of 1935. The *Criminal Law Amendment Act*, 1935 had just been enacted, and debate was in progress regarding the Conditions of Employment Bill, the basis for the *Conditions of Employment Act* which was passed in 1936. Under the Act quite stringent restrictions were placed on the employment of women aged 18 years and over, as well as on the employment of girls. These restrictions contrasted with the failure of the *Criminal Law Amendment Act* in the previous year to raise the age of consent to 18 years, as recommended by an expert committee, chaired by William Carrigan, QC. The resulting anomaly was that on the one hand a woman of 18 years or over could not work after 10 pm at night, or a girl after 8 pm, yet the age of consent was fixed at 17 years.

Helena Moloney from the Irish Women Workers' Union represented the feminist viewpoint, while the writer Alice Curtayne represented the more traditionalist view. Moloney commenced by saying, 'Wolfdogs, round towers, Celtic tracery, and Irish Womanhood (the latter an abstraction in capital letters), occupy about an equal place in the sentimental mind of the average male patriot' (Moloney and Curtayne, 1935: 558). Moloney suggested that there were disquieting signs that women were again to be segregated as a sex, 'and to have their lives ordered and restricted by the male portion of the population to suit the conditions of the mad world that exclusively male Governments have brought about'. She criticised the removal of the equal right of women to sit on juries, claiming that it was a definite break with the old tradition of Ireland which gave women equal place with men in administering the laws. She warned that women's right 'to labour even in such lowly occupations as she has previously followed is to be restricted in the alleged interests of male labour or in her own interests'. Moloney continued:

> Women are and have been exploited economically. Her political status until recently was a reflex of this economic bondage. The proposed 'Conditions of Employment Bill' as it

affects women will restrict their opportunities for labour in the future if not now, and gives power to the Minister of the day to define what a woman may or may not do. This will inevitably drive women into the cheapest and least skilled classes of labour, and sanction and intensify her present inferior position (Moloney and Curtayne, *ibid*: 598).

Nevertheless, Moloney continues, 'We agree that woman's place is the home, but she must do other things in order to have a home and preserve its sanctity and safety' (*ibid*: 598). In presenting her opposing view on women's status in Ireland, Curtayne did not focus specifically on the Conditions of Employment Bill, but rather on the 'principles of feminism'. She said that more women in the workforce would add to the unemployment problem, and concluded that the more attractive the labour market became for women, the more they would move out from the home. In this forecast she was prescient and in line with the analysis of economists decades later. Of her claim that feminists 'have made masculinity the ideal of womankind', she said:

> It tends to suppress the normal and rational division of human labour by removing woman from the family role to fling her into competition with man in public life. There then takes place that inversion of values which would make the choice of a profession, or a career, a thing superior to marriage or domesticity. ... The more attractive is the labour market made to women, the more inevitable is their drift from the home (Moloney and Curtayne, *ibid*: 599).

Women, reflecting on their circumstances and on the world around them, were thinking for themselves and, as Moloney had remarked, while accepting that a woman's place is in the home, a woman must do other things in order to have and to protect her home. Traditional voices were gradually added to the dissenting voices of the intellectual women. In 1939, two years after the passing of the 1937 Constitution, Alice Ryan, a future president of the ICA, said that members 'should challenge the man's saying "a woman's place is in the home" to "a woman's place is where she can best help her home"' (Ferriter, 1995: 17).

By the late 1950s the view was being expressed by a woman in a Church journal, *Christus Rex,* that the role of women should extend into the community. The contribution, by Ita Meehan, which had been delivered first at a Social Study conference, was significant at the time. According to Meehan, while woman is primarily a mother, though not exclusively in the physical sense,

> She must develop her own powers of soul and intellect. Now the powers of the intellect cannot be achieved by complete absorption in household tasks. ... Women must take themselves seriously. They must emerge somewhat from the privacy of the home, and take their proper place in the community side by side with man. ... What I am suggesting is that the home should be a woman's primary but not her exclusive sphere (Meehan, 1959: 98).

For those engaged in farming, the question of a 'woman's place' did not arise in the same way as it did among the working, business and professional classes in the towns and cities, because the home was the location of both family and business life. A commentary on the extent to which rural women were concerned with practical improvements in rural life, rather than ideological debate on the role of women, is given by historian Diarmaid Ferriter in his history of the Irish Countrywomen's Association (Ferriter, 1995). If there was no challenge to the view of a woman's place in rural Ireland, because the question did not arise, neither was there any great debate in either rural or urban areas about who was responsible for young children. It was accepted across the spectrum of opinion from the rural women to the early feminists that child-rearing was a woman's job. It was a commonly held view that men were not appropriate persons to deal with young children and therefore, for example, teachers in the earliest classes in primary schools have traditionally been women. The early feminists believed in the moral superiority of women and that this '… was inborn and a consequence of their function as mothers' (Harriss, 1992: 83).

For women, and for men, working in industrial and service occupations, generally at low rates of pay, the question of separate spheres of activity *did* arise. As the industrial revolution proceeded throughout nineteenth-century Britain the separation of the domestic from the public sphere was given legal sanction, and that law applied also in Ireland. Married women could not own property or make contracts in their own name, thus excluding them from business. By the end of the nineteenth century in England there were some who wished to forbid married women by law from going out to work. In 1901, Dr George Reid, concerned about the discrepancy between the drop in the overall death rate and the high infant mortality rate, used a phrase, 'neglect their home duties', which is almost identical to that used in the Constitution, and suggests some form of legal sanction:

> Now it is perfectly true that we cannot legislate as to how mothers shall feed their children, but surely we may reasonably expect the State to exercise some control in the case of those mothers who sometimes from necessity, but more frequently from inclination, neglect their home duties and go to work in factories (Reid, 1901: 410-12).

Trade unionists regarded the fact that women were prepared to work for lower rates of pay than men as a threat to men's jobs and livelihoods. In 1932, Louie Bennett, Secretary of the Irish Women Workers' Union, said that the employment of women in industry at low wages was 'a menace to family life'. Expressing her criticism of the use of women and girls as a source of cheap labour, she said:

> Naturally I have no desire to put a spoke in the wheel of women's employment. But this modern tendency to draw women into industry in increasing numbers is of no real

advantage to them. It has not raised their status as workers, nor their wage standard. It is a menace to family life, and in so far as it has blocked the employment of men, it has intensified poverty amongst the working classes (Quoted in Fox, 1957: 99).

The 1930s was the era of the Great Depression and of the Economic War with Britain. Jobs for men were given priority and gradually restrictions were introduced which limited the sphere of women's work outside the home. A marriage bar for women national teachers was introduced in 1933. The General Secretary of the Irish National Teacher's Organisation at the time, and subsequent author of the official history of the INTO, T. J. O' Connell, believed that an important motive behind the introduction of the bar was to gain the rural vote as, in rural areas, where two teachers were married to each other, their relative affluence was the cause of envy in those hungry times.

In his *Principles of Economics*, Alfred Marshall had no doubt regarding the economic value of mothers. In comparing the advantages of the artisan over the unskilled labourer, Marshall said that his parents were more likely to have been better educated and 'his mother is more likely to be able to give more of her time to the care of her family' (Marshall, 1920: 469). According to Marshall:

> If we compare one country of the civilised world with another, or one part of England with another, or one trade in England with another, we find that the degradation of the working-classes varies almost uniformly with the amount of rough work done by women. The most valuable of all capital is that invested in human beings; and of that capital the most precious part is the result of the care and influence of the mother (Marshall, *ibid*: 469).

Marshall proceeds to talk about the cost of production of efficient (male) labour in terms of the family:

> At all events we cannot treat the cost of production of efficient men as an isolated problem; it must be taken as part of the broader problem of the cost of production of efficient men together with the women who are fitted to make their homes happy, and to bring up their children vigorous in body and mind, truthful and cleanly, gentle and brave (Marshall, *ibid*: 469).

That such an approach to the role of women was taken at the time by the Professor of Political Economy in Cambridge serves to place Irish attitudes in context. The fact is that a view similar to that espoused by the Irish Catholic hierarchy prevailed among the liberal Protestant establishment at the time in Britain, and the quotation from Marshall's *Principles*, a hugely successful economics text, which dominated the study of economics for generations of students, at a time when Cambridge was the Mecca of the English-speaking economics world, bears out this fact.

Feminists in the 1920s and 1930s were strong supporters of motherhood. Although there were exceptions, such as Switzerland, where women were not granted the vote until 1971, the granting of female suffrage in most Western countries soon after World War I meant that a great goal had been reached for feminism and, accordingly, a shift in direction occurred during the 1920s. Feminists began to promote motherhood and the improvement of the conditions of mothers (Harriss, 1992). Following the carnage of the Great War there was renewed focus on population issues and on women's reproductive role. Increasing concern about the birth rate put feminists on the defensive. In nearly all European countries pro-family campaigns were mounted, often by feminists, in an effort to reverse the slide in birth rates. 'Mother's Day' was introduced in the US in 1907 and in Germany in 1922 while in France a special medal was introduced for mothers of large families. Increasingly all over Europe married women were barred from employment. Harriss gives the example of the German postal service where the total number of married women employed fell from 2,718 to 21 between 1922 and 1923. Working women in general were channelled into the 'caring' occupations while school curricula emphasised domestic economy for girls.

The concept of housewife implies a married woman with responsibility for the domestic sphere. The housewife, firmly on stage by the start of the twentieth century, was making a rapid exit at a rate of 340 per week by 1999 (*Quarterly National Household Survey*, 1st Quarter, 2000). The Hon. Miss ffrench was expressing a widely held view when she spoke to the Annual Assembly of the Laurel Hill Past Pupils' Union, in 1932, in Limerick, where the writer Kate O'Brien had been a pupil:

> The home is a Divine institution, and woman is the first teacher there, and is appointed by God to that exalted office. It is the temple of love that the enemy of the Church has sought to destroy. He seeks the destruction of the sanctity of home life by substituting for it the convenience and pleasures of parents, and where he succeeds, be it noted, a moral chaos flows, which betokens the departure of God. No direct attack is made, but wily, as of old, he dangles the forbidden fruit before woman, whispers to her that she should taste of the larger life, that her great powers are wasted in the drab sphere to which God has appointed her (ffrench, 1932).

The housewife, although producing a constant flow of goods and services, is not regarded as a producer in the economic sense. The national income accounts cover market production whereas non-market production includes the goods and services household members produce for their own consumption by combining their unpaid labour with the goods and services they acquire in the market. But, as pointed out in an OECD study, work done in the household both increases the value of purchased goods and services and 'contributes to the formation and upkeep of human capital. Its value is clearly substantial'

(Chadeau, 1992). National income accounting conventions have been strongly challenged by those who argue that by failing to recognise the economic value of women's household production services, the value of unpaid household labour is excluded from both national income and product accounts. Marilyn Waring also emphasises the absence of any measure of women's 'investment' in child-rearing and human capital formation (Waring, 1990).

For at least the first half of the twentieth century feminists, church leaders, political leaders as well as the general populace would have shared the view that motherhood was the ultimate calling of woman and of its proper link with marriage. The feminist critique of the statement in the Constitution regarding woman in the home centred on the implication that the home was the *only* fit zone of activity for women, as seemed to be contained in the expression 'by her *life* within the home'. The wave of feminism that developed in the 1960s and 1970s began to further scrutinise not just the concept of 'woman in the home', but also the concept of motherhood, which in time, some would argue, became part of a woman's 'right to choose'.

Breadwinners

The term 'breadwinner' first appeared in the Scottish census of 1871, where the procedure for classifying the occupations of husbands and wives differed from that used in England, Wales and Ireland:

> For the Scotch Census tables every class, order, and sub-order, is divided into earners, or to use the term in the Scotch Report 'bread-winners' and dependants. As regards the wives in Order IV of the Domestic class, whom the English tables assume to be help-mates, not merely in the husband's household but in the husband's business, the Scotch tables admit no presumption of the sort, but relegate these wives equally with the wives of no specified occupations to the dependent section of each order and sub-order, while the wives of specified occupations are tabulated in the bread-winning division of each order, sub-order, or specific calling (Census 1871, *General Report*: 67).

In studies of family change prominence is often given to changes in the role and behaviour of women, in particular regarding the labour force participation of married women and the decline in fertility. The change in the role of men has received less attention. The shift away from the function of men as sole family breadwinners, from at least the early 1970s, has come about both through the increased earning capacity of women and through the provision of state payments for unmarried mothers and deserted wives in lieu of a flow of income that might hitherto have been expected to come from a man's earnings. In agricultural communities throughout the world, women are substantial, sometimes the major, contributors to productive output, and they have contributed substantially to the agricultural output of Irish farms, although not recognised in the statistics. Children also have made an economic contribution.

Nevertheless, there has been widespread acceptance of the central role of the man as breadwinner.

Related to the economic superiority of men were their superior rights in law. Until late in the nineteenth century, a wife had no right to hold property in her own name separately from her husband. Husband and wife were regarded as one person in law, and the husband held all the property. By an enactment in 1882, a wife was permitted to hold property and to make a contract separately. In 1957, the *Married Women's Status Act* permitted one spouse to sue another in Court. Section 12 of that Act has been commonly used to determine proprietary rights to the family home. Married men also enjoyed a range of decision-making rights in relation to the upbringing of their children. For example, the father could determine in what religion his children were educated (see Kindersley case in Shatter, 1997). In the late 1940s the Isherwood and Begley cases, in which the mother had left home with the children, came before the Courts, and in both cases, the mother was instructed to return the children to their father. In ordering the return of the children in the Isherwood case to the father who was resident in England, Mr Justice Maguire said that it had been set down in Kindersley that '… the father has right in law to determine in what religion the child shall be educated and brought up' (*Irish Independent*, 16 January 1948).

In the Begley case, Mrs Begley, a Catholic, had left her husband, a member of the Church of Ireland, and taken the three children, the eldest of whom was aged eight, with her. Once more Mr Justice Maguire ordered the return of the children to the father. In his judgment, Mr Justice Maguire emphasised economic factors, although Mrs Begley claimed that the real issue was religious instruction and that she would have no difficulty getting employment. Mr Begley's mother gave evidence to support the claim that the children were being brought up as Catholics, stating that Brian, the eldest child, went to Confession at proper times and to Mass at Star of the Sea, Sandymount, every Sunday (*Irish Independent*, 20 January 1948). Mr Justice Maguire said that he

> … had a good deal of sympathy with the mother, but it was quite clear that it was not possible to have these children left in some house in Rathmines depending on the charity of some good woman while the mother was at work when the father was prepared to look after them and provide for their education (*Irish Independent*, 20 January 1948).

Until the Tilson case in 1950, Irish law tended to follow contemporary English law which in practice meant that the father's wishes regarding the education of the children prevailed. In its judgment the Supreme Court held that the common law rule whereby fathers enjoyed the sole prerogative of determining the religious education of their children was contrary to Article 42.1 of the Constitution (Hogan, 1988:311). The Tilson case centred on a marriage between a Catholic and a Protestant and a pre-nuptial promise by the Protestant father to bring up his sons Catholics. In delivering his judgment, Mr Justice Gavan Duffy said, '... for religion, for marriage, for the family and for the children, we have laid down our own foundations. Much of the resultant Irish standards are both remote from British precedent and alien to the English way of life' (Kennedy, 1989:71). On appeal, the Supreme Court, by four judges to one, affirmed the decision of Mr Justice Gavan Duffy. Mr Justice James Murnaghan stated:

> The true principle of the Constitution is this. The parents – father and mother – have a joint power and duty in respect of the religious education of the children. If they, together, made a decision and put it into practice, it is not in the power of the father or the mother to revoke such against the will of the other party (Quoted in Kennedy, 1989: 71).

It is worth noting that the emphasis in the Supreme Court decision was placed on the joint decision of the parents to bring up their children as Catholics and the fact that the decision could not be rescinded by one parent. The Supreme Court decision in 1951 would appear to be in accord with the principle of joint guardianship later enshrined in the *Guardianship of Infants Act*, 1964, and indeed to anticipate it.

For much of the twentieth century men who married were destined to become exclusive breadwinners for their wives and children. In the traditional wedding formula it was the man who pledged 'with all my worldly goods, I thee endow.' In 1907 the *Freeman's Journal* reported, 'The man who is worth his salt realises that his first duty is by the toil of his brains or his hands to make and keep a home for his wife and family. The woman can have no higher duty than to make that home happy' (Farmar, 1995: 34). In a letter to *The Irish Times* during the 1913 Lock-out, the breadwinner role was emphasised by AE (George Russell), when he accused employers of having 'determined deliberately, in cold anger, to starve out one-third of the population of this city, to break the manhood of the men by the sight of the suffering of their wives and the hunger of their children'. Character judgements were passed on men according as they were 'good providers' or not; failure to be a good provider implied that a man was somehow inadequate, or less manly. Writing in the 1950s, John D. Sheridan was in no doubt regarding the importance of the breadwinner, stressing his importance in economic development and for the early settlers in the New World: 'One of the greatest factors in economic development is the need to provide for wife and children. ... When the covered wagons rolled westward, the real driver was the infant at the breast' (Sheridan, 1954: 185).

For decades both the tax and social welfare codes were based on the assumption, sometimes explicit, sometimes implicit, that the family unit comprised a breadwinner father with dependent wife and children. The *Beveridge Report* which influenced the development of the Welfare State, not only in Britain, but in Ireland, asserted as fact:

All women by marriage acquire a new economic and social status, with risks and rights different from those of the unmarried. On marriage a woman gains a legal right to maintenance by her husband as a first line of defence against risks which fall directly on the solitary woman (Beveridge, 1942).

When in 1951, a decade after Beveridge, the Minister for Finance introduced his Budget, he said that since it was not possible to introduce an all-round improvement in tax allowances, he had decided 'that the best thing to do is to give relief where it is most needed – to the married man, especially the married man with children' (*PDDE*, 125, 1892, 2 May, 1951). This Budget was known as the 'Family Man's Budget' (Manning, 1999: 275). Trade unionist Sheila Conroy says that up to the 1970s, 'Society was geared to the family unit, whereby a woman went along in partnership with a man and she had no status of her own' (Heron, 1993: 31). Giving women who were working outside the home the same money as men was seen as a threat to the traditional position of wives and families (Heron, *ibid*).

Challenges to the 'Breadwinner Father' model of family life during the past two decades have come in both ideological and behavioural forms. In the early 1970s, equality legislation, and the removal of the ban on the employment of married women in the public sector, together with the changing values associated with the Women's Liberation Movement, were important contributory factors. In the mid-1980s the notion of a wife's economic dependency on her husband came under scrutiny when, in order to comply with EC regulations governing social security provisions, the Irish government adopted a revised definition of economic dependency. From 1985 a wife must be *mainly* dependent on her husband in order to be regarded as his dependant for social welfare purposes. This is a recognition of the *de facto* increase in the economic independence of many wives. More or less at the same time men's wages have become less adequate to support a family, as the concept of the 'family wage' has lost popularity. Research in Britain has shown that from the 1970s families increasingly depended on two wage earners to achieve a standard of living that would have been possible with one in the 1950s. Increasing owner occupation and the relative increase in house prices since the 1970s have also been relevant, as two-earner households could afford better housing and bid prices upwards (Fox Harding, 1996: 8). The breadwinner model also came under pressure due to the increase in unemployment between 1980 and 1995 when unemployment of males rose from 70,000 to 180,000, limiting the capacity of these men to act as breadwinners.

At a time when the male breadwinner model has been in decline, its origin and development is being subjected to careful examination (Creighton, 1996; Janssens, 1998). Depending on the value standpoint, the male breadwinner may be seen either as a symbol of women's emancipation or of women's dependency. It was an objective of early Trade Unionists to achieve a wage that would be adequate for a man to support himself together with his wife and children – a family wage. By this means women and children would be freed from economic necessity to engage in the workforce. Women could care for the home and children would have a work-free childhood. Mounting unemployment in the years of the Great Depression led to emphasis on the priority for men's jobs and restrictions on the entry of women, in particular married women, to the workforce. As freedom to work became restricted for women, the family wage was no longer viewed as a boon, but rather as a bulwark against equality. A goal of the Women's Liberation Movement in the 1960s and 1970s was equal pay for men and women and, in due course, a system based on equal pay for equal work was introduced, regardless of family circumstances.

Men and the Constitution

Article 40.1 of the Constitution states:

> All citizens shall, as human persons, be held equal before the law.

> This shall not be held to mean that the State shall not in its enactments have due regard to differences of capacity, physical and moral, and of social function.

According to the Report of the Constitution Review Group (CRG) in 1996, '… the second sentence has too frequently been used by the courts as a means of upholding legislation by reference to questionable stereotypes, thereby justifying discrimination against, for example, an unmarried person as compared with a married person (The State (Nicolau) v. An Bórd Uchtála [1966] IR. 567), and a man as compared with a woman (Norris v. Attorney General [1984] IR. 36)' (CRG, 1996: 228). Combined with Article 41 on the Family, Article 40.1 of the Constitution has justified preferential treatment of women *vis-à-vis* men in certain instances (Dennehy v. Minister for Social Welfare [1984] and Lowth v. Minister for Social Welfare [1984] ELR 119).

Leo Flynn, reférendaire at the Court of Justice of the European communities, has raised the question of how the Constitution views the role of men. He bases his analysis on two cases in particular, the Nicolau case in the 1960s and the Norris case in 1980s (Flynn, 1998). The Nicolau case centred on the adoption of a child born out of wedlock without reference to the wishes of the father, while the Norris case concerned the right to homosexual life. Nicolau was the natural father of a child born in London in 1960 to an Irish citizen. Despite the objections of the father, a Greek Cypriot, the mother placed the child for adoption and the Adoption Order was made in 1961. The core of Nicolau's case was that the *Adoption Act*, 1952 violated rights to equality and family life in the Constitution. Nicolau lost in both the High Court and the Supreme Court. In the Supreme Court the judgment delivered by Mr Justice Walsh dismissed Nicolau's claim to equal treatment under Article 40.1 (Flynn, 1998: 139). Walsh claimed that except where an unmarried man and woman were living in a common home in circumstances approximating to married life

> ... it is rare for a natural father to take any interest in his offspring [and] it is not difficult to appreciate the difference in moral capacity and social function between the natural father and the several persons described in the subsections in question (Quoted in Flynn, *ibid*: 139).

The judgment of the Courts was based on the particular construction of Irish men in the Constitution. 'From reading Nicolau and Norris, we have a better appreciation of what it is to be a proper Irish man and what the Constitution will recognise as such' (Flynn, *ibid*: 145):

> The Irish courts in this case are overwhelmingly concerned with legitimacy but once the child born outside marriage has been adopted the focus of this concern is on the legitimacy of Nicolau's position. His inconvenient reality having been erased, the courts can send out the message that men are either fathers and married or else they should disappear, and that there will be no space for the recognition of those who do not conform to this model (Flynn, *ibid*: 140-41).

Thirty years later the European Court of Human Rights found that the right to family life had been breached in a case where a child born outside marriage had been given up for adoption without consulting the father (Keegan v. Ireland 1994). The emphasis in Article 41 of the Constitution is on the protection of rights of the family unit rather than the rights resulting from a family relationship (CRG, 1996: 323). According to Article 8 (1) of the European Convention on Human Rights (ECHR), 'Everyone has the right to respect for his private and family life, his home and his correspondence.' In relation to Keegan, the European Court found that Ireland was in breach of Article 8 of the European Convention in that it failed to respect the family life of an unmarried father who had had a stable relationship with the mother of his child, in permitting the placement of the child for adoption without his knowledge or consent. As a result Ireland is obliged to give natural fathers to whom children are born in the context of 'family life', as interpreted by the European Court of Human Rights, a legal opportunity to establish a relationship with that child, including a legal entitlement to be consulted before the child is placed for adoption (CRG, 1996: 325).

The issue of discrimination against men under Article 41, due to the absence of any acknowledgement of the work of men/fathers in the home in the Article, has arisen in regard to Social Welfare entitlements. In Dennehy v. The Minister for Social Welfare (1984), Mr Justice Barron supported 'his conclusion that the failure of the State to treat deserted husbands in the same way as deserted wives for the purposes of Social Welfare was justified by the proviso in Article 40.1 (the recognition of a difference in capacity and social function)' (CRG, 1996: 333).

In July 1998 a case came before the Supreme Court regarding the treatment of a deserted husband, Tony Lowth, who had spent approximately fifteen years bringing up his children, Angela and Mark, then aged seventeen and sixteen years respectively. Lowth claimed that the *Social Welfare Act*, 1981 was unconstitutional since it denied the same benefits to deserted husbands as it granted to deserted wives, and therefore it did not treat all citizens equally as laid down in Article 40.1 of the Constitution. Lowth, who had given up his job to look after his children, had failed before the High Court in establishing that he was entitled to a payment similar to deserted wives' benefit from 1984-89. Mr Justice Costello '... found that the Oireachtas had taken a view that a married woman in Irish society fulfilled a different function to a married man and required greater help. This was based on the Constitution' (Coulter, 1998). The Supreme Court judgment in July 1998 upheld the 1993 High Court judgment of Mr Justice Costello that in 1984 the State was justified in holding that deserted wives had greater needs than deserted husbands, in turn justifying special payments to wives:

> ... the Supreme Court cited statistics from the 1970s to the 1980s showing that married women were less likely to be in the workforce and, therefore, less able to support themselves compared to men at that time. It held that women, if deserted by their husbands, were likely to require financial assistance (Coulter, 1998).

The protection of marriage in the Constitution was used as an argument by the Supreme Court to reject the claims in the Norris case to decriminalise homosexuality (Flynn, *ibid*). According to Norris, following years when homosexuality was excluded from public discourse, in the early 1960s the 'first chinks appeared in the curtain of silence' (Norris, 1998). This opening was due mainly to the debate that followed the work of Sir John Wolfenden and the *Commission of Enquiry into Prostitution and Homosexuality* in England and that led to the *Sexual Offences Act,* 1967, which removed criminal penalties from certain homosexual acts. The penalty for homosexual activity between males had been death by hanging prior to the introduction of the *Offences Against the Person* Act in 1861, an Act regarded at the time as a liberalising statute in that it involved a substantial reduction of the sentence. In 1885 the La Bouchère Amendment to the 1861 Act criminalised what it termed 'gross indecency' between males, described eighty years later by Sir John Wolfenden as 'a blackmailer's charter'; Oscar Wilde was among those convicted under its provisions.

In 1971 David Norris, then a lecturer in Trinity College Dublin, joined the group called 'The Southern Ireland Civil Rights Association', formed in response to the crisis in Northern Ireland. The atmosphere generated by the Civil Rights Movement in the United States and the Civil Rights Movement in Ireland in response to the discrimination against Catholics in the North helped Norris and some associates to found the Irish Gay Rights Movement (IGRM). In 1975 Norris and the IGRM decided to make a constitutional challenge. In 1976 they commissioned a legal brief from leading senior counsel Donal Barrington, later a member of the Supreme Court:

> Mr Barrington's opinion was positive in the sense that he believed we had an incontestable case intellectually although he was careful to warn us of the fact that due to the political complexion of the issues involved we would face an uphill battle in achieving the judgment we required (Norris, *ibid*: 10).

Before the case reached Court, Barrington was appointed to the High Court and his replacement as counsel was Mary Robinson, SC, later President of Ireland. Due to internal divisions within the IGRM, the campaign was relaunched under the banner of 'The Campaign for Homosexual Law Reform'. In November 1977 what became known as the 'Norris Case' opened in the High Court before Mr Justice McWilliam. The plaintiff was seeking a declaration that Sections 61 and 62 of the 1861 Act and Section 11 of the 1885 Act had automatically lapsed with the passage of the Irish Constitution of 1937 as a result of the conflict between these Sections and the provisions of Article 40, Section 1 and Section 2, guaranteeing the rights of the individual. Mr Justice McWilliam gave his decision on 10 October 1980, and, despite a number of favourable findings of fact in regard to the plaintiff's case, ... 'indicated that because of the Christian and democratic nature of this State despite all these findings he had to find in the government's favour' (Norris, *ibid*: 12).

Following the rejection of his case in the High Court, Norris indicated that he would appeal to the Supreme Court, and if necessary, to the European Court of Human Rights. In 1981 the European Court of Human Rights made a landmark decision in the case of Jeffrey Dudgeon. The Dudgeon case, which originated in Northern Ireland, had been taken in response to an incident of police harassment. The European Court found in favour of Dudgeon. In Norris's appeal to the Supreme Court, the Court divided 3:2 against Norris. The majority decision was signed by Chief Justice O'Higgins, with Mr Justice Finlay and Mr Justice Griffin assenting. The majority decision included the following: 'Homosexual conduct can be inimical to marriage and is *per se* harmful to it as an institution.' Referring to this point in the judgment, Norris claims that it

> ... justifies criminal penalties as a measure to protect marriage and which was so glibly agreed to by Mr Justice Finlay, conflicts strangely with his subsequent judgment in a nullity case, that the homosexuality of one of the spouses was sufficient to render the marriage null and void (Norris, *ibid*: 13-14).

Defeat in the Supreme Court opened the way to the European Court of Human Rights. By a very narrow majority the European Court found in favour of Norris.

It was several years before the Irish Government gave effect to the judgment of the European Court, when in 1993, the Minister for Justice, Mrs Máire Geoghegan Quinn, piloted *The Criminal Law Offences Act,* 1993, through the Houses of the Oireachtas with all-Party agreement, so that a Vote was not required.

Egalitarian model

Evidence of more egalitarian patterns in rural family life were found by Hannan and Katsiaouni in their study of farm families in the 1970s. They found that over one-quarter of the farm families in their sample had a 'modern' interactive pattern with a marked breaching of traditional sex roles in household and child-rearing tasks and with a joint consultative pattern of decision-making and a mutually supportive emotional structure (Hannan and Katsiaouni, 1977). By the end of the century the patriarchal, authoritarian model of the family was largely replaced by a more egalitarian model. The change is encapsulated in a striking manner in the motto selected by the United Nations for the International Year of the Family in 1994: 'Building the smallest democracy at the heart of society'. The concept of a democracy, the essence of which is 'one man one vote', would not spring to mind in relation to the generality of families in Ireland for much of the century.

Three factors occurred simultaneously in 1972-73 which contributed to the emergence of the egalitarian family model. Accession to the EEC in 1973 reinforced by the recommendations of the *Report of the Commission on the Status of Women* (1972) brought about equal treatment of women in the work-force, while at the very same time the first cohort of beneficiaries of free post-primary education, which was introduced in 1967, were graduating from second-level education from 1972 onwards, and women as well as men were equipped to avail themselves of the new employment opportunities in services, including the public services. A substantial impetus towards the egalitarian model of family was exerted by the trade union movement which had registered a shift in its traditional emphasis on the breadwinner model. In 1975, the annual conference of the Irish Congress of Trade Unions (ICTU) adopted the *Working Women's Charter* which sought full equality of men and women in the workplace and the provision of state-controlled crèches and day nurseries to enable mothers to engage fully in the workforce. The year 1975 was International Women's Year, and during the year a world conference was held in Mexico which adopted a Plan of Action for the UN Decade for Women.

Ten years later in 1985, to mark the conclusion of the Decade for Women, the Executive Council of ICTU prepared a new *Charter of Rights for Women* which contained a comprehensive list of measures necessary to achieve the declared goal of equality (ICTU, 1985: 20). The *Charter* reviewed the achievements of the previous ten years and highlighted the areas where demands remained unfulfilled. The two main areas outstanding related to pay, including the statutory protection of part-time workers who were mainly women, and the need to cater for working parents, especially in regard to child-care. In the words of the former Legislation and Equality Officer of ICTU, Patricia O'Donovan:

> To facilitate women entering and staying in employment, it is essential to provide child-care facilities. It is also essential to encourage increased involvement of men in sharing domestic and child-care responsibilities, through the introduction of paternity and parental leave (ICTU, *ibid*: 21).

One of the observable changes in family life is the degree to which child-care has come to be seen as a responsibility of men as well as women. Parallel to the man's responsibility as breadwinner was the acceptance of his freedom from what were regarded as 'domestic chores'. The reluctance of men to shop or to wheel a pram was evident in the 1950s: '... they would not be seen wheeling a baby or washing the dishes or anything like that. That is considered a woman's job' (Humphreys, 1966: 99). But as more women were drawn into the workforce, the newer generation of men increased their involvement at home (McKeown *et al*, 1998).

If what *The Irish Times* called the 'fifty-fifty' principle in marriage sixty years ago has now become standard, it has come about both as a result of choice on the one hand, and of economic necessity on the other. If the Constitution pledged the State to endeavour to ensure that mothers would not be forced out of the home to work, economic realities at the start of the twenty-first century indicate that the workforce participation of mothers is often necessary to secure a home in the first instance. From the 1970s onwards, Building Societies began to take account of the income of the spouse as well as that of the principal earner when allocating loans. In the late 1970s a fairly typical definition of household income for mortgage purposes would be the basic salary or wage of the husband including any regular additions such as overtime earnings and commission payments, and usually half of the wife's earnings would be allowed if derived from secure non-manual occupations such as teaching or clerical work in a semi-state company (Baker and O'Brien, 1979: 41-2). Local authorities would only give a loan if the breadwinner's wage was sufficient to repay the loan, but gradually the second wage was taken into account. The second wage was also taken into account in determining ceilings for loan approvals, but only if the wage was based on permanent employment. In July 1981 Ordinary loans under the Small Dwellings Acquisition Acts were restricted to married persons and persons about to marry (Circular B. C. 6/81, Department of the Environment). In a speech in the Dáil on 23 July 1981, the Minister for the Environment, Peter Barry, said that at that time about 22 per cent of new house borrowers from all agencies and a high proportion of purchasers of second-hand housing were single persons. He said, 'In the normal course the housing needs of families must take priority.'

Much has changed both in the housing market and in the pattern of family formation since then and the restriction subsequently lapsed. Given the rise in house prices, by the late 1990s first-time house purchasers often needed not only two salaries but contributions from parents and relatives to help with the purchase of homes while a new phenomenon emerged of three people pooling resources to buy a house together. In an assessment of housing needs carried out by local authorities in 1996, of those deemed eligible for local authority housing, 27 per cent were single persons, 32 per cent were households with two adults and children, while 41 per cent were households with one adult, predominantly a single mother, and children. An examination of the applicant status for those seeking local authority housing in 2000 indicates the extent to which the married couple has become a minority status. In one, not untypical county, late in 2000, married couples comprised less than 20 per cent of the applicants, while lone parents comprised over 33 per cent, common law husband and wife couples comprised 14 per cent and divorced and separated comprised over 12 per cent. These last three categories therefore amounted in total to 60 per cent of the applicants or three times the married share.[4]

5

Catalysts for Change

Changes in attitudes to marriage, motherhood and the role of women resulted from a complex range of factors, including the work of organisations and lobby groups which, often in pursuit of measures to support women in the home, transformed the role of women outside the home. Access to information, which helped to create the mood for change, came via the media, including magazines and radio. Television programmes, especially the *Late Late Show*, the longest-running show of its kind in the world, hosted by Gay Byrne, and the serials *Tolka Row* and *The Riordans*, brought changing lifestyles into living-rooms all around Ireland. Most significantly, job opportunities in both public and private services, and therefore access to independent income, increased from the 1960s onwards. Increased job opportunities, together with increased educational opportunities, following the introduction of free post-primary education in 1967, contributed to the greater financial independence of women, an objective of the Women's Movement that spread in Ireland in the 1970s.

Legislative changes governing conditions of employment were important in facilitating the participation of married women in the workforce. The choice for women was no longer marriage or a job; a combination of the two was possible. The earliest and most significant change in regulations governing the employment of married women was the removal, in 1958, by the then Minister for Education, Jack Lynch, of the bar against married women teachers in national schools, a bar that had been in existence since 1933. The change was made partly in response to arguments concerning the effects on family formation of improving employment opportunities for women, as suggested in the Reports of the Commission on Emigration, as well as in response to a shortage in the supply of trained teachers. In due course the complete removal of the marriage bar in every sector followed in the 1970s. The First Commission on the Status of Women in 1972 paved the way for the introduction of equal pay, while entry to the EEC copper-fastened this and other elements of the equality agenda.

Women's organisations and initiatives

Two defining features of many women's organisations and initiatives until at least the 1960s were that they were voluntary and that they focused mainly on the home and children. Before the expansion of state social services which got under way in the 1960s, the decades from the 1920s to the 1950s were years of extensive voluntary work. If the focus of activity of women's organisations was the home and issues related to the home, the fruits of their labours spread into the wider community. For example, a small organisation, *An Bhantracht le Forfhás Tionnscail* (Women's Industrial Development Association), by encouraging families to wear Irish clothes and to use Irish fabrics in the home, was also supporting Irish industry (*Irish Independent*, 26 April 1935). The two most important women's organisations – the Irish Countrywomen's Association (ICA) and the Irish Housewives' Association (IHA) – were based around the home. In the case of the countrywomen work and family life blended into a seamless whole, while among the housewives any efforts made in the public domain were directed towards improving the conditions of women in the home and their families. The United Irishwomen, as the Countrywomen were called from their foundation in 1910 until 1934, pursued practical patriotism, by trying to improve the conditions in which they and their families obtained their livelihoods. 'Rural Ireland for them was very much a business' (Ferriter, 1995: 9).

In 1907 the Women's National Health Association (WNHA) was founded by Lady Aberdeen, wife of the Viceroy. The Association focused on housewives and mothers as the key agents in improving the health of the population and reducing infant mortality through improved standards of hygiene and clean milk. The Association established a number of Babies' Clubs with a doctor and nurse attached to each one and, in 1916, opened the first school medical clinic. A remarkable initiative was the founding in Dublin in 1919 of St Ultan's Children's Hospital by Dr Kathleen Lynn and her friend Madeleine Ffrench-Mullen. St Ultan's cared for sick children from poor families, many without a breadwinner, as a result of unemployment or the death or absence of the father. Dr Lynn's philosophy centred on the belief that the child is the nation's most precious possession. She had clear views on child-rearing, saying that 'breast-milk is the baby's birthright' (Ó hÓgartaigh, 1997). In the 1930s St Ultan's helped to establish model tenement houses to break the cycle of deprivation and ill-health among poor families. In 1920 an Irish branch of 'Save the Children', which had its headquarters in Geneva, was founded; it was called *Saor an Leanbh* and aimed at ensuring adequate nutrition and care for children. Its projects included the 'adoption' of a child by subscribing a sum of money that would ensure adequate nutrition for a child for a year. *Saor an Leanbh* also worked as a lobby group to improve conditions for children through the provision of school meals. In the 1940s, Dr Angela Russell led a delegation regarding school meals to the Dublin Board of Health, which in turn decided to send a request to the Minister for Local Government and Public Health (Russell Scrapbook).

In 1924 the National Council of Women of Ireland (NCWI) was founded. Its honorary secretary was Mrs Lucy Kingston. It organised conferences and carried out educational work; it promoted reforms with special reference to women and children. In 1926, it sent a delegation to the Paris Congress of the International

Alliance and submitted a report there on 'Maternal Mortality in Ireland'. In 1935 the NCWI set up a *Standing Committee on Legislation concerning Women and Children*, and drew up a memorandum on women's work and status. In the same year, the Joint Committee of Women's Societies and Social Workers (JCWSSW) was formed and its joint honorary secretaries were Mrs O'Hegarty and Dr Angela Russell. The stimulus for the establishment of the JCWSSW came as a result of the decision by the government not to implement the recommendations of the Carrigan Report on Sexual Offences in the *Criminal Law Amendment Act,* 1935 (see Chapters 6 and 7 and Tweedy, 1992: 20). At its meeting on 20 March 1935 the Joint Committee decided to write to the Secretary of the Department of Justice, seeking a meeting with the Minister to protest against the failure to implement the recommendations of the Carrigan Committee. The Minister declined to meet the Joint Committee but, following a further request, eventually conceded to a meeting the following December (Department of Justice 8/20/1). The objective of the JCWSSW was to enable members to take joint action in matters of mutual interest, particularly social matters. It had a large number of member societies, some of which also belonged to the NCWI. The aggregate membership of Affiliated Bodies was 28,000. Members of the Joint Committee attended the Law Courts during the hearing of cases against women and children, and visited and made recommendations in connection with Industrial Schools and Reformatories. The Committee advocated the appointment of more Probation Officers, the establishment of a force of women police, and the restoration of the equal right of women to sit on juries.

Past Pupils' Unions represented another substantial group of women. The member Unions were spread throughout the thirty-two counties, the two oldest being the Sacred Heart Armagh Association, formed in 1908, and the Sacred Heart Roscrea Association, formed in the same year. In 1937 a Catholic Women's Federation of Secondary School Unions was formed comprising twenty-six Past Pupils' Unions of convent secondary schools, with a total membership of 3,300. The object of the Federation was to 'promote and foster Catholic social principles and action, especially from the woman's point of view, and in particular to promote and defend the interests, rights and duties of the family'.

When, in 1939, the government established the Commission on Vocational Organisation under the chairmanship of Dr Michael Browne, Bishop of Galway, to examine the possibility of social organisation along vocational lines, as proposed in the encyclical *Quadragesimo Anno*, a number of women's groups came together to make a submission. Representatives of the National Council of Women of Ireland, the Joint Committee of Women's Societies and Social Workers and the Catholic Federation of Secondary School Unions together formed a Joint Committee on Vocationalism (JCV) and submitted a Memorandum on 15 November 1940. The Joint Committee on Vocationalism used the term 'Home-maker' to describe the women they wished to see represented in any future vocational structures. The JCV pointed to the fact that, according to the 1936 Census, 25 per cent of the adult population of the country were 'Home-makers', 1,301 of whom were men and 552,176 were women, classified as 'Engaged in home duties'. In addition there were 2,482 men and 86,102 women working as domestic servants. By comparison the total number of women engaged in agriculture, industry, professions, commerce and as clerks and typists amounted to 227,000. The JCV made a two-part proposal. Firstly, it proposed that local groups of home-makers be formed which would be represented as a vocational group on local bodies, and secondly, that these local groups of home-makers, linked up by means of county and provincial committees, could provide the basis for representation in a Vocational Assembly.

In a nutshell the JCV were looking for representation in any new Vocational Assembly of the 'Woman in the home' of the Constitution. When the JCV gave oral evidence to the Commission they were charged by the Chairman, Bishop Browne, with being 'philanthropic ladies of leisure' engaged in 'slum work' (Clear, 1995). When the Commission reported, it recommended that women working in their own households be organised in some way to form a pressure group on government policy in relevant areas such as health, education, prices and public morality, but no permanent place for 'Home-makers' in any National Vocational Assembly was proposed, although representatives might be co-opted, if it were thought necessary. As Clear observes, 'the Commission's perspective on women's household work shows their evaluation of its importance, and crucially, the very faint consultative voice they were prepared to allow its representatives' (Clear, 1995: 186).

The founding of the Irish Housewives' Association (IHA) occurred the year following the rebuff to 'Home-makers' by the Commission on Vocational Organisation. In 1941, inspired by Dr Robert Collis, founder of the Marrowbone Lane Fund to help children when they came out of hospital, a group of women, led by Hilda Tweedy, drew up a Budget Petition addressed to the Minister for Finance.[1] Tweedy, together with some friends, including Andrée Sheehy Skeffington, Marguerite Skelton, Nancye Simmons and Sheila Mallagh, drew up what came to be known as the 'Housewives' Petition'. It was submitted with the signatures of 640 women in time for the Budget on 5 May 1941:

> We looked for special measures to ensure that the poor and unemployed would be safeguarded against the rise in the cost of living, measures such as a proportional increase in unemployment allowance, a free milk scheme for nursing and expectant mothers and the raising of the age from five to eight years of children of the unemployed eligible for the free milk scheme. We urged the government to organise a comprehensive plan embracing all existing schemes for communal feeding centres, including cooking centres and mobile kitchens (Tweedy, 1992: 14).

Among the signatories of the 'Housewives' Petition' were Louie Bennett, Secretary of the Women Workers' Union, and her sister, Susan Manning. It was they who suggested that the momentum generated by the Petition should not be lost and that an organisation should be formed to carry on the work that had been begun. The Organisation became the IHA. One of their early initiatives was a march through the streets of Dublin highlighting the special needs of children. They carried posters with slogans which included 'The Children must be Fed', 'War on TB', 'Pure Milk', 'Clean Food', 'Fair Prices', and 'Give the Children Dinner and not Bread'. During the campaign, members lobbied doctors, schools, TDs and members of Dublin Corporation. They received a variety of responses. Tweedy relates that on one occasion, 'When putting our case to the Schools Committee of the Corporation one Reverend gentleman said that we would be breaking up the sanctity of the home if children were fed at school!' (Tweedy, *ibid*: 17). Over the years the IHA contributed to a number of policy initiatives. As participants in an ad-hoc committee of women's organisations, established in March 1968, they lobbied for the establishment of the [First] Commission on the Status of Women (Tweedy, *ibid*: 36). In 1946 the IHA started their publication, *The Irish Housewife*, which continued until 1967, the year of the silver jubilee of the IHA. Between 1972 and 1980 the IHA produced another publication, *The Housewives' Voice*.

At the same time as women were finding a voice through the ICA and the IHA their voice was also beginning to be heard through the trade unions, notably the Irish National Teachers' Organisation (INTO). In the run-up to the General Election in 1948, the INTO engaged in a pointed advertising campaign to highlight the discontent of their members with the government led by Mr de Valera. One of the advertisements, headed 'Mr de Valera appeals to women!', listed six points regarding the attitude of Mr de Valera's government to women teachers:

1 Women placed on lowest grade of salary scales (1946)
2 Women principals NOW paid lowest grade Principals' grant – a new departure
3 Widows unfairly discriminated against in nature of allowances (1946)
4 Women compulsorily retired at 60 years of age (1938)
5 Women compelled to resign on marriage (1934)
6 Women in convent schools denied full pension rights
(*Irish Independent*, advertisement, 14 January 1948)

It was in the ICA and the IHA, Past Pupils' Unions, and other organisations, which were chiefly directed towards the support of women in the home and their families, as well as in professional bodies such as the INTO, that women honed the political skills of organisation and lobbying which would help to move them forward in public life. One member of the ICA argued persuasively in the 1930s that women could achieve more for their homes by getting out of them from time to time, '… as homemakers and homekeepers, women are all the better for getting out of them occasionally and when they meet in the guild they are talking about it, planning for it, returning always with some new scheme for it, and with renewed interest …' (Ferriter, *ibid*:18). In 1959 the ICA organised a major rural family conference. The themes included women in rural life, the family and the farm. In some notes written after the conference, former ICA president Olivia Hughes emphasised the objective that would be espoused by the Women's Liberation Movement in the 1970s – the gaining of some economic independence for women:

> I have been a farmer's wife since 1918 and kept the farm accounts for years. I have visited every county in the republic during the 3 years I was ICA president. I have been a member of the United Irishwomen and ICA since 1924. In 1955 I travelled for four months in the USA studying adult education in rural areas. *The countrywoman's chief need is for money which she can call her own* (Ferriter, *ibid*: 39-40).

A new phase in women's organisations came in the 1970s when the Irish Women's Liberation Movement was founded in Dublin. Among those who would become most widely known were journalists Mary Maher of *The Irish Times*, Mary Kenny of the *Irish Press* and Nuala Fennell, later a TD and Minister of State for Women's Affairs. In 1971 the group published a document entitled *Chains or Change*. Although the tone was different to that adopted by the pre-war women, a large part of the document focused on the handicaps that befell a woman who married. It listed areas of discrimination against women, drawing up demands for equal pay for equal work, equality before the law, equal access to education, and justice for deserted wives, unmarried mothers and widows. The mid-1960s coincided with a serious housing crisis, with much overcrowding and tenement accommodation still widespread. The Dublin Housing Action Committee was formed and when one of its members, Máirín de Búrca, also a member of Sinn Féin, proposed as one of the demands of the Women's Group, 'one family, one house', there was considerable debate:

> Mary Kenny, Nuala Fennell and others were exercised by this Sinn Féin demand, but Máirín swayed a sizeable acceptance of it when she argued that equality would mean little to women who didn't have any kind of decent living accommodation. Woman's place in Ireland was still in the home, so bad housing affected her more than anyone else (Levine, 1982: 155).

Chains or Change contained a summary of how, under prevailing conditions, married women experienced discrimination. The section entitled 'Five Good Reasons Why It Is Better To Live In Sin' was written by Mary Maher. The first reason for 'living in sin' was the existence of a marriage bar against women in many areas of employment. The second reason for 'living in sin' rather than marrying was that a married couple at the time was liable to a bigger tax bill than two single persons with the same income. Thirdly, on marriage, a woman lost any independent financial identity that she might have possessed. Following marriage, if a woman sought a bank loan or entered a hire purchase agreement, her husband's signature was required by way of endorsement. Marriage did not give a woman a legal right to any share in her husband's income, and even the entitlement to children's allowances was vested in him. The fourth reason was that, in the event of the marriage not working out, there was no legal exit route. A woman who left a marriage was presumed to have deserted her husband. Finally, Maher concluded that by 'living in sin' instead of marrying, a woman avoided being reduced to the status of property. 'The institution of marriage is something invented to preserve male superiority and a system of female chattels' (Levine, *ibid*: 157).

A memorable event in the Women's Liberation Movement was the dedication of an entire *Late Late Show* on RTÉ to the topic on 6 March 1971. The panel of speakers included Senator Mary Robinson, historian Mary Cullen, TV producer Lelia Doolin, trade union activist Máirín Johnston, and journalist Nell McCafferty. Members of Women's Liberation filled the audience and interacted with host Gay Byrne and the panel. Every aspect of *Chains or Change* was considered and debated. Speaking from the audience, Mary Kenny criticised the legislators. Her remarks led to the most dramatic event of the evening, the unscheduled arrival of the Fine Gael TD Garret FitzGerald, at RTÉ, requesting admittance to the Show. June Levine who was in the audience, while acknowledging the dramatic potential, resented the intervention:

> In the first place, it was obvious then that such a take-over could only happen on a woman's programme, and also that we were being used in a band-wagon bid for country-wide publicity for the Fine Gael Party. A free-for-all screaming match followed between Garret FitzGerald and various women in the audience (Levine, 1982: 164-5).

In due course many of the aims of the Women's Liberation Movement were realised; how much due to their efforts and how much to other factors, is impossible to measure. A study carried out a decade later suggested that very few housewives surveyed in 1984-85 identified wholeheartedly with the Women's Movement (Collins, 1986). Other organisations were founded in the 1970s and 1980s specifically with the needs of women who worked in the home in mind. The most significant of these was *Women in the Home* (WITH), founded by Norah Gilligan in Dublin. WITH is affiliated to COFACE, a European organisation of women in the home. *Women Working in the Home* was founded by Nora Bennis of Limerick. It focused on gaining practical support for women in the home and on the restoration of traditional values in family life.

Commissions on the status of women

On 7 November 1969 the ad-hoc Women's Committee received a letter from the Taoiseach, Jack Lynch, in which he said that he was recommending to the government the establishment of a National Commission on the Status of Women. The following day the Taoiseach announced the establishment of a Commission, when speaking to the annual dinner of the Soroptimists Club in Cork. Dr Thekla Beere was appointed chairman. Beere, the daughter of a Church of Ireland rector, had a remarkable career. A legal and political science graduate of Trinity College, she made history when she was appointed Secretary of the Department of Transport and Power, the first woman to become Secretary of a Department in Ireland. The Commission was to operate under the Minister for Finance, Mr Haughey. In February 1970 the ad-hoc committee sent a letter to Mr Haughey which raised the following points aimed at improving the financial situation of women:

(1) That the married woman, whether working inside, or outside the home, should have the same income tax allowance, i.e. for married couples the income tax allowance should be double the single person's allowance.

(2) That the joint income of a married couple is the result of their joint efforts and it is unfair that it should be regarded as the property of one for the purposes of estate duty. No estate duty on the surviving spouse's share should be payable until both spouses are dead.

(3) That adequate allowances for a widow and deserted or separated wife should be made, so that she may be in a position to keep her children with her (Tweedy, 1992: 43).

The terms of reference of the Commission on the Status of Women were published on 4 April 1970:

To examine and report on the status of women in Irish society, to make recommendations on the steps necessary to ensure the participation of women on equal terms with men in the political, social, cultural and economic life of the country, and to indicate the implications generally – including the estimated cost – of such recommendations.

Shortly after it was established, the Commission was requested by the Minister for Finance to prepare an interim report dealing with the question of equal pay, with particular reference to the public sector. In the event, and reflecting the needs identified thirty years ago, almost the entire Final Report of the First Commission deals with equal pay and other issues related to the employment of women, as well as aspects of politics and public life, land, taxation and social welfare as they impinge on women. The chapter in the Report entitled 'Women in the Home' totalled six pages. However, the Commission was keenly aware of the way in which circumstances were changing for women in the home and how these would further change if the Commission's own recommendations were implemented. Accordingly, the Commission made a strong recommendation for a special payment for women in the home. The Commission was aware and concerned about the fact that equal pay would lead to increased financial difficulties in single-earner, multiple person households, 'We are concerned, in particular, to ensure that the introduction of equal pay will not accentuate further the present undervaluation of the role of mother and housewife' (para: 392). The Commission pointed out that with the full implementation of equal pay, 'There is a serious deterioration in the relative standard of living of married couples with a number of dependent children where the wife is not working, and in the position of non-working widows with three or more children' (para: 396).

Focusing on the difficulties of the family with children and only one breadwinner, the Commission suggested that these difficulties might be addressed by increased child tax allowances for those paying tax and/or by adjustment of social welfare children's allowances or perhaps by the introduction of a minimum family income (para: 397). The Commission was specific as to the kind of remedy required:

> In our opinion the kind of upward adjustment in dependants' allowances which should be aimed at is £125 a year and we consider that the adjustment should be applied by way of State Social Welfare Allowance. We recommend accordingly, that a special allowance at the rate of £125 a year be paid to families where there is at least one child under 5 years of age or where, if there are two children or more, the youngest child is under 7 years of age (para: 401).

The Commission recommended that the special allowance be phased in at latest by 31 December 1977, to coincide with the phasing in of equal pay. In view of the cost of implementing the proposal, the Commission recognised 'that it may be necessary in the first instance to introduce measures to offset part or all or its benefits to higher income groups' (para: 404). The value of the suggested allowance of £125 per year in 1972 would be approximately £900 in 1998, or £75 per month.

The recommendation for a payment to women in the home caring for young children was the one major recommendation of the Commission that was never implemented. Furthermore, the child tax allowance which, in 1972, was 52 per cent of the single person's allowance for a child under 11, and 57 per cent of the single person's allowance for a child over 11, was gradually eroded by inflation until it was finally abolished by the Fine Gael-Labour Coalition Government in 1986. Children's allowances, now called child benefit, for the second and third child failed to keep pace with inflation over a long period, remaining higher in real terms in July 1973 than in July 1992. A recommendation regarding the vesting of the entitlement to children's allowances in the mother endorsed the demand in *Chains or Change* and was given effect in the *Social Welfare Act*, 1974. At the time about 80 per cent of children's allowances were in practice paid to women with the agreement of men. Changes were made in the method of taxation of married couples subsequent to the case of Murphy v. The Attorney General (1980) (see Chapter 9).

A key recommendation of the Commission was for the introduction of an allowance for an unmarried mother who rears her child herself. The introduction of this allowance in 1973 provided financial recognition for those who gave birth outside marriage and created an economic possibility for solo-motherhood. Other recommendations of the Commission included the establishment of an umbrella body for women's organisations. In due course this was established as the Council for the Status of Women, changing its name in 1996 to the National Women's Council.

In 1990 a Second Commission on the Status of Women was established with terms of reference almost identical to those of the First Commission, except that the Second Commission was asked to pay special attention to the needs of women in the home. Charles Haughey who, as Taoiseach, established the Commission, has suggested that the inclusion of the 'needs of women in the home' may have been partly due to the fact that the recommendation of the First Commission in this regard had not been fully implemented, and also due to representations seeking focus on women in the home.[2] The terms of reference were as follows:

(1) to review the implementation of the recommendations of the first Commission on the Status of Women as set out in that Commission's report to the Minister for Finance in December, 1972;

(2) to consider and make recommendations on the means, administrative and legislative, by which women will be able to participate on equal terms and conditions with men in economic, social, political and cultural life and, to this end, to consider the efficacy and feasibility of positive action measures;

(3) in the context of (2) above, to pay special attention to the needs of women in the home;

(4) to establish the estimated costs of all recommendations made; and

(5) to report to the government within a period of eighteen months from the date of its establishment.

Of the 603 submissions received by the Commission, the single item sought by the largest number of submissions was some payment for women in the home. In this respect the conclusion of Olivia Hughes, over thirty years earlier, that 'the countrywoman's chief need is for money she can call her own' remained valid. It might have been expected that the Second Commission would take up the unfinished business of the First Commission in regard to 'women in the home', but in a comment on the possibility of a payment for full-time homemakers, the Commission stated: 'In essence, the maintenance of a full-time homemaker, although of benefit to society, is primarily a private benefit to the earning partner, and as such could hardly be deemed to warrant a State payment' (Second Commission: 71). Nor did the Second Commission see fit to recommend any increase in child benefit:

> Following a thorough examination of the issue the Commission came to the conclusion that in *itself* increasing Child Benefit did not offer the most productive and effective return on investment made to improve the status of women. Such investment is better directed to specific supports for low income families, towards supports for childcare and eldercare and towards education and training opportunities for women (Second Commission: 78).

However, the *Minority Report* of the Second Commission (by the author) recommended the following:

> As a small step towards making up some of the leeway pointed to by the First Commission on the Status of Women, and with a delay of twenty years, it is suggested that Child Benefit be increased by £5 monthly in respect of all children at an annual cost of £65 million, together with an additional £10 monthly for children under five years at a cost of £40 million. This would effectively mean doubling of Child Benefit for the under fives. This extra £15 monthly or £180 per annum for the under fives contrasts with the £825 per annum (£125 in 1972 prices) mooted by the First Commission. It is a modest proposal (*Minority Report* of the Second Commission: 438).

In the event successive governments followed the path of increasing child benefit in the years since the Second Commission reported, culminating in a record increase of over 50 per cent in Budget 2001.

The Women's Movement in the 1970s encouraged women to limit their childbearing, and increase their labour force participation and their economic independence. This 'second wave' feminism contrasted to some extent with the first wave in the earlier part of the century. The first wave, which coincided with the revolutionary era in the national movement, emphasised women's right to participate in public life in the economic and political sphere, but a related strand focused strongly on the need for child and family support in public policy. Once women's suffrage was won and the most obvious direct block to women's participation in public life was removed, improvements in the domestic domain were sought by family feminists. At the start of the twenty-first century, the need to combine these two strands of public and home life is becoming apparent. The combination, or the sequencing, of work and family responsibilities is a high priority for women, and for a growing number of men also, as is the need to promote effective and harmonious relations between men and women in the joint challenges of parenting and income provision. In the early 1970s, feminists sought access to contraception; by the end of the 1990s, the attention of the Women's Movement focused on the provision of child care. On 14 November 1998, just weeks before the Budget, about one thousand parents and child care workers took to the streets of Dublin, calling for government action on child care. The march, organised by the National Women's Council of Ireland, commenced at the Garden of Remembrance in Parnell Square, and proceeded to Leinster House, where a petition was handed to Minister of State Chris Flood. Summing up the purpose of the march and the evolution of feminism from the days when legalisation of contraceptives was the goal, Nell McCafferty wrote, 'Back on the train – this time for childcare' (McCafferty, 1998).

Entry into the EEC

At the time of Irish entry into the EEC in 1973, the model of family life enshrined in the Constitution with the mother in the home and the father as the breadwinner reflected everyday reality. A little over 7 per cent of married women were in the workforce, not very much more than in 1926, and the social welfare code was based on the model of a married man with a dependent wife and children. Membership of the EEC hastened the emergence of a different model of family life, one based on equality legislation and the participation of both partners in the workforce, so that dual earner households increasingly became the norm. Membership of the EEC contributed to a series of significant changes in regulations governing the employment of women and the entitlement of married women to individual social welfare payments. These measures by and large strengthened women's economic independence outside marriage. On 31 July 1973, the marriage bar in the civil service was ended. The *Anti-Discrimination (Pay) Act*, 1974 came into operation in December 1975 and established the right of men and women to equal pay for equal work. The *Employment Equality Act* came into operation on 1 July 1977, and prohibited discrimination on grounds of sex or marital status in recruitment, training or provision of opportunities for promotion. The *Unfair Dismissals Act* protects employees, including pregnant employees, from unfair dismissal, while the *Maternity Act*, 1981 provides maternity leave and the right to return to work for pregnant employees.

The first European Commissioner for Social Affairs, and therefore the person responsible for introducing equality provisions at European level, was an Irishman, Dr Patrick Hillery. At the Heads of State Summit in 1972, German Chancellor Willi Brandt called for a Social Action Programme and it fell to Dr Hillery to devise the Programme. His priorities were clear from the outset. He recalls saying to his *chef de cabinet*, Ed Fitzgibbon, 'Put the women in there first.' However, two things bothered him. Firstly, a married woman friend who was well qualified, but had left her job to care for her family, told him that she had no desire to be pushed out to work. He believed that 'extreme feminists wanted to drive women out of the home', and he did not want women to be obliged to enter the workforce, or to be made to feel in any way inferior if they did not go out to work. The second thing that bothered him was the consequences of mothers working outside the home for the care of children. He recalls remarking to Mr Crijns, a Dutch colleague, 'Some day you are going to have a situation where there will be no one to take care of the children.'[3]

A problem with the EEC Equality Directives, according to Dr Hillery, was that they were *limited* to the workforce. The insertion of Article 119 into the Treaty of Rome, from which equality legislation flowed, was originally made for *competition* reasons. Dr Hillery says that it was specifically inserted to prevent low paid women workers in any one EEC state undercutting men workers in other member states. Article 119 held that women had to get the same pay as men if they were doing the same work. As time passed, the number of jobs equally suited to men and women, and not dependent on physical strength, increased and the merits of the women's own case on grounds of fairness emerged clearly. Dr Hillery emphasises that the motivation behind equal pay changed from the original motivation based on competition to one based on fairness and equal treatment. He clearly recalls the days when women accepted small pay: 'When I was young, a woman making a few bob here and a few bob there – she would be delighted with herself. It wasn't a big principle to get the same pay as men.' As Dr Hillery sees it, women were put into the home in the Constitution, having been taken out of the schools on marriage as a result of the marriage bar, and then they were given equality in Europe. But the origin for equality in Europe lay in 'competition rules and at some stage our motivations changed, and when people don't spot the change they get lost in what they are about.'[4]

The media

Women's magazines which began to proliferate in the late nineteenth century had become a significant cultural phenomenon by the 1930s. According to historian, Catherine Conway, there were six Irish magazines in the 1930s devoted to women's interests (Conway, 1997). The two which enjoyed the longest life-span were *Model Housekeeping* which appeared first as *Everyday Housekeeping* in 1927 and survived into the 1960s, and *Woman's Life* which lasted from 1936 into the 1940s. The magazines, which essentially catered for a middle-class audience, had a wide readership. In 1937 *Woman's Life* sold nearly 20,000 copies per issue, reaching 30,000 copies in 1938. The magazines dealt with issues relating to the home: household tasks, including cookery, cleaning and gardening; motherhood and child rearing, as well as beauty hints. Through the 1940s and 1950s women's magazines continued to focus on home-based topics, on beauty and romance, and they had widespread appeal. Reflecting on her reading in the 1950s, journalist June Levine remarked: 'Two magazines in particular I had read since my early marriage, *Woman* and *Woman's Own*. ... They were like trade magazines; they reflected my interests, my work problems, my aspirations' (Levine, 1982: 40).

An overriding theme in the magazines was that happiness and personal fulfilment were to be found in romantic love culminating in marriage:

> One of the primary quests in life for Irish women was to be the search for the right man. ... Wives were given the key to happy and successful marriages. The view of relations between the sexes is unashamedly romantic and sentimental, reinforced by the fiction which in many cases took up the bulk of the space of the magazine. There was a Mr Right for every woman and as long as the hero and heroine were truly in love, in spite of the vagaries of Fortune, they always lived happily ever after (Conway, 1997).

Sixty years later women's magazines were still helping women in their search for Mr Right, but Mr Right was no longer synonymous with a husband. Mr Right now symbolised 'fulfilling sex'. According to journalist Ann Marie Hourihane, writing in 1997:

> It is certainly true that many women's magazines (245,000 of which are brought into Ireland each month) seem obsessed by sex, and advertise the fact with bad puns and a lot of exclamation marks. Looking for It, Dressing For It, Wondering If He's Good At It, Wondering If You're Too Good At It, combined with more anatomical detail about It than even mid-wives need – this is part of the diet presented by magazines like *Company, Cosmopolitan and More!* (Hourihane, 1997).

There is ample evidence that marriage was prized by Irishwomen. Referring to her youth in the early years of the century, Joan Dunn recounts:

> For girls, the main thing they looked forward to was marriage and you never thought of marrying above your class. The girls then mostly worked in factories. ... There used to be an old saying around here when I was a girl: 'Make sure you get a Guinness' man – he's money dead or alive.' That was because Guinness gave a widow's pension (Humphreys, 1966: 119).

For Joan and John Dunn and for the society in which they lived – they married in 1923 – the essence of marriage was to beget children and to raise a family as a simple matter of God's will. One reason why they did not marry at an earlier age – they were both aged twenty-nine years at the time of their marriage – was to be secure enough financially to be able to provide for whatever children they did have. To have had no children would have been 'stark tragedy' and a matter of commiseration by friends and neighbours (Humphreys, *ibid*: 119-20). This view is endorsed by Levine who summarised her own life goal in the 1950s as follows: 'The core business of my life was GETTING MARRIED' (Levine, *ibid*: 12). When she worked in Dublin in the early 1960s, she found the ambition to marry was very strong among her women friends: 'They'd have jumped at anything to get a man to the altar, and some of them did. ... And my friend was putting her all into her husband hunt. So were her peers' (Levine, *ibid*: 91-2).

In the early 1950s, a priest sociologist, Edmund Murray, claimed that 'Ireland's women want marriage and long for family life more than anything else in the world' (Murray, 1954: 72). Extolling the qualities of Irish women, Murray said that few 'Irish maidens' lacked the six gifts demanded by the legendary Cúchulain when he was courting Emer; beauty, singing, needlework, sweet speech, wisdom and chastity. In his essay, Murray quotes an Irish woman who had been a teacher in Bristol before her marriage to an Englishman, as saying, 'but what girl wants to spend the whole of her life slaving away as a frustrated school ma'am?' On this view marriage was a more glamorous option than teaching, at any rate. At the same time, however, McNabb, researching in the Limerick rural area, detected signs of change in the attitudes of women to marriage. Girls in the late 1950s were setting the agenda for change in marriage, seeking greater personal and emotional fulfilment. McNabb found evidence that the country girl was turning away from the land as she objected to the 'muck and dirt' of farm life. Also, 'There is a certain amount of propaganda on the part of the mother to dissuade the daughter from following in her footsteps' (McNabb, 1964: 221). In Dublin, by the late 1940s, there was some indication that young girls were seeking to enter occupations that had been traditionally limited to males and to 'consider marriage somewhat of a "drag"' (Humphreys, 1966: 237-8). According to Walsh, women's attitudes to marriage within an agricultural context had been changing over a long period (Walsh, 1995). Girls in rural areas tended to remain longer at school than boys and their education at post-primary level was almost exclusively provided by religious orders that spread rapidly in Ireland throughout the late nineteenth and early twentieth century. Refinement and 'lady-like' behaviour was a priority in convent schools. Birmingham observed, 'Year after year our convent schools are sending out young women eager to be ladies and utterly dissatisfied with a life spent in churning butter and baking cakes' (quoted in Walsh, 1995).

Radio provided a medium of particular interest to housewives who could access programmes as they continued on their daily round in their homes. Radio serials mirrored family change. An early serial, *The Foley Family,* dealt with simple issues from minding a neighbour's dog to getting a cheque book. In the 1950s serial *The Kennedys of Castlerosse*, marriage remained the ultimate objective of the heroine, Ellen. By the late 1970s-1980s, in the serial *Harbour Hotel*, a new, liberated type of woman, Miss O'Connell, retains her maiden name following her marriage and runs a hotel business. In *Harbour Hotel* none of the key women characters is completely satisfied with a 'full-time housewife' role. The 'Women Today' programme, and later 'Liveline', both hosted by Marian Finucane, raised many issues concerning women's lives. Together with the Gay Byrne radio show, these programmes afforded to women in particular the opportunity to carry out debate over the airways. Since the late 1990s, 'Liveline', hosted by Joe Duffy, has tended to draw an increasing number of men into discussion of everyday matters.

The advent of television, in particular the opening of Telefís Éireann in 1961, provided a new forum for the access of ideas. Unlike other forms of media – newspapers and radios, which can be read or listened to in trains or buses – the greater part of TV viewing is done in people's own homes. Of course TVs are viewed in public places but in the main TV is viewed by consenting persons in private. How effective or influential has it been in changing ideas and patterns of behaviour in relation to family matters in Ireland? A dynamic relationship exists between all forms of media – newspapers, magazines, radio, cinema, television, the internet – and the socio-economic structures that both produce and consume their messages. What is presented in the media both springs from, and influences society. In the first half of the century when the majority of people left school at the end of primary level, the transmission of behavioural norms occurred chiefly in the family, in the national schools, and from the pulpit – the home, the school and the church. Priests, together with national teachers, were the educated leaders of local communities, both rural and urban. As the century progressed an additional source of behavioural norms developed within the media and gradually grew in strength, presenting a counter-culture to traditional Catholicism. By the late 1960s, when second level education was extended to all, a questioning of Church teaching in areas of sexual and family morality had already begun.

The media, according to communications expert Martin McLoone, consciously tried to foster change. McLoone has argued that there was an ideological agenda at work in RTÉ in the 1960s and 1970s which aimed to make a 'liberal and social democratic' insertion into Irish culture, a culture that had hitherto been dominated by nationalist, Roman Catholic elements (McLoone and MacMahon, 1984: 68). According to another media expert, Luke Gibbons, programme makers did not at the outset of RTÉ confront sexual issues in current affairs programmes or documentaries '… but rather negotiated them indirectly through areas such as the live chat show or television serials which were more open-ended and less susceptible to the array of political and legal controls which pervaded Irish television from the outset' (Gibbons, 1984: 22).

The circulation of English Sunday newspapers had grown rapidly in Ireland after World War I. In 1930 the *News of the World* came to the attention of the Censor because of its reporting of divorce court proceedings in England. This led to its being banned between July-September 1930 when a special Irish edition was produced. But it was the advent of television that would be the midwife to the most profound changes in Irish family life and thus, in Irish society. Dáil Deputy Oliver J. Flanagan once famously remarked that there was no sex in Ireland before RTÉ. Before Telefís Éireann made its first broadcast on New Year's Eve 1961, apprehension was expressed about its possible impact in the area of family life and family values. The Ninth Annual Summer School of the Social Study Conference took place in 1961 on the theme 'The Challenge of Television'. At the Conference reservations were expressed about 'the possible impact of television on two crucial areas of Irish life: the family and the farming community' (Gibbons, *ibid*: 26). With keen insight the Social Study Conference argued, in a submission to the Pilkington Committee on Broadcasting, then sitting in the UK, that the main impact of television on values and attitudes derived from programmes in serial form:

> The misgivings about drama, and the identification of the serial as the Trojan Horse of Irish television smuggling in alien attitudes and values; the apprehension about the demise of positive images of the family unit farm, and of traditional female roles, all seem to point towards the inevitable introduction of a farming serial such as *The Riordans* (Gibbons, *ibid*: 24).

RTÉ's first major serial, *Tolka Row* (1963-68), centred on the Nolan family which had moved from tenement rooms in the Liberties to a new Corporation estate. Jack Nolan is a garage foreman. Rita, his wife, is the central character. As wife and mother she rules the household. She is a peacemaker and a loyal friend '... the combination of mother figure and tea-pot is the absolute assurance of community comfort, understanding and support' (McLoone, *ibid*: 64). The Nolan household reaches out to an extended family. 'The family ... not only infiltrates the workplace but also becomes ... a kind of surrogate welfare state, a point of intersection for the various affective and social ties which bind the community' (Gibbons, *ibid*: 31).

Tolka Row ended with the emigration of Jack Nolan to a job in Coventry. As unemployment and emigration lead to the denouement, Rita, whose task has been to support the home, cannot fulfil her task without a support system from the State. According to McLoone, this idea and the enlargement of Rita to 'Mother Ireland' has immense ramifications. Following a generation in which the Catholic hierarchy opposed state interference in social and family matters and condemned the Mother and Child scheme:

> ... Tolka Row is implicitly condemning the State for its failure to provide just such a support system, bringing attention to its failure to develop the necessary social democratic mechanisms that would keep Rita Nolan within her community. Despite the myths of 'frugal self-sufficiency' and intrinsic rural virtues, Mother Ireland needs the type of English welfarism that the nationalist consensus has always denied (McLoone, *ibid:* 65).

Tolka Row, produced to provide an outlet for the voice of working-class Dublin, succeeded in reconfirming the notion of city life, implicit in the idealisation of rural life, as the site of disharmony and communal breakdown. In the ideology of de Valera's Ireland the belief that, in some sense, the Irish way of life was superior to that of 'pagan England' helped to sustain the people, even if it was not really true. The countryside was associated with wholesome youth and the nationalist struggle; the city with moral snares and the class struggle. In a culture dominated by romantic ruralism, 'the mere presence of the city and the urban working-class on television was an important cultural shift'. When de Valera spoke to the nation at the opening of Telefís Éireann, he could not resist a clear reference to the BBC, then available in many Irish homes: 'And the competition unfortunately is in the wrong direction so standards become lower and lower.' At its most simple the countryside is identified as the site of traditional values where men and women live and work in harmony with nature; the city is somehow unnatural – a place of alienation and immorality. But it's not so simple. In reality there is a greater interrelation between city and rural cultures than a simplistic opposition permits. As rural dwellers moved to the towns and cities they brought their rural ways with them. Gibbons discusses the question of residual rural characteristics in urban families, referring in the process to Humphreys, who posits 'radical continuity between the general pattern of the family in Dublin and the rural community' (Humphreys, 1966: 234). In 1980 RTÉ screened a seven-part adaptation of James Plunkett's novel, *Strumpet City*, set in Dublin between 1907-14, with its climax, the Lock-out of 1913. Central to *Strumpet City* are mothers and their families. What will the families eat during the Lock-out? The hungry families are caught between the ideology of socialism and the property rights of the bourgeoisie.

It was a serial drama based on rural, not urban life, however, which did most to open debate on traditional family values. *The Riordans* exploded the romantic representations of rural family life by introducing a range of controversial moral issues. The first episode of *The Riordans* was screened on 4 January 1965, continuing for fifteen years and approximately five hundred episodes until the final episode was broadcast on St Stephen's Day 1979. The original intention of *The Riordans* was didactic, to encourage modernisation in farming, but it led to a discussion on, and a questioning of, traditional values, especially those associated with rural family life. For half of the fifteen-year run of *The Riordans* over half of all the households in Ireland that possessed TV sets were classified as 'rural' rather than 'urban'. In 1966, one year after the serial commenced, 56 per cent of households with TV sets, or 288,000 households, were in rural areas. In 1971, six years after the series began and shortly before Ireland joined the EEC, 51 per cent of households with TV, or 355,000 households, were in rural areas. When the series ended rural households still accounted for 45 per cent of total households with TV sets. *The Riordans* dealt with life on a family farm on the outskirts of Leestown, a village near Kilkenny. In the words of author Wesley Burrowes, the Riordan family, which the audience saw at the outset, were as follows:

Tom Riordan, a strong farmer; his wife Mary, absorbed in her family; one son Benjy just back from Agricultural College, waiting, not very patiently, for his chance to use his knowledge; the other son Michael at the University, studying to be an engineer.

There is a daughter Angela, engaged to an Englishman of whom all the family are very wary. The younger sister Jude is a nurse in a Kilkenny hospital (Burrowes, 1977: 4).

The early programmes showed the interaction between the characters, the strains between Benjy and his father, the peace-making role of Mary, and their relationships with neighbours. Gradually the programmes began to focus on controversial moral and social issues, a task to which it was well suited: 'The interdependence of home and production on the family farm enables the Riordans to explore complex social and economic problems in the very process of delineating personal and emotional relationships ...' (Gibbons, *ibid*: 36).

The programme introduced one of the most sensitive issues in rural family life, the links between property, farm ownership and marriage at the very time of the debate on the Succession Bill (see Chapter 9). Eventually Benjy marries Maggie, a barmaid whose early life was spent in an orphanage. Gibbons says that the serial brought to the surface 'with almost relentless zeal every possible transgression of the traditional Irish family enshrined in the 1937 Constitution' (Gibbons, *ibid*: 39). The list included illegitimacy, 'mixed marriage', i.e. marriage between those of different religions which was not favoured by the Catholic Church, adoption – 'mixed marriage' couples were prohibited from adopting children under the *Adoption Act*, 1952 – marriage breakdown, divorce, cohabitation or 'living in sin', and the idea of a 'kept woman'. The serial also included a discussion on the concept of annulment in the Catholic Church. When the question came up, Mary Riordan disagreed with it, even though it was approved by the Church. Thus a central figure, Mary, was beginning *to think for herself* about Church teaching. Mary speaks of 'this annulment nonsense' as she is forced to think through the problem rather than accept pat answers to complex questions. This move towards independent thinking signalled the tentative beginning of post-Vatican II Ireland.

Another example of a character, again a woman character, in the *Riordans* thinking things through for herself, relates to Maggie's attitude to contraception. When difficulties began to surface in Benjy's and Maggie's marriage:

> ... it became clear that the age of innocence had finally passed in representations of family and rural life in Ireland. The 1974 season revolved around the contentious theme of contraception, precipitated by Maggie's decision to go on the Pill, following the complications which attended the birth of her first child (Gibbons, *ibid*: 41).

When Maggie consulted Father Sheehy she was told that there were no pat answers and that the last resort was personal conscience. This screen encounter took place at a time when the *Humanae Vitae* debate was still alive and some years before contraceptives became legally available in 1979, although the Pill was available on prescription as 'a cycle regulator'. Father Sheehy was probably fairly typical of many priests at the time who refused to follow the traditional approach of black and white answers:

By disengaging the rural family from the cycle of inhibition, authority and conservatism in which it had been traditionally enclosed, it made deep inroads on a dominant ideology which looked to the family – and indeed the family farm – as the basic unit of Irish society (Gibbons, *ibid*).

Subsequent serials, *Bracken, Glenroe* and *Fair City,* would all add ingredients of change. In *Bracken* there was an eclipse of the mother figure while 'father figures, far from being centres of authority and action, are repeatedly brought down in the world and reduced to a state of abjection and powerlessness' (Gibbons, *ibid*: 47). But it was *The Riordans* that defined an era. *The Riordans* both opened up and reinforced debate already taking place on key areas of values and beliefs in the wider society. The questioning, which earlier had been limited to a small group of writers and intellectuals such as Sean O'Faolain, and the contributors to *The Bell*, now spread to the masses via television.

6

The Role and Status of Children

The Democratic Programme adopted by the First Dáil on 21 January 1919 stated:

> It shall be the first duty of the Republic to make provision for the physical, mental and spiritual well-being of the children, to secure that no child shall suffer hunger or cold from lack of food, clothing or shelter, that all shall be provided with the means and facilities requisite for their proper education and training as citizens of a free and Gaelic Ireland.

A chasm exists between the Democratic Programme of the First Dáil and the 1937 Constitution in regard to children. While the Democratic Programme placed the care of children as 'the first duty of the Republic', the 1937 Constitution sought to protect 'the Family' from any interference by the State, other than in exceptional cases of parental neglect. There are a number of references to 'the child' or 'children' in the 1937 Constitution; two references in Article 42 which deals with Education, and in Article 42.3.2°, the State, as guardian of the common good, requires that children receive a minimum education, moral, intellectual and social. Under Article 42.5, the State, in exceptional cases where parents fail in their duties towards their children, shall endeavour to supply the place of the parents, taking account of the 'natural and imprescriptible rights of the child'. Article 45.4.2° refers to the economic abuse of children, stating:

> The State shall endeavour to ensure that the strength and health of workers, men and women, and the tender age of children shall not be abused and that citizens shall not be forced by economic necessity to enter avocations unsuited to their sex, age or strength.

The focus of Article 41 is on the rights of the family as a unit and on the protection of the family from intervention by the State, rather than on the rights of individual members of the family (CRG, 1996: 326). The *Report on the Kilkenny Incest Investigation,* chaired by Mrs Justice Catherine McGuinness, suggested that 'the very high emphasis on the rights of the family in the Constitution may consciously or unconsciously be interpreted as giving a higher value to the right of parents than to the rights of children'. The Report recommended an amendment to the Constitution which would include 'a specific and overt declaration of the rights of born children' (CRG, 1996: 326).

Attitudes to children have changed in fundamental ways during the course of the century. Changes relate to the growing awareness of children's rights, including the rights of children born outside marriage, as distinct from the rights of the family or of parents, and to the economic status of children, in turn related to the increased number of years spent in full-time education. The manner of dealing with children has also changed, the attitude towards corporal punishment providing a clear example. This chapter will review in turn, the economic status of children, the abuse of children, changes in the minimum legal age of marriage and the age of consent, the change in attitudes to births outside marriage, and finally, the question of child-care.

Economic status of children

The biggest change in regard to children has come about as a result of their changing economic status, a major, if neglected key to understanding aspects of changing family life. There is much evidence that children were exploited for their labour in the past. Over the course of the nineteenth century, fundamental reforms, culminating in the Shaftesbury Acts, guaranteed minimum protection of children. In the late Victorian era an idealised version of childhood began to emerge, and to some extent, exist, among the privileged classes, but economic conditions in Ireland meant that a work-free childhood was the exception rather than the rule.

The changing economic position of children is linked with two factors in particular: the move away from agriculture and the extension of formal education which means that children are dependent on their parents for economic support for a longer period. In 1961 employment in agriculture still exceeded employment in industry. As late as 1964 only 36 per cent of 16-year-olds and 14 per cent of 18-year-olds were in full-time education. In the small farm context as it existed until World War II, children were an important economic resource. While still at school children worked on the farm. The economic value of rural children to their parents and the nation was stressed by the president of the Irish Vocational Education Association (IVEA) fifty years ago, at a time when tillage and turf production made heavy demands on rural juvenile labour, sometimes interfering with school attendance (IVEA, 1947: 24). A boy or girl who obtained employment away from home was expected to send money home. This was done faithfully by thousands of Irish emigrants, who sent home what journalist John Healy called the 'slate money', or what national income accountants styled 'emigrant's remittances' (Healy, 1978). A letter from an emigrant child that did not contain money was called an 'empty letter' (Carbery, 1937). Writing about his native Donegal in the early years of the century, Patrick MacGill says, 'Maura The Rosses did not want a loan from her son, she simply wanted money that was hers by right. It is only when the young marry that parents' claim to the wages ceases' (MacGill, 1983: 194).

Ita Healy, a primary school teacher, who grew up in Achill, recalls that in the 1940s young people who went to work in England sent the bulk of their earnings home. The women held the purse strings and managed the meagre family resources. On one occasion a young man, Johnny McGinley, back home from working in England, got 6 pence (6d) from his mother to go to a dance. The admission charge was 4d. On his return from the dance, he gave her the 2d change, even though the money was earned by him.[1] Patrick Kavanagh recounts how in the 1920s an old man of eighty turned a deaf ear to the request for a shilling from his 50-year old son:

'Give me a shillin',' I overheard the son ask the old man.
'Now what would ye be wantin' with a shillin'?' the father said. He put his hand in his pocket, but he kept it there (Kavanagh, 1971: 183).

The Killanin Committee (Killanin, 1918-19) on primary education highlighted poor levels of school attendance and recommended the enforcement of school attendance combined with a total prohibition on paid labour up to the age of fourteen years. In the same year the House of Commons raised the school-leaving age to thirteen years in the UK. The *School Attendance Act*, 1926 required every child to attend school from the age of six until fourteen years, that is eight years of compulsory schooling. Children between the ages of 14 and 16 years could be required to attend classes in certain circumstances. The school leaving age remained at 14 years until 1972 when it was raised to 15 years.

An Inter-Departmental Committee on Raising the School-leaving Age (IDCRA), which reported in 1935, found the position in Ireland was closely similar to that in other European countries. A key issue for the Committee was the link between agricultural occupations and the school-leaving age, in particular 'how far juvenile labour is indispensable to the farming community' (IDCRA, 1935:11). At the 1926 Census there were 16,500 juveniles, 13,000 of whom were boys, aged 14 and 15 years engaged in agricultural occupations, representing about half of the total of 14 and 15 year olds in the agricultural community. In 1926 one quarter of all young persons aged 14 and 15 years were in occupations, 30 per cent of the boys and 17 per cent of the girls. Agricultural occupations were dominant for the boys and non-agricultural occupations for the girls.

The overwhelming majority of young persons in agricultural occupations were sons and daughters, or other relatives, of farmers. When the occupation of juveniles by farm size was examined, 8,000 worked on farms under 30 acres in size. The importance of juvenile family labour to farmers varied by area. It was of little importance in a county like Cork, but of great importance on the small holdings along the Western seaboard. In County Clare, for example, there were large numbers of smallholders entirely dependent on family labour and 'many such farmers look forward to the time when the eldest boy will be 14 years old, and it would be a serious matter to them if the school-leaving age were raised'. The Committee viewed juvenile labour in agriculture as 'indispensable and its withdrawal would be a serious hardship to parents' (IDCRA, 1935: 16). The importance of the contribution of children to family income was also remarked on by the Commission of Inquiry into the Reformatory and Industrial School System which reported around the same time as the Inter-Departmental Committee on the School Leaving Age. The Report of the Commission remarked that at a time when the statutory minimum period of detention in a Reformatory was three years, Justices were often reluctant to commit for three years a young person who, but for his sentence, might be contributing to family income (Department of Education, 1936: 15).

Robert O'Connor tells how the seasonal migration of small farmers in Roscommon was made possible by the work of their wives and children (O'Connor, nd: 4-5). In the 1950s children remained an important resource as workers in the farm economy, as signalled by the Emigration Commission: 'In agriculture, the additional labour available in a large family, from the time children are able to work on the land until they obtain employment away from home, is a valuable aid to increased production' (Commission on Emigration, 1954: 99). Girls as well as boys were expected to work, although girls were viewed as of less economic value than boys:

> Children begin to help in the house at an early age. Drawing water seems to be the chief occupation of boys. As girls grow older, they share a great many of the household chores or look after younger children. When a daughter reaches sixteen, if she remains on the farm, she must do a full day's work, and too often her life is one of unrelieved drudgery. There is an almost oriental attitude to girls. They are favoured by neither father nor mother and accepted only on sufferance. This is, perhaps, too strong a conclusion, and it would be better to say they are loved but not thought of any great importance (McNabb, 1964: 230).

In the Dáil Debates in relation to the *Succession Act,* 1965, which took place around the same time that McNabb was writing, John A. Costello highlighted the shoddy treatment sometimes meted out to daughters in comparison with sons:

> There was a man who had seven daughters and finally a son was born and the son was the apple of his eye. He explained, as the boy grew up, what he was going to do for him: he would send him to the best school and then to university, and his attitude was summed up when he said: 'You would like to do the best you can for the one child you have.' The seven daughters were in the halfpenny place (*PDDE* 213: 481).

Until the 1930s, when wages and conditions of work were fixed by law, the common method of recruiting farm labour was by hiring. Local authorities hired out certain illegitimate children who were in their care. For example, in 1930,

112 children were hired out by local authorities, the largest number being in Co. Clare, where 27 children were hired out (LGD, 1930-34: 131). McNabb describes the situation in the Limerick area, where the last hiring fair took place in Kilmallock in 1939, as follows:

> On 17th March, boys and girls from the upland regions of Kerry or West Limerick gathered in the market-places of East Limerick towns and offered themselves for hire. If they were minors, the parents bargained with the farmer. The period of hire was from St Patrick's Day to the end of November. Conditions of employment included board and lodging and a lump sum ranging from £15-£30 per year, depending on the quality and experience of the worker. The money was paid either to the parents or the worker at the end of the year (McNabb, 1964: 200).

The following are some comments of workers who had been hired in their youth:

— One thing I must say about my mother; she was hard, but she never let me go cheap.
— We suffered nothing but hardship, working long hours with poor diet.
— I remember working on a farm where the mistress was so mean she would save the left-overs for us. I was so hungry that I ran away.
— We were slaves, but in our own way we were happy.

One woman who was hired out, Dora Maguire, described the Derry hiring fair in a letter to a friend. At first sight there was the appearance of a holiday, but beneath the surface there was anxiety, poverty and despair. The fair took place in the principal square. Girls and boys from fourteen years and women stood in the centre of the square:

> Each carries his or her worldly goods, some have smart suit-cases, others have brown paper parcels – a good many only what they stand up in ... People who wish to hire are mostly middle-aged men – farmers – a certain number of women, a few elder daughters from private houses, hotels, etc. They walk up and down and walk round girls, examining them from every aspect. If the face and body please – the question is put: Are you for hire? Then begins the bargaining, if the person for hire is not a novice. Often the paper parcel is handed to the employer, and a time for meeting fixed. If girls are out for the first hire, they are too shy to bargain, and probably ask no questions at all, and have no redress afterwards. The parents and guardians are not present. A good many boys and girls are hired for outdoor work with pigs, cows, etc. – the rest for inside domestics. The usual bargaining is for six months at £6 to £11, often paid at the end of the six months (Fox, 1935: 175-6).

Liam O'Donnell tells the story of hiring in the Co. Cork region where he was born the son of a small farmer in the village of Milford in 1923. The main hiring fair took place at Charleville on 10 January each year. The length of hiring was from January to Christmas Eve. The usual pay was £18 per year for a 16-year old boy; older lads could get up to £35, with £50 in exceptional cases. Girls got far less. Prospective servant boys and girls came to the Charleville Fair from the surrounding counties of Limerick, Clare, Kerry and Waterford. At the Fair they were inspected for strength and good physique and checked for useful skills in order 'to work ... or should I say slave ... for the better-off farmers, and use their paltry wages to help their own families who were often living in desperate conditions'. Despite the hardship endured the servant boys retained affection for their homes and for their own families. O'Donnell describes how an important excursion was to buy a penny stamp and a copybook for two pence or three pence in order to send a letter home. Even though many needed help to write, 'The boys were always anxious to let them know back home how they were getting on' (O'Donnell, 1997: 63).

Servant boys often worked up to eighty hours a week, working more than twelve hours a day for six days a week and approximately six to eight hours on Sunday with no day off. O'Donnell recalls that when he started working on farms in the late 1940s the first breakthrough in improved working conditions was the half-day on Saturday. Some of the old men were reluctant to take their half-day in case they would lose their jobs. Many of the farmers resented any regulations. O'Donnell recalls hearing some of them saying, 'I'd rather sell out my cattle and farm than give the servant boy a half-day.' It took many years to get the law governing conditions of employment on farms properly enforced.

In addition to the economic contribution of young people in farm families, there was a good deal of employment of 14 and 15 year olds outside agriculture. Of a total of 120,000 aged 14 and 15 years in 1926, 30,000 were in primary schools, 18,000 in post-primary schools, 16,000 in agricultural occupations, 12,000, or 10 per cent in non-agricultural occupations, and a remarkable 44,000 who were neither in employment nor at school. In non-agricultural employment the number of girls employed exceeded the number of boys and the number of juveniles employed rose markedly between 1925 and 1934. For example, in the Dublin area there were 1,400 juveniles aged 14 and 15 years employed in 1925 and 2,700 juveniles employed in 1934. In both years nearly three-quarters were girls. In certain industries such as clothing and footwear, the proportion of juveniles to adults was very much higher for women than for men. The Inter-Departmental Committee on Raising the School Leaving Age observed that this was only to be expected. 'Women retire from industrial occupations on marriage. Their average occupational life is very much shorter than that of men – possibly not half of it – and larger numbers of juveniles are needed annually for the maintenance of normal recruitment' (IDCRA, 1935).

Louie Bennett of the Irish Women Workers' Union knew the reasons why employers favoured 14 and 15 year olds. Women and girls predominated in the tobacco, sweet, chocolate and jam factories as well as in tailoring, Jacob's biscuits and in several laundries in the 1920s and 1930s:

But the most serious complaint Irish women workers have at the moment is the difficulty a trained worker has in holding her job after she is 18 or 19 years of age. Labour Exchange returns show that in the past few years there has been a very considerable increase in the jobs offered to girls of 14 and 15 years old. ... Women's industries are largely run on juvenile labour – largely because the wages are lower. It is not necessary to stamp insurance cards for juvenile employees (Fox, 1957: 24).

Bennett argued, 'The position could be considerably improved by making it illegal to employ children under 15 or 16 years of age, and by fixing the maximum proportion of juvenile to adult labour which any one factory or workshop may employ' (Fox, *ibid*: 25-26). Much of the employment of 14 and 15 year olds was 'blind-alley' employment, in 'dead-end' jobs. Nearly half of the boys were employed as messenger boys and one quarter of the girls were in domestic service. The Committee was clear that 'Boys and girls who enter blind-alley occupations at the ages 14-15 are compelled to do so through economic necessity' (IDCRA, 1935: 23). Although about one-third of juveniles were neither in employment nor at school, and it was unclear what they were doing, an influential factor in deciding against a recommendation to raise the school-leaving age was the potential hardship that would ensue for poor parents who depended on the labour of their children. Another objection was the potential cost to the State:

The most serious economic issue that would arise from the raising of the school-leaving age and the withdrawal of juveniles from employment would be the hardship which it would cause parents whose circumstances are poor.

... It seems to us almost inevitable that if juveniles were compelled to go to school instead of to work there would be a demand for maintenance allowances for the disemployed juveniles – a demand which the state would find difficulty in refusing. The cost of a scheme of maintenance allowances would be prohibitive (IDCRA, 1935: 26).

Even if the cost were not prohibitive, there was a philosophical argument against such a scheme: 'We think it would be entirely wrong in principle to start young people in life with the conception that the State is responsible for their support.' The Inter-Departmental Committee, although it did not recommend raising the school-leaving age, believed that there would be an advantage in keeping unemployed or idle young persons at school not just to 15, but to 16 years, the usual time for entry into employment. The question of unoccupied juveniles would be addressed a decade later by the Commission on Youth Unemployment (CYU), which was established in May 1943 by Seán Lemass, Minister for Industry and Commerce. The Commission, which reported eight years later in 1951, was chaired by Dr John Charles McQuaid, Archbishop of Dublin. It recommended that the school-leaving age be raised ultimately to 16 years, and as a first step that it should be raised to 15 years. The Commission considered that the policy most likely to yield the best results and, at the same time, cause minimum inconvenience to families dependent on juvenile labour, would be to raise the school-leaving age area by area, according to local conditions. In the event it would be a further twenty years before the school-leaving age would be raised to 15 years in 1972. The Commission, aware of the economic hardship of poor families, was generally in favour of support for these families via children's allowances and maternity and child welfare and other services (CYU, 1951: 29). The Commission dismissed the objection that such help would lessen parental responsibility:

> A difficulty seen by some is that helping the children tends to lessen the sense of responsibility of parents for the maintenance and upbringing of their offspring. But to the average poor mother of a growing family the assistance received encourages her to feel that she is not fighting a losing battle against circumstances, and the attitude of the children towards society, when they grow up, is not embittered by the recollection of early years of almost unbearable poverty (CYU, ibid: 29).

Demand from parents for more education for their children was evident from the steady rise in enrolments that pre-dated the introduction of free post-primary schooling. In 1929, 38 per cent of 14-16 year olds were in full-time education. The proportion rose to 42 per cent in 1944 and to 51 per cent in 1962; by 1995 it had reached 95 per cent. In 1946, the share of 14-19 year olds in full-time education was 24 per cent. By 1966 the share had risen to 41 per cent (OECD Survey, 1965; Fahey, FitzGerald and Maître, 1998). In the decade 1985 to 1995 the proportion of 17-year-olds in full-time education rose from 65 per cent to 78 per cent, while the proportion of 18-year-olds rose from 41 per cent to 61 per cent. At the foundation of the State only a tiny proportion of 19-year-olds were in full-time education; by the close of the century just one in two were so engaged. The number of girls sitting public examinations, which was well below that of boys early in the century, surpassed boys by the end of the century. Before 1922 girls accounted for between 25-30 per cent of those sitting for the examinations of the Intermediate Board. Participation of girls rose in the 1930s and 1940s so that by the early 1950s there were as many girls as boys sitting the Intermediate Certificate examination. By the late 1980s more girls than boys were sitting the Leaving Certificate examination.

The proportion of gainfully occupied males aged 14-19 years rose between 1926 and 1946 but has since declined, while the proportion of gainfully occupied females in the same age group was higher in 1961 than in 1926, but has declined since then. In 1946, 71 per cent of males 14-19 years and 68 per cent of females 14-19 years were gainfully occupied. By 1991 only 31 per cent of males and 24 per cent of females aged 15-19 years were so occupied. Because of the raising of the school-leaving age in 1972, the data for 1981 and 1991 refer to the age group 15-19 years. Between 1981 and 1991 the proportion of males aged 15-19 who were in the labour force fell steeply from 49 per cent to 31 per cent while the share of females fell from 38 per cent to 24 per cent.

The conditions of employment of young persons are regulated by a number of Acts. *The Employment of Women, Young Persons and Children Act,* 1920, gave effect to Conventions adopted at a general conference of the International Labour Office (ILO). It fixed 14 years as the minimum age for admission to employment in any industrial undertaking or shop, other than one in which only members of the same family were employed. Under the *Conditions of Employment Acts,* 1936 and 1944, employment in industrial work of those under 14 years was prohibited and the option was provided to limit the work of persons under 18 years and of females in industrial work. Further legislation governing the employment of young persons was introduced in 1977 and again in 1996. The *Protection of Young Persons (Employment) Act,* 1996 brought Irish legislation into line with that in the EU.

With the decline in the importance of agriculture and increased urbanisation, the issue of child poverty and child maintenance, possibly not as stark an issue in a rural setting in which children contributed to output, came to the fore. The introduction of Children's Allowances, for the third and each subsequent child in 1944, was an early recognition of the special difficulties of large families (see Chapter 9). In the past two decades a considerable amount of research has been carried out by the ESRI, the Combat Poverty Agency and the Family Studies Unit at University College Dublin on the relative deterioration of the economic situation of families with children. Households with children face a disproportionate risk of poverty (Nolan and Farrell, 1990; Nolan and Callan, 1994). In 1994 a study published by the Combat Poverty Agency made estimates on the cost of rearing children of different ages and argued in favour of increased child support (Carney *et al*, 1994). A measure of the degree to which attitudes have changed since the Commission on Youth Unemployment *Report* is found in the view taken by the researchers regarding the costs of children. They maintain that there are two kinds of costs associated with children. Firstly, there are the direct costs of food, clothing, education and other living costs. Secondly, there are indirect costs such as income foregone by parents who care for children, or the costs of child care when parents do in fact work outside the home. There is no suggestion regarding income foregone *by the child,* or loss to family budget on that account, or to the loss of child labour on family farms, which was so important in earlier decades.

Secret societies: the abuse of children

Examples exist of those who grew up in institutions, under the care of religious orders, who have been successful in life and who have acknowledged good done on their behalf by members of these orders. A striking example of this is Sheila Williams Conroy who was the first woman to be elected to the Executive of the ITGWU in 1955, and in 1976 became the first woman to chair a state company when she was appointed chairman of RTÉ. After her birth in 1918, Sheila Williams was fostered out to a family in Bantry until she was six years old. Her mother was dead and her father away at sea and she had no other family. After First Communion Sheila was taken into a home run by the Sisters of Mercy in Cóbh. Although it was a bleak institutional place, 'Some of the nuns were very kindly, others very strict' (Heron, 1993: 13). At one stage she required a course of 'injections costing a guinea a time – a huge sum for the nuns to find in those days' (ibid). The nuns encouraged Sheila's interest in confectionery-making and got her a job in a bakery, even though it was owned by a Protestant family. Sheila Williams Conroy, still active in her eighties, is a very exceptional woman, but others were not so lucky.

A distinguishing feature of late twentieth century Ireland was the flushing into the open of some dark social secrets. In an earlier era the media shared in the collective silence, when according to former editor of the *Evening Herald*, Brian Quinn, some journalists 'allowed cowardice to rule' (Quinn, 1999). In recent years the media deserve credit for providing a voice for many a hitherto silent scream. If, as Bentham remarked, 'Publicity is the soul of justice', nowhere has this been truer than in areas where the authority of the family, church and state had long remained unquestioned, in particular concerning the treatment of children. In May 1999 a three-part series produced by Mary Raftery, entitled *States of Fear*, was broadcast on RTÉ. It shocked viewers with accounts of how children had been abused physically and sexually in industrial schools. Later in the same year Raftery, together with Eoin O'Sullivan, a lecturer in social policy in Trinity College, published a book on the topic which included harrowing testimonies of survivors of the system (Raftery and O'Sullivan, 1999). How could these abuses have happened in state-sponsored institutions? Who knew? One aspect that merits reflection is the fundamental one of the extent to which both the law and its *modus operandi* were inadequate or even counter-productive. Another aspect is the extent to which some of those in positions of responsibility chose to suppress information on the mistaken view that the public were better off if they did not know about the situation. Both these aspects are well illustrated by the contents of the Carrigan Report on Sexual Offences (1931) and the reaction of the Department of Justice to the Report, a Report that was never made public on the advice of the Department. The memorandum of evidence from the Commissioner of the Civic Guard to the Carrigan Committee included the following:

> That there was an alarming amount of sexual crime increasing yearly, a feature of which was the large number of cases of criminal interference with girls and children from 16 years downwards, including many cases of children under 10 years;

> That the police estimated that not 15 per cent. of such cases were prosecuted, because of

(1) the anxiety of parents to keep them secret in the interests of their children, the victims of such outrages, which overcame the desire to punish the offenders;

(2) the reluctance of parents to subject their children to the ordeal of appearing before a public Court to be examined and cross-examined;

(3) the actual technical embarrassments in the way of a successful prosecution of such offenders owing to (a) the difficulty of proof, from the private nature of the offence, usually depending on the evidence of a single witness, the child; (b) the existing law, or the rule of practice in such cases, requiring corroboration, or requiring the Judge to warn the Jury of the danger of convicting the accused upon the uncorroborated evidence of the witness (Carrigan, 1931: 14).

Carrigan pointed to the ways in which the prevailing judicial processes operated to the detriment of children, leading to their sometimes being treated as accomplices in a crime rather than victims of an outrage (Carrigan, *ibid*: 28). The Report pointed to the fact that procedures were protracted and put

... a strain upon the child, under which not infrequently she or he breaks down, and the prosecution fails or must be abandoned. ... Indeed it may be believed that the frequency of assaults on young children is to some degree attributable to the impunity on which culprits may reckon under this protection (Carrigan, *ibid*: 26).

The Department of Justice strongly advised against the publication of the Carrigan Report, saying that even if the contents of the Report were true it was better not to give them currency. In a telling remark regarding the evidence of children, the memorandum from the Department of Justice stated:

It is understood that many competent authorities have grave doubts as to the value of children's evidence. A child with a vivid imagination may actually live in his mind the situation as he invented it and will be quite unshaken by severe cross-examination (Department of the President, S 5998, Department of Justice memo, 27 October 1932: 10).

Child abuse is rooted in the unequal power relations between children and adults. Parents, priests and carers have emerged as the cruellest abusers of children and, as O'Mahony says, helped to dissolve the 'Myth of Irish Social Virtue' centred on the family, the caring institutions and the Catholic Church. Two of the most notorious cases of child abuse are the Kilkenny Incest case and the McColgan ('The West of Ireland Farmer') case. In the Kilkenny Incest case a father raped and beat his eldest daughter over a long period. The girl gave birth to her father's child at 15 years of age. In the McColgan case the father regularly abused his children and tried to force his son to have sexual intercourse with his sister. In both cases the mothers were unable to prevent the abuse. In his assessment of these extreme cases O'Mahony shows how the fathers abused behind a veneer of respectability. 'The West of Ireland farmer' was noted for projecting himself 'as a great family man, leading his wife and three children to the front of the village church every Sunday' (O'Mahony, 1996: 232). O'Mahony remarks that these cases, '… reflect on the structures and values of Irish social and family life and the assumptions normally made about them. These men have exploited the popular faith in the family myth in an extreme manner and by their example subverted it' (O'Mahony, *ibid*: 231-2).

An attempt to comprehend child sexual abuse within families must take account of the social context which includes 'the latitude allowed to the individual family by society and the status and power bestowed on the father within that family' (O'Mahony, *ibid*: 235). In an analysis of the McColgan case, Harry Ferguson, Professor of Social Policy and Social Work in University College Dublin, argued that the case must also be judged in the context of accepted professional practices belonging to a different era. According to Ferguson, the McColgan case spanned a period – 1979 to 1984 – when awareness of child abuse was only beginning to dawn: 'The first guidelines on how professionals should deal with the new phenomenon of "non-accidental injury" to children were issued in 1977, while it was another 10 years before procedures even dealt with child sexual abuse' (*The Irish Times*, 26 January 1998). According to Ferguson, professional emphasis was placed on trying to sort out 'inadequate' parents. This was at a time 'when the kinds of child sexual abuse that we now know to have been going on were almost literally unthinkable'. According to Deputy Alan Shatter, however, there was no excuse for the inaction of the Health Board in the McColgan case; the Board could have taken action under the 1908 *Children's Act*. Under Section 58 of that Act, a care order could be made where parents failed to exercise 'proper guardianship':

> There should be no doubt that the information disclosed to the North-Western Health Board in the 1979-1984 period detailing the physical violence and sexual abuse suffered by the McColgan children should have resulted in the health board taking care proceedings (*The Irish Times*, 5 February, 1998).

Following the broadcast on RTÉ in 1996 of a documentary entitled 'Dear Daughter', dealing with abuses in Goldenbridge orphanage, a former Sister of Mercy, and one-time head of Carysfort Teacher-Training College, Teresita Durkan, attempted to establish a context for Industrial Schools. The Goldenbridge complex had, according to Durkan, started in the 1850s 'as an industrial school, a female convict refuge and a laundry'. Durkan taught in the primary school close by the Industrial School between 1959 and 1964, although she never taught in the Industrial School itself. No longer a nun and writing from Valparaiso in Chile, where she now works, Durkan stated:

It came as no surprise to me that sad personal experiences – which were almost inevitable under a national child-care system that was poor, penny-pinching, under-staffed, socially condescending and dismally provided for – should become the focus of public concern (Durkan, 1997).

Another feature of the context is the fact that corporal punishment, which would now be regarded as physical abuse, was accepted as a method of discipline in schools for the first three-quarters of the century. Joyce, in *Portrait of the Artist*, describes it taking place at Clongowes, an upper middle class Jesuit boarding school. It was a *sine qua non* of a Christian Brothers' education and it occurred in convent schools also (Kerrigan, 1998). It was widely used in reformatories and industrial schools. One past pupil of a Christian Brothers' school, former Secretary of the Department of Finance, Seán Cromien, says that when he was a schoolboy, modern ideas about corporal punishment were not held, even by the boys. Cromien believes the boys 'preferred to be punished physically to being kept in after school and particularly preferred it to being lectured sarcastically by the teacher'.[2] Change came partly as a result of a campaign to abolish corporal punishment in schools, and partly because of the spread of a more child-centred approach to education from the 1960s onwards. In 1998 a judgment in the European Court of Human Rights outlawed corporal punishment of children at home. The judgment resulted from a case in which a young boy had been severely punished physically by his step-father (*The Irish Times*, 23 September, 1998).

In 1946 Monsignor Flanagan, associated with 'Boys' Town' in the United States, criticised the use of corporal punishment in Irish institutions. The following year, James Dillon, regarded as among the more enlightened of the members of Dáil Éireann, challenged the monsignor for his use of language, '... which appears to give the colour of justification for the cartoons in the American papers where muscular warders are seen flogging half-naked 14 year old boys with cat-o'-nine tails' (*PDDE*, 27 March 1947: 343). Dillon challenged Monsignor Flanagan to investigate more closely his allegations and if he found them to be untrue, he should correct the grave injustice he has done to '... respectable men who are members of the Irish Christian Brothers, to the warders in our prisons and to the warders in the Borstal, and to the other individuals who are looking after young persons in the various places of detention provided by the State' (*PDDE, ibid*: 344).

On the general issue of juvenile delinquency, Deputy Dillon suggested that parents were too anxious to protest if their offspring were physically punished by teachers:

One of the reasons is that, if a national school teacher gives a child a slap, he may find himself involved in something like the Nuremberg trial. By the time Papa and Mamma have finished describing the massacre that took place, Belsen fades into insignificance beside the scenes that took place in the national school, and a fat stump of a child is sitting beside them, ready to get up and tell his story like a man.

... the national teacher who beats the child and is then brought to court on that account, is singled out, and, even when she is going to Mass, people can say: 'That is the teacher who was up for beating the child' (PDDE, ibid: 351).

Deputy Dillon's comments, which might be interpreted as trivialising the sufferings of those in Belsen while mocking a child who was fat and short of stature, would be regarded, at least, as politically incorrect today. They did not cause any uproar in Dáil Éireann in 1947. In fairness to Deputy Dillon he also made what by today's standards would be regarded as enlightened and fair points in the same speech. For example, he pointed to the poor social background of most juveniles who came before the courts, saying that the families of the well-to-do had ways of protecting their children from the law, sometimes by paying for the damage their children had done: 'But take a young kid from Gloucester Street who takes it into his head to break a window. Very quickly the Guards pick him up and admonish him ...' (PDDE, ibid: 349).

The roots of the present system for children in care go back to the nineteenth century when provision for the protection and care of children was covered by Acts including the Abandonment of Children Act, 1861 and the Offences against the Person Act, 1861. In the mid-nineteenth century the only public provision for children was in workhouses. By 1820 a whole range of Catholic orphanages existed. In general these were bodies that boarded out children, rather than taking them into institutional care, as would become the pattern later. Under the Reformatory Schools Act, 1858, a number of existing voluntary institutions and homes were certified as suitable for the reception of young offenders committed by the courts. The Act also provided for the inspection of institutions and for the payment of grants from public funds for the maintenance of the children in these institutions. At one time there were ten Reformatory Schools, five of which were for girls. By 1944, due to the decrease in the number of committals by the courts, only two reformatories remained. These were St Joseph's, Limerick, for girls, conducted by the Sisters of the Good Shepherd, and St Conleth's, at Daingean, Co. Offaly, for boys, conducted by the Oblates of Mary Immaculate. In 1944 St Anne's School, Kilmacud, Dublin, conducted by the Sisters of Our Lady of Charity of Refuge, was certified as a Reformatory School for young girl offenders, 'with marked tendencies to sexual immorality' (Government of Ireland/Kennedy Report, 1970: 1).

Shortly after the Reformatory School system was introduced it was realised that a different type of school to cater for neglected, orphaned and abandoned children was needed. Accordingly, the Industrial Schools were established, first in Scotland, and later in Ireland in 1868. On the introduction of the Industrial School system to Ireland:

The Local Authorities were unwilling to contribute to the establishment of these schools or even to contribute to the maintenance of the children. As a result various Religious Orders were requested to undertake the work. Where an Order was willing to do so, and where they provided suitable premises, those premises were certified as fit for the reception of children in care (Government of Ireland/Kennedy, *ibid*: 2).

During the next thirty years, from 1868 to 1898, the number of certified Industrial Schools increased to seventy-one, caring for approximately 8,000 children. Sixty-one of the Schools were in the 26 County area, five for Protestants and fifty-six for Catholics. The *Children Act*, 1908 was a landmark in child care, at the time representing a new charter for children. Under that Act children could be detained by the district courts for being 'found wandering', being 'illegitimate' or lacking 'proper guardianship'. It gave the Minister for Education broad responsibility in regard to children in Reformatories and Industrial Schools. In addition to children placed in institutions, many children were boarded out and fostered. According to Barrett (1955) there were 'over 10,000 normal healthy dependent children in institutions and in foster homes throughout the State' in 1955. Barrett argued in favour of increased family liaison work for children in care, maintaining that family-care work in the homes of children in institutions was far from satisfactory. As family rehabilitation was rare, the child spent his or her formative years in an institution and accordingly 'he has no normal home life; he has none of those things which matter most in the child's development' (Barrett, 1955). Due to a variety of factors, including population decline, improvements in living standards, better social services, adoption and boarding-out of children, the number of Certified Industrial Schools declined to twenty-nine in 1970, catering for 2,000 children. In 1970 the Kennedy Report pointed to the lack of love and security in the lives of the children in institutions (Government of Ireland/Kennedy, *ibid*:13).

In 1934 the Minister for Education, Tomás Ó Deirg, set up a Commission of Inquiry into the Reformatory and Industrial School System under the chairmanship of the Senior Justice of the Dublin District Court, Mr G.P. Cussen. The Commission found that the reasons for admission of children to Industrial Schools indicated 'that in the main the problem is one not of criminal tendencies, but of poverty' (Department of Education, 1936:10). In 1934, 6 per cent of admissions were due to serious offences, 6 per cent were due to failure to attend school, while 88 per cent were due to poverty and neglect. The broad conclusions of the Report expressed reasonable satisfaction with the system: 'The children are on the whole suitably housed, fed and clothed, and their treatment is in general kindly and humane' (Department of Education, *ibid*: 20). The children's diet was found to be adequate, although insufficient milk was served to meet the needs of growing children, and butter was seldom provided. The regime of silence at meals and, in some cases, in the workplace, which operated in a number of schools was judged to be unduly harsh and should be discontinued.

The Report pointed to the need for improved medical attendance and inspection. The Report recommended that in no case should the number of children exceed 250 in a school. At the time Artane boys' school in Dublin was certified to take 800 boys and had an average of about 700 at any one time. The Committee found that few of the teachers – religious or lay – were trained and that the salaries for lay teachers were very poor. Most of the children graduated to low-level jobs; the majority of girls became domestic servants, while the majority of boys became labourers. Sometimes the children were treated as juvenile labourers by the institutions in which they lived, rather than as trainees, in that they were expected to do agricultural, domestic and other work for the institutions. At the time the state grant was two shillings per week per child (Department of Education, *ibid*: 41). Notwithstanding the serious defects highlighted, the overall tone of the Report was congratulatory rather than condemnatory.

The fact that the conclusions of the Cussen Report differed so markedly from the Kennedy Report thirty years later can be explained partly in terms of the change in what was considered an acceptable standard of care for children in Industrial schools, in turn related to the improvement in living standards in the interim. The difference could also be due to the fact that the investigation carried out by District Justice Kennedy was more thorough, and focused more on the emotional welfare of children as distinct from minimum physical requirements. At any rate by the mid-twentieth century the whole concept of care of children was subjected to fresh examination. Donogh O'Malley, when Minister for Education in the 1960s, realised not only the limited nature of the powers vested in him by the 1908 Act, but also that the Act was no longer suitable for prevailing conditions, and accordingly set up a committee of inquiry under District Justice Eileen Kennedy. According to the Kennedy Report, O'Malley 'felt that the Community was not doing all it should to help underprivileged children, particularly those who had been placed in these schools' (Government of Ireland/Kennedy, *ibid*: 4).

In a special survey that the Committee carried out regarding the background of the children in Industrial Schools, it was found that only about 18 per cent of children were known to the school to have parents who were married, alive and living together. However, in only 1.5 per cent of the cases were the father and mother known to be dead, while 30 per cent of the children had one parent who was dead. About 19 per cent of the children were known to be illegitimate, while in an astonishing 51 per cent of cases the schools said they did not know whether one or other or both of the parents were alive or dead. In the case of the Reformatories, over half the children were known to have parents who were alive, married and living together. Between 1900 and 1970 at least 70,000 children were detained by the Courts in Industrial Schools. Of the 51 per cent of children in industrial schools where it was not known if parents were alive or dead, it is certain that many were the fruits of extra-marital unions. The unmarried mother is a defining figure in regard to the Industrial Schools and Orphanages.

The Report of the Kennedy Committee was a strong indictment of the system of reformatories and industrial schools. It urged the abolition of the existing system of residential care and its replacement with group homes 'which would approximate as closely as possible to the normal family unit. Children from one family, and children of different ages and sex should be placed in such group homes' (Government of Ireland/Kennedy, *ibid*: 6). The Report also recommended proper training for staff, the transfer of administrative responsibility for child care to the Department of Health, all law relating to child care to be updated and incorporated into a composite Act, the age of criminal responsibility to be raised to 12 years and the system of payment to the Reformatory and Industrial Schools on a capitation basis to be replaced by a system based on agreed budgets. With regard to the training of staff, the Kennedy Report stated that most of those working in Industrial Schools and Reformatories had no proper qualifications for their work. 'Their only previous experience may have been in teaching, nursing or mission work and to expect them to put into practice the principles of child care without adequate training is expecting the impossible' (Government of Ireland/Kennedy, *ibid*: 13). It is difficult to find hard evidence on the priorities for human resource allocation within the religious orders, but Eoin O'Sullivan of Trinity College, based on conversations with some members of religious orders, has suggested that the less able members of religious orders were put to work in the Industrial Schools and Reformatories. He believes that in the Sisters of Mercy, for example, the more able nuns taught in the private schools.[3] Since the Kennedy Report was published the training of child-care workers has been considerably improved.

From 1868 to 1984, the capitation fee system was the method used to finance the Industrial Schools. Despite their very low level, the payment of capitation fees was an incentive to keep children within an institution, rather than to seek alternatives, such as foster care. The *Public Assistance Act*, 1939 enabled Public Assistance Authorities to pay, or contribute to the cost of maintenance in a suitable school or institution, or in a foster home, for a 'child who is illegitimate, deserted or otherwise destitute and deprived of a normal home'. Of those children not boarded out the great majority were placed in industrial schools and a small number in orphanages. When the Emigration Commission reported in 1954, the 'approved maximum rate of payment for children in industrial schools is £1.10s.0d. per week'. In July 1968 the capitation rate in Industrial Schools was raised from £3.37p (67/6d) per week to £4.12p (82/6d.) per week, and in the Reformatory Schools the figure was increased from £3.57p (71/6d.) to £4.32p (86/6d). Two years after the Kennedy Committee commenced its deliberations, in 1969, the rates were doubled. The capitation system remained in place until 1984.

In 1980 the *Final Report of the Task Force on Child Care Services* (TFCCS) was published. It raised the most basic issues regarding the child and the law. Could the constitutional protection of 'the family' ever be an actual impediment to the protection of children? The Report referred to the ruling of the Courts (*in Re* Doyle, an Infant, 1955), that the right of the State to withhold a child from his parents' control lasts only for as long as the parents continue to fail to provide for the child's welfare. The Report referred to a submission from the Council for Social Welfare, a Committee of the Catholic Bishops' Conference. This submission pointed to the change in thinking that was beginning to take place in Irish law in relation to the interests of children. The submission quoted examples of legal decisions which, it suggested

> ... would seem to indicate the way in which Irish law is developing to ensure that the interests of children are more appropriately protected and that the old-fashioned attitude which accepted parental rights as paramount *vis-à-vis* children's rights is now an outdated approach (TFCCS, 1980: 213).

A Supplementary Report to the main Task Force Report emphasised even more strongly the need to address the rights of the child (O'Daly and Ó Cinnéide, 1980). The *Child Care Act*, 1991 gave the Minister for Health administrative responsibility for child care. The Health Boards have duties and powers to protect the welfare of children and to provide child care and family support services. At present, responsibility for co-ordinating policy on child care is held by the Minister of State for Health and Children. The Minister is assisted by a multi-departmental team of officials. The age of criminal responsibility remains at seven years, as it was at the start of the century. At a meeting of the UN Committee on the Rights of the Child in Geneva in January 1998, the Minister of State for Foreign Affairs, Liz O'Donnell, admitted on behalf of the government that its childcare agencies could not cope with the number of young children who need help. The government claimed that it could not raise the age of criminal responsibility from seven to twelve because to do so would place 'an intolerable burden on our social services'. However, in the Children's Bill, published in autumn 1999 the government announced plans to raise the age to twelve years as recommended in the Kennedy Report in 1970. Time will tell how effective the administrative reorganisation of the child care services proves to be, but it will never be possible to know how much, if any, abuse of children might have been avoided if the Carrigan Report which spoke with crystal clarity on the matter of child sexual abuse seventy years ago, had been published and publicly debated.

Age of marriage, age of consent

The age of consent, i.e. the age at which sexual intercourse may take place legally outside marriage, differs from the legal minimum age for marriage. Until 1986, the minimum legal age for marriage was lower than the age of consent, but since then the age of consent has been lower than the legal age for marriage. In 1972 the minimum age of marriage for females was raised to 16 years, bringing it into line with that of males. In 1986 the marriage age for both males and females was raised to 18 years. Up to 1935 the age of consent was 16 years when, following the *Criminal Law Amendment Act*, 1935, it was raised to 17 years. In 1993 the age of consent for homosexual relations was fixed at 17 years also, following a period since 1861, when under the *Offences against the Person Act* passed in that year, homosexual activity was illegal.

Table 6.1: Legal age of marriage and age of consent, 1863-1993

Marriage	Age of consent
1863–1972	*1885–1935*
Males–16 years, females–14 years	16 years
1972 Marriage Act	*1935 Criminal Law Amendment Act*
Males and females–16 years	17 years
1986 Family Law Act, Sect. 31	*1993 Criminal Law Offences Act*
Males and females–18 years	Re Homosexual relations–17 years

Source: Department of Justice

The civil law in Ireland relating to the minimum age at marriage reaches back to the common law of England, itself based on the canon law of the Church prior to the Reformation. Permitted ages at marriage according to Church law, which covers a world-wide range of cultures, and Irish civil law, vary. The permitted minimum age for marriage under the canon law of the Catholic Church was 12 years for girls and 14 years for boys prior to 1918. The selection of 12 and 14 years as minimum ages for marriage reaches back beyond canon law to Roman law. The Code of Justinian established a presumption that puberty was attained at the age of 14 in the case of males and at the age of 12 in the case of females. This presumption was imported into canon law in the Middle Ages, and from there it found its way into the common law tradition which was originally heavily indebted to canon law for its prescriptions on marriage. In medieval canon law capacity for marriage was largely, though not exclusively, judged in terms of physical fitness; hence marriage before the age of puberty was deemed invalid. The presumption that puberty had not been reached before the ages of 14 and 12 years could, however, yield to contrary proof. The law invalidating marriage at an earlier age was qualified by the clause *nisi malitia suppleat aetatem* (unless malice, i.e. sexual wrongdoing, supply the age). Thus a boy who fathered a child before he was fourteen or a girl who became pregnant before she was twelve, was considered as physically capable of marriage. There was also another qualifying clause *nisi prudentia suppleat aetatem* (unless discretion, supply the age) indicating that some consideration was given to mental maturity also.

The ages of 14 and 12 remained the minimum legal ages for marriage until the first code of canon law, which came into effect in 1918. This code retained 14 and 12 as the legally presumed ages of puberty but raised the ages for valid marriage to 16 and 14, effectively drawing a clear distinction between the age of puberty and the age for valid marriage. The current code of canon law, which came into effect in 1983, gives no age for presumed puberty. It retains the earlier code's minimum ages for valid marriage. However, canon law recognises the great variety of cultures that exist and it allows the local Bishops' Conference to establish a higher age for marriage. Examples of such higher ages are found in Canada where the age is 18 for both males and females; England and Wales where it is 16 for both males and females in accordance with civil law, and the Philippines where it is 20 for males and 18 for females. The position in Ireland since 1986 is that the minimum age at marriage in civil law is two years higher for a male and four years higher for a female than in canon law. However, until 1972 the minimum permitted age was higher in canon law than in civil law.

The last quarter of the nineteenth century was a period of major importance with regard to the law governing sexual offences. The *Criminal Law Amendment Act,* 1885, popularly known as 'Stead's Act' after W.T. Stead, a prominent journalist, was a watershed. Stead was the author of an article in the *Pall Mall Gazette* in 1885, 'depicting an epidemic of child prostitution' (O'Malley, 1996: 5). The 1885 Act increased the age of consent, which had been 13 years since 1875, to 16 years, and outlawed the procurement of women and girls for prostitution. For the first sixty years of the State, 1922-81, there was only one significant Act dealing with the control of sexual behaviour – *The Criminal Law Amendment Act*, 1935. The 1935 Act increased the age of consent for females to 17 in relation to unlawful sexual intercourse, and established 15 years as the age below which no person of either sex could consent to an act constituting indecent assault.

Evidence of the incidence of under-age sexual activity exists in the number of births to girls aged 16 years and under (Table 6.2). In 1980 there were 52 births outside marriage to girls aged 15 years and under, while there were 153 such births to girls aged 16 years. Between 1960 and 1990 the number of such births rose from 32 to 62, and from 44 to 172 respectively. This was at a time when the age of consent is 17 years. The data are puzzling in one respect. How were there 11 marital births in 1980 and 4 in 1990 to girls aged 15 years and under, at a time when the minimum age of marriage was 16 years? Could these births have resulted from marriages celebrated in Church ceremonies where the permitted minimum age for marriage is lower than that recognised by the State?

Between 1992-96, 127 Irish girls aged 15 years or under travelled to Britain for abortions; approximately 25 per annum. During the same period 215 girls aged 15 years and under gave birth. In 1997 national attention focused on the case of a 13-year-old girl from the travelling community who became pregnant as a result of rape. Following High Court proceedings in what came to be known as the 'C case', Mr Justice Geoghegan granted permission for the girl to travel to England for an abortion. Clearly teenagers below the age of consent, and indeed below the school-leaving age are engaging in sexual intercourse. Sexual activity among young people was confirmed by an EU and Southern Health Board study of 800 young people aged between 15 and 24 years, which was published in November 1997. More than one fifth of females and one third of males claimed to have had sex before the age of 16 years ('Teenage Sex', *Sunday Tribune Review*, 30 November 1997). According to a survey by Dr Juliet Skinner, St James's Hospital, one third of women with sexually transmitted diseases are under the age of 20. Thirty two per cent of those attending a sexually transmitted diseases clinic are teenagers (*Evening Herald*, 28 March, 1996).

Table 6.2: Births to mothers aged 15 years & under, and aged 16 years, 1960–90

Year	15 Years and Under			16 Years		
	Non-marital	Marital	Total	Non-marital	Marital	Total
1960	32	8	40	44	22	66
1970	19	9	28	51	55	106
1980	52	11	63	153	43	196
1990	62	4	66	172	6	178

Source: Central Statistics Office

Changing attitudes to extra-marital births

Until the 1980s when the rights of extra-marital children and the rights of their parents became a focus of law reform, the main official interest in illegitimacy centred on the cost of maintenance. As far back as the *Bastardy Act, 1610*, the language was condemnatory. The Act attributed extra-marital births to 'lewdness' and 'bastardy was a great dishonour to Almighty God'. The weight of social control fell on the woman as her pregnancy was visible, whereas the man's fatherhood was not. Morality aside, the practical objection to bastardy was that 'great charge ariseth upon many places within this realm' because of it (Dennis and Erdos, 1993: 16). The Catholic liberal Daniel O'Connell was strict in regard to this issue. Shortly after O'Connell's election to the Commons in 1828, an Irish Bastardy Bill was introduced to equalise treatment in England and Ireland. O'Connell opposed the Bill, arguing that to enable unmarried women to secure maintenance for their children, as the Bill proposed, 'from whichever unmarried man they nominated as the father would undermine Irish (as it had already undermined English) sexual morality' (MacDonagh, 1991:

316). O'Connell apparently assumed that the father of an illegitimate child would be an 'unmarried man'. He appealed directly to at least two Irish bishops for their aid in denouncing the proposed measure.

The monumental *Commission of Inquiry into the Conditions of the Poor in Ireland* which was chaired by Richard Whately, the Church of Ireland Archbishop of Dublin, had a great deal to say about attitudes to, and the treatment of, unmarried mothers. The Commission found that the unmarried mother was a social outcast, whose 'stain was never forgotten, and the memory of which lingered for generations'. Her option was work, if possible, to support her child, but 'Begging and prostitution were successive as well as complementary occupations, and the progress might be either way' (Connell, 1968: 57). Under an Act of 1863 (26 and 27 Vic., cap.21), the poor law authority was empowered to recover from the putative father the cost of maintenance of any illegitimate child under 14 years of age who had become a charge on the rates. The proceedings were by civil bill as in the case of recovery of a debt, and the father could stop the proceedings by payment of the amount claimed plus costs. A decree could not be given unless the mother was examined and her evidence corroborated. The key point was that the Act only became operative *when a child became a charge on the rates,* but it gave no personal redress to the mother who could not compel the father to make any contribution. An indirect remedy available to the mother was an action for seduction brought by a parent, guardian or employer and based on loss of service (LGD, 1930-34: 123).

An illustration of the attitudes towards unmarried mothers in the 1920s is provided by the following extract from the *Report of the Department of Local Government and Public Health* in 1922:

> Special mention is due to efforts of the Sisters of the Sacred Hearts of Jesus and Mary to deal with the very difficult problem of the unmarried mother. They have established at Bessborough, a short distance from the City of Cork, a Home for the reception and reformation of girls who for the first time have had illegitimate offspring, or as they are usually designated – first offenders. The Sisters believe they can influence these cases best by keeping them dissociated from those who have lapsed a second time or oftener.

The Local Government (Temporary Provisions) Act, 1923 brought the administration of the Public Assistance services into Irish law and provided a framework for dealing with unmarried mothers. The Galway County Scheme would have been broadly representative. Unmarried mothers were divided into two classes: (a) First offenders, to be dealt with in the same institution as children and (b) Old offenders to be sent to a Magdalen Asylum. The Act stated:

> Unmarried mothers who come within Class (b) shall be offered an opportunity of relief and retrievement in the Magdalen Asylum, Galway, upon such terms and conditions as may be agreed on between the Executive Committee and the sisters in charge of the

Magdalen Asylum. If necessary the Committee may make arrangements with other Institutions. Persons in Class (b) who refuse to enter such Institutions as may be selected shall not be allowed under any circumstances to become chargeable to the public rates.

The *Report of the Department of Local Government and Public Health*, 1930-34 continued to emphasise the importance of specialised homes for unmarried mothers. It argued that specialised homes where appropriate training could help to restore self-respect to the mothers were important, and desirable on economic grounds also; otherwise the mothers were in danger of becoming a permanent burden on the ratepayers.

The language used about unmarried mothers during the first half of the twentieth century in Ireland was marked by the colours of crime and sin. Phrases like 'rehabilitation of the mother' or 'girls who have fallen again' occur regularly (LGD, 1934-37: 179). Because of attitudes at home, girls often fled to England when they became pregnant. The following was recorded in 1937:

> During the year many applications were received from English Public Assistance Authorities and English Rescue Societies for the repatriation of Irish unmarried mothers who having become pregnant in this country went to England for their confinement. Through the co-operation of the various boards of health and public assistance and of the Catholic Rescue Societies in Dublin it was possible to make suitable provision for all such cases who were willing to return (LGD, 1930-34: 129-30).

According to the *First Report of the Department of Health*, 1945-49, two Public Assistance Authorities, the Dublin Board of Assistance and the Galway Public Assistance Authority, maintained homes for unmarried mothers and children, located at Pelletstown in Dublin and Tuam in Galway. In addition there were three institutions run by religious orders at Castlepollard in Co. Westmeath, Mallow in Co. Cork and Roscrea in Co. Tipperary. The Public Assistance Authorities paid a capitation grant for the maintenance of the mothers and children. Efforts were made to foster out the children and when the children were boarded out, the mother was free to leave the institution. In 1949 there were 614 mothers and 1,014 children in the institutions run by religious orders. Public Assistance Authorities also sent children to Industrial Schools, if they were not boarded out. In 1949, 2,325 children were boarded out.

In recent years there has been criticism of the treatment meted out to unmarried mothers and allegations have been made that some mother and baby homes were almost prison-like institutions. But there was another view. Journalist and writer Dorine Rohan, who was sharply critical of Church attitudes towards sexual matters in the 1950s and 1960s, writes:

> I visited one of these homes and found the atmosphere and facilities most pleasant and homely. Many of the girls having far more comfort than they would have in their own

homes. They had the choice of a room of their own if they wished, or to share with a companion. The nuns who run it are delightfully human and kind towards the girls in their plight, and eager to save them the anguish and misery they would have endured had they run away to England as many of them do (Rohan, 1969: 56).

In 1930 the *Illegitimate Children (Affiliation Orders, Act), 1930* was passed. The object of this Act, for which the Minister for Justice was responsible, was to make the fathers of illegitimate children liable for their support. The Act enabled the mother, whose evidence had to be corroborated, to bring proceedings in her own name. If the mother succeeded, an order could be made for the payment of a weekly sum for the maintenance and education of the child until he/she reached 16 years. Payment could also be made to cover expenses related to the birth of the child and other charges. While the Act of 1863 was repealed, a local body (authority) giving relief to an illegitimate child, or a mother, could apply to the District Court for an affiliation order.

The non-marital family does not feature in the Constitution. However, in a case in 1946, which concerned custody of an illegitimate child, Mr Justice Gavan Duffy said that he regarded 'The innocent little girl as having the same "Natural and imprescriptible rights" (under Art.42) as a child born in wedlock to religious and moral, intellectual, physical and social education' (Kelly, 1980: 497). Whatever about the equal rights of illegitimate and legitimate children to education, when it came to property it was a different matter. In January 1984, the Supreme Court ruled that illegitimate children had no succession rights in respect of their father's estate where their father died intestate. An unmarried man died intestate, leaving a daughter, sisters and a brother. It was argued on behalf of the daughter that the *Succession Act, 1965* should be interpreted to permit an illegitimate child to succeed to his/her father's estate where the father had died intestate. If this was not accepted, it was argued, the Act was unconstitutional in that it discriminated against the child. The Supreme Court held that the *Succession Act* distinguished between legitimate and illegitimate children, and that the Act gave no rights of succession to a father's estate to an illegitimate child. The Court rejected the view that such an interpretation of the Act was unconstitutional. In 1983 the Law Reform Commission made a recommendation that the legal status of illegitimacy be abolished and in 1987 the *Status of Children Act* was passed (see Chapter 9).

Caring for children: who cares?

Mothers have always been the key figures in child care, sometimes on their own, sometimes supported by the wider family network, and sometimes with domestic help. In traditional farm families in the early twentieth century, '... A man *never* attended to small children. Should the wife be ill or die, another woman must come at once to take care of the children' (Ó Danachair, 1962:188). The child of a successful business or professional man, or a large farmer, was often reared with the help of a nanny prior to despatch to a boarding school that might be located in England or Ireland. Domestic labour was cheap and plentiful in those days and, indeed, until after World War II. The status of domestic work was always low and as factory jobs became available, girls shunned such labour. The Emigration Commission referred to, in their opinion, the mistaken view that

> ... domestic service was a despised form of employment, requiring the minimum amount of skill or intelligence. So far from this being the case, domestic employment, particularly where it involves the care of children, is not only a responsible undertaking, but one requiring for its proper performance a relatively high degree of intelligence, adaptability, judgment and skill (Commission on Emigration, 1954: 172).

Rowthorn tells us that, in the late twentieth century, 'In Britain, it is assumed that it is normally best for young children to live with their mother' (Rowthorn, 1999: 679). He backs this up with a judgment of the House of Lords:

> The award of custody of a four-year-old girl to her mother was justified by Lord Jaucey as follows: 'Nature has endowed men and women with different attributes and it so happens that mothers are generally better fitted than fathers to provide for very young children. This is no more discriminatory than the fact that only a woman can give birth. ... In normal circumstances, and I stress the word normal, a mother is better able than a father to fulfil the needs of a very young child' (Brixey v. Lynas, House of Lords (Scotland), 4 July 1996) (Rowthorn, 1999: 679).

The widespread demand for child care as a state service, however, is an indication that it is no longer taken as axiomatic that responsibility for the care of a child, even in the early years of life, rests with the mother. Pressure for state child care has come from a range of sources including the Majority Report of the Second Commission on the Status of Women (1993), the National Women's Council of Ireland (1998), and ICTU, so that it is easy to forget that such a demand was not only undreamed of by socially active women throughout most of the century, but would have been considered a decidedly second-best option, and is so described by the First Commission on the Status of Women:

> In dealing with the question of the provision of day-care facilities for babies and young children, we wish to stress that we are unanimous in the opinion that very young children, at least up to 3 years of age, should, if at all possible, be cared for by the mother at home and that as far as re-entry to employment is concerned, the provision of day-care for such children must be viewed as a solution to the problems of the mother who has particularly strong reasons to resume employment (Commission on the Status of Women, 1972: Para. 310).

Early feminists accepted that child-rearing was the task of women, but argued that women deserved support with the task. Rathbone highlighted the fact that wages took no account of family needs and that men were the principal recipients of wages (Rathbone, 1924). In order to ease the poverty of families, the state would have to take some economic responsibility for children. Rathbone wanted mothering to be judged worthy of financial reward and for income to be transferred from men to women. Looking to the Continent, she pointed out that family allowances had been introduced in France and Belgium, and argued that paying benefits to mothers would be an important recognition of the social value of child rearing. At the time this was a radical proposal and met with sharp opposition from, amongst others, economic historian Alexander Gray (Gray, 1927).

The nature and extent of public financial support for children has evolved against a background that included the curtailment of child labour alongside the extension of compulsory education:

> Many of these states had come during the nineteenth century to extend and enforce the dependence of children, establishing universal schooling and prohibiting child labour. Patterns of economic development, demographic changes, and protective legislation made it difficult in some countries for mothers to earn as well, creating a familial cycle of poverty in which the period of greatest dependence coincided with the family's smallest capacity for self-support (Pedersen, 1995: 3-4).

By the mid-1970s in Ireland, the Trade Union Movement was urging state provision of child care. The *Working Women's Charter*, adopted at the annual conference of ICTU in 1976, stated that Congress would campaign for, and appeal to all trade unionists, to further the following principle: 'The provision of State-controlled crèches, day nurseries and nursery schools with adequately-trained personnel. Provision of after-school and holiday care facilities and school meals' (ICTU, 1982: 148). At its annual conference in 1979, ICTU adopted a motion calling on the government to encourage and develop child-care facilities, especially for pre-school children. In 1980 Congress made a submission to the Minister for Health recommending the establishing of a National Co-ordinating Committee to plan and make provision for child-care facilities. This was followed in 1982 by a submission in which Congress argued that the demand for child-care facilities in future would be mainly determined by the increased participation of women in the workforce. Congress recommended 'that the provision of child-care facilities be regarded as a social service to be provided by the state' (ICTU, *ibid*: 152).

A couple of years before Congress made their submission on child care, Dr Patrick Hillery was piloting employment equality legislation in Europe. He recalls his acute awareness at the time that the issue of child care would arise as a consequence of equality legislation and that a gap was being left in that regard.

He thought, 'Some day there is going to be a result from this legislation and no solution is visible.'[4] He did not favour the enterprise crèche attached to the place of work because it would tie a woman to a particular job, and thought that some form of government-sponsored child care might be necessary. Flexible working hours might help, but that would also depend upon the employer. Flexi-time, job sharing, career breaks as well as parental leave, have gone some way in this direction. Hillery concludes that we are now living in 'a double salary society' and that crèches need to be government-controlled or local authority-controlled to ensure a certain standard. He has a strong personal philosophy about child care which is of interest not only because he was once Minister for Education and Social Affairs Commissioner, but also because he is a doctor, married to a doctor, a parent and a grandparent who today does a school run for a grandchild:

> My own thing about children was that you must be there. You just don't go home and ask 'How did you get on at school today?', because there are times when children want to talk and if you're not there, you're not there and they won't talk when you say you are ready to listen. You have to be around when they are really bothered about something and to listen – or then it gets buried in their subconscious. They need somebody there (Interview with Dr Hillery, 14 December 1998).

Former Taoiseach Garret FitzGerald, who did much to encourage participation of women in public life, holds the view that, 'It is better for children if women didn't work. But you can't say that women shouldn't work because of that. They must make their own choice.'[5] The views of both Hillery and FitzGerald merit reflection because both men contributed significantly to the environment in which child care is coming to be regarded as the norm.

In February 1999 the *Partnership 2000 Expert Working Group on Chidcare Report* was published by the Department of Justice, Equality and Law Reform. It recommends tax relief towards child care costs as well as subsidies for low earners for whom tax relief would not be relevant. In formulating policy the government will have a number of objectives to consider, first of which must be the welfare of the child. Other concerns include support for parents who wish to work as well as for those who wish to care directly for their own children. In an increasing number of contemporary families the main carer for the child or children is the father. Given the traditional approach to child care with the almost exclusive emphasis on women, fathers who are primary carers may face obstacles, including prejudice. Whether the government could or should try to influence parental behaviour needs to be debated, since there is no such thing as a neutral policy.

7

Family, State and the Moral Teaching of the Catholic Church

Two themes are central to this chapter: (i) the link between the moral teaching of the Catholic Church and the law of the land, and (ii) the relationship between the moral teaching of the Catholic Church and behaviour patterns of Catholics in Ireland. In regard to the first theme a shift has occurred from a position of close coincidence between the teaching of the Church on moral issues and the civil law, to one of clear differentiation between the two. In regard to the second theme, a shift, related to the legal-moral shift, has occurred in behaviour patterns from one of broad conformity with Church teaching on family and sexual matters, to an *à la carte* position. This at any rate is the overall picture; the detailed picture is more complex. Two features that emerge on closer observation are firstly, that a rigid clerical/lay divide is an oversimplification and secondly, that on a number of issues, Catholics have on a variety of occasions adopted positions different from those directed by their pastors.

A conservative laity, an independent laity

To draw a line between the clergy and the hierarchy on the one hand, and the bulk of the people on the other, and to label one conservative and the other progressive is incorrect. The truth is not so simple. The writer Sean O'Faolain remarks that the worst censors in Cork were among the laity; in fact on one occasion O'Faolain said, 'the tough common-sense and humanity' of the bishop distanced him from lay censors in regard to a performance of dance (Whyte, 1980: 29). If the great majority of clerical figures espoused conservative views in social as well as moral matters, one of the most advanced proposals for reform of the social services was made in 1945 by a bishop, Dr John Dignan of Clonfert, while some of the most conservative and cautionary utterances emanated from Seán MacEntee, Minister for Local Government in the 1940s, although MacEntee's daughter, Máire Mhac an tSaoi, believes that his conservatism was based on financial pragmatism, rather than on anti-interventionist ideology.[1] Among the hierarchy, as among the laity, there were those who tended to look more backwards than forwards in family matters, and *vice versa*. De Valera and some influential clerics were in many matters relating to the family, essentially backward-looking, yearning for a rural society peopled by small-farm families. Dr Lucey of Cork and Dr Browne of Galway tended this way; but others were forward-looking, including Dr Dignan, Bishop Birch and, at a later stage, Bishop Kavanagh, a Dubliner who understood the urban world, and who was chief author of the ground-breaking pastoral *The Work of Justice*, published in 1977. Among the laity, prominent conservatives included Dr James McPolin, Deputy Patrick Belton and Deputy Oliver J. Flanagan. A few were ahead of their time, including León Ó Broin, who was an ecumenist, and Frank Duff, the pioneer of lay participation in the Church.

It was the view of one of the revolutionary leaders, Kevin O'Higgins, that 'We were probably the most conservative-minded revolutionaries that ever put through a successful revolution' (*PDDE*, 2: 11). In an essay entitled 'The Social Revolution that never was', Patrick Lynch identifies rural conservatism in the fact that by 1916 the former tenants were for the most part farmers, while rural Ireland had profited from the introduction of the Old Age Pension in 1908 (Lynch, 1966). In the wake of the Parnell débâcle politicians vied for the support of the clergy because where the priests went the people would frequently, but by no means always, follow. More than half a century later, in 1951, Noël Browne was fully prepared to accept the moral teaching of the Catholic Church. His quarrel was with the 'social teaching' of the Church, not with the 'moral teaching'. Browne's educational background was a-typical of Irish politicians in that he had spent some time at an English public school and was a graduate of Trinity College Dublin. With few exceptions, Whyte's observation is correct: 'Churchmen and Statesmen were moulded by the same culture, educated at the same schools, and quite often related to each other'(Whyte, *ibid*: 366). If Noël Browne was prepared to accept the Church's moral but not social teaching, the leader of Browne's Clann na Poblachta Party, Seán MacBride, as well as the Taoiseach, John A. Costello, were fully committed to accepting the social teaching also. Perhaps the deadliest critic of the Mother and Child proposals was a Limerick layman, Dr James McPolin. In the abortion and divorce referendums of 1983, 1986 and 1995, deeply conservative elements were to be found among the laity. A small group of immensely influential persons, who until recent years were for the most part practising Catholic laymen of conservative outlook, were the judges of the High and Supreme Courts. An important member of this group was Mr Justice George Gavan Duffy, a member of the High Court from 1936-46 and President of the Court from 1946 until 1951. In 1950 he heard the famous Tilson case (see chapter 4 above).

If a strict clerical/lay divide is an oversimplification, so too is the notion of a docile laity, completely accepting of clerical direction. Contrasting the ban on contraception in Church teaching with the widespread use of contraceptives by Catholics, Becker says that 'it illustrates that religious doctrines will be disobeyed when they run strongly against the interests of Church members' (Becker, 1989: xiv). In a survey in rural Limerick in 1964, McNabb arrived at a similar conclusion in a different context (McNabb, 1964). The practice of Catholics, including Irish Catholics, acting according to their own interests, Church teaching notwithstanding, is not new. McCullagh says that in the nineteenth century, 'Irish Catholics were not prisoners of their Church. They were prepared to ignore those aspects of its teaching, such as the encouragement of early marriage, which did not suit them' (McCullagh, 1991: 209). Rather than Catholic ideology shaping Irish society, Irish Catholics in the late nineteenth century used 'selected parts of their Church's teaching to support an ideology which had been chosen for material rather than spiritual reasons' (McCullagh, *ibid*: 209). *À la carte* Catholicism is not an invention of the late twentieth century. Throughout the nineteenth century sections of the laity displayed an independence from their clergy on a number of issues; Daniel O'Connell was an important influence (Kennedy, 1973: 36).

In the 1840s the Young Irelanders sought to put political objectives above sectarian religious ones, while the Fenian leadership argued that 'people must learn to draw a clear line between ecclesiastical authority in spiritual and temporal matters' (Inglis, quoted in Kennedy, 1973: 36). The Fenian Movement was strongly opposed by the Catholic hierarchy, yet it received considerable support among the people, especially among farm labourers and the urban working class. In the early days of the Land League, Michael Davitt, a Fenian, was denounced by a Catholic archbishop. As the Land League grew it gained support not only among the people, but also many priests became supporters, despite continued disapproval by the hierarchy. In 1882, at the behest of the British government, the Pope sent a letter to Irish bishops forbidding Catholics to subscribe to a 'national tribute' to Parnell; Catholics subscribed abundantly. And when Parnell died, Catholics defied their clergy to attend his funeral. 'Symbolic of the relations between the hierarchy and the Parnellites was the clerical ban on attendance at Parnell's funeral in Dublin. In spite of the ban, over 100,000 persons attended, but not a single priest' (Kennedy, *ibid*: 38).

The hierarchy also opposed the wish of the Gaelic League for the introduction of the Irish language as a compulsory subject in schools. In 1909 Fr O'Hickey, Professor of Irish at Maynooth, was dismissed because of his support for compulsory Irish. After the 1916 Rising the hierarchy opposed Sinn Féin, and when in 1918 the British government proclaimed Sinn Féin an illegal organisation, Catholic clergy denounced Sinn Féin. But in the subsequent General Election Sinn Féin won seventy-three seats, Unionists won twenty-three, all in Ulster, and moderate Home Rulers won only six seats. An expression of independence from the hierarchy was made by de Valera himself. In September 1922, following the deaths of Arthur Griffith and Michael Collins, the Bishops issued a Pastoral letter condemning the Republicans' campaign and decided to deny the Sacraments to those who actively resisted the Provisional Government. In later years de Valera claimed that, on the first occasion when he met a Pope face to face, he protested against the course of action taken by the Bishops towards the Republicans. 'I told the Holy Father that I was as loyal a

Catholic as the Bishops – even as the Holy Father himself – and he had no answer' (Farragher, 1984: 140).

Fourteen years after the passing of the Constitution when the Mother and Child crisis climaxed in 1951, it seemed as if the power of the Catholic hierarchy was never greater. By and large secondary education was controlled by religious orders and the ban on the entry of Catholics to Trinity College by the hierarchy remained. Yet Catholics went to Trinity, some with permission, using excuses like failure to satisfy the compulsory Irish requirement for entry to the NUI Colleges. Other examples of Catholics following their own wishes include the occasion in the mid-1950s when Yugoslavia, then behind the Iron Curtain, came to play football in Dublin. The Archbishop of Dublin forbade the people to attend the match, but they went in large numbers. Another example occurred on the small island of Inis Oírr, off the west coast of Ireland in 1960. A ship was wrecked but lives were saved thanks to the islanders. The cargo of the *Plassey* wreck, as it came to be known, included bales of brightly coloured material. The parish priest declared from the pulpit that it was mortally sinful to take any of the cargo. However, during the coming months children all over the island wore brightly coloured items of clothing.

Moral teaching of the Church on the family

The distinction between the moral and the social teaching of the Church was widely drawn before the Second Vatican Council and has persisted in some shape to the present day (Whyte, 1980; Ryan, 1979; Fahey, 1998). In the late 1940s, the President of University College Cork, Alfred O'Rahilly, who was subsequently ordained a priest, published separate volumes on *Moral Principles* and *Social Principles* (O'Rahilly, 1948). Moral teaching referred to right and wrong, whereas social teaching left some room for discussion regarding different forms and methods of social organisation that might be subject to change in changing circumstances. The Church claimed infallibility in regard to its moral teaching that was binding under pain of sin. In *A Catechism of Catholic Doctrine* (1951), published with the *imprimatur* of Archbishop John Charles McQuaid, it is stated: 'The Church is infallible, that is it cannot err, when it teaches doctrines of faith and morals to be held by all the faithful.'

Liam Ryan uses the distinction identifying two fundamental issues, (i) the relationship of the Catholic moral code and the law of the State and (ii) Catholic social teaching on the nature of the State and the rights of voluntary bodies (Ryan, 1979: 3). Ryan says that the first of these involves the problem of law and morality set in a Catholic context, while the second concerns the rise of 'the omnicompetent, benevolent or, perhaps, totalitarian State and the rights of the Church in education, health and welfare' (Ryan, *ibid*: 3). When Ryan turns to 'Moral Questions', he takes up the issue of contraception:

In the halcyon days of the 1930s when governments were ready to employ the power of the State in safeguarding Catholic moral principles, the Criminal Law Amendment Act of 1935 had prohibited the sale and importation of contraceptives. In the McGee Case of 1973 the Supreme Court had declared the ban on importation unconstitutional, and the Church was faced with the prospect of inevitable amending legislation (Ryan, 1979: 11-12).

More recently, sociologist Tony Fahey has written of

> ... the conventional, though rather arbitrary, definition of 'social policy', which links it to questions of distribution of material resources and services in society. It thereby excludes a whole range of social issues (such as family and sexual matters) on which the Catholic Church has for long exerted an influence. In Catholic circles, these latter issues are often classified as 'moral' rather than 'social', and while this is a forced distinction, I will follow it here ... (Fahey, 1998: 1-2).

Following the publication of *Quadragesimo Anno* in 1931, the bishops directed attention towards building up a social order in accordance with Catholic principles. In 1937 a Chair of Sociology and Catholic Action was founded at Maynooth and Father Peter McKevitt was appointed to the Chair; he remained in the position until 1953. McKevitt published widely on social issues, his main work being *The Plan of Society*, based on his sociology course in Maynooth. A number of bishops stand out as key figures in Catholic social thinking from the 1930s to the 1960s, notably Bishop Michael Browne of Galway who chaired the Commission on Vocational Organisation, Dr Cornelius Lucey of Cork who was a member of the Commission on Emigration and who wrote a minority Report, as well as Dr McQuaid. In 1941, McQuaid founded the Catholic Social Services Conference, now called *Crosscare*, and in 1943 the government appointed him Chairman of the Commission on Youth Unemployment. De Valera, in his later years, remarked that what swayed him in favour of McQuaid becoming Archbishop of Dublin 'was his competence in the social question' (Farragher, 1984: 191). Among the next generation, Dr Conway, later Primate of All Ireland, Dr Philbin, a Maynooth Professor and later Bishop of Down and Connor, and Dr Daly, also later Primate, were among the best known. Philbin was an acknowledged source of inspiration for T.K. Whitaker in writing *Economic Development* in the 1950s.

Joe Lee has characterised the concentration of bishops' pastorals 'on the soft sexual option' as morbid: 'A morbid preoccupation with occasions of sin in dance halls would dominate pastoral pronouncements throughout the twenties and thirties' (Lee, 1989: 158-9). The perception remained until the 1960s when one husband expressed the following view in a survey on marriage: 'Sex is the only sin in Ireland. You can go to Confession and say you got drunk or were uncharitable and it doesn't matter. You are just "a hard man". But anything to do with sex, and the gates of hell are wide open for you' (Rohan, 1969: 75). In the early years of the century many pastoral letters of bishops did indeed stress sexual morality, but intemperance was regarded as the biggest pastoral problem. At a time when wages were small and families large, spending the wage packet on drink could mean malnourishment, even starvation, for a family. Here the bishops held common cause with the Labour leader Jim Larkin, who succeeded in bringing to an end the custom whereby dock workers were paid in the public house. Following the Great War, bishops' pastorals spoke with much greater intensity about sexual morality (Whyte, 1980: 27-8). One explanation for this preoccupation with sexual matters is that they are at the centre of family life and that family life was the principal, indeed almost exclusive, concern of the bishops for decades. Commenting on the significance of the Mother and Child affair, the Jesuit sociologist Alexander Humphreys remarked:

> For the fact that it directly concerned family life and that the hierarchy primarily objected to it as investing the State with excessive power over families as well as individuals indicates the main direction in which episcopal influence is exerted. The primary and almost exclusive concern of the bishops has been to preserve Catholic moral standards of family life (Humphreys, 1966: 54-5).

The denunciation of sexual sins was accompanied by an idealisation of the family based on marriage. A not untypical example is found in *The Plain Gold Ring: Lectures on Home,* by Robert Kane, SJ, (Kane, 1910). Kane's book was based on a series of lectures he had given in St Francis Xavier's church in Dublin and in several centres in the UK. The lectures were presented under six headings: 'The Hallowed Bond of Home', 'Husband and Breadwinner', 'Home's Queen and Helpmate', 'Unhappy Homes', 'The Homeless', and 'The Cradle and the Grave'. The book was dedicated, with her permission, to her Royal Highness, Princess Louis Ferdinand of Bohemia. Kane sent a copy of his book to Queen Mary, with an accompanying letter, saying:

> It is well known with what high reverence your majesty cherishes the beloved bonds of Home, and my feeble attempts to vindicate the sacredness of these bonds may not be without interest. In the second place I should wish to express my humble recognition of the glorious fact that, while in our modern world the holiness of marriage and the happiness of home are being so much ignored or even contemned, we have had upon the throne of England three successive Queens, Queen Victoria, Queen Alexandra and Queen Mary whose names will be embalmed in History as ideal types of 'Home's Queen and Helpmate' (Kane papers, Jesuit archives).

In an unusually harsh passage Lee is critical of an idealisation of the family in theory which was unsupported in practice by positive measures:

> Censorship purported to protect the family, but no measures were taken to prevent the continuing dispersal of families ravaged by emigration. Ireland continued to be

characterised by a high incidence of mental disease, by hideous family living conditions in its urban slums, and by a demoralised casual working class, urban as well as rural. Few voices were raised in protest. The clergy, strong farmers in cassocks, largely voiced the concern of their most influential constituents, whose values they instinctively shared and universalised as 'Christian' (Lee, *ibid*: 159).

To judge by the submissions to the Second Commission on the Status of Women in 1990, many women shared the view that, rhetoric notwithstanding, little of a practical nature had been done to support the traditional married 'woman in the home'. The following submission was not untypical:

On behalf of women who marry and give up work to run a home and look after children here we are today twenty or more years later – no jobs, worse still no stamps, no dole – my husband is on pension, I have nothing. Most women of my age are the same: we devote a quarter of our lifetime rearing children and in some cases as in mine grannie and grandad need looking after as well.

We should have some kind of allowance, i.e. we should be allowed weekly stamps – our husbands can claim dole or stamps when work ceases, but married women who devote their lives to full time rearing of their children are too old for the job market, too young for pension; we are in a limbo, 'THE NO NOTHING CLUB' (CSW/SUB/33).

State-Church consensus

From the foundation of the State to the enactment of the 1937 Constitution a broad consensus existed regarding the values that should inform laws and policies. This led to a close similarity, though not identity, between the teaching of the Catholic Church and the laws of the State. The two major political parties, though recently engaged in armed conflict, were at one on these issues:

Mr Cosgrave refused to legalise divorce; Mr de Valera made it unconstitutional. Mr Cosgrave's government regulated films and books; Mr de Valera's regulated dance halls. Mr Cosgrave's government forbade propaganda for the use of contraceptives; Mr de Valera's banned their sale and import. In all this they had the support of the third party in Irish politics, the Labour party (Whyte, ibid: 60).

Despite close correspondence between Church teaching and State laws it would be inaccurate to depict the State in the 1920s and 1930s as merely providing a rubber stamp for the moral teaching of the Catholic hierarchy and clergy. In the middle of the nineteenth century marriage law in England and Ireland began to diverge. The British Parliament specifically exempted Ireland from the innovations concerning marriage and divorce that were introduced into England after 1857. While in that year the *Matrimonial Causes Act* legalised divorce *a vinculo* in England, a series of special Acts from 1844 to 1871 maintained the prohibition on divorce *a vinculo* in Ireland. Private Acts were passed in the United Kingdom for divorces of Irish couples before 1921. It was the introduction in the Senate in 1925 of the standing order to ensure that no further such bills would be passed by the Oireachtas that gave rise to a famous speech by W.B. Yeats in defence of the right to divorce. The Constitution of 1937 fortified the extant legal position by proscribing the introduction of legislation permitting divorce. Even a Papal decree of dissolution of a marriage that is *ratum, non consummatum* (i.e. decree of dissolution of a validly contracted, but unconsummated, marriage), which is sometimes granted by the Church, was not recognised in Irish law. Unless a separate civil nullity decree is sought and obtained, both parties, although canonically free to marry following a church nullity, were not free to marry according to the civil law prior to the passing of the divorce referendum in 1995.

Other differences exist between canon law and civil law in regard to marriage. For example a case occurred in the 1920s in which a man was sentenced to six months imprisonment for bigamy under the civil law although Catholic Church authorities regarded him free to marry. The man, a Catholic, had married in a Protestant church in England in 1922, and shortly afterwards he left his wife. In 1927 he married another woman in a Catholic Church in Ireland. According to the State the true marriage was the first marriage, while according to the Catholic Church the second marriage was the valid one. Another case in the 1940s was similar. In both cases the 'Catholic' marriage was staunchly defended by Dr William Conway, who stated: 'We are here concerned merely with showing that the attitude of the Church in regarding as mere empty form certain ceremonies which the civil law regards as true marriages, is a simple and logical deduction from divinely revealed truth' (Conway, 1946: 361). Conway insisted that 'no contract of marriage by a Catholic shall be valid which is not made in the presence of a duly authorized priest' (Conway, *ibid*: 364), although he did remark in a footnote that 'There are exceptions to this rule in certain very unusual circumstances which need not concern us here'.

Forty years later, in the context of a referendum to introduce divorce, a similar issue regarding the validity of a marriage where a previous valid civil marriage had been annulled by the Catholic Church would lead to a sharp exchange between a delegation from the hierarchy led by Cardinal Tomás Ó Fiaich, successor to Cardinal William Conway as Catholic Primate of All-Ireland, and the then Taoiseach, Dr Garret FitzGerald. In a subsequent letter to Dr FitzGerald in 1990, Cardinal Ó Fiaich was apparently concerned with these 'very unusual circumstances', when he wrote:

The possibilities which we had in mind ranged from a formal declaration at the time of, or even as part of, the ceremony, disclaiming any civil significance, to the conducting of the ceremony in the absence of an episcopally ordained minister, as provided in Canon 1112 (the delegation of a lay person to assist at marriage) or in Canon 1116 (marriage in the presence of witnesses alone) (Ó Fiaich, 1991: 648).

The case of contraception

The background to the introduction by the State of a ban on the sale and importation of contraceptives under the *Criminal Law Amendment Act*, 1935 illustrates the complexity, as distinct from the caricature, of the relationship between clergy and laity and between state law and Catholic moral teaching. As a result of statutes passed for England and Scotland in 1922 and 1928 and for Northern Ireland in 1923, the law with regard to sexual offences against young persons was relatively more lenient in the 26 Counties than in Great Britain and Northern Ireland. On 17 June 1930 a Committee was appointed by the government to consider if the *Criminal Law Amendment Acts* of 1880 and 1885 required modification, and to consider if new legislation was required to deal with juvenile prostitution. The Chairman of the Committee was William Carrigan, KC; the other members were Rev John Hannon, SJ; Very Rev H.B. Kennedy, Dean of Christ Church; Surgeon Francis Morrin; Mrs Jane Power, a Commissioner of the Dublin Union; and Miss V. O'Carroll, Matron of the Coombe Hospital. The Committee thus included one clergyman from the Roman Catholic Church and one from the Church of Ireland; of the four lay members, two were women. The composition of the Committee was well balanced to reflect different perspectives. The Committee viewed itself as operating in a distinct context, emphasising the 'secular aspect of social morality': 'Under the terms of our Reference we had to consider the secular aspect of social morality which it is the concern of the State to conserve and safeguard for the protection and well-being of its citizens' (Carrigan, 1931:4).

The Report of the Carrigan Committee which was completed on 20 August 1931, and which painted a bleak picture of the standard of 'social conduct' in the country, was never released to the public. Carrigan made the general observation that the problems described in the Report were related to indigenous factors and that 'the cure is to be found in home remedies', an expression which would find its echo fifty years later in the remark of Mr Charles Haughey regarding 'an Irish solution to an Irish problem', in the context of the repeal in 1979 of the provisions of the *Criminal Law Amendment Act*, 1935 in relation to contraception. The twenty-one recommendations of the Report included one 'That the sale of contraceptives should be prohibited except in exceptional circumstances' (Carrigan, 1931: 41). Earlier in the Report, Carrigan had recommended in regard to contraceptives 'that the articles in question should be banned by an enactment similar to the Dangerous Drugs Act, 1920' (*ibid*: 37). In an Addendum to the Report, however, Rev John Hannon, SJ, said that he understood the 'exceptions' did not include contraceptive 'appliances':

> I take them [the exceptions] to apply only to certain drugs, which, though commonly used for contraceptive purposes, may also be used for other medicinal ends. The

suggestion is that such drugs should be excluded 'by an enactment similar to the Dangerous Drugs Act, 1920'. That they should not be excluded altogether is due only to the fact that they may be required for medical purposes other than contraception. Hence the 'exceptional conditions' indicated in the 'Summary of Recommendations' are to be taken to mean occasions when drugs commonly used for contraceptive purposes are required by the medical profession for the treatment of disease.

... My object, then, in sending this *addendum* is to state that the Report does not make exception for the sale of contraceptives *as such* in any circumstances (Carrigan, 1931: 45).

The wish to ban contraceptive and abortifacient material was by no means confined to Catholics. On 26 September 1931 Victor Hanna, a wholesale distributor, with premises at 69-70 Mount Street, Dublin, wrote as follows to Mr J.A. O'Rourke, a Dún Laoghaire pharmacist who had shortly before proposed a motion against contraception at a meeting of the Pharmaceutical Society of Ireland: 'No doubt you know I have never stocked such articles while acting as a wholesaler, nor did I ever stock them when acting as a retail chemist. In fact on every possible occasion I always use my influence to discourage the sale in every possible way' (Department of Justice 8/20/1, 26 September 1931).

A copy of Mr Hanna's letter in the files of the Department of Justice is marked in red ink: 'V.E. Hanna *is not* a Catholic.'

At a meeting of the Executive Council on 2 December 1931 the Carrigan Report was referred back to the Minister for Justice with a request for the 'considered views of the Minister'. A general election was called in February 1932 and a new government led by Éamon de Valera took over from Mr Cosgrave's government. Mr James Geoghegan, SC, was appointed Minister for Justice. On 27 October 1932 a 14-page foolscap Report, severely critical of the Carrigan Report, was delivered to the Executive Council. The unequivocal recommendation of the Minister for Justice was that the Carrigan Report should not be published; that it contained sweeping statements against the state of morality in the Saorstát which, even if true, should not be given currency by publication (Department of the President S 5998, 27 October 1932). Regarding contraceptives, the memorandum found 'difficulty in ascertaining the relevance of this subject to the terms of reference' (*ibid*: 13).

The Executive Council decided to set up an all-Party Committee of Deputies to consider on a 'strictly confidential' basis what action should be taken in light of Carrigan. The Committee was chaired by James Geoghegan, Minister for Justice. The Seventh Dáil was dissolved on 22 December 1922 and, following a general election early in 1933, Mr Ruttledge was appointed Minister for Justice, but Mr Geoghegan, still a Dáil deputy, chaired the new Committee of Deputies dealing with the Carrigan Report, as he had done with the similar Committee of the previous Dáil. The Geoghegan Committee recommended a more lenient approach than Carrigan in regard to the age of consent, recommending that it be raised to 17, not 18 years. However, on the matter of contraceptives, *both* Carrigan and Geoghegan were *less* drastic in their recommendations than the subsequent Act. The Geoghegan Committee held that a complete ban on contraceptives might be unduly severe.

When the Criminal Law Amendment Bill had been drafted, a letter dated 13 November 1933 from S.A. [Stephen] Roche, Assistant Secretary, Department of Justice to the Secretary of the Executive Council, was accompanied by a short memorandum, dated 10 November 1933, which referred to 'a difficulty which has arisen'. According to the memo, the Geoghegan Committee recognised that drugs used for contraceptive purposes were also used for other purposes and decided that there should be no prohibition of drugs or substances capable of use for contraception; they limited their recommendations to contraceptive appliances:

> They felt, however, that it would be unduly severe on persons who did not regard the use of such appliances as improper, and who were advised by their Doctors to employ them, to prohibit completely the importation and sale of such appliances. Head 16 [of the proposed Bill] accordingly contemplates that qualified medical practitioners may prescribe and supply such appliances to their patients (Roinn an Taoisigh S 6489 A, 10 November 1933).

Under the proposed Head 16 – in the 1935 Act contraceptives would be dealt with under Head 17 – it was provided that there should be a general prohibition against the sale or distribution, and importation for sale or distribution, of contraceptive appliances. Qualified medical practitioners should have power to prescribe and to supply such appliances to their patients. The quantities required by such practitioners would be imported under licence granted by the Minister for Local Government and Public Health. Registers of supplies received and prescribed would be required to be kept by doctors and should contain full particulars of the persons to whom such appliances were supplied. The registers would be open to inspection by any Medical Inspector duly authorised by the Minister for Local Government and Public Health.

According to the communication from Roche to Geoghegan, when the draft Heads of the Bill were circulated to the Department of Finance and to the Department of Local Government and Public Health, they were agreed to by the Minister for Finance, Seán MacEntee, but an objection to Head 16 was raised by the Minister for Local Government and Public Health, Seán T. Ó Ceallaigh. The Roche memo states:

> The Minister for Local Government and Public Health has, however, informed the Minister for Justice that he is unable to concur in head 16 in so far as it empowers qualified medical practitioners to prescribe and supply the appliances in question to their patients (Roinn an Taoisigh S 6489 A, 10 November 1933).

No explanation is given for the Minister's inability 'to concur in head 16'. However, there is little doubt that there would have been support for Ó Ceallaigh's position in some circles. For example, the Department of Justice files contains a letter from Fr Devane, SJ, to Mr Browne (Domhnall de Brún), Secretary of the Department of Justice, dated 7 June 1933. Devane's letter which cited American and Swedish precedents – in Sweden contraceptives had been banned in 1911 – included the following:

> It may be well to have some such precedents lest some of those who have not studied this difficult problem may think that all this is an affair of prudes. I especially refer to those uneducated Catholics who owing to their reading have become largely mentally paganised and who assume an attitude of – as Catholics – unprincipled superiority and materialist liberalism. We regard contraception from the same angle as we do divorce and abortion as inherently and essentially immoral, and as we do not make provision for those who believe in these latter as justifiable by passing special laws for them so also in the case of contraception. Before the advent of Hitler in Germany there was a determined movement made by some pagan degenerates of the uneducated classes to make abortion legal and books and plays of a propaganda nature were not uncommon. Of course in Russia where materialism is accepted as fundamental Abortion clinics are growing rapidly and the practice is now legalised (Department of Justice 8/20/1, 7 June 1933).

On 14 February 1934 John Duff wrote from the Department of Justice to James Geoghegan communicating the decision of the Executive Council regarding the recommendations of the Committee of Deputies:

> The question of contraceptives seems to have given a very considerable amount of trouble and it is only in the last few days that a decision was finally reached. It has not been communicated to us in writing but it amounts to this: all appliances and substances for contraception are to be definitely prohibited and no exceptions whatsoever are to be made (Department of Justice 8/20, 14 February 1934).

It may be of significance that Duff states that the decision of the Executive Council had not been communicated in writing, as it clearly differed from the recommendation of the Geoghegan all-Party Committee. Time was apparently allowed for the Geoghegan Committee to react because on 19 February 1934 the Minister for Local Government and Public Health, Seán T. Ó Ceallaigh, sent a hand-written note to the Minister for Justice:

> Has that Dáil Committee on Criminal Law Act been summoned yet to reconsider matter of contraceptives?
> If so, has it come to any decision?
> I am being pressed to speed up the matter (Department of Justice 8/20, 19/2/34).

Ruttledge replied on 21 February, saying that the Committee members had been notified, but that he was not sure what they would do. He said that he intended to go ahead with the main bill and that Ó Ceallaigh could sponsor a separate Bill on contraceptives. Four months later, on 15 June 1934, the Criminal Law Amendment Bill was approved by the Executive Council. On Saturday 16 June at 11 am Stephen Roche, Assistant Secretary in the Department of Justice, received a phone call from Seán Moynihan, Secretary to the Department of the President, in which Moynihan said that the Executive Council decided at its meeting the previous evening that before the text was circulated to Deputies, members of the Geoghegan Committee should be given the chance of 'meeting and formally approving' the Bill (Department of Justice 8/20, 16 June 1934).

The Geoghegan Committee met on 19 June in Room 106 in Leinster House to consider the 'White Print of Draft Bill'. Present were: James Geoghegan, Chairman; the Attorney General, Conor Maguire; W. Thrift, Desmond FitzGerald, William Davin, James Dillon and James Fitzgerald-Kenney, i.e. all members were present except Dan Morrissey. Professor Thrift of Trinity College said that Section 17 [regarding contraceptives] did not follow the recommendations of the Committee. He disapproved of the Section. It was finally decided by the Committee not to make any recommendation on the subject to the Executive Council. The way was now clear for the Bill to be introduced into the Dáil and this was done on 21 June 1934.

At the Second Stage of the Bill on 28 June 1934 Deputy FitzGerald-Kenney who, as Minister for Justice, had established the Carrigan Committee, and as an opposition deputy was a member of the Geoghegan Committee, made a statement regarding the all-Party accord on the Bill:

> This Bill is really the work of a Committee, formed from all Parties of this House, which was an entirely non-political Committee. There are certain things in this Bill which I, personally, may not or do not entirely approve of. In a matter of this kind, naturally, it is absolutely impossible to get every mind to agree on every detail. The Bill, however, is the result of the best effort of every member of that committee to bring in the best possible Bill that could be brought in under the circumstances (*PDDE*, 53, 1248-1249).

At the Committee Stage on 1 August 1934, Deputy Rowlette said:

> ... one cannot overlook the fact that there are cases in which contraceptives are employed by many people for what they believe conscientiously to be quite legitimate purposes. ... The problem not infrequently arises where a respectable married woman is in ill-health. She is told that her health or her life may be endangered should she again have to undergo the trials of pregnancy and childbirth. ... In such a case two alternatives are open to her. There is the alternative of abstaining from marital

relations. The other alternative … is the adoption of contraceptive measures to prevent pregnancy occurring (*PDDE*, 53, 2018-2019).

Deputy Rowlette proceeded to argue: 'That is a matter which she herself must decide by her own conscience.' He pointed out that there were a number of people in the country who did not view the use of contraception as contrary to morality, and that, 'It is questionable whether it is either feasible or just to try to enforce moral principles by statute' (*ibid*: 2019-2020). Rowlette concluded that in so far as Section 17 did prevent contraceptive measures, '… it would be likely to lead to an increase in crimes such as criminal abortion and infanticide' (*ibid*: 2020).

On 9 August 1934 the Bill was passed by the Dáil and sent to the Senate. On 12 December the Bill was referred to a special committee. The 9-member committee, chaired by Senator Brown KC, was appointed on 20 December. On a motion proposed by Senator Kathleen Clarke, the committee voted 5-3 in favour of the deletion of Section 17. In the Senate debates Mrs Clarke explained the reasons why she opposed Section 17 (*Seanad Debates*, Vol. 19, 1247 *et seq*). She was strongly supported by Senator Gogarty, but her view did not prevail. Mrs Clarke was the widow of Tom Clarke who had been executed for his part in the 1916 Rising. Following their marriage in 1898 they lived in the United States until 1907 and it was in part as a result of her experience of life there that she opposed Section 17.

On 20 February 1935 the *Criminal Law Amendment Act* passed both Houses of the Oireachtas and the King's Assent was sought from Domhnall ua Buachalla who had been appointed Seanascal,[2] in place of the Governor General, James Mac Neill. On 28 February 1935 the Act was marked 'Sígnighte ag an seanascal' and initialled by the Private Secretary to Domhnall ua Buachalla. The Clerk of the Dáil agreed to accept it provided the Secretary to the Department (of the President of the Executive Council) agreed, which he did.

The fact that Professor Thrift of Trinity College was the one member of the Geoghegan Committee who held out against a total ban on contraceptives pinpoints a difference in view between a Protestant and Roman Catholics on the matter which would reappear twenty years later at the time of the Emigration Commission when differences emerged between Roman Catholic and Church of Ireland clergy on the matter of family size and family planning. The Majority Report maintained that the downward trend in size of family was unwelcome and that every effort should be made to arrest the trend. This view was not shared by all the Commission members. Two clergymen, one Church of Ireland and one Roman Catholic, Rev A.A. Luce and Rev C. Lucey, held quite different views from each other. Dr Luce favoured smaller families, while Dr Lucey did not.

In a Reservation to the *Report* Rev Luce states:

A temporary halt in the rate of natural increase is necessary at the present juncture. … The Report (para. 166) *suggests* the right inference, but fails to adopt it. The right inference is that the Quiverful families of Victorian days are not, in general, possible or desirable today ... I dissociate myself from the unqualified and unargued condemnation of contraceptives (paras. 166 and 458) (Luce, 1954: 230-31).

Dr Lucey thought differently:

The many spiritual and cultural advantages of family life and the intrinsic worth of human beings hardly need to be pointed out in a Christian society and although the trend towards smaller families has not been as pronounced here as in most other countries, it is imperative that attention should be drawn to it and every effort made to arrest and reverse it (Lucey, 1954(a): 340-41).

The path towards the repeal of the ban on the sale and importation of contraceptives did not come to an end until 1979 when, as a result of the McGee case, the sale of contraceptives to married people was permitted (see Chapter 9). In 1985 the marriage limitation was abolished, although an age minimum of 18 years was retained, which does not, however, seem to have been enforced. It is the judgement of Garret FitzGerald that the extent to which Catholic Church teaching influenced State policies turned out to be counter-productive. He argues that the Catholic Church held back change in a way that built up pressures which eventually made gradual change impossible and by implication obstructed the preparation of some kind of appropriate response to change:

But what was not foreseen was if you build up pressure behind a dam, and the dam bursts, you get a flood whereas previously you would have had a stream and the flood destroys in the process, and that's what has happened. I can see why that was not foreseen by the Church, and it wasn't, certainly not, by the State either. But it has created a very real problem for us.[3]

FitzGerald believes that the problem was intensified by the fact that the 'dam burst' coincided with the Church's holding the position on contraception that it did in *Humanae Vitae,* a position which FitzGerald regards as 'non-credible in rational terms': 'And once the Church took up a position which was non-credible in rational terms its authority over the whole sexual area disintegrated. At the worst moment for us, when pressure on the dam was great already, you suddenly put a hole in the dam. ... Everything fell.'[4]

It is the view of FitzGerald that:

... the extent to which the Irish value system depended on the Catholic Church and had no great independent backing in civil society and no rational backing, turned out to be a major problem. When Church authority disappeared a rational basis for some ordered way of controlling sexual relationships wasn't there. Where there has been reliance on Catholic teaching to inform legislation, it can be argued that, as that reliance wanes a problem arises as to what alternative values can or should inform legislation. Resolving this problem is not helped by positing 'rational' and Catholic values as opposed alternatives when in fact Catholic values have in large measure been interpretations of rational values, sometimes perhaps, over-elaborated.[5]

In the event, by the time *Humanae Vitae* was published in 1968, a sea change had taken place among clergy and laity. By degrees the laity came to disregard the encyclical while the bulk of the clergy fell silent.

Authoritarianism and the drift in behaviour

Ireland in the early twentieth century was a land where people appeared to know their place – masters and servants, teachers and pupils, parents and children, shepherds and flock. Obedience to the clergy was stressed, but frequently it was combined with a genuine closeness between priests and people, a closeness that reached back to the penal days and was cemented by the fact that the priests were drawn from the people, from the small peasant farmers and from the bigger farmers as well as from the business classes. In the political sphere young men in particular showed, that by joining politically motivated secret organisations proscribed by their priests, they had not abandoned their independence. Women would in time register their independence in another sphere, that of the family, and in issues related to contraception, birth outside marriage, and abortion.

The authoritarian strain in Irish culture that permeated the religious sphere and was evident in father-son relationships, in pupil-teacher relationships as well as in priest-people relationships was by no means uniquely Irish. In France, for example, the fear of family decline was widespread among sociologists including Comte, Le Play, de Tocqueville and Durkheim. It was believed that paternal authority was eroded by State intervention and the full restoration of patriarchal authority, which had been lost in the wake of the Revolution, was recommended (Gauthier, 1996: 22). Le Play was a proponent of the larger patriarchal peasant family model. The farm wife tended to be subordinate to her husband, because the small farm economy depended on centralised control, while children were subordinate to both parents. In some Irish households the woman might be the dominant partner, in which case a son's name might be linked to that of his mother rather than to that of his father, as in the classic case of Jimín Mháire Thaidhg (Ó Danachair, 1985: 109). But this was the exception and in general the male heads of families were the true 'local authorities'. Paramount among the values and beliefs of rural dwellers was the desire to keep the farm – the basis for economic survival – intact. This was matched only by belief in Catholic Church tenets, deeply embedded in historical tradition, because they had

... been accepted by generations of countrymen – and indeed by virtually all Irishmen – as supreme intrinsic values and goods in their own right. These are the Catholic beliefs and values which make up his religion and which have such a constant modifying effect upon the organization of his family and community that without them the Irish countryman and his family can never be fully understood (Humphreys, 1966: 23-4).

The effects of religious tradition on behaviour in Ireland have never been systematically studied. Humphreys, at the time of his study, 1949-51, found that secularism did have some influence on the countryman but that much reliance was placed on the teaching power of the Church as voiced by the clergy, with much emphasis on formal religious and sacramental activity. The countryman, '... inclines to a jaundiced view of sex and a generally ascetic outlook which places a high premium on continence, penance and, in most spheres of life, on abstemiousness' (Humphreys, *ibid*: 260). While Arensberg and Kimball attribute the countryman's attitude to sex to the structure of life in rural Ireland, Humphreys adds in Church influence. The first generation of urban dwellers tenaciously held to the faith of their rural fathers and the basic set of religious values of the countryman survived the transition to the city.

The breakdown of social and family bonds during the civil war contributed to the subsequent assertion of 'the immense authority of the Church on the majority in the Free State in the area of faith and morals' (MacCurtain, 1989: 243). The influence of the Church was rendered the stronger because of the absence of an educated laity. The Catholic Church, indirectly through its influence on the Catholic majority and directly through its influence upon Catholic members of government, 'Is without peer in terms of power' (Humphreys, *ibid*: 52-3). Statements issued by the hierarchy reflected the tone of the papacy. Professor Liam Ryan of Maynooth writes:

With Leo XIII, with Pius XI and Pius XII one is never allowed to forget that they are laying down the law. One finds exactly the same admonitory tone in social and political statements of Irish bishops of the period; and the message too is the same – that mankind goes astray even economically and politically whenever it ceases to look to the Church for guidance (Ryan, 1979: 6).

According to sociologist Tom Inglis, the system of primary education launched in the nineteenth century under which the Church became the main provider of education instilled a sense of discipline:

But because the Catholic church was the means behind this new system of moral discipline and social control, Irish Catholics became socialised into an ideology of spirituality, frugality and celibacy. This ideology was maintained through practices which centred on individuals surrendering to the interests of Church, family and community, and through an uncritical commitment to traditional rules and regulations (Inglis, 1987: 5).

When Pearse wrote about the Irish education system, he called it a 'murder machine'. The prevailing educational ethic was based on criticism, fault-finding, correction and chastisement. He suggested that the 'Murder Machine' appealed to certain members of the Catholic hierarchy, pointing out that when John Dillon declared that one of the first tasks, if Home Rule were achieved, would be a recasting of the education system, 'The declaration alarmed the Bishop of Limerick, always suspicious of Mr Dillon, and he told that statesman in effect that the Irish education system did not need recasting – that all was well there' (Pearse, 1912:10). In an article in the *Irish Review* in 1913 Pearse tried to bring together the Church view as expressed by Dr O'Dwyer and the political view expressed by John Dillon. He argued that Dr O'Dwyer was really concerned to maintain the machinery of the system, or at least a portion of that machinery, and he could accept that, but the machine needed to be imbued with a new spirit, as Mr Dillon appeared to suggest. Above all Pearse wanted freedom in a renewed Irish education system: 'Freedom to the individual school, freedom to the individual teacher, freedom as far as may be to the individual pupil. Without freedom there can be no right growth; and education is properly the fostering of the right growth of a personality' (*ibid*: 13).

To the ears of a bishop of a recently Romanised and rule-oriented Church, this surely sounded alarm bells. If education fostered freedom would the laity stray away from the rules and go out of control? The authoritarian strain in Irish culture is no mystery to Pearse. It derived from an education system in which the teacher sought to dominate his pupils by the imposition of his will on them. The teacher in turn was constrained by a system of competitive examinations with payments made on the basis of results. The hierarchy was not unsympathetic to this system – some of them were the successful products of the system – as it encouraged obedience to authority and snuffed out freedom of enquiry. While Pearse sought to inspire and encourage individuality through education, the hierarchy sought conformity. Bishops' pastorals issued after Independence were filled with expressions of dismay regarding the low moral fibre of the people, and the need to reinforce parental authority in face of onslaughts from indecent influences:

The bishops found cause for dismay in many different areas. Their pastorals abound in denunciations of intemperance, gambling, perjury, crimes of violence – many other evils. But there was one sphere in particular which aroused their alarm. By far the most prominent topic in their published statements was the decline in sexual morality (Whyte, 1980: 24).

The media were a root cause of the bishops' worries. The cinema, and especially certain English newspapers whose circulation was increasing in Ireland in the 1920s, were all suggesting new ideas and lifestyles and behaviour to a hitherto more sheltered flock. Occasions of sin were multiplying and concern regarding Irish moral decline in the 1920s and 1930s was by no means exclusive to the Catholic clergy. *The Irish Times* expressed alarm that the reputation of Ireland for 'her men's chivalry and her women's modesty' was in danger:

> There is irony in the fact that at this very time, when the Free State Government has declared war on English newspapers, the Irish newspapers are forced, almost daily, to touch matters which are both wicked and disgusting. We have published during recent weeks reports of trials, and statements by judges and magistrates, which suggest that in many parts of the twenty-six counties, especially in the South and West, the standards of sexual morality are lamentably low.
>
> The abominable crime of rape figures often in the police reports. Infanticide is common – one judge has described it as 'a national industry' – and the reports of cases in which unmarried mothers have been brought to trial for this crime indicate a general looseness of manners, a contempt of moral decencies, that are a wholly new feature of Irish life (*The Irish Times*, 2 March, 1929).

The Irish Times also deplored the softening of parental control. Prior to the passing of the *Guardianship of Infants Act* in the UK in 1927, parents could forbid their children under the age of 21 to marry. Under the 1927 Act, minors desiring to marry, but failing to win their parents' consent, could summon their parents to a police court and compel them to show cause for their refusal. *The Irish Times* expressed concern that Ireland should not stray down that particular path:

> In England as in Ireland, thoughtful people lament the decline of parental authority. It is being demonstrated everywhere by the lax conduct of boys and girls, by deplorable marriages, by the pitiful records of police courts. In such conditions the burden of English parenthood will not be relieved by the Guardianship of Infants Act, which the wisdom of Parliament has added to the Statute Book ... it seems that parental control over minors has become a dead-letter in the most important affair of life. ... We hope and believe that in this matter the Oireachtas will not imitate the mother of Parliaments (*The Irish Times*, 17 March 1927).

The Carrigan Report also attributed the decline in the standard of social conduct to a loss of parental control (Carrigan, 1931: 12), while according to Archbishop Gilmartin of Tuam, 'Parental control had been relaxed, and fashions bordering on indecency had become a commonplace' (Whyte, *ibid*: 25). The most energetic criticisms probably emanated from Bishop O'Doherty of Galway. In one of the bishop's sermons he deplores the craze for dancing, and advises fathers: 'If your girls do not obey you, if they are not in at the hours appointed, lay the lash upon their backs. That was the good old system, and that should be the system today' (Whyte, *ibid*: 26). Such a statement might be dismissed as the observation of an eccentric were it not the serious advice of the Bishop of Galway who was reflecting, if in somewhat extreme form, the general teaching of a hierarchy that was oriented towards the exercise of power, authority and control. The darker side to this type of mentality, and the purveying of such a violent approach to obedience, was that it led to actual physical cruelty, falsely exerted, and justified as duty.

The economic growth of the 1960s brought options for children who were no longer so heavily dependent on the family farm and its code of conduct; with increased educational and job opportunities, young people could assert much greater independence from their families. By 1973 one of the most enlightened members of the hierarchy, Bishop Birch of Kilkenny, could write:

> ... The inherited idea of parental authority over subordinates, wife, children, servants ... is disappearing, or more correctly, is already gone. According to this the husband was the head of the house; wife and children were totally subject to him; the man was much nearer to a dictator than a partner in the home. ... Families are becoming more democratic; and democracy implies difference of views, conflict and compromise (Birch, 1973: 490).

Bishop Birch pointed to other changes in families. There was a disturbing increase in marital desertion and 'increasing numbers of demands by Irish husbands and wives for decrees of nullity' (Birch, *ibid*: 485). Wives and mothers as well as children were gaining freedom, and trying to restore the social customs of the past, which were in many ways faulty, would be intolerable. The wife 'will not be the manual drudge she was' (Birch, *ibid*: 487): 'For many families in Ireland life is not based on a family business, farming or trading. The wife may work outside the home. If she works at home, she expects similar payment for her share. This is a great change which is being reflected in marriage' (Birch, *ibid*: 487)

Distrust of the laity

Allied to authoritarianism was a distrust of the laity, unless carefully supervised. Examples of lack of trust of the laity are to be found in the attitude of some of the hierarchy to the Legion of Mary (Ó Broin, 1982), the ban on the attendance of Catholics at Trinity College, and the attitude towards lay teachers in schools. Regarding the ban on attendance by Catholics at Trinity College, which lasted until the early 1970s, not only could the laity not be trusted 'against the danger of perversion', the notion that lay Catholics might actually have an active role in evangelisation was not within the imagination of at least some Church authorities.

The lack of trust in lay teachers is made clear by the attitude of members of the hierarchy to the vocational education system that was outside Church control. Although the vocational schools were providing for the least well-off and were directed towards supporting small family farm life, as well as providing educational escape routes from rural Ireland, they were heavily criticised by Church authorities. Robert O'Connor who spent years as a vocational school teacher writes:

> Vocational education ... was strongly opposed by the Catholic Church and its ally, the *Irish Independent* which in leading articles invariably referred to the vocational schools as 'godless' institutions. The Commission on Vocational Organisation chaired by Bishop Michael Browne of Galway was very scathing about the system. ... The Commission's Report when it came out reflected the bishop's views (O'Connor, nd. 3: 6-7).

Nowhere is the lack of trust in the Catholic laity by Church authorities in Ireland more potently illustrated than by the attitude of two Archbishops of Dublin to the great modern lay movement founded within the Archdiocese of Dublin – the Legion of Mary. In its *Handbook*, the Legion states that it is

> ... at the disposal of the bishop of the diocese and the parish priest for any and every form of social service and Catholic action which these authorities may deem suitable to legionaries and useful for the welfare of the Church. Legionaries will never engage in any of these services whatsoever in a parish without the sanction of the parish priest or of the ordinary (Legion of Mary, 1993:11-12).

Yet the Legion of Mary met with clerical obstacles in the Archdiocese of Dublin in which it was founded. In his biography of the Legion founder, Frank Duff, León Ó Broin who knew Duff intimately, shows that the early development of the Legion was hindered by the withholding of approval by Archbishop Byrne. While Dr Byrne had 'tolerated' activities carried on by the Legion, and a number of priests worked with the Legion in their personal capacities, Duff encountered difficulties in obtaining spiritual directors for Praesidia (Legion branches) due to the lack of formal approval (Ó Broin, *ibid*: 32). The Archbishop also refused permission to have a Retreat in the Legion-run Morning Star hostel for its 'down and out' residents.

Fortunately for the Legion, and for the subsequent history of the Church, Duff had a powerful lay ally in the President of the Executive Council, W.T. Cosgrave, who opened doors for him with Cardinal Bourne of Westminster, with the nunciature in Dublin, and in Rome. Fortunately also, Duff found another powerful ally in Dr Joseph MacRory, the Bishop of Down and Connor, whose diocese embraced the city of Belfast, and who was later to become Archbishop of Armagh. In 1927, Dr MacRory gave *carte blanche* for the Legion to go ahead in Belfast. Despite Duff's enthusiasm for the appointment of Dr McQuaid as successor to Dr Byrne, trouble soon flared under the new régime, this time in the form of censorship of the contents of *Maria Legionis*, the journal of the Legion of Mary. The problem occurred over the publication of an account of legionary work in the famed 'Monto' area of Dublin. A series of articles appeared under the title 'Bentley Place', written by Duff. According to León Ó Broin, who was editor of *Maria Legionis* at the time, Duff made a personal appeal to complete the series, 'but was given a blank refusal'. As a consequence the full story of legionary work in the prostitution heartland of Dublin would not appear in English until published in book form in America by the Montfort Press in 1961, under the title *Miracles on Tap* (Duff, 1961). It was not without significance that sexual matters were at stake. The laity could not be trusted to read such accounts, or perhaps it could not be admitted that such activities existed in Dublin. It is significant that in a Survey of *Religion, Culture and Values* in Ireland in the 1960s, an area of criticism existed among Catholics with third level education regarding the manner in which the lay potential in the Church was ignored by the clergy (Biever, 1976: 444-5).

Attendance at the sacraments

In Ireland emphasis on formal religious and sacramental activity has been strong, with practice of religion closely equated with attendance at Sunday Mass. According to the Catechism, 'the whole liturgical life of the Church revolves around the Eucharistic sacrifice and the sacraments'. There are seven sacraments: Baptism, Confirmation, Eucharist, Penance, Anointing of the Sick (formerly known as Extreme Unction), Holy Orders and Matrimony. The Catechism stresses the role of the priest:

> The ordained priesthood guarantees that it really is Christ who acts in the Sacraments through the Holy Spirit for the Church. ... The ordained minister is the sacramental bond that ties the liturgical action to what the apostles said and did and, through them, to the words and actions of Christ, the source and foundation of the sacraments (CCC: 257).

Reception of the Sacraments has ensured a priestly presence at many of the key lifetime events – events which are also *family* events. Sociologist Máire Nic Ghiolla Phádraigh says, 'Eucharist is also celebrated at major rites of passage which are essentially family occasions. Secular funerals are very rare events' (Nic Ghiolla Phádraigh, 1995). Attendance at daily Mass had, for many housewives, a valuable social dimension associated with neighbourhood communication. In the days before telephones were widespread a chat after Mass allowed time to catch up with local and family news. It is safe to say that a majority of Irish people were born in a Catholic hospital, baptised in a Catholic church, educated in a Catholic school, married in the presence of a Catholic priest and will be buried following a Catholic funeral. From the cradle to the grave the priest or bishop is a key figure. The vast majority of Irish families for much of this century could identify with the Dunn family:

The Dunns are deeply conscious that their family is a religious society of a sort. It began as such when Joan and John were married at a nuptial Mass in the local parish, fully aware that the contract they made was a religious and, indeed, a sacramental one. As the children were born, they were incorporated into the religious life of the family by the rite of baptism. And each major stage of their physical and social growth has been made to coincide with religious development in the reception of the Sacraments of Penance (their first Confession), first Communion and Confirmation (Humphreys, *ibid*: 104).

The Sacraments are generally conferred in public. They are 'outward signs of inward grace'. In the early 1960s, an American Jesuit, B.F. Biever, confirmed the importance of outward signs of respectability in Irish society (Farmar, 1991: 154). The penalty for non-attendance at Mass, especially in a small rural community, could come via isolation and condemnation. Non-attendance at mass was very visible: 'the black sheep is very conspicuous in the country' (Murphy, 1952). Furthermore, there was the threat of spiritual condemnation for failure to partake of the Sacraments. Sean O'Faolain in a famous, if harsh, judgement, declares:

> The Maynooth Parliament holds a weapon which none of the other institutions mentioned holds: the weapon of the sacraments. ... But when the Catholic Church, through its representatives, speaks, he (the Taoiseach) realises, and the Roman Catholic public realises, that if they disobey they may draw on themselves this weapon whose touch means death (O'Faolain, 1951).

The reasons why Irish people partook of the sacraments to such an extent cannot be explained by the desire for public respectability. Traditionally Irish people were proud of being Catholics, having received their beliefs from ancestors who had endured the oppression of the penal laws. At government level, where a majority of the Cabinet were also committed Catholics, the public dimension of religious observance was important. In dealing with the Vatican in the period preceding the introduction of the 1937 Constitution, the Secretary of the Department of Foreign Affairs, Joseph Walshe, was instructed to stress that 'in practice the Catholic Church will be the Church associated with the State on public occasions':

> In the past ministers in a body have annually attended Mass on St Patrick's Day at the Catholic Pro-Cathedral; the Government and members of Parliament have attended a special Mass on each occasion in which a new Parliament meets after the dissolution (from *pro memoria* given to Walshe for use in discussions in the Vatican, quoted in Keogh, 1995: 134).

This practice came to an end in 1997 when, at the suggestion of President Mary Robinson, an Ecumenical Service was held in Dublin Castle for the opening of the 38th Dáil. Following President McAleese's election as President a Mass which she attended was celebrated by the Archbishop of Dublin in Westland Row Church.

Changing public opinion

Pope Pius XII once remarked that there had to be a place for public opinion in the Church. His remark must be set in the context of a Church where the bishops and priests were seen as presenting rules and regulations for a compliant flock. In an interesting insight into the way in which lay Catholics in rural Ireland viewed the priest, just at the end of Pius XII's reign, McNabb notes the following:

> People pay heed to his advice and wishes. It is very exceptional for them to oppose him openly. There is a limitation to the priest's range of power in as much as he cannot go against the preferred tendencies: these would derive from traditions of inheritance, marriage and education (McNabb, 1964: 196).

Challenges to the primacy of the Church in determining behaviour in the family and sexual spheres came from the mass media – newspapers, radio, cinema and television, but it is difficult to measure in any precise way the shift away from Church influence. One approach is to examine market research and attitude survey work. The early 1960s saw the flowering of a number of market research and public opinion polling organisations. Irish Marketing Surveys, Lansdowne and the Market Research Bureau of Ireland (MRBI), were the leading organisations and the leading players included John Meagher, John Lapère, Leslie Collins and Jack Jones. While much of the work was product and service oriented, political polling became a regular feature. Questions on social/moral issues have tended to be fairly superficial in many general surveys, without great breadth or depth. Generally one or two questions in the social/moral area would be included within a mixed bag of questions, mostly in the context of when the media deem a question, or questions, to be topical. Some relevant findings emerged from polls conducted by MRBI in 1983 and 1987 for their twenty-first and twenty-fifth anniversaries. Perception of sources of influence was assessed at two levels:

(i)   in *general terms*, by enquiring which of four groups, home and family, the media, the Church or government and politicians, had the most influence on the respondents' thinking and opinions.

(ii) in *specific terms* where respondents were asked to relate the extent to which each specific group most influenced their thinking on a range of subjects which included marriage and family life, divorce, abortion and the Northern Ireland problem.

Home and family were still by far the most important sources of influence, but their importance dropped sharply between 1983 and 1987. By contrast, the perceived influence of the media rose markedly, with the influence of the Church falling slightly (MRBI: 1983, 1987). With regard to the *specific* issues of marriage and family, divorce and abortion, the influence of the Church was much stronger than overall. In regard to divorce, 40 per cent regarded the Church as the major influence on their thinking in both 1983 and 1987. On the subject of divorce, an inkling of future change was to be found in the first major survey of Irish values and attitudes which was carried out as part of the European Value Systems Study (Fogarty *et al*, 1984). It found that although there was strong support for the institution of marriage among the Irish, '... they increasingly reject the principle that marriage must be for life' (Fogarty, *ibid*: 40).

Both the hierarchy, through their research unit at Maynooth, and CORI (Conference of Religious of Ireland, formerly CMRS, Conference of Major Religious Superiors), have undertaken a number of surveys. The research unit at Maynooth undertakes regular surveys of Mass attendance, while CORI, then CMRS, were involved with the first European Value Study in Ireland (Fogarty *et al*, 1984). In addition individual religious orders have had a variety of surveys carried out, generally unpublished. Overall it may be said that there is an increased awareness, and utilisation of, opinion polling in Church circles, while at the same time the influence of the Church on thinking and opinions has declined since 1980. Until around 1990, Ireland remained, according to surveys, a country with a uniquely high record of Mass attendance among the countries of Europe. The *European Values Survey*, 1990 registered only a slight drop in the numbers claiming to attend Mass at least once each week, from 87 to 85 per cent since 1980. With the resounding success of a referendum to insert a ban on abortion in the Constitution in 1983 and the defeat of the first referendum to remove the constitutional ban on divorce in 1986, it might even have seemed possible that there was a strengthening of attitudes which coincided with Church teaching. However, the election of Mary Robinson, pioneer of liberal causes, as President of Ireland in November 1990, indicated that the tide was flowing in the liberal direction.

The years immediately following Mrs Robinson's election saw a series of highly publicised scandals among the clergy, generally associated with sexual matters, but which included financial and managerial deceits also. It was against this background that an MRBI poll for the *The Irish Times* in December 1996 found that weekly Mass attendance had fallen to 66 per cent of those polled compared with 85 per cent six years earlier in 1990. Looking to the likely future of the Church in twenty years time, less that 30 per cent believed that the great majority of the people would be practising Catholics, while 70 per cent believed that the majority would be Catholic only in name. In February 1998 a *Prime Time*, RTÉ/MRBI poll showed a further drop in weekly Mass attendance to 60 per cent, with the lowest attendance rates in the most economically deprived areas. A majority surveyed disagreed with official church teaching on contraception, divorce, priestly celibacy and women priests.

In 2000, the distinguished sociology professors and priests Andrew Greeley and Conor Ward published an analysis based on the religion module of the International Social Survey Programme carried out in some twenty-five countries including Ireland in 1998. The authors concluded: 'If attitudes to sex and authority are important indicators of Christianity, then religion among the Irish is in decline' (Greeley and Ward, 2000: 582). They found that the proportions of the Irish people thinking that premarital sex, extra-marital sex, same sex relationships and abortion when there is a strong chance of a serious defect in the child, are always wrong, declined significantly since the previous survey in 1991. However, they also found that with regard to acceptance of core teachings, for example on Mary, the Irish continued to be deeply religious (*ibid*: 582).

8

Catholic Social Thought and the Family

The Catholic social movement, focused on the reconciliation of social divisions and the reformulation of social patterns which emerged in the wake of industrialisation, was slow to develop in Ireland by comparison with continental countries such as Germany, France, Holland or Belgium. None of these countries had a social problem so profound and so unique as the Irish land struggle that engaged the energies of the people, of many of the priests, and of some of the bishops. Following the settlement of the land question with the *Irish Land Act* (the *Wyndham Act)* in 1903, interest began to turn towards the 'social question'. The Great War in which thousands of Irishmen fought and died, the Rising of 1916, and the events that unfolded subsequently, interrupted concentration on the social question. The objective of this chapter is to determine whether a body of Catholic social thought relevant in particular to the family existed, how it evolved and what, if any, was its influence on policy in Ireland.

Social thought

In the late nineteenth century in the United Kingdom, of which Ireland then formed a part, at the time *Rerum Novarum* (1891) was published, the dominant ideology was economic liberalism. Socialism was waiting in the wings. But reality was more complex. During the so-called age of *laissez-faire*, governments in Britain displayed quite a vigorous concept of economic and social responsibility by introducing Factory Acts, Poor Law Acts, Railway Regulation Acts, the Bank Charter Act and Land Acts – to mention only a few. *Rerum Novarum* provided a critique of both socialism and capitalism; while it defended the right to private property, it strongly defended the rights of workers to a living wage. Forty years later, *Quadragesimo Anno* proposed the principle of 'subsidiarity', of the state granting help (*subsidium*) to, but not replacing, smaller bodies, foremost of which was the family. Another forty years later, when *Humanae Vitae* was published, a period of unequalled expansion of state activity in the realm of family life in Ireland was about to commence. It seemed a long way from the original preoccupation with 'the living wage' as the concern of the employer.

Joe Lee has commented trenchantly on the absence of thinking on economic and social policy among the post-Independence generation:

Those responsible for the formulation of social policy had little contact with the supply of ideas in Ireland, much less in the wider world. Catholic thinking, or assumed Catholic thinking, or selected Catholic thinking, may have influenced some. However, what is striking about social policy in the first generation of independence is not the demand for Catholic principles among policy-makers, but the general indifference in policy formulation to any social thought, Catholic or otherwise (Lee, 1989: 578).

Lee's judgement is severe when one thinks not only of the rudimentary state-building that preoccupied the minds and energies of that generation, but also of the work of bodies such as the Tariff Commission 1926, the Currency Commission 1927, the Poor Relief Commission 1925-26 and the Report of Inquiry into the Housing of the Working Classes of the City of Dublin, 1939-43, all of which were reflective, analytical documents. The Report of the Banking Commission (1938) was teeming with ideas. It even included a note by Bishop MacNeely and Professor George O'Brien on the relevance of papal encyclicals to the terms of reference of the Commission. Indeed a case could be made that the thought and analysis contained in some of these early commissions, including the Commission on Emigration (1954), has not been surpassed. In the first generation of Independence, although the civil service was small in numbers, it contained men of exceptional intellect, including Joseph Brennan, J. J. McElligott, Maurice Moynihan and Stephen Roche. The man primarily responsible for the establishment of the new civil service was Sir Cornelius Gregg. He and his private secretary, Frank Duff, were both past pupils of Blackrock College. All of these men were Catholics, unlikely to be indifferent to papal teaching in policy formulation. Brennan, McElligott and other leading civil servants at the time maintained the British tradition whereby civil servants did not publish their ideas in articles. Rather they put their ideas into draft legislation. Several priests also contributed to social thinking, through their writings, and also through participation in Commissions of Inquiry. Fr Canavan, SJ, chaired the Commission on Housing in Dublin, Dr McQuaid chaired the Commission on Youth Unemployment and Bishop Browne chaired the Commission on Vocational Organisation. Nor were Ministers devoid of ideas. In his obituary of Patrick Hogan, George O'Brien, Professor of Political Economy at University College Dublin, wrote that 'the economic policy of his party was inspired principally by his ideas' (O'Brien, 1936: 353). Hogan started from the assumption that agriculture was, and would remain, the most important industry in the Free State.

O'Brien served on three Commissions which considered different aspects of Irish agricultural problems – the Commission on Agriculture 1922, the Economic Committee 1928 and the Derating Committee 1929; in addition he served on the Fiscal Inquiry Committee 1923, which had the agricultural issue in the background. O'Brien makes the telling point that the abstention of the anti-Treatyites handicapped debate, and thus the teasing out of ideas, 'When Parliamentary criticism and discussion would have been useful, the main opposition party abstained from the Dáil' (O'Brien, 1962: 12). Credit for the survival of the State in its early difficult years is attributed by O'Brien to a number of exceptionally clever and courageous ministers, to the loyalty of the Civil Service, and to members of important Commissions set up to examine the difficult economic problems of the new State, but he gives the greatest credit to the ordinary people who got on with their daily work.

Because the first Pope to take up the 'social question' was Leo XIII, it should be no surprise that the Jesuits were among the foremost thinkers on the matter in Ireland. Leo XIII, who became Pope in 1877 at the age of sixty-seven, had been sent, when only eight years old, to the Jesuit College at Viterbo, and at fourteen years to the Roman College, again under the Jesuits. In Ireland, a group of Jesuits, notably Fr Lambert McKenna, author of a book on James Connolly, became increasingly concerned with the conditions of labour. In 1912, following the foundation of *Studies*, serious articles relating to the relevance of Catholic thinking to social and economic concerns began to appear on a regular basis. The very first issue of *Studies* contained an article entitled 'The Future of Private Property', by the poet-professor Tom Kettle, who would die at the Somme. From the early 1920s *Studies* 'became increasingly concerned with the problems thrown up by self-government' (Meenan, 1962: 1). Debate was overtaken by events which culminated in the strike led by Jim Larkin, the Lock-out of 1913, and the labelling of Larkin as a communist. A particular concern of the Catholic social movement was the continued adherence of the working class to the Church in view of the competing attractions of socialism and communism.

Catholic thinkers, including Robert Kane, SJ, believed that socialism posed a threat to the family. Kane, a well known preacher, who became blind shortly after ordination, was a nephew of Sir Robert Kane, author of *The Industrial Resources of Ireland* (Kane papers, Jesuit archives). Kane's Lenten lectures in Gardiner Street Church in 1910 provoked a response from Connolly, in a pamphlet entitled *Labour, Nationality and Religion.* In denouncing socialism, Kane claimed:

> Socialism would ruin the home firstly, because it would rob the father of the home, of his God-given right to be master in the citadel of his own home; secondly, because it would banish home's queen from what ought to be her kingdom; it would break the marriage bond which alone can safeguard the innocence and stability of the home; it would make the wife of the home practically a tenant at will; thirdly, because it would kidnap the child (Quoted in Connolly, 1910: 30).

In a further passage in his Lenten Lectures, Kane expressed ideas which, unwittingly, as Connolly suggested, had much in common with socialism:

> The reason of the family is in the insufficiency of man alone to secure the right development of human nature. The reason of civil society is in the insufficiency of the

family alone to attain that fuller perfection of human nature which is the heritage of its birth, but which it can only reach through the help of many homesteads united into one common weal. Hence, civil society is only intended by Nature to be the helper of the family, not its master; to be its safeguard, not its destroyer; to be in a right true sense its servant, but in no sense its owner (Quoted in Connolly, *ibid*).

Connolly claims, with irony, to have read over the passage several times to satisfy himself that it was not a quotation from some socialist writer. Both Kane and Connolly agree on the 'insufficiency of the family alone', but differ on the implications for the State. Connolly sees that 'insufficiency' as conferring a duty on the State 'to provide for the care, education and physical and mental development of the child', while Kane views the State as a threat to the independence of the family.

Two concepts were central in Catholic social thought on the family in the early twentieth century: the 'living wage' and 'subsidiarity', identified respectively with the Papal encyclicals *Rerum Novarum* (1891), and *Quadragesimo Anno* (1931). Both concepts support the independence of the family unit and resistance from state 'interference'. In the second half of the century a marked shift occurred, reflected in the views of the Irish hierarchy, from condemnation of state 'interference' in the family to calls upon the state to guarantee a minimum income for every household, regardless of circumstances. This shift in thinking was underpinned by the Encyclical of Pope John XXIII, *Mater et Magistra*, 1961, which provided the first comprehensive treatment by a Pope of social issues since *Quadragesimo Anno*.

A living wage

The determination of the wages of the new property-less proletariat was the burning social issue in industrialising societies in the nineteenth century and provided the backdrop for *Das Kapital*. The conventional wisdom in political economy was typified by the supply and demand approach of the Manchester School[1] which argued that a free contract between employer and worker would determine wages. But since, in a world without developed trade unions, the bargaining position of the worker was weak relative to the strength of the employer, justice required more than supply and demand. The issue was taken up within the Catholic Church which provided a coherent body of thinking on the subject, with a strong ethical base. In an analysis of family, work and wages in the Stéphanois region of France between 1840 and 1914, Michael Hanagan observes that 'The Catholic church was first to locate the working-class family as a key point of intervention' (Hanagan, 1998: 142).

In proposing the concept of a *living wage* in *Rerum Novarum*, Pope Leo XIII owed much to the work of Bishop William von Ketteler of the Rhineland, who outlined the demands of the working classes for improved wages, shorter working hours and days of rest. Allied demands were for the prohibition of child labour in factories, and 'that women, especially mothers of families, be prohibited from working in factories'. Nor should young girls be employed in factories, because 'girls can work for far lower wages because they require less to live on, and ... therefore, wholesale girl labour must of necessity have a damaging effect on the wages of men' (von Ketteler, 1926: 638). One hundred years later, trade unionist Inez McCormack would denounce the concept of a family wage because she regarded it as anti-egalitarian:

> We are asking you to join with us in rejecting the concept of a family wage. ... Suddenly the notion of a family wage, of interest in the family, has become extremely important to the Thatcher government and to this Government. I would suggest that their interest is not in the family. Their interest is increasing a pool of cheap labour because if you accept the concept of a family wage, you accept that there is such a thing as a breadwinner who should earn a decent wage and other people who shouldn't. Those other people are largely women and part-time workers (McCormack, 1983: 67).

The substance of the living wage teaching was that, while it is proper for employers and employees to freely enter into wage agreements, in the words of *Rerum Novarum*, there is 'a dictate of nature more ancient and more imperative than any bargain between man and man, namely, that the remuneration of the worker should be sufficient to enable him to live in reasonable and frugal comfort' (Ryan, 1926: 688). The Pope thus entered an important moral caveat that the wage contract must not be such as to deprive the worker of at least that amount of wages which would enable him to achieve a minimum adequate living standard, and thus placed the right to a living wage above the right to a free contract. That the wage must be sufficient for a man to support a wife and child dependants, was endorsed by Pope Pius XI in *Casti Connubii*, where he writes:

> Such economic and social methods should be adopted as would enable every family to earn as much as, according to his station in life, is necessary for himself, his wife and rearing of children. ... To deny this or make light of it is a grave injustice and is placed among the greatest sins by Holy Writ, nor is it lawful to fix such a scanty wage as would be insufficient for the upkeep of the family in the circumstances in which it is placed.

In the English speaking world, Rev John A. Ryan of the Catholic University in Washington was the foremost exponent of the concept of the living wage, and the author of a book on the topic in the 1920s. Ryan believed that a living wage needed the support of the law:

> The only method of bringing about living wages universally is that of legislation. That is to say, the State should make it illegal for any one to pay less than what competent

authorities will determine to be a living wage. That means in the case of a man a wage sufficient for decent support of himself and family, and in the case of a woman, remuneration sufficient for decent individual support. In times past there have been a few Catholics who have declared that this is socialistic, or that it was not in accordance with Catholic teaching. I do not know now of any Catholic of importance who is making such an assertion. It seems to me as clear as any proposition can be that this device of a legal minimum wage is a proper intervention by the State, according to the Catholic principles of political ethics. The Catholic doctrine of the State is not the *laissez faire* theory (Ryan, 1926: 695).

In Ireland a prominent exponent of the theory of the living wage was Professor Edward Coyne, a Jesuit priest and a sociologist, and a founder of the Workers' College, subsequently known as the College of Industrial Relations. He also founded the extra-mural Department in UCD in 1949. Firmly opposed to state intervention in family matters, he was a strong supporter of workers' rights. Writing to a fellow priest in 1948 Coyne said, 'There can be no doubt from the three great Papal documents – *Rerum Novarum, Quadragesimo Anno* and *Casti Connubii*, – that an employer is bound in some way to pay a family wage to an adult normal working man, doing a normal day's work' (Coyne, 1948). Coyne expresses the view that the 'norm Family' in most countries is a man, wife and three children. In his letter Coyne discusses family size as well as his strong opposition to the State taking over the responsibilities of the breadwinner:

> With regard to the size of the family, it is obvious that the norm family, not a particular family, is to be accepted as the standard. In most countries this would be a man, his wife and three children. Personally I would accept that as the only standard by which to judge the nievau of the family wage. With utterly exceptional families of 10 or 12, it is obvious that the older members will be earning money while the younger ones are still unable to do so. But normally it would be a comparatively short period of time when the father would have to support completely five children or more.
>
> I am utterly opposed and I think it completely false and most dangerous in practice, to allow the state to come in as the normal means for increasing the family wage. Once we admit that we give away our whole case against communism (Coyne, *ibid*).

Associated with the idea of a living wage was the idea of endowments for child dependants. Fr John Canavan, a confrère of Coyne's, proposed a system of family endowments to deal with the problem of child dependants. Difficulty arose because not every industry could afford to pay each worker a family wage. His solution was that adopted in a number of European countries at the time, whereby a standard wage was fixed appropriate for a single man. Employers then paid a further allowance for a wife and for each child under, say, fourteen years. The total wage bill paid by an employer in an enterprise was divided in such a manner that married men with families received more than bachelors. A form of family endowment or *allocations familiales*, had been introduced in France in the nineteenth century by Léon Harmel in the Val-des-Bois (Crawford, 1925). The system was first introduced on a firm footing by a few Catholic employers in Grenoble in France during World War I, in particular at the Joya ironworks. From there it spread to Belgium, Germany, Austria and other countries (Canavan, 1926: 701-3).

The Living wage and the Shannon Scheme

The question of a living wage was brought into sharp focus in the 1920s when a dispute arose regarding the wages offered to the workers on the Shannon Scheme, which involved the State in a project to harness the river Shannon for purposes of hydro-electricity. The Free State government had contracted the German engineering firm Siemens Schukert to undertake the project. The wage rate for the workers was fixed at a level slightly above the prevailing rate for agricultural labourers (Manning and McDowell, 1985: 41-2). A bitter dispute ensued in which effectively the workers were defeated. Although the Labour Party, then in Opposition, supported the Shannon Scheme, the leader of the Party, an Englishman, Thomas Johnson, moved the following motion in the Dáil on 3 November 1925:

> That the Dáil demands that before proceeding further with the Shannon Electrification Scheme all necessary steps shall be taken to ensure that the rate of wages paid to workmen engaged therein shall be such as will enable a man to provide a decent standard of living for himself and his family (*PDDE*, Vol. 13, Col. 38, 3 November).

In introducing the motion, Johnson referred to the deplorable conditions of workers in the years before World War I, saying that workers should never be forced to return to such standards. Workers on the Shannon Scheme were being offered 32/- (32 shillings) per week for a week of 50 hours, while Johnson had hoped for a wage of 50/- per week. Before the war labourers were being paid between 13/- and 18/- per week. Allowing for the rise in prices since the war, the cost of living in 1925 was about 188 points above the pre-war level; a wage of 32/- effectively meant a reversion to a pre-war wage of about 17/- per week. Johnson demanded:

> Are you assuming that every workman in this country engaged on public work, or work of a public constructional kind, must be an unmarried man? Do you make the assertion that no man shall get married or that no man shall have a family, or are you willing to concede this, that the family is the unit of social life in Ireland and is to be maintained as such? (*PDDE*, Vol. 13, Col. 42, 3 November).

The crucial point of Johnson's speech was that the wage on the Shannon Scheme was inadequate to support a man and his dependants. Emphasising his theme, Johnson said:

Now we have the implied confession that they [the Government] are hoping to build a new Ireland upon the basis of unmarried men. There was a statement in the Dáil of 1919, a declaration of social policy, subscribed to by the members of that Dáil, some of whom are present on the Ministerial benches, which said that in Ireland we 'shall not suffer that any child shall go hungry or cold, from lack of food or clothing or shelter'. Now we understand what was at the back of their minds when they made that declaration – a mental reservation that there were to be no children! ... We are going to have a State based on bachelordom (*ibid*: Col. 44).

In a passage that summarises Johnson's objections to the underlying economic philosophy of the Scheme, he continued:

Your whole scheme seems to be to adapt the worst features of the old political economy of the Manchester School. Labour is a commodity to be bought at the lowest price and any instrument can be used to drive down the price of labour, ... You are trying to compete the unmarried with the married (*ibid*: Col. 45).

Deputy Morrissey, in seconding the motion, added some strong political punches. He remarked: 'It seems rather a funny thing to read in the newspapers statements made by Ministers who are in receipt of £32 per week, in which they tell us 32/- per week are sufficient as a wage for a workman' (*ibid*, Col. 46). Turning his attack on to general government economic policy, Morrissey complained that the overriding priority of the government appeared to be the reduction in taxation. He said that to achieve this goal the government was dismantling every piece of social legislation that had been introduced by the British. Already the old-age pensions had been reduced and outdoor relief had been reduced. The President, Mr Cosgrave, claimed that the workers on the Scheme were being paid more than agricultural labourers in the two counties in the immediate neighbourhood of Shannon. Morrissey countered that the position of the Shannon men differed from that of agricultural labourers, in that the majority of the 3,000 men at Shannon would probably have to maintain both themselves at Shannon and their wives and children at home, whereas the agricultural labourer would just have a single home to maintain. The President conceded that a case might be made to the Minister for Industry and Commerce on that point. The President moved an amendment to the motion so that it now read:

That the Dáil is satisfied that, in connection with the Shannon Electrification Scheme, steps have been taken to ensure that the rate of wages paid to workmen engaged therein shall be such as will compare favourably with the rates paid in other occupations in which the same kind of labour is employed (*ibid*, Col. 58).

The President's amendment, which shifted the ground away from the concept of a living or family wage, to one of comparability with wages in other employments, was carried by thirty-nine votes to eighteen. Its passage followed a fascinating debate during the course of which the Labour Party leader challenged Deputy Heffernan as to whether the Deputy would 'accept Pope Leo's proposition, which is "frugal comfort"' as the basis for determination of the appropriate wage.

Five weeks later, on 10 December 1925, Senator O'Farrell of the Labour Party introduced a motion into the Senate comparable to that introduced by Deputy Johnson in the Dáil. Among those who contributed to the debate was Senator Farren who had first hand experience of working on a somewhat similar scheme 'at the other side of the water'. He said that the worker on the Scheme

> ... gives to that scheme his blood and sweat and he does not get sufficient to send home enough money to pay the rent of his little house. Then you talk about Christianity and about the State. ... we accept the principles with regard to a living wage as laid down in *Rerum Novarum. Rerum Novarum* is the Encyclical on labour that was issued by the greatest Churchman in our generation, the late Pope Leo XIII. In that Encyclical he laid down what the conditions of life ought to be for the meanest worker (*ibid*: Cols. 57, 58).

In an attempt to defend the link that the government had made between the wages of workers on the Scheme and comparable wages for agricultural labourers, Senator Gogarty said:

> It was not so much the fault of the government that wages were restricted as the capacity of the country to pay them. When I say that, I mean that in the long run every sheltered trade must press on the one that is unsheltered, that being agriculture. Eighty per cent of these people hold less than 40 acres, and you cannot prevent farmers from sweating their children. All agricultural labour is sweated labour. There is nothing to prevent a farmer utilising the help of his family. If the Labour Party were able to protect the children I would support them (*ibid*: col. 67).

Before the vote on the motion was taken, the Minister for Industry and Commerce pointed out that at the time there were 212,000 agricultural labourers, most of whom were striving to maintain families on wages from between 20-25 per cent less than the Shannon workers. In addition there were at least 250,000 holders of uneconomic land holdings, most of whom were trying to maintain families on about 50 per cent of the level of the Shannon workers' wages. He warned that if wages at Shannon were increased the money would have to be raised in the first instance by the people who pay most of the taxes of the country, namely the agricultural community, especially the small farmers. Senator O'Farrell's motion was defeated by twenty-one votes to ten.

In reflecting on the fate of the Shannon workers, it is notable that the strongest supporters of the workers' cause, and therefore, the strongest supporters of Catholic teaching in this instance, were members of the Labour Party. From the perspective of the 'Celtic Tiger', it is all too easy to criticise the government's tough economic stance in the 1920s, but it was a different era, and there was no shortage of men available for work at the going rate. Labour costs were critical at a time when machinery and equipment were primitive by current standards. The 32/- shillings per week compared with the 40/- per week recommended for a man and wife by Beveridge, nearly twenty years later, by which time, after an initial rise, the purchasing power of money had fallen by one-third. In the future, when funds were more readily available, governments would prove more than willing to spend; but at that time, fiscal rectitude, what Deputy Morrissey correctly identified as the government's priority to cut taxation, won the day. However, at a higher pay level than that of the Shannon workers, i.e. in the civil service, the government took the notion of the family wage on board.

Pay differentiation in the civil service

The question of a family living wage also surfaced at a different level, that of civil service workers. On the take-over of government from the British in 1922 pay was differentiated on a sex basis, that is, different pay scales existed for men and women. In 1925 a major innovation was made when sex differentiation was abolished for the general service and replaced with a scale for single persons, both men and women (Scale A), and a scale for married persons (Scale B), which effectively applied to married men, as women left the service on marriage when they received a marriage gratuity. In effect what happened in 1925 was that married men continued to receive the man's rate (Scale B) while new male entrants, who were single persons, were put on the former woman's rate (Scale A). The Scale A rates were equivalent to between 80-90 per cent of the Scale B rates. The savings that ensued from reducing the single man's rate to the former woman's rate were paid instead to married men in the form of children's allowances. In other words pay operated on the lines of family endowments or *allocations familiales*.

The changes described were not made in respect of the professional and technical ranks which, with one exception, continued to be paid sex differentiated rates. The exception related to those working in Institutions of Science and Art who were paid on the basis of a marriage differential; the rationale for this was that they sat a similar examination to the general service administrative grades on entry to the Service. By the time the Devlin Committee reported in 1969 both marriage and sex differentiation were the object of criticism. According to Devlin:

> We have had representations against both marriage differentiation and sex differentiation. Women consider sex-differentiation iniquitous, bachelors are opposed to marriage differentiation and married men on sex-differentiated scales want marriage differentiation with children's allowances (Devlin, 1969: 106).

Following Irish entry to the EEC in 1973 sex differentiation and allowances for children were abolished, yielding one pay rate regardless of sex or marital status.

If the concept of the living wage formed the basis of pay differentials in the Civil Service, the story of the Shannon workers shows how financial priorities overrode its implementation. Those who were sufficiently well-off to pay income tax benefited from tax-free allowances for children under the income tax code which could be interpreted as in keeping with the living wage concept. The introduction of children's allowances on a limited basis in 1944 was a step in shifting the cost of providing for children away from the direct employer to the 'indirect employer', that is, the State. If in need of updating in light of changing social realities, the living wage concept is still present in Catholic social teaching, occurring, for example, in *Centesimus Annus* of Pope John Paul II. Catholic social teaching has long realised that one of the things which working people should be enabled to do, with the help of the 'indirect employer', is to spread their incomes to provide for sickness, accidents and old age. However, the teaching has not come to terms with the idea of spreading income across the life cycle so as to cover the high costs of children, especially the first child, when mothers are likely to reduce their labour force commitment to care for their children. Nor did the teaching take cognisance of the increasing number of families in which both mother and father are in paid employment.

Restrictions on the employment of women
At a time of heavy unemployment of male breadwinners, restrictions on the employment of women were seen as a method of rationing the available jobs to those whose need was perceived to be greatest. The use of tariffs, prevalent in the 1930s, to create male employment would be negated if women were prepared to work for lower wages. When de Valera became Taoiseach in 1932 unemployment was a huge social and economic problem, not only in Ireland, but throughout the developed world. In 1931 in the United States the number unemployed was 8.3 million. On 2 March 1932, as the result of the critical Sligo-Leitrim constituency was awaited, the 'most vital single constituency election in recent Irish history' (*Irish Press*, 3 March, 1932), the *Irish Press* announced under the heading 'Workless Army Still Growing', that 'The Irish Free State has 18% more unemployed this winter'. In December 1930 the registered unemployed amounted to 25,622, while in December 1931 the figure had risen to 30,865, the bulk of them 'breadwinner men'. Fifty years later, registered unemployed would exceed 300,000, but in 1931, 31,000 was probably more frightening.

The marriage bar against married women teachers in national schools was introduced in 1933. The General Secretary of the Irish National Teachers' Organisation (INTO) at the time, and author of the official history of the INTO, T.J. O'Connell, believed that an important motive behind the bar was the gaining of the rural vote, because in rural areas where two employed teachers were married to each other, their relative affluence was the cause of envy. In October 1932, the Catholic Bishops' Conference considered the rule but decided not to express an opinion. In fact, some bishops, both Catholic and Protestant, were opposed to the bar, while others favoured it (O'Leary, 1987: 48, 50, 52). The bar remained in force until 1958 when it was removed by Jack Lynch when he was Minister for Education. In 1936 the *Conditions of Employment Act* was passed. It was 'An Act to make further and better provisions for regulating and controlling the conditions of employment of workers engaged in industrial work, and to make provision for divers matters connected with the matters aforesaid' (14 February 1936). The Act contained many items that were in complete sympathy with current Catholic social teaching. Three categories of worker were defined in the Act – an 'Adult worker', 18 years and over, a 'Young person', 14-18 years and a 'Woman', 18 years and over. An interesting feature of the Act, one that reflected contemporary mores, was the option to substitute certain listed Holidays of Obligation of the Catholic Church, such as Ascension Thursday or Corpus Christi for the public holiday of 'St Stephen's Day – when it falls on a weekday, or for Easter, Whit, or August Monday bank holidays'.

Restrictions on employment of female workers were set out in Section 16 of the Act as follows:

16 (1) The Minister may in respect of any form of industrial work, after consultation with representatives of employers interested in such form of industrial work and with representatives of workers so interested, by order make regulations either –
  (a) prohibiting the employment of female workers to do such form of industrial work, or
  (b) fixing a proportion which the number of female workers employed by any employer to do such form of industrial work may bear to the number of other workers so employed.

16 (3) If, when any regulations made under this section are for the time being in force, any employer employs a female worker or a number of female workers in contravention of such regulations such employer shall be guilty of an offence under this section.

Further restrictions were imposed in Section 46 of the Act regarding the employment of women at night:

46 (1) Notwithstanding any provisions of this Act, other than the provision empowering the Minister to make exclusion regulations, it shall not be lawful for any employer to permit any woman to do for him any industrial work at any time between the hour of 10 pm on any day and the hour of 8 am on the following day or to permit any woman to commence to do for him any industrial work on any day until after the

expiration of eleven hours from the time at which she ceased to do industrial work on the previous day.

In Section 47 of the Act restrictions on night work between the hours of 8 pm and 8 am were imposed on young persons, 'unless such young person is a male young person and is so employed under and in accordance with regulations made by the Minister under this section'. All of the provisions introduced under the *Conditions of Employment Act*, 1936 were in keeping with the tenor of Catholic social teaching (von Ketteler, 1926).

Subsidiarity

The key document which set forth the principle of subsidiarity was the encyclical *Quadragesimo Anno* of Pope Pius XI, issued in 1931 to celebrate the fortieth anniversary of *Rerum Novarum*. The Pope and his advisers, aware of the darkening shadow of totalitarianism in Europe, sought to emphasise the rights of individuals and smaller groups. The concept of subsidiarity was developed in the German Koeningswinter Circle, a group of Catholic intellectuals interested in political economy who had a major influence on the author of *Quadragesimo Anno,* the Jesuit priest Oswald Von Nell-Breuning, and on the evolution of Christian democracy in pre- and post-war Germany (Weigel, 1992: 232). In Ireland, Edward Cahill, SJ, saw as one of the main aims of the Catholic Social Movement the reorganisation of the public life of the nation in accordance with Catholic standards. He interpreted the social movement as a means of breaking away from British economic liberalism, and replacing it with a Catholic emphasis on the family headed by the breadwinning father, as the central unit group of society.[2]

The core of *Quadragesimo Anno* was emphasis on the individual human person as both the source and end of society. The purpose of social relationships and of human communities is to give help, *subsidium*, to individuals as they realise their human development. The State should not, except in exceptional circumstances, remove or replace the individual; rather the State should try to provide the conditions for the exercise of individual responsibility. Decision-making should be at the 'lowest' possible level in society. The key passage in the encyclical is the following:

It is true, as history clearly shows, that because of changed circumstances much that formerly was performed by small associations can now be accomplished only by larger ones. Nevertheless, it is a fixed and unchangeable principle, most basic in social philosophy, unmoveable and unalterable, that, just as it is wrong to take away from individuals what they can accomplish by their own ability and efforts and then entrust it to a community, so it is an injury and at the same time both a serious evil and a disturbance of right order to assign to a larger and higher society what can be performed successfully by smaller and lower communities. The reason is that all social activity of its very power and nature should supply help (*subsidium*) to the members of the social body, but may never destroy or absorb them.

To its advocates, the principle of subsidiarity represented a bulwark against the State taking control over the lives of its citizens. At the time of the Mother and Child crisis, Dr Cathal Daly, then a lecturer in Queen's University, and later Cardinal, wrote: 'The family in the welfare state is in grave danger of being injured as fatally by state benevolence as it formerly was by state neglect. It can be killed by too much kindness; too much of the wrong-headed kindness, which violates its nature, its dignity, and its independence' (Daly, 1951).

This sort of thinking informed the Irish Constitution of 1937. It influenced education, health and social welfare policy, where Church teaching stressed that the State had the right to intervene only in a subsidiary capacity. A thought-provoking comparison can be made between the 1937 Constitution and the Democratic Programme of the First Dáil, 1919. The Democratic Programme, of which the Labour Leader, Thomas Johnson, was the most influential draftsman, had a strong socialist thrust. It placed on 'the Republic', as its first duty, the well-being of children. The small farmers who formed a large segment of the community, and who had recently won the right to land ownership, were not attracted to socialism, and were wary of an extended role for the State. The principle of subsidiarity was one that appealed to these new small proprietors and also suited de Valera's purposes; by supporting the principle of subsidiarity de Valera was both following Church teaching and endorsing the principle of private ownership which, after generations of exclusion, was embedded in the Irish psyche.

An instance of the Supreme Court striking down a Bill relating to property on the grounds of undue intervention by the State into the affairs of the family would occur in relation to the *Matrimonial Home Bill*, 1993. In 1993 the Second Commission on the Status of Women recommended a régime of community property including joint ownership of the family home and joint entitlement to all income (Second Commission, 1993: 454). The *Matrimonial Home Bill*, 1993 sought to give effect to joint ownership of the family home. In a case determined following a Presidential referral under Article 26 of the Constitution, of the Bill to the Supreme Court, the Court affirmed the constitutional right under Article 41 of a married couple to make a joint decision as to the ownership of the matrimonial home. The Court ruled that the Bill, which prescribed automatic joint ownership, amounted to a disproportionate intervention by the State which violated 'the rights of the family' and constituted 'a failure by the State to protect the authority of the family'. The Bill was held to be repugnant to the Constitution and, as a consequence, it could not become law (Shatter, 1997: 721).

Church authorities who argued against State intervention in the family in the sense of the State providing services for families which they could provide for themselves, *did,* however, support legal interventions when those legal interventions were in line with church interests and teaching. Fahey has suggested that bringing the State into the family via the public provision of education was probably the biggest ever State 'intervention' in the family (Fahey, 1992). Fahey shows that legal sanctions to compel parents to send their children to school regularly were widely applied in Ireland from the 1920s to the 1950s. Child labour in the context of small family farms was an accepted feature of rural life but the authorities sought to outlaw paid child labour. This latter goal is a background feature in the understanding of compulsory schooling. The *School Attendance Act*, 1926 required the attendance at school for every day of the school year for 6-14 year olds. Enforcement for the most part was entrusted to the police. Both Church authorities and teachers agreed with the measures which were based on the *School Attendance Act, 1926.* During this period Church authorities had considerable power over primary education through the system of local managers, generally the parish priest.

Subsidiarity and the family in the 1937 Constitution

In his study of the Constitution, John Kelly describes Articles 41 and 42 which deal with the Family and with Education as being among the most innovative in the entire Constitution (Kelly, 1980: 483). The Constitution of 1922 contained nothing about the family and marriage, and its references to education were more limited. A former President of the High Court, Mr Justice Costello, has pointed out that explicit reference to the family, which was a novel feature in the 1937 Constitution, was subsequently made by the United Nations in the Declaration of Human Rights, by the Council of Europe, by the Organisation of South American States and by the Organisation of African Unity (Costello, 1988). In their study of family policy in the European Union, Hantrais and Letablier say:

> In most member states, the normative institutional framework of the family is embodied in the national constitution. In Finland, France, Germany, Greece, Ireland, Italy, Luxembourg, Portugal and Spain, the constitution recognises the family as a social institution and undertakes to afford it protection (Hantrais and Letablier, 1996: 26).

If at a general level support for the family was expressed in the Constitution, support in a pragmatic way was far less clear. It is the view of former Taoiseach Liam Cosgrave, concerning some of this section of the Constitution, that you 'could not implement it even if you tried'.[3] The implication that, for example, protecting mothers from the economic necessity to work outside the home was, to an extent, window dressing, proved to be the case. Nonetheless a comparison of the text of Article 41 of the Constitution with extracts from papal encyclicals shows a virtual identity. De Valera could thus import the teaching of the Vatican into the Constitution, without following its logic in practice by supporting mothers in the home.

Article 41.1.1° states:

The State recognises the Family as the natural primary and fundamental unit group of society – as a moral institution possessing inalienable and imprescriptible rights, antecedent and superior to all positive law.

This echoes Pope Leo XIII in *Rerum Novarum*:

> The family is a society limited, indeed in numbers, but no less a true society, anterior to every kind of State or nation, invested with rights and duties of its own, totally independent of the civil community.

Article 41.1.2° states:

The State, therefore, guarantees to protect the Family in its constitution and authority, as the necessary basis of social order and as indispensable to the welfare of the Nation and the State.

This would certainly meet with the approval of Pope Pius XI who wrote in *Casti Connubii*:

> Those who have the care of the State and of the common good cannot neglect the needs of married people without bringing great harm upon the State and upon the common welfare.

The phrase 'social order' in Article 41.1.2° merits comment, echoing as it does *Quadragesimo Anno*, known as the *Encyclical on the Social Order*. In the *Preamble* to the Constitution, the attainment of 'true social order' is one of the objectives for which the Constitution is adopted. The phrase 'social order' also appears in Article 45.1 regarding the Directive Principles of Social Policy, as well as in Article 41.1.2°.

Article 41.2.1° and 41.2.2° states:

In particular the State recognises that by her life within the home, woman gives to the State a support without which the common good cannot be achieved.

The State shall, therefore, endeavour to ensure that mothers shall not be obliged by economic necessity to engage in labour to the neglect of their duties in the home.

These sentiments fit perfectly with those of Pope Pius XI:

Intolerable and to be opposed with all our strength is the abuse whereby mothers of families, because of the insufficiency of the father's salary, are forced to engage in gainful occupations outside the domestic walls, to the neglect of their proper cares and duties, particularly the education of their children (*Quadragesimo Anno*).

According to Pope Pius XI a first duty of the State in providing for the common good is to protect and strengthen family life:

Not only in those things which regard temporal goods is it the concern of public authority that proper provision be made for matrimony and the family, but also in matters pertaining to the good of souls: namely, just laws should be made for the protection of chastity, for reciprocal conjugal aid, and for similar purposes (*Casti Connubii*: 62)

This papal teaching would certainly fit in with Article 41.3.1° and 41.3.2°:

The State pledges itself to guard with special care the institution of Marriage, on which the Family is founded, and to protect it against attack.

No law shall be enacted providing for the grant of a dissolution of marriage.

The Beveridge Report and the shift from 'non-intervention'

The publication of the *Beveridge Report* in Britain in 1942 and the determination of the British government to build a welfare state were met with a mixed response in Ireland. In the realm of social thinking subsidiarity was the order of the day and undue state intervention in the family, to the extent of relieving the breadwinner of his responsibilities, smacked of socialism. In the world of practical politics, however, with a high degree of poverty and deprivation in society, to fall behind the level of social provision in the sister island, where the people were engaged in fighting a world war, could call into question the value of Independence. In a symposium held by the Statistical and Social Inquiry Society of Ireland in 1943, following the publication of the *Beveridge Report*, a strict interpretation of the subsidiarity principle appeared in the contribution of Edward Coyne, SJ:

The second great danger of certain types of social services from a moralist's point of view is that men may easily lose moral stamina. ... Hunger or its fear, the love of wife and family, the hope of a secure old age are nature's way of calling forth the best that is in man (Coyne, 1943).

Although they hardly realised it, Beveridge shared their concern. Patrick Lynch has drawn attention to the common ground between Catholic sociologists and Beveridge on this matter (Lynch, 1953). In 1953, ten years after Coyne's paper to the SSISI, Beveridge observed:

The term 'Welfare State' was unfortunate in that it suggested to many people that responsibility for the welfare of individuals and families rested with the government. The right view was that men must depend for welfare on themselves; the aim of the Beveridge report was to secure for every one an income both when working and out of work, sufficient to provide the bare necessities of life for the worker and his dependants, leaving the spending of this income as the responsibility of the individual (*The Times*, 23 May, 1953, quoted in Lynch, *ibid*: 253).

The Professor of Sociology in Maynooth, Peter McKevitt, welcomed the recognition in the Report of the principle 'that the welfare and security of the worker are put in the first place' (McKevitt, 1943:149), and praised the good points in the scheme. However, he was worried about creeping totalitarianism and whether a succession of State interventions would not eventually undermine individual freedom. Bishop Dignan was pragmatic in his reaction saying, 'I suppose the State *must* step in and assist but the less it interferes with the rights of the family the better' (Dignan, 1945:33). Caution was evident in the *First Report of the Department of Social Welfare, 1947-49* (1950), which stated: 'The main objective of social welfare schemes administered by the State is to help the individual when, through no fault of his own, he is in danger of being overwhelmed by poverty.' Emphasis was placed on the idea of individual and family responsibility in the 1949 *White Paper on Social Security.* In a discussion on the desirability of a system based on flat rate contributions and benefits, the view is taken that the State has done its part by providing for basic requirements:

The flat rate system, which is now well established here, can be held to conform with this view, subject, perhaps to an extension of the plan of additions to benefit, based not on salary or wages, but on family needs. This basis is felt to be more in accord with Christian principles, and, indeed, may be related to the special recognition given in the Constitution to the family as 'the natural, primary and fundamental unit group of society' (Department of Social Welfare, 1949).

The ideology which was wary of state intervention in family matters was buttressed by a reluctance for the State to become involved on financial grounds. The fiscal policy of the Free State government, 1921-32, was directed towards low taxation and low expenditure, for 'It had long been an article of faith that Ireland had been over-taxed under British rule and the country could be administered much more cheaply under native rule' (Meenan, 1970: 246). Financial caution was the order of the day at least until the economic upsurge of the 1960s. In *Economic Development*, high taxation was described as an impediment to growth (Department of Finance, 1958: 24).

Dr Dignan's plan

Following the publication of the *Beveridge Report*, it was feared that improvements in social services in the UK would lead to the Republic falling behind Northern Ireland. The most significant plan for reform put forward at the time was that of Dr John Dignan, Bishop of Clonfert. In 1936 the government established the National Health Insurance Society which took over the administration of health insurance under the National Insurance Acts from a number of small societies. Dignan was appointed Chairman. In autumn 1944, Dignan addressed the National Health Society's Committee of Management, outlining his proposals for a scheme of national health insurance. The proposals were published in a pamphlet, *Social Security: Outlines of a Scheme of National Health Insurance* (Dignan, 1945). Dignan favoured the insurance principle, suggesting the unification of existing insurance services for sickness benefit, widows' and orphans' benefit and unemployment benefit and the addition of medical treatment benefit under the enhanced social insurance scheme. Self-employed workers would be entitled to join the scheme on a voluntary basis. The reason for Dignan's preference for insurance-based social services was that they were in line with Catholic teaching on the rights of the family. Insurance schemes, while assisting the family, did not supplant its functions:

> By the natural and divine law, the father of the family is bound to maintain his home for himself, his wife and his family: no authority, not even the State, can relieve him of this duty and privilege. Care must be taken then in any scheme of Social Services claiming to be Christian not to attempt to relieve him of this obligation to support his family: all we should do is to assist him so that he can the better meet his family and social obligations (Dignan, *ibid*: 7-8).

Reaction to the Dignan Plan was revealing. One contemporary account said:

> The desirability of a comprehensive system of social security is now generally accepted by all who understand the requirements of a properly organised community. That such a project should be sponsored in Ireland by a Churchman of Dr Dignan's standing is an augury (Lynch, 1945: 389-90, 394).

The Irish Times welcomed the Plan, saying, 'Whatever its reception may be from the doctors, the hospitals and the insurance companies, it bids fair to furnish a model for the social legislation of the future' (*The Irish Times*, 18 October, 1944), as did the annual conference of *An Ríoghacht* (*The Standard*, 20 October, 1944). The main Opposition parties, Fine Gael and Labour, welcomed the Plan; however, the Minister for Local Government and Public Health dismissed the scheme as impracticable. MacEntee's basic objection to Dignan was an economic one. MacEntee, who had nominated Dignan as chairman of the National Health Insurance Society, replaced him as chairman in 1945. Dignan who had described the existing social services as unchristian, tainted by Poor Law legislation, and reeking of degradation now found himself denounced by the Minister. It was all the more trying for Dignan because in the days when the bulk of the Bishops were unsympathetic to Fianna Fáil, Dignan and Browne of Galway were exceptions. The treatment of Dignan merits reflection. It is the case of a churchman who was in advance of the lay authorities on a matter of fundamental social importance.

The stand-off between the Minister and the Bishop was recalled in the debate on the National Health Insurance Bill in March 1947, by William Norton, leader of the Labour Party, who referred to MacEntee's repeated attempts 'to justify himself in that unseemly dispute in which he was involved with his Lordship, Most Rev Dr Dignan' (*PDDE*, 19 March 1947, 2336). A little later, on the occasion of the introduction of the Social Welfare Estimates, there was praise for Dr Dignan when Deputy Murphy of the Labour Party, said that the

> ... welcome improvement in the social code for the most deserving sections of the people is in great vindication of the action of another distinguished Irishman in the recent past, a distinguished member of the Irish hierarchy, Dr Dignan, who paved the way for what has been done here this evening and whose report and recommendations aroused in the country perhaps more interest than anything that happened in recent years (*PDDE*, Vol. 105, Col. 452, 27 March, 1947).

Deputy Murphy regarded the Minister's proposals as 'the first limited steps' towards implementing Dr Dignan's proposals:

> It is true that what the Minister has put forward in this House is a very pale imitation of what was outlined by Dr Dignan in his famous and, may I say, historic report, but at least it is a recognition now, in spite of many symptoms that appeared in the country at that time, that the line he took on that occasion was the only one that could be taken in the circumstances if the obligations of the State in this connection were to be honoured and realised (*ibid*, Col. 452).

Deputy Murphy concluded by expressing the hope that at some future time the Minister would come before the House 'for approval of all the proposals originally outlined in the Dignan Report' (*PDDE*, 27 March 1947, 456). Dignan's contribution, rebuffed in the short term, helped to remove ideological barriers to State intervention. The financial ones which greatly troubled MacEntee would gradually crumble as resources became available. Once the dyke was breached, expenditure would grow in a swelling wave so that the move from a 'Plimsoll line' approach (Kaim-Caudle, 1964: 23) to a 'Pay-related Welfare State' would be achieved.

Mother and Child

Meanwhile, the Irish Medical Association, whose members were anxious to safeguard fee income from private patients, published its own plan for a health insurance service for the middle classes. In the Health section of the Department of Local Government and Public Health, key figures, most notably the Chief Medical Adviser, Dr James Deeny, were working on plans to improve services. Apart from a Free Milk Scheme for necessitous mothers, which had been introduced in 1933, the principal social welfare services provided for mothers and children at the time were those provided by voluntary groups, for example the John's Ambulance Brigade, which ran feeding centres for mothers. The Catholic Church, in particular in the Archdiocese of Dublin following the appointment of John Charles McQuaid in 1940, initiated a major programme of help for mothers under the auspices of the Catholic Social Services Conference. Dr McQuaid's initiatives, which were ably administered with the co-operation of religious orders and layfolk, were developed partly in response to the avalanche of letters written by mothers to his predecessor, Archbishop Byrne, imploring help (Earner, 1999). A novel feature provided by the diocese was a Maternity Ambulance that could access outlying areas with large Corporation housing estates, such as Crumlin. Parishes were encouraged to sponsor 'Bonny Baby' contests to promote sound nutritional and health practices. These events were held in parishes such as the large working-class parish of Crumlin in County Dublin, where the redoubtable Canon Hickey was parish priest, during the 1940s and 1950s.

Impetus to focus on health services for infants and mothers derived from the sharp rise in infant mortality in the war years, from 66 per 1,000 births in 1939 to 83 per 1,000 in 1943. This particular rise, in opposition to the long run decline, was due to a severe outbreak of gastro-enteritis in 1943. In 1944 MacEntee formally delegated responsibility for the public health wing of his Department to his Parliamentary Secretary (Junior Minister, or Minister of State), Dr Conn Ward. Ward, who had been in charge of this wing since Fianna Fáil came to power in 1932, presented a Public Health Bill to the Dáil in 1945 (Whyte, 1980; Barrington, 1987; Horgan, 2000). Among its recommendations, it proposed very wide-ranging powers to combat infectious disease, as well as a new scheme for mother and child care. A unified scheme for all mothers and children up to the age of 16 years was to be provided by dispensary doctors to all who chose to avail themselves of it, regardless of means. School inspections of children were to be compulsory. In comparison to schemes elsewhere, the Irish scheme was unique in a number of respects: there was no choice of doctor, and it was highly centralised:

> In short, one can say that in the Public Health Bill 1945, the bureaucratic, centralising traditions of the Department of Local Government and Public Health had passed all bounds. The scheme produced by this department in an overwhelmingly Catholic

country was probably further away from Catholic principles than any scheme produced anywhere in the world at this time (Whyte, 1980: 134).

The Fine Gael Party opposed the Bill basically on the grounds that it 'violated Catholic social teaching' (Whyte, *ibid*: 135). There were no protests from the bishops, however, and it is possible that the Bill might have been passed into law but for the allegations of corruption against Ward in regard to business dealings in County Monaghan, allegations that led to his resignation. A new Health Bill, very similar to the 1945 Bill, was introduced in 1947 and passed into law in August as the *Health Act, 1947*. Deputy James Dillon, at that point an Independent Deputy, argued that part of the Act, including that relating to the compulsory health inspection of school children, infringed the natural rights of parents and on 3 December he launched a case in the High Court seeking a declaration that certain sections of the Act were unconstitutional. Senior counsel for the case were Paddy McGilligan, former and future Minister for Finance; Cecil Lavery, later Attorney General and member of the Supreme Court; and John A. Costello, the future Taoiseach. It later emerged that in October 1947 the hierarchy had objected to the Bill (*PDDE*, 125, 733, 12 April 1951). Whyte asks why the hierarchy objected to the 1947 Bill but not to the similar 1945 Bill, and answers that it was the tradition in the Custom House where the Department of Health was based that, notwithstanding similar proposals in the 1945 Bill, the particular phrase of the 1947 Act which '... caused all the trouble was that in safeguarding the health of women in respect of motherhood and for their education in that respect' (Whyte, *ibid*: 148).

A critical role in opposing the Bill was played by Dr James McPolin, the County Medical Officer in Limerick. McPolin who was born in Hilltown, Co. Down, worked in the Medical Corps in the British Army during World War I, sustaining injuries at the Somme. He later worked in the Mater Hospital in Belfast but, following the pogroms against Catholics in the 1920s, moved to Limerick where he was appointed County Medical Officer of Health. McPolin had a deep interest in the social and moral teaching of the Church and was an avid student of papal encyclicals. One of those who influenced him was Monsignor Arthur Ryan of Queen's University. Among those who were regular visitors to his home in Limerick to discuss a range of issues, including medical ethics and the primacy of the family in society, were Dr Trevor MacNamara from Drumcollagher, an activist in the Irish Medical Association, and a young priest, also from Drumcollagher, Fr Jeremiah Newman, later Bishop of Limerick. Broadly speaking, this group saw socialism as a threat. When the Health Bill, with its proposals for a universal health scheme for mothers and children, was introduced, McPolin saw red. McPolin, realising that the bishops had more power than lay people, took the initiative to alert the bishops to the dangers which he envisaged in the Bill. A message on the matter from McPolin to the Bishop of Limerick, Dr O'Neill, was contained in an envelope conveyed by McPolin's youngest son, James, who carried it on his bicycle to the Bishop's Palace in Limerick where he was received by Dr O'Neill in person, who accepted the letter from the boy.[4] McPolin criticised the Bill saying that it threatened professional secrecy between patient and doctor:

> Thus it will, for instance, compel all records of personal and family life of TB patients, and all similar records concerning mothers and children, to be carefully filed by the doctors according to a scheme laid down by the Minister, and then handed over to the Public Authority. The public authority will then use these records to examine and direct the doctors' activities and also for statistical purposes. ... Gone is our professional independence. We become medical policemen, the health secret agents, of a State department (McPolin, 1947: 5).

McPolin continued his argument by stating that wives and husbands have an intimate life of their own and that the doctor would find it extraordinarily unpleasant 'writing down the confidences entrusted to him and handing them over to the Public Authority'. Family privacy was the other side of the professional secrecy coin.[5] At the height of the Mother and Child crisis the privacy aspect was emphasised by Dr P.J. Delaney, Secretary of the IMA, when he said, 'We favour the maintenance of complete privacy of medical records and the preservation of doctor-patient relations' (*Sunday Independent*, 15 April, 1951).

McPolin also objected to the Bill on the grounds that it obliterated a whole section of private practice for doctors:

> Again, the proposal to provide a State service for mothers and children destroys a whole field of private practice. Well-to-do patients are to be offered this service free of charge, the doctor being paid by the public authority. ... It is difficult to see how we can expect the presence of the necessary conditions for the personal services of a doctor to a patient if he is forced to lose his own interest in his private practice by the proposal in the Bill to take this away in regards to mothers and children without any question of compensation. ... It is difficult to expect good will in return for an act of injustice (McPolin, *ibid*: 11-12).

McPolin was prepared to follow his principles even if his job was placed on the line. Speaking at a County Council meeting in February 1951 on a resolution from Waterford County Council suggesting that all dispensary medical officers be retired at sixty-five, McPolin said:

> There is some kind of underground organised vendetta against the doctors of this country. Here is a printed document circulated anonymously aimed at destroying our rights.
>
> And I have got a letter from the Minister for Health threatening me with the loss of my job because I wrote an article for a local newspaper. These kinds of covert attacks on doctors are most unfair (*Sunday Independent*, 11 February 1951).

The anonymous document to which McPolin referred was entitled 'Is It Needed?' and was delivered to many Dublin households in January 1951. It contained a strong attack on the medical profession, alleging that one reason why doctors were objecting to the Mother and Child scheme was because of income tax implications. According to Noël Browne's biographer, John Horgan, few people doubted that Browne was the author of the document (Horgan, 2000: 122-3).

When Noël Browne became Minister for Health in 1948, he set about bringing in a scheme to give effect to the Mother and Child provisions of the 1947 Health Act. It has been argued that the crux of the Mother and Child scheme, and one of the rocks on which it perished, was the absence of a means test, an element of subsidiarity. A statement of the principle of subsidiarity is to be found in a letter dated 10 October 1950 from the Catholic hierarchy to the then Taoiseach, John A. Costello:

> The right to provide for the health of the children belongs to parents, not to the State. The State has the right to intervene only in a subsidiary capacity to supplement, not to supplant. It may help indigent or neglectful parents; it may not deprive ninety per cent of parents of their rights because of ten per cent necessitous parents (*The Irish Times*, 13 October 1951).

As far as the doctors were concerned, the absence of a means test meant their incomes were threatened; for the Church, Catholic social teaching was breached. However, the means test was not, so to speak, an 'infallible' rock on which the scheme might perish. Noël Browne pointed out in a memorandum in relation to points raised in a letter from the Bishop Staunton letter (10 October 1950), and sent to Staunton by the Taoiseach on 27 March 1951, that no means test operated in relation to primary education, the treatment of infectious diseases or the payment of children's allowances.

In Dr McQuaid's letter, on behalf of the hierarchy, 5 April 1951, such a comparison was simply described as a 'fallacy' (Whyte, 1980: 446). In regard to children's allowances, although they were paid to all regardless of means, when they were introduced in 1944, a 'clawback' of the child tax allowance was introduced for those liable to pay income tax, i.e. the better off at the time. The idea of the 'clawback' came from T.K. Whitaker, then a young civil servant, and secretary to the committee on children's allowances. He recalled that he had great difficulty persuading the Revenue Commissioners, in particular Mr Rice, to take the idea on board.[6]

The existence of an effective means test for children's allowances in the form of a 'clawback' raises an intriguing question. If the hierarchy assumed that there was in effect a means test (clawback) on children's allowances, whereas most people assumed that there was no means test, why could not a similar arrangement have been made in regard to the Mother and Child scheme for those liable to pay income tax? Among those who believed that an honourable compromise was possible by the introduction of some insurance element to the scheme were the Labour leader, William Norton and the trade unionist Donal Nevin. Nevin says that he and Norton met Browne to put their case concerning the insurance element and that Browne listened to what they had to say, but said little himself. When Nevin and Norton left the meeting with Browne the evening papers were already on sale on the streets with headlines announcing that Browne had resigned as Minister for Health.[7]

From the point of view of the hierarchy there was the other rock, that which 'Custom House tradition' regarded as causing most trouble: the element relating to 'education in regard to motherhood'. In the letter, dated 10 October 1950, written by the Secretary to the hierarchy, James Staunton, Bishop of Ferns, to the Taoiseach, John A. Costello, setting out the objections of the hierarchy to the Mother and Child proposals, the 'social' teaching of the Church is not mentioned, although 'social policy' is mentioned once, while 'moral' appears on three separate occasions in relation to 'teaching', 'questions' and 'issues' (Whyte, *ibid*: 424-5, for text of letter). Following this letter from the hierarchy the scheme was a dead duck. On 5 April 1951 the hierarchy's decision on the scheme was delivered to the Taoiseach. It included the following:

> The Hierarchy cannot approve of any scheme which, in its general tendency, must foster undue control by the State in a sphere so delicate and so intimately concerned with morals as that which deals with gynaecology or obstetrics and with the relations between doctor and patient.

The letter went on to state that 'the Hierarchy must regard the Scheme proposed by the Minister for Health as opposed to Catholic social teaching', listing seven specific objections. Browne himself made the distinction between the social and the moral teaching of the Church, claiming that his scheme did not breach the moral teaching, and Costello in his letter to the Archbishop of Dublin on 9 April 1951, informing him of the Government's decision to withdraw the scheme, said that the Government had agreed 'to defer to the judgement so given by the hierarchy that the particular scheme in question is opposed to Catholic social teaching'. However, it is abundantly clear from the Staunton letter that the bishops viewed the scheme as contrary also to the *moral* teaching of the Church.

Outside the Dáil, Browne had his supporters. Donal Nevin recalls a meeting in College Green, which he helped to organise along with May Keating (wife of the artist Seán Keating), Peggy Rushton and Sheila May Greene and 'dissident elements in the Labour Party' to 'protest at the killing of the Mother and Child scheme'. It was presided over by Mrs Tom Kettle, and all the speakers were women. Nevin says that the meeting was never reported in the newspapers.[8] It is possible that it is the same meeting referred to by Hilda Tweedy:

My own particular memory of this period was, somewhere along the line, being on the back of a lorry in College Green, Dublin, with the two honorary secretaries of the IHA, Ruth Deale and Kathleen Swanton, all eager to show IHA support for the scheme. Dr Noël Browne was there and several other supporters and a considerable crowd of people (Tweedy, 1992:73).

Following the government decision to withdraw the scheme, there was widespread acceptance of the authority of the bishops on all sides within the Dáil. This included Browne himself, who in his resignation speech declared:

Furthermore, the hierarchy has informed the government that they must regard the mother and child scheme proposed by me as opposed to Catholic social teaching. This decision I, as a Catholic, immediately accepted without hesitation. ... While, as I have said, I as a Catholic accept unequivocally and unreservedly the views of the hierarchy on this matter, I have not been able to accept the manner in which this matter has been dealt with by my former colleagues in the Government (*PDDE*, 125, 667-667, 12 April 1951).

Browne's close ally, Jack McQuillan, likewise accepted the ruling of the hierarchy. Whyte remarks: 'Even if one assumes that Dr Browne and his friends took this line from policy rather than from inner conviction, it is still significant. It shows that in their belief it was not electorally profitable for an Irish politician to appear to be in conflict with the church' (Whyte, *ibid*: 233).

The role of the Catholic bishops was critical in the demise of the Mother and Child Scheme in its original form, but the role of the medical profession should not be minimised. There is little doubt that some of the top men in Fine Gael, including the Taoiseach, would have been sympathetic to the medical profession, not least because of personal friendships which existed amongst them, for example the friendship between John A. Costello and the influential medical professor, Oliver FitzGerald. Dr Tom O'Higgins, deputy leader of Fine Gael and Minister for Industry and Commerce, was of the opinion that Browne had bitten off more than he could chew by taking on both the Catholic hierarchy and the doctors: 'Time and again I told him such a scheme could not be worked by the Civic Guards and if it were not worked by doctors then it was no scheme and could not be worked by anyone else' (*Sunday Independent*, 29 April 1951).

If bishops and doctors both opposed the Scheme, Browne's harshest critic was surely Seán MacBride, the leader of his own party, Clann na Poblachta. Addressing the fifth Árd Fheis of the Clann in July 1951, MacBride claimed that, 'There had been a clever and unscrupulous intrigue to disrupt the Party, in which the Mother and Child Scheme had been just the issue chosen by Dr Browne' (*Sunday Independent*, 1 July 1951). MacBride, who could not be viewed as an impartial witness, threw restraint to the wind and charged that Browne had perpetrated 'probably the greatest hoax ever played on an unsuspecting public' (*Sunday Independent*, 1 July 1951).

Expansion of the welfare state: towards a minimum income

The 1949 White Paper (Department of Social Welfare, 1949), was haunted by the spectre of malingering and moral degeneration through 'dole' payments to the unemployed. In the 1940s and 1950s it would have been difficult to imagine the shift in emphasis that would take place from a job as the ultimate source of income towards a minimum income independent of work. Brendan Walsh sets the change in context as follows:

> Nothing in the intellectual climate of the late 1950s would have led us to anticipate the explosive growth of the public sector that was to occur in the following two decades. The Irish catholic hierarchy were very hostile to any measure that could be interpreted as socialist. ... By the 1970s several bishops were arguing that the state had a duty to tackle the poverty and inequality that were widespread in Ireland (Walsh, 1986: 62, 66).

The rebuff to Dignan, followed by the Mother and Child episode, contributed to the air of caution regarding State 'intervention' which persisted throughout the 1950s, a lean decade in terms of availability of resources. By contrast a period of expansion in social services would occur between the introduction of free post-primary education in Autumn of 1967 and the introduction of pay-related benefits for a range of contingencies from April 1974. The period included Irish accession to the EEC and the associated increase in availability of funds. In the 1970s the ratio of social welfare expenditure to GNP rose from 7.6 per cent to nearly 12 per cent (Kennedy, 1997).

For the hierarchy the turning point came with the pontificate of Pope John XXIII, specifically with his encyclical *Mater et Magistra*. The change in papal style that operated during his pontificate, as well as the content of papal writings, had an impact.

Liam Ryan captures the change succinctly:

> With *Mater et Magistra* we are in the world of the Welfare State with the pope inviting it to provide for people in a manner that would have seemed an infringement of human rights a decade earlier. With Pope Paul the argument is taken a step further. In *Octogesima Adveniens*, written to commemorate the eightieth anniversary of *Rerum Novarum*, the social problem is defined not in moralistic and individualistic terms but in structural and collectivist terms. What is basically wrong is the 'system', and so a change of mind and heart is not an adequate solution. The solution, of its very nature, must be political, because it is precisely the task of politics to build the structure of society (Ryan, *ibid*: 6).

Two of the fundamental assumptions on which the growth of the Welfare State was based were the norm of full employment and the centrality of a breadwinner male with dependent wife and children. No sooner, however, was the Welfare

State established in Ireland, than both labour market conditions and family patterns began to change in a radical manner. The changes included the steady rise in unemployment, a loss in the popularity of marriage, and an increase in the labour force participation of married women. But in the early 1970s the concept of the male breadwinner was still that on which the welfare system hinged. There was no cross-party disagreement on this. In the Estimates debate in 1974, Frank Cluskey, Parliamentary Secretary to the Minister for Social Welfare, referred to how delays in processing claims 'can cause real hardship to a man and to his wife and children' (*PDDE*, Vol. 273, Col. 1332, 21 June 1974). Later in the same debate he referred to the 'hardship occasioned by the illness or unemployment of the breadwinner' (*ibid*: Col. 1337), while the Opposition Spokesman, Pádraig Faulkner of Fianna Fáil, referred to the hardship of widowhood where 'The initial stage of widowhood is a frightening experience. The breadwinner is gone and the widow is left to face the future alone with her children' (*ibid*: Col. 1371).

The breadwinner concept remained central, even as an important shift was set in train from a literal emphasis on providing for the needs of oneself and one's family by the fruits of one's work, towards the right to a minimum level of subsistence guaranteed by the state. On the occasion of the introduction of the Social Welfare Estimate in the Dáil in 1974, Frank Cluskey quoted with approval from a statement on social policy of the Council for Social Welfare of the Catholic Hierarchy, '… the principle of a guaranteed income related to the cost of living index, for each household, whatever the circumstances, ought to be accepted' (Council for Social Welfare, 1972). This represented a defining moment in social policy as emphasis was now firmly placed on the right to a minimum income guaranteed by the state, as distinct from previous policy emphasis on the right to provide for one's own livelihood as set forth in the Directive Principles of Social Policy in the Constitution. The document to which Cluskey referred, *A Statement on Social Policy*, was produced by a Working Party of the Bishops' Council for Social Welfare. The Working Party was chaired by Professor James Kavanagh, Professor of Social Science in UCD, later an Auxiliary Bishop of Dublin. Apart from Professor Kavanagh and the Bishop of Ossory, Dr Peter Birch, all of the other members of the Group were laypersons. They included the Director of the Institute of Public Administration, Tom Barrington; Séamus Ó Cinnéide, the pioneer of modern poverty studies in Ireland; Helen Burke and Clare Carney from the Social Science Department in UCD; Anthony Coughlan from Trinity College; as well as Trade Union representatives, health and social workers, and the President of the St Vincent de Paul Society. The document, cast in the language of the social scientist, is clearly imbued with Christian values. It takes as the overall objective of a programme of social development the promise contained in the Proclamation of Easter 1916 that the new state would have the aim of 'cherishing all the children of the nation equally'. A key recommendation concerned the immediate acceptance of the principle of a guaranteed minimum income:

The principle of a guaranteed minimum income, related to the cost of living index, for each household, whatever its circumstance, ought to be accepted. It would then be the task of the social services to ensure that incomes did not fall below this national minimum. There are various ways of achieving this, for example by higher and more selective child allowances, or by the introduction of some form of Family Income Supplement (Council for Social Welfare, 1972: 12).

The Group listed a number of specific categories requiring particular forms of help in addition to the minimum income. These included single parent families, deserted wives, widows, the disabled, the unemployed, the poorly paid employed and the aged.

The provision of a minimum income for all was essentially what was guaranteed in the *Beveridge Report*. It is a more limited concept than that of a basic income as discussed in the *Report of the Expert Working Group on the Integration of the Tax and Social Welfare Systems,* 1996, and in the work of the Conference of Religious of Ireland, *Towards an Adequate Income for All* (CORI, 1994). The basic income concept implies an income for all regardless of means whereas a minimum income refers to a threshold level below which no one should be allowed to fall. The Directive Principles of Social Policy in the Constitution include the following:

> The state shall, in particular, direct its policy towards securing: That the citizens (all of whom, men and women equally, have the right to an adequate means of livelihood) may through their occupations find the means of making reasonable provision for their domestic needs.

The principle enshrined in this part of the Constitution, which stresses the rights of individuals to provide for their needs via *their occupations*, is quite different in emphasis from that in the Bishops' Council for Social Welfare regarding a minimum income whatever the circumstances. This shift in ideology represents a shift from Catholic social teaching of the 1930s towards a more socialist post-Vatican II emphasis in keeping with the principles of the Beveridge Plan and, significantly from an Irish perspective, endorsed by the encyclicals of Pope John XXIII. The hierarchy moved from a position that emphasised selectivity, subsidiarity, and self-supporting families to one that endorsed guaranteed state provision regardless of labour force attachment. Evidence that politicians were influenced by Church teaching at that time is found in a number of sources, for example, in the Fine Gael *Just Society* document published in 1965, in which it is noted that 'most people in public life will state their acceptance of the teachings contained in the Papal Encyclicals'.

The document further stated: 'The social and economic thought of the Fine Gael Party has been informed and moulded by the social doctrines contained in the Papal Encyclicals.' Fine Gael identified two dangers; the first was that acceptance might simply mean lip service, while the second danger was the possible use of papal principles as an excuse for inaction. The document continued, 'We accept the principle of subsidiary functions and in our plans for reform we will be guided at all times by this principle. It is our responsibility as laymen in politics to learn and appreciate these principles' (Fine Gael, 1965: 4). In an article published in *Studies* in 1964, some months prior to the publication of the *Just Society*, the future leader of Fine Gael, Garret FitzGerald, wrote:

> From the Christian tradition we must continue to draw not only a sense of purpose but also a firm hold on the principles of faith and morals which are not to be minimized or played down in any misguided effort to reach a spurious accommodation with agnostic thought ... emphasis on the role of the family in society and not mere lip-service to it (FitzGerald, 1964: 339).

CMRS/CORI

Father Seán Healy, co-director with Sister Brigid Reynolds of the Justice Office of the Conference of Religious in Ireland (CORI), notes that there were two defining influences on the change in the attitudes of Catholic Church authorities to the involvement of the State in the provision of social services.[9] The first was the huge increase in State funding for education which followed in the wake of free post-primary education, associated with Donogh O'Malley. Church authorities realised that increased State funding for education combined with the decline in personnel in the religious orders signalled a changing world. The second influence was the 'arrival' of Vatican II in Ireland in the 1970s, some years after the closing of the Council, which led the religious orders to examine their roots and the objectives of their founders. Many discovered, or rediscovered, the concern of the founders for the poor and those on the margins of society.

In 1981 The Conference of Major Religious Superiors, as CORI was then called, established a Justice Commission and in the following year, a Justice Office. The Office was located on the Jesuit campus at Milltown Park in Dublin; its first Director was Fr Bill McKenna SJ, with Sr Brigid Reynolds as Deputy Director. Fr McKenna had been Director of the College of Industrial Relations, and it was entirely fitting that this new initiative would be headed by a Jesuit, thus maintaining the long Jesuit link with social policy in Ireland. In 1983 Fr Healy, recently returned from a decade in Northern Nigeria, became director of the Justice Office; since 1986 he has been co-director with Sr Brigid Reynolds. The idea with which Healy and Reynolds are most closely identified is that of a basic income for all. The idea came to Healy partly as a result of his experience in Africa. At twenty-six years of age he was appointed a parish priest. His parish covered 2,000 square miles and forty-seven churches. It contained no big cities. While everyone worked, no more than ten people had a paid job, leading Healy to the view that the only work respected in western culture is that which is paid.

Returning to Ireland where unemployment was rising he felt a need to redefine work to include a great deal of unpaid work. From this insight his commitment to a basic income developed.

With the notable exception of the Mother and Child episode, Church influence did not operate as a result of any direct pressure from the hierarchy upon the legislature; rather because Catholic social teaching was part of the air breathed by the legislators. It is the belief of former Taoiseach Liam Cosgrave that there is no evidence for the charge that the hierarchy interfered, or attempted to interfere, in policy matters. When he was Taoiseach two bishops came to see him concerning the hunger strikers in the Curragh, but they came quietly and he would not budge. The only other episcopal intervention Cosgrave recalled related to a bus strike at the Clontarf dépot in Dublin in 1950, which happened as a result of two bus workers leaving the ITGWU to join the National Union of Railwaymen, a British union. In the context of the strike Cosgrave saw Archbishop McQuaid on six occasions within a fortnight, three times in Drumcondra and three times in the Archbishop's residence in Killiney. Following his intervention in the earlier Teachers' strike, the Archbishop had become something of a court of appeal to workers, but he gradually dropped out of that role. Regarding the Mother and Child issue, Cosgrave believes that the affair was badly handled on all sides, but that only one voice has tended to come out over the years, that of Noël Browne.[10] In his biography of Noël Browne, John Horgan describes that voice as 'sometimes prophetic', but also 'wayward, headstrong, often self-congratulatory and self-indulgent' (Horgan, 2000: 294).

9

Family and Government

The changes in family patterns which have accompanied the modernisation of the Irish economy have been closely associated with changes in government policy towards families. In this chapter government measures which affected the family are divided into two broad categories: measures of a redistributive kind that affect the resources available to families, and measures that define the rules within which families operate. The first set of measures encompass many of the expenditure programmes identified with the welfare state: pensions for the old, the widowed and the orphan, children's allowances, and allowances for unmarried parents. They also include taxation measures. At the outset special mention is given to the great Land Acts under which land was transferred from the landlords to small proprietors under land purchase schemes. Legislation defines the framework within which families exist and function, a framework that is finely delineated in Shatter's *Family Law* (Shatter, 1997). Key Acts include the *Succession Act*, 1965, the *Family Law (Maintenance of Spouses and Children) Act*, 1976, the *Family Planning Act*, 1979, the *Status of Children Act*, 1987, the *Judicial Separation and Family Law Reform Act*, 1989 and the *Family Law (Divorce Act)*, 1996, as well as a range of equality legislation enacted subsequent to Irish entry to the EEC.

The shift away from agriculture as the primary means of earning a livelihood for the majority of the people meant a shift away from a social security system based on the family. Meenan summarises the transition neatly, saying that a social revolution occurred within an economic revolution:

> The problems of dependency in youth as well as in old age were tackled within each family to the extent that its resources permitted. Moreover, the farm constituted a constant occupation for the members of the family who remained on it. ... Matters are very different when an increasing part of the labour force works for direct monetary reward, outside the social structure of the family. In a cash economy, much greater attention must be paid to problems such as provision for old age and sickness, assistance to widows, the health and education of the young; ... It is essential to understand that an economic revolution entails a social revolution (Meenan, 1970: 281-2).

The earliest twentieth-century example of the State assuming financial responsibility for family members by way of an income payment was the provision for old age pensions under the *Old Age Pension Act*, 1908. Subsequent milestones included the introduction of Widow's and Orphan's Pensions in 1935, Children's Allowances in 1944, Deserted Wife's Allowance in 1970 and Unmarried Mother's Allowance in 1973. The earliest innovation made by the government *vis-à-vis* families this century, however, related not to the provision of services, but to the provision of land (Fahey, 1998a), and land was the *sine qua non* of marriage and family formation for a majority of Irish people in the early years of the century.

Land and family: the *Irish Land Act*, 1903

The Land Act of 1881, introduced when Gladstone was Prime Minister, went a good distance towards meeting the claims of tenants:

> ... it provided fixity of tenure by the institution of statutory tenancies, a fair rent by a process of judicial review, and acknowledged a right to free sale of the unexpired portion of a lease. It conceded at last to the rest of Ireland the tenant-right on which much of the prosperity of Ulster had been built (Meenan, *ibid*: 11).

The year 1903 in which the *Irish Land Act*, known as the Wyndham Act, after George Wyndham, Chief Secretary of Ireland, was passed '... is one of the pivotal dates in Irish history, and the Land Act marked the highest point of the Conservative government of Ireland. Arthur Balfour was largely justified when, thirty years later, he asked, "What was the Ireland the Free State took over? It was the Ireland we made"' (Meenan, *ibid*: 15). The *Land Act* of 1903 which made tenant ownership effective was the foundation stone for an entire era and an entire society when the small proprietor and his family became identified with the concept of 'Irishness'.

Under the pre-1921 British Land Acts, chiefly the *Irish Land Act*, 1903, and the *Irish Land Act*, 1909 (the Birrell Act), over 316,000 tenants purchased holdings amounting to 11.5 million acres out of a total of 17 million acres in the country. The advances paid for the purchase of the land were about £100 million. Another 750,000 acres of 'untenanted' land, the bulk of which was in congested districts, was distributed among 35,000 allottees. Until the *Land Law (Commission) Act*, 1923, the land purchase scheme was a voluntary one, based on agreement between landlords and tenants with the help of finance from state bodies. The political will to introduce *compulsory* purchase for the remaining three million acres of land was reflected in a Bill introduced in Westminster in 1913, but it failed to pass into law during the Home Rule crisis (Wylie, 1975: 38). A Bill introduced in 1920 also failed to pass into law. Compulsory purchase was central to the 1923 Act. Since then the remainder of the tenanted estates, amounting to over 3 million acres and about 114,000 holdings, were transferred to the tenants subject to payment of land annuities under the *Land Act*, 1923 and subsequent Acts. A further 2 million acres were redistributed to relieve congestion (Wylie, 1975: 38; Sammon, 1997: 279). The programme of land distribution, as distinct from land purchase, proceeded rapidly in the late 1920s and reached its zenith in the 1930s. The effect of the Land Acts, in particular the *Irish Land Act*, 1903, but also the Acts of 1909 and 1923, was to create a class of small farm proprietors which formed a conservative core in Irish society and strongly supported property rights (Lynch, 1966). The rights of private property which had been entrenched in the 1922 Constitution were extended further by de Valera in 1937 (FitzGerald, 1998: 360).

The *Old Age Pension Act*, 1908

In the 1830s, the Royal Commission on the Conditions of the Irish Poor, chaired by the Protestant Archbishop of Dublin, Richard Whately, left no stone unturned in its study of poverty. The Commission did not recommend the introduction of the English Poor Law system with workhouses and outdoor relief – but in the spirit of Keynes before Keynes, argued in favour of schemes to increase employment. The government did not accept Whately's proposals. Following a six-week trip to Ireland by George Nicholls, a member of the English Poor Law Commissioners, the government adopted the Nicholls proposal for a poor law in Ireland with a workhouse system and related tests of destitution (Ó Cinnéide, 1969:288). On 31 July 1838, the *Poor Law Relief (Ireland) Act* was passed. By the end of the nineteenth century the only State assistance provided for the elderly was within the ambit of the Poor Law. In 1872 the introduction of a pension for working men over sixty years of age was proposed (Longfield, 1871-76: 107-8), but it was not until 1908 that the *Old Age Pension Act* was passed (Carney, 1985). The pension was payable on a graded scale at the age of seventy; the maximum rate was five shillings per week for those whose income did not exceed £31.10.0 per annum. The *Old Age Pension Act* came into force on 1 January 1909 and by February 1909, 177,000 pensions had been granted in Ireland, representing 4.1 per cent of the population, compared with 370,000 persons in England, representing 1.1 per cent of the population. Since compulsory registration of births only began in 1864, determination of age was open to debate. The number of recipients in Ireland 'staggered the statisticians' and fraud was suspected (Carney, *ibid*: 496), although the proportion of old people in Ireland was higher at the time than in England and poverty was greater. In 1911 there were 243,000 recipients of the weekly old age pension in the 32 Counties at a total annual cost of £2.7 m. In 1919, following the Great War, the old age pension was doubled, increasing to a maximum of ten shillings weekly.

At Independence, expenditure on old age pensions was one of the largest single items in the expenditure of the new government. In 1924, £3m. was spent on 124,000 pensions in the 26 Counties, representing around 10 per cent of total central government expenditure. Because of the relative importance of expenditure on pensions, the issue of old age pensions recurred constantly in parliamentary debates throughout the 1920s and 1930s, and '... parliamentary question time was taken up largely with questions regarding the old age pension. The names and addresses of claimants were given in every case together with the fullest details of family and finance' (Carney, *ibid*: 498). The most memorable episode associated with the old age pension was its reduction from 10/- (10 shillings) to 9/- in Ernest Blythe's 1924 Budget, as part of fiscal retrenchment. The shilling was not restored until 1928. The pension remained unchanged for a further twenty years until it was increased to 17/6 in 1948. Under the *Old Age Pension Act*, 1932, means test requirements were eased. Relaxing the restriction on the assignment of land with a valuation of over £10 to an heir was seen as an effort to 'let the young fellow grow up'; Senator Comyn expressed the hope that it would prevent 'that gliding into old bachelorhood' which he considered to be one of the greatest evils then besetting Ireland (Carney, *ibid*: 506).

An important decision from the point of view of the family unit, taken in 1932, was the disregard of the value of board and lodging provided by his/her family for a pensioner as part of his/her weekly income; although it became customary to assess the value of board and lodging at a nominal income of one shilling a week. Cases had been cited in the Dáil 'where an old person had moved to live alone in a small cabin or had had to move prematurely to live in an institution, because the children could not afford to maintain him without the income from the pension' (Carney, *ibid*: 507). By 1951 the number of recipients was 151,000 and total annual expenditure was £7m. The issue of board and lodging was highlighted in 1966, by which time the old age pension was £2/12/6 weekly, when an extra 5/- weekly was granted to pensioners who had no other income. This created a difficulty for pensioners who were receiving board and lodgings from their families and who, accordingly, had a nominal income of one shilling weekly. James Dillon, TD argued that the regulation was anti-family. He questioned the justice of a situation where the young people kept their father or mother in the house and as a result:

> The aged parent should be denied the five shillings simply because the children, the son and daughter-in-law, allow them the use of the hag – the bed in the kitchen? ... it actually suggests that we are encouraging the daughter-in-law and the son to put their parents out (*PDDE*, Vol. 226, Col. 2395, 2 March 1967).

In 1973 provision was made for pensioners to have income of up to £4 per week and still receive the old age pension. The limit was subsequently increased and the custom of attributing a nominal one shilling weekly income for board and lodging was dropped. Restrictions on the assignment of land to children, which limited access to the pension for parents, and acted as a deterrent to the marriage of children, were eased gradually. Following Irish entry to the EEC, it became a policy objective to actively encourage the transfer of farms to younger family members in order to increase farm productivity.

Widow's and Orphan's Pensions, 1935

The care of widows, orphans and neglected children caught the attention of social reformers in the late nineteenth century when several papers were presented to the Statistical and Social Inquiry Society relating to child welfare and the treatment of widows (Daly, 1997: 3). Many widows were forced into the workhouse because only widows with two or more dependent children were allowed outdoor relief. The *Poor Law Relief (Ireland) Act*, 1847 authorised the Poor Law Guardians to give either outdoor or indoor relief to certain classes, including destitute widows having two or more legitimate children dependent on them (Ó Cinnéide, 1969: 284-308). Widows, if able-bodied, and widows with only one legitimate child, were assisted in the workhouse only.

A Commission on the Relief of the Sick and Destitute Poor including the Insane Poor (Poor Relief Commission), was established in 1925 and reported in 1927. Item 3 of its terms of reference was to examine the law and administration affecting the relief of (a) Widows and their children; (b) Children without parents; (c) Unmarried mothers and their children; and (d) Deserted children. At the time widows and their children, who were without means of their own, were supported by home assistance. The Commission recommended the adoption of a 'Scheme of Mothers' Pensions payable by the State'. This was based on a scheme operating in a number of American states whereby maintenance grants were made 'in respect of children under a fixed age to a widowed or deserted mother who has not the means to feed, clothe and house her children adequately' (Ó Cinnéide, 1969). The Commission also recommended that a scheme of widows' pensions similar to the one that had been introduced in Britain in 1925, be introduced in the Free State.

The 1927 Report acknowledged the inadequacy of poor relief and 'the injury to the self-respect of a widow reduced to destitution by the death of her husband, who was compelled to parade her poverty every week at the office of the Assistance Officer' (Soffe, 1997: 8). A Committee of Inquiry into Widow's and Orphan's Pensions was established by the Minister for Local Government and Public Health and reported in 1933. At the time there were over 10,000 widows in receipt of home assistance. The majority report of the Committee recommended the introduction of a non-contributory widow's pension funded by the Exchequer. There were two minority reports; one recommended the introduction of a contributory pension scheme, while the other recommended improvements in home assistance provision for widows. The government opted to introduce both a contributory and a non-contributory pension under the *Widow's and Orphan's Pensions Act*, 1935. At the time slightly less than one-third of the male population of insurable age was covered by social insurance. Under the 1935 Act certain categories of employed persons became compulsorily insured for the purposes of widow's pensions; it was also possible to make voluntary contributions. The non-contributory scheme was subject to a means test. A non-contributory pension could not be paid to a widow under 60 years unless she had a dependent child. The qualifying age for widows without children was reduced to 55 in 1937 and subsequently to 40 years. Thirty-one years later, in October 1966, a widower's contributory pension was introduced. Prior to 1968 there was no provision for the widows of civil servants who died in service. The pensions of husbands were deemed to die with them and the only entitlement for their widows and children was a lump sum payment. In 1968, when Charles Haughey was Minister for Finance, changes were made which introduced pension rights for future widows. This change came about partly as a result of a campaign waged by two young widows of civil servants, Rita Fay and Winifred Delaney. These two women then helped to organise the 'pre-1968 widows' to lobby for their inclusion into the scheme. Eventually these widows were granted an *ex-gratia* payment equal to one-eighth of their husbands' salary. Finally in 1986 they were granted the full pension.

The distinction between widows with and without children was considered by Beveridge. He favoured support for widowed mothers. He did not favour the idea of a pension for life for a childless widow – 'if she is able to work, she should work'. Although he was concerned about older widows without children who could find difficulty entering the workforce, he was reluctant to make exceptions to his general principle, '… That any person physically fit for work should be entitled to retire from work upon pension before reaching the minimum pension age of 60 for women or 65 for men cannot without grave danger be admitted in any scheme for social insurance'. By 1995 total expenditure on widow's pensions was £400 million, or 10 per cent of total social welfare expenditure. Contributory pensions accounted for the bulk of the payments. In 1950 there were 15,600 recipients of the widow's contributory pension and 27,000 recipients of the widow's non-contributory pension; by 1995 the numbers were 94,700 and 19,100 respectively.

Children's Allowances, 1944

Following the introduction of the old-age and widows' pensions, attention was turned to 'family welfare' in the sense of the welfare of dependent children and their families. The *First Report of the Department of Social Welfare* states:

> The earlier schemes show concentration on making provision against the immediate risks which threatened the economic security of the individual and his dependants and survivors. When considerable advances had been made in this direction, it was possible to turn to the apparently less pressing problem of raising the standard of living of the family. It became clear that measures were required to remove the relative disadvantages in material circumstances which harassed parents of families, and thus to mitigate the handicaps arising from parenthood (Department of Social Welfare, 1947-49).

The introduction of children's allowances had been under consideration for at least five years; James Dillon was the first Dáil Deputy to argue in favour of their introduction. On 23 November 1938 he asked the Minister for Industry and Commerce whether statistics were available showing 'the number of children under 16 years in families the heads of which enjoy an annual income of £250 or less, and, if so, what is the number of such children in Éire' (*PDDE*, 73, 851, 23 November 1938). The Minister, Seán Lemass, replied that statistics were not available according to the income of heads of families. Dillon was on the trail of seeking out, and helping, poor families. In March 1939 he pointed to the fact that the better off people in the community who paid income tax benefited from child tax allowances while those too poor to pay tax got no such benefit:

> If the income tax payer in this state, the person with an income of over £250 a year is entitled to go to the Government and say: 'Because I have a child, you ought to relieve a certain part of my income tax,' surely the man who has 27/- a week has a better right to go to the Government and say: 'Because I have a child, bring me somewhere near the income of the person you are excusing from taxation on account of his child.' That is an unanswerable claim, but the answer given to it at present is that the money is not there (*PDDE*, 75, 405-407, 30 March 1939).

Dillon's plan for a scheme of children's allowances sprang from his desire to tackle poverty where it was most acute – in poor families with many children. The greatest social problem was that children were hungry. Dillon recalled to the Dáil the sight of children going to school with a slice of bread and jam because they could not afford butter. He asked:

> Who are the people who suffer most from poverty today? Are they not the poor parents of a big family? The person who has really got his back to the wall is the person whose income is only 30/- or 35/- a week and who has ten children. That is the real difficulty (*PDDE*, 75, 406, 30 March 1939).

In November 1939 a Cabinet Committee on Family Allowances was established. Its membership included Seán T. Ó Ceallaigh, Minister for Local Government and Public Health, as well as Frank Aiken and Seán Lemass. The secretary of the Committee was a civil servant, Brian O'Nolan, better known as the literary genius Myles na gCopaleen, or Flann O'Brien. As the progress of the committee was slow Lemass became impatient and he drafted a report for government outlining a scheme of children's allowances, and proposing that an inter-Departmental committee be established 'to prepare the heads of the necessary legislation' (Ó Cinnéide, 1994: 5). Strong objections on the basis of principle to a general scheme of children's allowances came from the Secretary of the Department of Finance, J.J. McElligott, who said:

> The principle has not been generally accepted that the State has responsibility for the relief of poverty in all its degrees – the principle underlying any social measures

undertaken by the State in this country up to the present is that the State's responsibility is limited to the relief of *destitution*, i.e. extreme cases where employment and the minimum necessities of existence are lacking (Lee, 1989: 28).

Notwithstanding the objections of McElligott, the government followed the Lemass proposal to establish an inter-Departmental Committee, chaired by O.J. Redmond from the Department of Finance; its secretary was T.K. Whitaker. The Committee submitted its report to government in October 1942. It recommended the introduction of a contributory and a non-contributory scheme of allowances. The non-contributory scheme would be means-tested and would vary between the city and rural areas. In these recommendations, it was following existing precedents. Widows' and orphans' pensions had been introduced on both a contributory and non-contributory basis in 1935, while different rates of unemployment assistance were paid in urban and rural areas. The contributory scheme aimed to be self-financing, while the non-contributory scheme would be financed by cuts in food and agricultural subsidies, and in income tax allowances. The government gave Lemass the go-ahead to prepare legislation. However, a major political and administrative row now erupted. Ó Cinnéide takes up the story:

> Behind the scenes a major political and administrative battle ensued. Children's Allowances were resolutely opposed by the more conservative element in the Government, led by Seán MacEntee, now Minister for Local Government and Public Health, and by the Secretary of the Department of Finance. They each marshalled all the ideological and political arguments they could to oppose Lemass's proposals (Ó Cinnéide, 1994: 6).

In March 1943 memoranda were submitted to the government by the Departments of Finance and Local Government and Public Health. Both these memoranda focused on how children's allowances might conflict with Church teaching. The Finance memorandum stated that ' … Catholic writers stressed again and again their dislike of the present-day increase of State interference in the private lives of families and have stated their fears that family allowances may tend further in this direction and towards "the socialisation of children"' (D/Taoiseach, S12117B, 11 March 1943).

The memorandum from the Department of Local Government and Public Health concluded as follows:

> It can be shown that the moral objections to a scheme of family allowances are greatest (a) if the scheme is non-contributory in character, (b) is universal in application and (c) if the distribution of allowances is not related as strictly as possible to the actual needs of the recipients. If therefore a scheme of family allowances is to be adopted the Minister for Local Government and Public Health would urge very

strongly that, whatever be the initial limitations on the scope of the scheme, it should be contributory in character and the allowances paid under it should be related as closely as practicable to the actual family circumstances of the beneficiaries (D/Taoiseach, S12117B, 16 March 1943).

In June 1943 a General Election took place following which the return of Fianna Fáil to Office depended on the support of Independents. Proposals for children's allowances were included in the election programme of the Clann na Talmhan Party which, led by Joseph Blowick, returned thirteen Deputies to the Dáil. When the Children's Allowances Bill came before the Dáil in September 1943, its contents differed markedly from the proposals of the inter-Departmental committee. The scheme would be a non-contributory one only, paid to all families regardless of means, and paid in respect of the third and each subsequent child. For taxpayers there would be a 'claw-back' of the child tax allowance. It is striking that Lemass totally ignored any opposition to children's allowances allegedly based on Church teaching as set out in the memos from the Departments of Finance and Local Government and Public Health.

Speaking in the Dáil, Lemass said that the Bill was not based on the Committee's Report:

That inter-Departmental Committee was set up exactly three years ago, on 22nd November, 1940. It was set up following long consideration of this problem by the Government. The report of the committee was received on a subsequent date and it was very carefully considered by the Government. We decided that the recommendations contained in it were inadequate to meet the situation and it became necessary to depart from them and work on a new basis (*PDDE*, 92, 230-231, 24 November, 1943).

Speaking on the introduction of the Second Stage of the Children's Allowances Bill on 23 November 1943, Lemass gave a clear exposition of its contents. He said that the earliest record of children's allowances could be found in the equalisation funds established on a voluntary basis by employers in particular industries, mainly in France and Belgium. He said that some countries, like Italy and Spain, operated contributory schemes, but that these were limited to those who work for wages. In Australia, New Zealand, Germany and France, there were State schemes paid for out of taxation. Lemass stressed that the *raison d'être* of the scheme sprang from the needs of large families. He referred to the observations of the Beveridge Report on the relationship between poverty and family size saying, 'It is, I think, necessary to emphasise that the basis of the whole case for the establishment of a children's allowance service is the need of large families' (*PDDE*, Vol. 92, Col. 23, 23 November 1943).

Lemass spelled out the financial implications of the Bill, stating that the cost would be met from current revenue and not from borrowing. He said that voting for the Bill placed a moral obligation to vote later on in the Budget for the taxation necessary to pay for children's allowances. The proposals would cost £2.25 million per year. By way of illustration of the magnitude of that sum, expenditure on unemployment relief in the previous year cost £2m, while total expenditure on all social services cost £8m, or £10m, if unemployment relief expenditure was included. To raise £2.25 m. in taxation would involve 1/- in £ increase in income tax, 1/- in the lb on tobacco, 2d on a lb of tea, 1/2d on a lb of sugar and 1d on beer. Lemass explained why the government opted for the scheme outlined in the Bill. The government did not select a contributory scheme because of the very high proportion who were not employed for wages. Of approximately 480,000 heads of families – married men, widows and widowers – 219,000 earned wages. The remaining majority were mainly farmers. There would be no means test for the practical reasons that the implementation of such a test would be both difficult and costly. However, child tax allowances would be reduced for taxpayers. Lemass explained, 'It is proposed to offset the benefit that may be secured by persons in the income-tax paying class through the inauguration of the children's allowance scheme by a reduction in the allowance now made in respect of children under the income tax code' (*PDDE*, Vol. 92, Col 35, 23 November 1943).

Speaking in the debate, the Leader of the Opposition, W.T. Cosgrave, suggested that the Bill did not go far enough. He would have liked to see the proposals combined with a contributory scheme, and he said that the Beveridge proposals went further to secure minimum income (*ibid*, Col. 46). But Deputy James Dillon expressed his satisfaction at the advent of the Bill: 'I have been trying to get it introduced for five years and, tonight, I see the realisation of that ambition' (*ibid*, Col. 102-103). At the same time, however, Dillon said that the ideal would be an adequate family wage:

> In our rejoicing at what I regard as something closely approximating to a great revolution, which will be brought about by this Bill when it becomes an Act, we should not lose sight that family allowances, desirable as they are, are only a second best. The ideal, as I see it, in a Catholic country, would be to ensure that every person who did an honest day's work would receive for that labour a wage sufficient to enable him to rear a Christian family. If we could realise that it would be a very much better way of meeting the whole question of the special responsibilities of the fathers of families, than the method enshrined in this Bill (*PDDE*, 92, 103, 23 November 1943).

Dillon said that he welcomed the Bill for something far more important than the half-crown allowance: 'It is the recognition of a great principle. It is the recognition that, in our community, there should be no penalty for exercising a Christian man's right to marry and raise a family, in so far as the community can help it' (*ibid*, Col. 106). Dillon said that he saluted the Bill because it recognised the principle of the family wage and the desire to do the next best thing to providing a family wage directly, when it was not possible for the employer to provide a family wage for the earner. Dillon also welcomed the Bill because children's allowances would not be means-tested, saying 'I also salute it [the Bill] because it has abolished the means test. This is, I think, the first piece of social legislation on the Continent of Europe which has abolished the means test' (*ibid*, Col. 106). Dillon utterly rejected any suggestion that the allowance might be paid in the form of vouchers for food or other goods. The family should have discretion as to how the money would be spent:

> The beauty of this Bill is that it bolts and bars the door against the bureaucrat. It strengthens the citadel of the family against the Government. It places a complete and absolute discretion in the hands of the parents to use this income as they think best for the benefit of the children, and I earnestly hope that, while we might do something by handing it to the mother, we would not go an inch beyond that in any form of dictation or interference in the way the total family finances are to be administered by the parents (*ibid*, Col. 109).

An interesting contribution to the Debate came at the Committee Stage of the Bill from Deputy Liam Cosgrave who had been elected to the Dáil in the June General Election at the age of twenty-three. He proposed that children's allowances should be paid to mothers, but this was rejected by Lemass. This is of special interest because it was only a few years since the Constitution had been passed which talked about supporting women in the home. Yet when the opportunity arose, it was rejected. Child benefit would not be paid directly to mothers until thirty years later when, in 1974, Cosgrave was Taoiseach. Speaking at the Committee Stage of the Bill on 2 December 1943, Cosgrave said, 'the person in closest touch with the actual needs of the children, is either the mother or the female guardian operating in the mother's place …'(*PDDE* 92, 577). For this reason and also because of the danger that in some cases, if the allowance was paid to fathers, 'it may be spent either on gambling or on drink' (*PDDE*, 92, 577), he was proposing that the allowance be paid to the mother. The words of Cosgrave's proposed amendment were as follows:

> Where such person has complied with the prescribed conditions as to identification there shall, during the said payment period, be paid to the mother or other female relative or guardian functioning in the household as a house-keeper, or subject to the discretion of the investigation officer, to the person who has so applied (*PDDE*, 92, 577-578).

Lemass at once rejected the amendment:

> Mr Lemass: I would urge the Dáil very strongly to reject this amendment. I take it the main purpose is to ensure the payment of the allowance to the mother rather than to the father and that –

Mr Larkin: Why not make it optional?

Mr Lemass: – the proposal to leave it to the discretion of the investigation officer is only incidental to the main proposal. I would not agree to that at all, in any event (*PDDE*, 92, 578).

Among the reasons Lemass gave for rejecting Cosgrave's amendment was the fact that the amendment implied that fathers were not to be trusted. He did not see why the State should interfere with the father who was head of the household. After all, the father could decide to give the money to the mother or the housekeeper as he saw fit. 'I hold that in questions concerning the family, we should keep Government or State interference down to a minimum. That is why I urge that this amendment should not be adopted' (*PDDE*, 92, 579).

Dillon and several other speakers, including Deputies Tunney and Blowick, supported the idea that the allowance might be paid directly to the mother of the child, as did Jim Larkin who pointed to cases where men passed on meagre sums from their wages to the mothers of their children:

… the general feeling in the world today is that the mother should get an adequate wage for the work that she does: that the mother is entitled to a wage just as the father is entitled to his wage. It would appear to me that we have been too impressed by this 'father complex', as I might call it. I have known of cases of men earning £4 or £5 a week – men with large families – handing £1 a week over to the wife and spending the rest on themselves (*PDDE*, 92, 582).

Lemass thought that paying children's allowances to the mother could set a dangerous precedent which could force the government to do the same in the case of food vouchers, or of child allowances under the *Unemployment Assistance Act*. In essence, Lemass saw children's allowances as an adjunct to a *man's wages* to meet the needs of large families. He said that there would be provision to pay the allowance to someone other than the father in cases where there was evidence that the father had neglected the children. A discussion ensued as to how neglect might be determined and Lemass said that he would accept the judgement of a parish priest; he was not for turning:

… we should not depart in the slightest from the principle that the father is the head of the family and entitled to receive the benefit obtainable under this Bill. If we were to depart from that principle in this case, we should be, for the first time, attacking the integrity of the family. That is my own belief (*PDDE*, 92, 590-591).

Children's allowances, introduced in 1944 for the third child aged under 16 years, were extended to the second qualified child in July 1952, and to all qualified children from November 1963 which coincided with the introduction of a new Turnover Tax. Under the *Social Welfare Act*, 1973, the qualifying age for children's allowances was raised to 18 years for children in full-time education, in apprenticeships, or disabled. The total number of families in receipt of children's allowances has risen from 132,000 in 1944 to about 500,000 at present, while the total number of children in respect of whom the allowance is paid has risen from 321,000 to over one million.

Unmarried Mother's Allowance, 1973

In ideological terms the provision of a State allowance for the unmarried mother was like stepping on to a new planet. Henceforth the unmarried mother would be a visible, recognised member of Irish society. The allowance was introduced following a recommendation of the Commission on the Status of Women (1972). The Commission considered that, '... there should be some financial support available to an unmarried mother who keeps her child, particularly when the child is very young and she cannot resume employment' (Commission, 1972, para. 388). Accordingly, the Commission recommended that an unmarried mother who keeps her child should be entitled to a social welfare allowance at the same rate and on the same conditions that apply to a deserted wife, for a period of not less than one year after the birth of the child. The allowance was introduced for a much longer period than the minimum recommended by the Commission. Subject to a means test, it is paid until the child is aged 18 years, or 21 years, if in full time education. In 1989 a comparable allowance was introduced for male lone parents. In November 1990 these payments together with some others were amalgamated under the title of 'Lone Parent's Allowance'. All recipients of Unmarried Mother's Allowance, Deserted Husband's allowance and Widower's Non-contributory Pensions transferred to this scheme, as did recipients with children on Widow's Non-contributory Pension. At the end of December 1996 Lone Parent's Allowance, Deserted Wife's Allowance, Deserted Wife's Benefit and Prisoners Wife's Allowance were discontinued for new claimants. A new unified payment, One-Parent Family Payment, was introduced for all parents who are bringing up children on their own.

The number of recipients of unmarried mother's allowance has grown steadily from 2,000 mothers with 3,000 child dependants in 1974, to over 11,000 mothers with 14,000 eligible children in 1985, to 37,215 unmarried mothers with over 51,000 children in 1996, at a cost in excess of £150 million. In 1996, 291 fathers with over 300 children were in receipt of a Lone Parent's Allowance. In 1997 there were 59,000 recipients with just 95,000 eligible children, that is almost 150,000 beneficiaries, of the new amalgamated One-Parent Family Payment, at a cost of £267 million.

Taxation of families: the Murphy Case 1980 and Budget 2000

Personal allowances under the Income Tax Code as well as allowances in respect of dependent children existed at the foundation of the State. In April

1986 the tax allowances in respect of children, which had been reduced over a number of years, were abolished. At the time of their abolition, the Minister responsible for Social Welfare was the Labour Deputy Barry Desmond, and the Taoiseach was Garret FitzGerald. FitzGerald remains firm in his opposition to child tax allowances. He believes that they are regressive because they are worth more to higher income earners. It must be noted, however, that at the time of their abolition, by far the largest category of beneficiaries of child tax allowances were paying at the then lowest marginal tax rate of 35 per cent. In 1985/86 of the total of 258,000 claimants for tax allowances in respect of 709,000 children, 63.6 per cent of claimants, claiming for 63 per cent of children, paid tax at 35 per cent, compared with 22.7 per cent of claimants, claiming in respect of 23 per cent of children, who paid tax at 48 per cent. Only 13.6 per cent of claimants, claiming in relation to 14 per cent of children, paid tax at the highest marginal rate of 60 per cent. While recognising that to earn the sum equivalent to cash child benefit, the higher income earner would need to earn a larger sum of pre-tax income than the lower rate tax-payer, FitzGerald believes that the way to deal with this is to tax child benefit.[1] A suggestion to tax children's allowances was a feature of the child benefit proposals of FitzGerald's Fine Gael-Labour Coalition of 1983-86, but it met with an unpopular response and was shelved. Ten years later in the Report of the Expert Group on the Integration of the Tax and Social Welfare Systems, chaired by Donal Nevin, published in 1996, it was suggested that taxing child benefit might be deemed unconstitutional on the grounds that the benefit was the income of the child (Expert Working Group, 1996: 46). Nevin suggests that where the woman received the payment, but the tax was levied on the income of the man, there would probably be pressure to increase wages.[2]

One former politician with unrivalled experience in this area is Charles Haughey. Haughey was Minister for Finance in the late 1960s as well as Minister for Health and Social Welfare from 1977 until 1979 when he became Taoiseach. Haughey says that in his time in politics the question of focusing children's allowances came up frequently. He said there were always difficulties in deciding where the cut-off point might be, while the administration of a means test can be costly. Furthermore women say, 'Look, this is the only thing we get as women into our own hands. Just leave it that way.'[3] Regarding child tax allowances, Haughey would not agree with the general recommendation of the Commission on Taxation to abolish all personal allowances, including those for children. He believes that the overriding message of the Commission to 'Simplify, simplify, simplify' failed to take account of social and economic complexities, and of the necessity for a degree of complexity in the system to ensure greater social justice.[4]

The provision of child tax allowances is an attempt to take account of the number of child dependants who must be supported from a given pay packet and is based on the concepts of horizontal and vertical equity. Horizontal equity in this context concerns the position of families with children *vis-à-vis* families without children, but with the same income, while vertical equity concerns the position of families with different numbers of dependants, e.g. one, three or five children, and with different levels of income. During the early years of the State the benefit from such allowances was limited due both to the high proportion engaged in farming and the low level of incomes generally. With the introduction of the PAYE system from 6 April 1960, and the increase in the number of income tax payers, the allowance extended to a large sector of the population. During the 1920s the child tax allowance was equivalent to between one quarter and one fifth of the tax allowance for a single person; in the 1930s the allowance for a child rose first to 40 per cent and then to 48 per cent of the single person's allowance. The position of a child relative to a single person reached a peak of 67 per cent in the years 1956/57 to 1959/60. It declined relatively in the early 1960s, recovered again in the late 1960s and then declined steadily to just under 7 per cent in 1982 at which level it remained until its total abolition in 1986. Relative to the allowance for a married couple the child tax allowance reached a peak of 34 per cent for a child under 11 years and 38 per cent for a child aged 11-16 years in 1967/68 when Charles Haughey was Minister for Finance (Kennedy, 1989). Not surprisingly a study of the changing burden of personal taxation in Ireland over the period 1946 to 1976 showed a particularly large proportionate increase in the taxation of couples with children (Ó Muircheartaigh, 1977). In 1989, when Albert Reynolds was Minister for Finance, a limited tax exemption of £200 was introduced for children in low-income families. Since 1994 the exemption has been £450 for the first and second child and £650 for the third and each subsequent child.

The budgets in the late 1960s, the Haughey years in the Ministry of Finance, reflected the ethos of the time by supporting the marriage-based family. For example in the 1967 Budget the child tax allowance for children under eleven years was increased, while the allowance for children over eleven, already at a higher level, remained unchanged. There was a reference in the budget to the fact that increasing the child tax allowance was costly, and also, interestingly, there was a reference to the new costs that were falling to the Exchequer, following the introduction of free secondary education, which would benefit older children. In the 1968 Budget, the Minister gave a special increase of £100 in the personal allowance for married men in the year of marriage because 'Financial problems of young people getting married are considerable'. In the 1970 Budget the wife's earned income allowance was increased so that 'The combined married allowance and wife's earned income relief will then be twice the single allowance', i.e. it would be twice the single allowance where both husband and wife were earners.

The method of taxation of married couples was altered following the case of *Murphy v. The Attorney General* (1980) in which a Dublin couple, Frank and Maura Murphy, both national school teachers, took a case against the State, challenging those provisions of the *Income Tax Act*, 1967 which resulted in a husband and wife paying more income tax on their combined salaries than they would pay on their two separate salaries, if they were not married. The central challenge of the case was against compulsory aggregation of the salaries of husband and wife for tax purposes. In his judgment, Mr Justice Hamilton stated that the provision of Section 192 of the Act was contrary to the principle underlying the remainder of the Act, that was, the principle of individual taxation on an individual income. In no other circumstances was provision made for deeming an income, which an individual did not himself earn or receive, as his income for income tax purposes. The provision only applied in the case of married couples living together; it did not apply in the case of any other individuals living together. Consequently it was clear that the provision, and the method of assessment caused by it, was based on the circumstances of marriage and the fact that the married woman was living with her husband. As such, it was an exceptional provision that discriminated against married persons. By virtue of the provisions of Article 41 of the Constitution, the State pledged itself to guard with special care the institution of marriage. By entering the married state a woman did not surrender her right to work. It was not a matter in which the State was entitled to interfere, by way of prohibition of the exercise of the right or the imposition of a penalty, should the right be exercised. Mr Justice Hamilton said that he was satisfied that provisions of the income tax code which increase the tax bill as a result of marriage were unconstitutional. The High Court judgment of Mr Justice Hamilton was subsequently upheld in an appeal to the Supreme Court.

It is the view of Trade Union leader, and biographer of Jim Larkin, Donal Nevin, that the Murphy judgment was 'daft'. As a consequence of the judgment the personal tax allowance for a single person could not be increased without a double increase for a married couple, and, according to Nevin, pressure for pay increases were coming from single people as a result. 'Single people always bore the brunt of it [high taxation] anyway. It was really most oppressing as far as single people were concerned because of this daft Murphy judgment which says that the allowances have to be double for a married couple.'[5]

In June 1981, shortly after the Murphy case, the Fine Gael election manifesto promised the introduction of a measure that would convert part of the allowance paid to husbands into a tax credit of £500 per annum, representing a cash payment of £9.60 weekly, to wives. According to Garret FitzGerald it was difficult, from the data available to the tax authorities, to identify the spouses working at home with no income of their own, and therefore it was necessary to invite such spouses to apply for the payment (FitzGerald, 1991: 293). Reaction to the proposed scheme was interesting; it was welcomed by a leading Dominican priest and lecturer in University College Dublin, but treated with scorn by Noël Browne. In an interview shortly after the scheme was announced, Browne said, 'I was deeply shocked at the Fine Gael assessment of £9.60 a week as a woman's worth. I felt it an extraordinary intrusion into the family in a society which professes horror at interference by the State in the family' (*The Irish Times*, 7 July, 1981). By contrast, Fr Fergal O'Connor defended the scheme in a letter to the newspapers:

> What a pity that the plan to transfer half the tax credit (£500 p.a.) to the spouse at home (mostly women) has become a political joke. Has anyone asked how many wives were prevented by jibes and force from claiming it?
>
> It is, without doubt, one of the most radical social changes introduced into this country. The roots of most forms of discrimination against women lie within the family and the property attitudes cultivated there by law and opinion. The proposed transfer is a direct challenge to some of these attitudes, and will help to establish the principle that wives who stay at home have an equal moral claim to their husband's wages or salaries (*The Irish Times*, 19 February 1982).

In the event the take-up for the scheme was very small and when the FitzGerald-led Fine Gael-Labour Coalition fell subsequent to the Budget early in 1982, the incoming Fianna Fáil government dropped the idea.

At the beginning of the twenty-first century a fresh debate has opened regarding the taxation of couples. ESRI researchers questioned the justification for the provision of double bands and allowances where there is only one income (Callan and Farrell, 1991; Fahey, 1998b; Callan *et al*, 1999). At the ESRI Conference, Budget Perspectives, held on 27 September 1999, Callan stated: 'It is now time to consider a change in policy direction introducing greater independence in the tax treatment of husbands and wives, and restricting the transferability of bands and/or allowances' (Callan *et al*, 1999:42).

In a comparison with the UK Callan showed that marginal tax rates facing single persons at incomes between about £15,000 and £35,000 were substantially higher in Ireland than in the UK, while one-earner couples face similar marginal rates in the UK and Ireland up to about £28,000 per year (or, for two-earner couples up to a joint income of £28,000). Callan concluded that a shift in the Irish tax system ... 'towards greater independence in the tax treatment of husbands and wives has many attractions and should be considered seriously' (Callan, *ibid*: 44).

The question of transferability of bands and allowances was among the items examined by a Working Group established in 1997 by the Minister for Social, Community and Family Affairs (Working Group, 1999).[6] The Group failed to reach agreement on the transferability of allowances for married couples. Some members of the Group supported the restriction of transferability and favoured diverting the money thus saved into child benefit and related child-care areas. The representatives of the Department of Finance and the Revenue Commissioners, however, held as mistaken, the premise that the existing treatment of marriage in the tax code was a subvention to child care. They opposed the proposal, pointing out that it could result in an increased tax bill of up to *£60 per week* for a married one-earner household without children. A significant number of married households with children would also suffer a net loss.

In Budget 2000, introduced on 1 December 1999, the Minister for Finance, Charlie McCreevy, opted for the individualisation route when he announced that complete individualisation would be achieved over the course of three budgets. The nub of the Minister's proposal for Budget 2000 was to widen the standard rate band for a single person from £14,000 to £17,000 and to double that to £34,000 for a two-income married couple, but to leave the band for one-income married couples unchanged at £28,000. When the individualisation programme was completed in 2002, other things being equal, the single-income couple would continue to pay the higher tax rate at £28,000, while the two-income household could have income of £56,000 before being hit by the higher rate. The individualisation proposals were seen as a reward to women in the workforce *vis-à-vis* women in the home.

Public reaction to the individualisation plan was dramatic. The letter columns of the newspapers were filled and the airways were jammed with objectors composed of a coalition of women in the workforce and in the home. In the teeth of parliamentary opposition from Fianna Fáil backbenchers as well as Independent TDs, Mr McCreevy introduced a compensatory allowance of £3,000 in the Finance Bill for a stay-at-home spouse looking after children, the aged or handicapped, and other dependants. In Budget 2001, Mr McCreevy continued on the individualisation route.

Property and family: the *Succession Act*, 1965

At the time the *Succession Act* was passed in 1965 there was a 50 per cent intestacy rate, and it was one of the objectives of the Act to address intestacy by laying down rules regarding the division of property. At the core of the Act was the freedom of the testator to dispose of his property as he wished regardless of his dependants. The need for the *Succession Act* sprang mainly from the failure in practice for provision to be made for widows, especially in the case of the farming community. Prior to the passing of the Act it was possible for one spouse to exclude the other from benefiting from his or her estate. For example, a man could leave his farm to a male relative, without any provision being made for his widow. Under the rules of intestate succession a distinction existed between the rights of inheritance of husband and wife, of father and mother and of males and females. It was possible, for example, for the 'heir at law' (generally the eldest son) to inherit certain property in preference to the wife and other children. Dr Patrick Hillery recalls occasions in the course of his medical practice when, in the days before the *Succession Act*, he might be asked to help a dying man to make a will. In the rural culture of the time men would often think of leaving money for masses to be said for them after death, before they would think of leaving money for their wives. 'I'd ask, "What about your wife?" and he would say, "Ah, she has enough"; and I'd keep at him. They would be leaving money to priests to get masses said.'[7] While Dr Hillery believes the *Succession Act* was a great Act, not everyone was impressed by the attempts to improve the treatment of women. Deputy Joseph Leneghan claimed that the Bill as originally devised was an attempt to introduce 'perverted petticoat legislation into the House' (*PDDE* 213: 576).

The *Succession Act* entitles a surviving spouse to a proportion of the estate of the deceased spouse whether or not a will exists. If there is no will the surviving spouse is entitled to the whole estate if there are no children, and to two-thirds or the estate if there are children, while the children receive one-third. Even if there is a will, the surviving spouse is entitled to half of the estate if there are no children and one-third if there are children. The *Succession Act* was formally introduced into the Dáil by the Minister for Justice, Mr Haughey, on 17 June 1964. More than twenty years later he would say in an interview:

> The biggest political battle was on the Succession Act. Up to then a man was totally free to dispose of his property in whatever way he wanted and I brought in this requirement that he had to give a third to his spouse and a third to his children. It aroused terrific hostility (*The Irish Press*, 16 May, 1986).

Reflecting on this over a decade later Mr Haughey said that he was not sure that it was the *biggest* political battle but that there had been great opposition to the proposals, including a good deal of opposition from women and from *within* Fianna Fáil. He first began to reflect on the issue of wills as a result of approaches from the Church to alleviate the position with regard to the sums of money that were left to say masses. He clearly recalls being approached about money left to say masses at the high altar at Killarney Cathedral, and how it was physically impossible for the requisite number of masses to be said as requested. He then began to look into the situation with regard to inheritance and 'he became incensed by what he saw, by what the position was, that a man could ignore his wife in his will'. Roger Hayes, Assistant Secretary of the Department of Justice when Haughey was Minister, was 'even more passionate' about the issue and they set to work devising a solution. Asked if there had been any Church opposition, he said no and that furthermore the Archbishop of Dublin, John Charles McQuaid, would have favoured caring for women and children.[8]

Haughey was predisposed towards the plight of widows as a result of personal experience. He was twenty in 1945 when his father died at the age of forty-five leaving a widow and seven children. His father had 'not been in the picture for ten years before that' due to a serious illness, disseminated sclerosis, and the task of rearing a large family and caring for her husband, fell to Mrs Haughey. Haughey says, 'I'm sure there was a residue of that [experience] in my thinking.'[9] Haughey's attention to the needs of widows was apparent not only in the Succession Bill but also in measures regarding public service pensions for widows and orphans in the Budgets of the late 1960s when he was Minister for Finance.

When in October 1964 Haughey became Minister for Agriculture, it fell to the new Minister for Justice, Brian Lenihan, to steer the Bill through the Oireachtas. There was broad cross-Party agreement on many aspects of the Bill. In the words of Deputy Brendan Corish, Leader of the Labour Party, it was 'not the sort of Bill that should engender any hostility between any of the three Parties in the House' (*PDDE* 213: 412), while Deputy Seán MacEoin of Fine Gael described as 'a shocking state of affairs' the case of a man with a large, valuable estate who deliberately 'left his widow or children out of the picture' (*PDDE* 213: 405). However, there was strong opposition to aspects of the Bill, both inside and outside the Dáil. The Incorporated Law Society opposed it, favouring instead the then prevailing British system under which family members could seek redress in the Courts, but which remained a discretionary system. It is an irony that the Succession Bill was opposed by Fine Gael in the Dáil, in the Seanad, and in its *Just Society* document which claimed in the section dealing with law reform that 'such follies as Fianna Fáil's Succession Bill will find no place in such a programme'. Fine Gael pledged itself to a rejection of the Fianna Fáil Succession Bill. One reason for what today looks like a surprising approach by Fine Gael was that lawyers are generally conservative and Fine Gael contained a number of lawyers who at the time would have raised their eyebrows at the idea of a law overruling the wishes of a testator.[10] However, in the Dáil Debates, John A. Costello, former Taoiseach and father of Declan Costello, principal author of the *Just Society*, made a major contribution in which he praised many aspects of the Bill. His contribution to the debate was acknowledged by Fianna Fáil Deputies, including Vivion de Valera and Seán Flanagan. Vivion de Valera who had his own reservations about aspects of the Bill remarked, 'I want to join hands again with Deputy Costello in his constructive approach to the Bill' (*PDDE* 213: 514), while Seán Flanagan referred to Costello as 'a kindly, magnanimous and altogether brilliant man' (*PDDE* 213: 1046).

Garret FitzGerald who opposed the Bill in the Senate – 'I was in the Senate. I was in Fine Gael. We opposed it' – is not a supporter of property rights between generations.[11] According to a paper he delivered in the Shelbourne Hotel in 1968, later published in *The Irish Times* (FitzGerald, 1969), and reiterated thirty years later, FitzGerald believes the accumulation and transmission of property between generations impedes progress towards an equitable society, and that there is 'no moral basis whatever for transfer of property between generations':

> In so far as you accept the transmission of property to the next generation which has no moral basis whatever to start with, but given that society will not work unless you have that, society insists on it, despite the fact that there is no moral basis. ... I don't rule out the transmission of a dwelling, of modest amounts, reasonable to do that. ...

Having said that, if somebody dies and leaves their home or other property to somebody other than their wife and children that is wrong.[12]

Speaking in the Dáil in December 1964 on the second stage of the Bill, Mr Lenihan took a very different view regarding the transmission of property. He described the Bill as one of the most important measures of law reform ever to come before the House and argued that a justification for the Bill was the support of the family. Calling on Article 41 of the Constitution regarding the Family and the contribution to the life of the State given by the woman in the home, he said, 'These principles cannot be reconciled with a system of law which allows a man to ignore the mother of his family and to leave his property to strangers' (*PDDE* 213: 339). Thus Lenihan presented the Bill as a contribution to the support of the family and to women, as pledged in the Constitution, saying that there were no real and valid grounds for the view that freedom of testation is a fundamental right:

Freedom of testation has come to be regarded by some people as a fundamental and inviolable right inherent in property. In fact there is no real moral or historical basis for this view. On the contrary, the protection and preservation of the family as a continuing institution demands that the right to dispose of the property by will should be subordinated to the just claims of the testator's spouse and children. In a country such as ours which recognises the very special position of the family as a moral institution forming the necessary basis of social order, freedom to disinherit one's wife and children is a paradox which cannot be defended on any ground (*PDDE*, 213, 335-6).

Mr Lenihan said that old Irish law knew nothing of freedom of testation, and that the will was introduced by the Church in order to allow a person to bequeath a portion of his property – the 'dead's part' – for ecclesiastical or charitable purposes (*PDDE* 213: 337). He remarked that the 'sanctity of inheritance as the great safeguard to family security' was a recurring theme in the history of property and, in a striking sentence, he observed that 'Laws of succession are but an attempt to express the family in terms of property'. He said that in drafting the Succession Bill, the aim had been to devise a system of succession suitable to Irish needs, and compatible with the traditions, beliefs and values of the Irish people. The Succession Bill represented a departure from British practice, and was more in keeping with the 'Custom of Ireland', which had been abolished four years after the Treaty of Limerick, as the Penal Laws were launched. According to the 'Custom of Ireland' only one-third of an estate of a deceased person was subject to disposition by will. If a man died leaving a wife and children, his estate was divided into three equal parts, with one-third for his wife, one-third for his children, and one-third to be disposed of at will (*PDDE*, 213, 337). As an experienced lawyer John A. Costello was keenly aware of the hardship caused by the freedom of testation which then existed:

I have seen cases of wives, after a lifetime of service, being rather badly treated, if not very badly treated … we all know from our own experience the extraordinary habit of some people … who want to control their family from the grave.

… We know of the little settlements made on marriage in this country. Writing is drawn up almost in common form. Very often when a will is made, if there is not a settlement of that kind, provision is made for one particular son. He has to provide again very small fortunes for the sisters. The widow is relegated to the use of one room, the grass of a cow, wet or dry. She is to be given the use of the horse and car to bring her to Mass on Sunday. She is to be maintained in the condition in which she was heretofore maintained … to that type of farmer and to that type of outlook, the provisions of this Bill must have been not merely academic but a shock (*PDDE*, 213: 481, 483).

During the Debate, Deputy Seán MacEoin asked Mr Lenihan if there had been any consultation with Catholic social and moral thinkers on the contents of the Bill. The Minister assured Deputy MacEoin that he had taken the very best moral and canon law advice available, including 'some of the top Catholic theologians in this country also' (*PDDE* 213: 410), and that the advice fully endorsed the provisions of the Bill:

The influence of Canon Law on the law of succession has always been very great. Provisions providing for legal rights to specific shares for a widow and children are to be found in all countries in the Catholic tradition. … There is an endorsement of the essential rights of the family in this Bill (*PDDE*, 213: 1062).

Following further lengthy debate the Bill was declared carried in the Dáil on 7 July 1965. There was an extensive debate in the Seanad also, in the course of which two women senators, Miss Mary Davidson and Mrs Kit Ahern, expressed their support. Senator Davidson described the Bill as 'a fair and just measure' (*Seanad Debates* 59:445), while Senator Ahern said that 'He (the Minister) has at least tried to ensure that part of the promise made at the altar – with all my worldly goods I thee endow – will be carried through' (*Seanad Debates* 59:463).

Family Planning Act, 1979: 'an Irish solution to an Irish problem'

In 1914 when the American social reformer Margaret Sanger introduced the term 'birth control' in a publication called *The Woman Rebel*, she was naming the phenomenon that would become a major catalyst for social change. In 1921 London's first birth control clinic opened, while two years later the National Birth-rate Commission in the UK recommended sex education in schools and homes. Doubtless with an eye on happenings in the UK, the *Censorship Act*, 1929 in Ireland made it illegal to advocate the use of contraceptives. The development of birth control devices continued apace and in 1934 Durex condoms were first produced. Alarm bells were ringing in Ireland and Edward Cahill wrote to de

Valera the same year concerning the availability of contraceptives, saying, 'Civil law and government cannot indeed make or even keep a nation moral. They can however keep a check on unfair temptations or allurements to vice' (Cahill, 1934). In the following year Section 17 of the *Criminal Law Amendment Act*, 1935 prohibited the sale and importation of contraceptives.

The discovery of the so-called 'safe period' in the 1930s led to permission for the use of the 'rhythm method' of family planning by Catholics. In the late 1940s and early 1950s in Dublin, family planning practices – both by the rhythm method and by continence – were reported. In a survey at the time a young couple in which the husband was a clerical worker said that they practised birth control. The husband said, 'People have to curtail their families. ... The cost is terrible and this business about free maternity service is bunk. It is inefficient and no one is going to avail himself of it unless he is a pauper' (Humphreys, 1966: 211). The wife in a different couple agreed: 'I think people practise family control. The women talk about it quite a bit and I know several girls who say they do. They'll often mention the fact that they are trying to limit the family and that they will be disappointed if they have another baby too soon' (Humphreys, *ibid*: 211).

The practice of this type of family limitation was borne out by contemporary medical evidence as well as by a number of priests who said that control by rhythm and continence was on the increase while contraception was virtually non-existent. Contraception was a taboo. When in March 1935 Dr Halliday-Sutherland gave a public lecture in the Gaiety Theatre in Dublin in aid of the Central Catholic Library, the following report appeared in *The Catholic Times*, published in London:

> It was a pity that those responsible for the lecture selected as the subject for the major portion of the address the question of Birth Control. This evil is almost unknown and certainly not prevalent in Ireland. In these circumstances, a public lecture on it is very much out of place (*The Catholic Times*, London, 29 March 1935).

In 1954 two Americans, Dr Pincus and Dr Rock, while researching the causes of sterility, discovered a drug which brings about in a woman's body what occurs naturally during pregnancy – the suppression of ovulation. In 1960 G.P. Searle Co. introduced Envoid 10, a commercially developed oral contraceptive in the US. Church authorities and theologians became heavily involved in discussing the anovulant pill and the moral questions related to its use. Ten years after the discovery of 'The Pill' it was being prescribed in Ireland as a 'cycle-regulator', a 'side-effect' of which was that a woman taking the Pill did not become pregnant. The publication in 1968 of the Papal Encyclical *Humanae Vitae*, which declared the use of any form of artificial birth control as contrary to Church teaching, triggered an immense debate throughout the Catholic Church in the developed world, including Ireland. Ten years earlier, on 7 April 1958, family planning received the support of the Church of England.

Because the contraceptive pill was prescribed as a 'cycle-regulator', it was exempt from the law which prohibited the importation and sale of contraceptives. The right of access to other methods of contraception became an important battleground between Catholic traditionalists and the younger generation of liberals. A key figure among the new generation was a young barrister, Mary Robinson, a Trinity graduate, who had been radicalised while engaged in post-graduate studies in Boston in the mid-1960s. In 1969 the first Family Planning Clinic opened in Dublin and began to supply contraceptives. While it was illegal to sell contraceptives, the supply of contraceptives was made possible by 'voluntary' donations from clients. Numbers attending the clinics began to grow; according to the then Senator Mary Robinson, speaking in the Senate in December 1976, two centres in Dublin run by the Irish Family Planning Association (IFPA) had seen 30,000 clients in 1976 (Whyte, 1980: 404). This total amounts to approximately 60 clients per working day.

Increased demand for contraception, evident from the number of prescriptions for the Pill, and the numbers attending the Family Planning Clinics, which were gradually developing a network throughout Ireland, was accompanied by a change in public opinion. This was apparent from the increasing numbers who, according to responses given in opinion polls, favoured the legalisation of contraceptives (Whyte, *ibid*: 404-5). Judging that the tide was turning, in 1971 Senator Mary Robinson and fellow Trinity College Senator Trevor West, together with Senator John Horgan, endeavoured to introduce a Bill in the Senate which would permit the importation and sale of contraceptives. It failed to get a first reading by twenty-five votes to fourteen votes. Senator Robinson and Senator Horgan both subsequently joined the Labour Party. At a time when Fianna Fáil under Jack Lynch, and Fine Gael under Liam Cosgrave, supported traditional values, the Labour Party in the 1970s attracted a number of younger aspirants anxious to cut their teeth on a liberal agenda.

As there was no sign that the Legislature would take the initiative and change the law, a group of women decided to take the law into their own hands, and the law turned a blind eye on them. On 22 May 1971, when a contingent of women arrived at Connolly Station on their return from a trip to Belfast, a trip that had been expressly undertaken to purchase contraceptives, the authorities chose to ignore them. The government simply decided not to enforce the *Criminal Law Amendment Act*, 1935 on the occasion. Even when the women marched to the nearby Store Street police station, the gardaí took no action. Enormous publicity ensued. On the *Late Late Show* that evening, two of the shoppers, Mary Kenny and Colette O'Neill, spoke about the need to make contraceptives legally available. In the following year, 1972, two Labour Party TDs, Dr John O'Connell and Dr Noël Browne, introduced a further Bill in the Dáil aimed at repealing the 1935 ban, but it was defeated on first reading by 75 votes to 44. In July 1974, in the Dáil, two Labour deputies, Justin Keating and Barry Desmond, spoke respectively of contraception as a positive good and as a human right.

A further attempt late in 1973 by Senators Robinson, Horgan and West to reintroduce their Bill in the Senate succeeded. The granting of a first reading to the Bill led to an interesting statement by the Catholic hierarchy. While condemning contraception, 'They disclaimed any suggestion that the state was obliged to defend by legislation the moral teaching of the Catholic Church' (Whyte, *ibid*: 407). Their argument hinged not on Catholic teaching but on the effects on society of a liberalisation of the law on contraception. In a statement issued by the hierarchy in November 1973, reflecting on possible changes in the law, they accepted that the State was not obliged to uphold the moral teaching of the Church in its legislation: 'There are many things which the Catholic Church holds to be morally wrong and no one has ever suggested, least of all the church herself, that they should be prohibited by the State' (*Irish Independent*, 26 November 1973).

The basis of the bishops' case against the legalisation of contraception was its effect on the quality of life in Ireland. If politicians and people could be convinced that contraception would have undesirable social consequences, rather than simply conflicting with the teaching of the Catholic Church, then support might come from those who would not necessarily support Catholic Church teaching. At any rate the shift in emphasis by the hierarchy opened the door to the possibility of passing legislation on contraception without creating a direct Church/State clash. This collective approach of the hierarchy contrasted sharply with a number of statements by individual bishops, including those of Dr McQuaid in 1971, and of Dr Newman of Limerick in 1976, who both roundly condemned the possible legalisation of contraception. Dr Birch of Kilkenny took a more open approach. In a letter to newspapers in 1972, he indicated that one could not expect to defend morality by legal prohibitions:

> I don't think we can hope to defend morality by enactment. We can only win people to it. I believe that these enactments are a hard edge behind which we hide, and which we use to free ourselves from responsible effort. As Christians … we must begin by being ourselves convinced of the value of Christian morality and of our personal and communal responsibility in it and to it (Ryan, 1993: 86).

The Legislature delayed action, and a legal campaign, which ended in the Supreme Court, was launched. Towards the end of 1973 matters were brought to a head with the Supreme Court judgment in the case of *McGee v. The Attorney General*. Mrs McGee wished to obtain contraceptive material that she and her husband could use together in private. With that objective she placed an order for such material which was in due course impounded by the Customs. The Irish Family Planning Association supported Mrs McGee's case in which Mary Robinson acted as counsel. The action was dismissed by the President of the High Court, Mr Justice O'Keeffe. In a far-reaching decision, delivered by Mr Justice

Brian Walsh, in which many American decisions were cited, the Supreme Court held, on appeal, that there was a right under the Constitution to marital privacy and Mrs McGee won her case. The McGee case was a key example of the Courts leading and the politicians reacting in introducing social change. The judgment also represented a shift towards a less traditionalist Supreme Court.

It fell to the Cosgrave-led Coalition of Fine Gael and Labour to act in the wake of the McGee case. When the Fine Gael Minister for Justice, Patrick Cooney, introduced a Bill providing for the control of importation, sale and manufacture of contraceptives, Fianna Fáil opposed the Bill and Fine Gael allowed a free vote as a matter of conscience. According to Garret FitzGerald, then a Cabinet member, the Bill '... was not strictly a Government Bill but one introduced by the Minister for Justice, Pat Cooney, on his own account, a distinction that I am afraid was far too subtle for many people to grasp' (FitzGerald, 1991: 309). The Bill was defeated by 75 votes to 61. Seven Fine Gael deputies voted against the Bill, including the Taoiseach, Liam Cosgrave, and the Minister for Education, Dick Burke. No further attempts to legislate were made during the life of the Coalition. Cosgrave has been criticised for not informing his colleagues in advance of his voting intentions, but he believed that to have done so '... would have wrecked the Bill. I wrecked it anyway. But I would have pre-empted their right to decide'.[13] The accuracy of Cosgrave's judgement is borne out by FitzGerald's allegation that once Cosgrave had voted '... some who had not yet passed through the lobbies decided to follow him' (FitzGerald, ibid: 309).

For Cosgrave, a free vote was what it said. Cosgrave thought it wrong to have contraceptives freely available and that a substantial number in the country at the time were in agreement with him. Apart from his private judgement, he recalls that a strong argument at the time in favour of contraception was that it would prevent the spread of sexually transmitted diseases, yet sexual diseases are more prevalent today so he does not see evidence that contraceptives have been successful in this regard.[14] Dr Fiona Mulcahy, consultant in the State's main clinic for sexually transmitted diseases at St James's Hospital in Dublin, has described the increase in syphilis in the city as 'epidemic', while Dr Derek Freedman, genito-urinary physician, gives as a main reason for the increase in syphilis, the fact that there are now more sexually active young people (The Irish Times, 28 November 2000).

When Fianna Fáil under Jack Lynch were returned to office in 1977, responsibility for legislation on contraception was transferred from the Department of Justice to the Department of Health where the Minister was Charles Haughey. Haughey had been in the political wilderness since the events of 1970 surrounding the Arms Trial, and Lynch in handing Haughey the matter of dealing with the Supreme Court judgment and the fall-out from the McGee case, was handing him a potentially poisoned chalice. Haughey describes the Family Planning battle as 'Probably a more seriously politically acute battle' than that surrounding the Succession Act. This was because people who were opposed, sometimes in a very hostile manner, to the legalisation of contraceptives were genuinely sincere in their opposition; they were not simply opposing on political grounds. Opponents included personal friends and close political associates: 'political friends and allies convinced that what we were doing was wrong'. Haughey says that the real battle was inside the Fianna Fáil Party, and inside the Government.[15]

Haughey set about a systematic consultation process with interested parties, inviting representatives of all the Churches, including the Catholic bishops, to discuss the matter. Margaret Hayes, who in 1995 became the second woman in the history of the State to become Secretary of a government Department, was an administrative officer in the Department of Health at the time. In 1977 she had just entered the General Medical Services Division of the Department of Health, having spent two years in the Collector General's Office:

> I was given a project the minute I arrived which was the Family Planning Bill. Charlie Haughey was the minister at the time and one of his priorities was to deliver on this legislation which was outstanding since the Magee judgment of 1973 (it said there should be legislation for contraception). There had been a few false starts and Charlie Haughey said that he would try to sort it out (O'Toole, 1995).

Margaret Hayes has described how she was given the task of identifying who should be consulted, and of organising the consultations and helping to achieve compromise. She was also involved with the process of drafting the legislation and preparing responses on any matters that might arise as the Minister steered the legislation through the Dáil and Seanad. The work spanned the period from spring 1978 until the legislation was enacted in the summer of 1979. Hayes then worked on the implementation of the legislation, which included licensing arrangements for the importation of contraceptives:

> It [the legislation] was popularly known as the Irish solution to the Irish problem. The key phrase in the bill was that contraception was to be available on prescription for *bona fide* family planning purposes. We felt that it was as far as we could go in terms of public acceptability but it did pave the way for subsequent amendments (*ibid*).

According to Hayes, Haughey took a 'hands-on' interest and was 'very involved in what was a very tight team'. Finally in July 1979 the anti-contraception laws were removed and the legislation passed without any confrontation between Church and State.

The *Status of Children Act*, 1987

In 1984 the Supreme Court ruled that illegitimate children had no succession rights in respect of their father's estate where their father died intestate. An unmarried man died intestate, leaving a daughter, sisters and a brother and it was argued on behalf of the daughter that the *Succession Act,* 1965 should be interpreted to permit an illegitimate child to succeed to her father's estate. If this was not accepted, it was argued, the Act was unconstitutional in that it discriminated against the child. The Supreme Court held that the *Succession Act* distinguished between legitimate and illegitimate children, and that the Act gave no rights of succession to a father's estate to an illegitimate child. All persons had to be treated equally before the law but the distinction made between the rights of children born in and out of marriage had to be considered in the light of the Act, one of the purposes of which was to safeguard the inheritance rights of married persons and of the children of a marriage. The Court ruled that the Oireachtas, by acting to protect the legitimate family, was acting in accordance with Article 41 of the Constitution.

In 1983 the Law Reform Commission had argued that existing law could not be justified in protecting the institution of marriage by denying the rights of innocent persons, namely, 'children born outside marriage', and in the opinion of the Commission the Constitution would not require such a conclusion. The Law Reform Commission made a far-reaching proposal 'that the legislation remove the concept of illegitimacy from the law and equalise the rights of children born outside marriage with those of children born within marriage'. The Commission were aware that this would mean the recognition of the parental relationship 'in cases which the law in many countries has been reluctant to recognise – namely where children are born as a result of adulterous or incestuous unions'. The Commission stated, 'in our view it should be open to the mother, a man alleging that he is the father, the child, or any person with a proper interest, to take proceedings seeking a declaration as to parenthood.' The Commission recommended that in proceeding to establish parenthood the father and the mother should be compellable witnesses, and that it should be possible to ask for a declaration of parenthood 'at any time during the joint lives of the parent and child, and where either dies, within six years of the death, where a share in the estate is being claimed'.

The *Status of Children Act* was passed in 1987. The principle underlying this Act is to place children whose parents have not married each other on the same footing, or as nearly so as possible, as the children of married parents in the areas of guardianship, maintenance and property rights. The non-marital child will first have to prove his/her claim in Court. The Act provides a means of appointing the father of a non-marital child as joint guardian with the child's mother by applying to a Court. Where the mother consents and the father has been entered on the births' register as the father, joint guardianship can be effected with the minimum formality. The non-marital children of a testator are also given the right to apply for just provision under the *Succession Act*. It is worth noting that the *Status of Children Act*, 1987 differs in at least one important feature from the recommendations of the Law Reform Commission on the matter of illegitimacy. The main difference is that the Law Reform

Commission recommended *prima facie* that the father of an illegitimate child should be in the same position as the father of a legitimate child and that it was up to the mother to apply to the Court if this position was to be altered. The *Status of Children Act* puts the onus the other way.

Judicial separation, 1989; divorce, 1995

Judicial separation or *divorce a mensa et toro* was available in Ireland since 1870, when under Section 7 of the *Matrimonial Causes (Ireland) Act*, 1870 the High Court was given power to grant a judicial separation. The *Courts Act*, 1981 extended the jurisdiction to grant judicial separations to the Circuit Court. Sometimes separations occurred on the basis of voluntary agreement between the couple, while on other occasions an amalgam of barring orders, maintenance orders and custody orders featured. Although the Law Reform Commission had recommended in the early 1980s that separation should not be fault based, until the passing of the *Family Law Reform and Judicial Separation Act* in 1989, the basis of judicial separation was fault based. To obtain a decree against a spouse, a plaintiff had to prove that the defendant was guilty on one of the following: adultery, cruelty or unnatural practices. The *Family Law (Maintenance of Spouses and Children) Act*, 1976 had introduced a significant shift away from fault based procedures when adultery was made a discretionary bar to maintenance rather than an absolute bar. The *Family Law Reform and Judicial Separation Act*, 1989 resulted from a private members' Bill introduced by Alan Shatter, TD. It was the first private member's Bill to pass into law for over thirty years. The Act established the right to a judicial separation even when one party to a marriage opposed such a separation and had been guilty of no matrimonial misconduct.

Under the *Matrimonial Causes Act*, 1857, which was law in Ireland at the time of Independence, divorce could be obtained by way of a private bill in the Westminster Parliament. Although there was no reference to marriage or the family in the 1922 Constitution, the Attorney General, Hugh Kennedy, favoured allowing divorce for those who wanted it, thus providing freedom of choice for the Protestant minority. Three private divorce bills were actually presented in Ireland. However, in 1925 the Free State government carried a motion in the Dáil to make it impossible for such Bills to be introduced in future. Mr Cosgrave said:

> I have no doubt but that I am right in saying that the majority of people in this country regard the bond of marriage as a sacramental bond which is incapable of being dissolved. I personally hold this view. I consider that the whole fabric of our social organisation is based upon the sanctity of the marriage bond and that anything that tends to weaken the binding efficacy of that bond to that extent strikes at the root of our social life (*PDDE*, 10: 158, 11 February 1925, quoted in Whyte 1980: 37).

Mr Cosgrave's opposition to divorce was not sectarian. While he personally viewed marriage as a sacramental bond, incapable of dissolution, he also argued that the entire social fabric depended on the strength of the marriage bond. To weaken marriage would weaken society. Likewise, in 1937, when de Valera introduced his draft constitution to the Dáil, he emphasised the social dimension to the stability of marriage:

> Then, we have in this Constitution also the family. We refer to the family, and make it quite clear that in our view the fundamental group of the State – in a sense the most important group of the State – is the family. We pledge the State to protect the family, to protect it in its constitution and in its rights generally. This is not merely a question of religious teaching; even from the purely social side, apart altogether from that, I would propose here that we should not sanction divorce. Therefore no law can be passed providing for divorce (*PDDE*, 67: 63, 11 May 1937).

Between the enactment of the Constitution in 1937, and the New Ireland Forum which operated between May 1983 and May 1984, a fundamental change took place in the attitude of the hierarchy. In their submission to the New Ireland Forum, the hierarchy stated: 'The Catholic Church in Ireland totally rejects the concept of a confessional state. We have not sought and we do not seek a Catholic State for a Catholic people.' The Declaration on Religious Liberty of the Second Vatican Council contributed to the position adopted by the hierarchy (Riordan, 1995: 125), as did unfolding developments in Northern Ireland. In addition, the changed behaviour of the Irish people indicated that legal restrictions had failed to deliver outcomes in tune with Church teaching. Marriages were breaking down. Garret FitzGerald, who is against divorce personally, claims that the reason why he wished to introduce divorce in 1986 was in order to protect marriage. He believed that marriage was being undermined through the frequency of second unions, which were recognised by neither Church nor State. He says that he was against divorce as long as it could be avoided. According to FitzGerald the debate in 1986 was between two groups of people whose views he did not accept. On the one hand there were those who claimed divorce to be a 'civil right', and on the other the Church was saying that the floodgates would open. FitzGerald says that the idea of divorce as a civil right is, 'A nonsense. You can't have a civil right to break a contract that was indissoluble. That's a contradiction in terms.' With regard to the Church argument, 'Marriage was being destabilised through the absence of divorce.' He says that in the debate only one person, a bishop, dealt with his point, and did so ineffectively in two sentences, in the opinion of FitzGerald who claims, 'I was the only person who was right, which I must say, I don't normally feel.'[16] He believes that in 1986, 'Property was the fact that defeated the divorce referendum. No doubt about that.'

An advocate of the claim that divorce *did* represent a civil right was the Irish Congress of Trade Unions. At the Annual Conference of ICTU in 1982, the following resolution was adopted:

Conference, recognising that the irretrievable breakdown of marriage can and does occur and that because of this divorce is and should be recognised as a civil right, calls on Congress to campaign for and support the necessary legislative steps to be taken by the Government towards this end (ICTU, 1986: 200).

In January 1984, the Executive Council of ICTU forwarded a submission to the Oireachtas Joint Committee on Marriage Breakdown and met the Committee in May 1984 to discuss the details of their submission in which they reiterated the view that divorce was a 'civil right' (ICTU, 1984: 1). Congress concluded its submission by saying that in defining divorce as a civil right, it was signalling that access to divorce should not be denied because of lack of financial means. In December 1985 the Executive Council agreed to take steps to promote the introduction of divorce, including the issue and circulation of 150,000 Divorce Handbills which were to be launched publicly by Congress. Ten years later in the divorce referendum in 1995, Congress again played an active role, though of this occasion ICTU Handbills stressed 'The Right to Remarry'.

Carol Coulter, writer and legal affairs correspondent of *The Irish Times*, has shown that the government's campaign to legalise divorce in the 1990s was largely waged on the pragmatic grounds that a growing number of marriages were breaking down, and that the number of separated people in second unions was rising, while there was an absence of debate on the nature of values that should inform the law. The 1986 Census was the first census to provide information on the breakdown of marriage. Prior to 1986, information on marital breakdown had been published in *Labour Force Surveys*. In 1986 over 37,000 persons were returned as separated; by the time of the 1991 census, 34,000 women and 21,000 men were classified as separated. According to the 1993 Labour Force Survey, 39,000 women were numbered as separated. In advocating an end to the constitutional ban on divorce the government claimed that approximately 80,000 persons were affected by marital breakdown. The Report of the Second Commission on the Status of Women (1993), recommended the removal of the ban.

In proposing the introduction of divorce legislation prior to the 1995 referendum, the government and the Department of Equality and Law Reform which sponsored the constitutional amendment, relied heavily on the growth in the number of married people who were separated. The government publication *The Right to Remarry* also relied heavily on the number of separated persons as the basis for constitutional change. The basis for the government campaign rested on pragmatism, rather than ideology. Coulter has argued that the social base for the ideology of the anti-divorce lobby had been eroded by changing social realities:

Social, attitudinal, and legislative changes had brought about a situation where lone parents made up a significant, and no longer stigmatized, minority, where many married women with children worked outside the home and favoured a sharing of responsibility in providing for the family and in domestic tasks between partners. The presentation of female dependency as either the ideal or the norm was no longer acceptable (Coulter, 1997: 293).

The introduction of divorce legislation in the form of the *Family Law (Divorce) Act*, 1996, on 27 February 1997, following a referendum which was carried by a wafer-thin majority, opened the door to re-marriage for those whose marriages have broken down. In its editorial on 28 February 1997, *The Irish Times* hailed the arrival of divorce with enthusiasm:

> The introduction of divorce yesterday is a milestone in Ireland's social development and the culmination of a long campaign to modernise our social legislation. The right to divorce joins the right to contraception, homosexual expression and freedom to travel for abortion in a liberal agenda of change that has taken a generation to complete (*The Irish Times*, 28 February 1997).

On the 'This Week' radio programme on Sunday 29 November 1998, John Bruton, Taoiseach at the time the divorce referendum was passed, claimed credit that in an interview 'in this studio' prior to the vote, his contribution had been responsible 'for swinging it'.

According to the 1996 Census, close to 95,000 persons have experienced marital breakdown (Census 1996, Vol. 2). This includes 78,000 who are separated, 10,000 who are divorced, and 6,600 who remarried, following the dissolution of an earlier marriage. Although the majority reside in cities, separated people are spread throughout the land. The highest proportion of separated people, 9 per cent of the ever-married, live in Dublin, followed by 8 per cent of ever-married in Limerick, with the proportion down to 3 per cent in Roscommon and Cavan. Many more women are listed as separated than men. In the category 'deserted' 23,000 women described themselves as deserted, compared with 6,000 men. The peak age for separation appears to be from the mid-30s to the mid-40s. The number of separated women is over 1,700 for each year between ages 35-47; while for men there are over 1,200 separated for each year between the ages 29-48. Marriage breakdown is also happening at very young ages. Seven men and four women aged seventeen years are described as separated, with twenty-five men and forty-two women separated by age twenty years.

Since the introduction of divorce, demand for divorce has climbed. The demand was slow to manifest itself, with less than five hundred applications and one hundred grants of divorce up to mid-1997. But in the three-year period from August 1997 to July 2000 there were well in excess of 6,000 grants of divorce.

Looking back over the twentieth century the Irish people have, via their government, directed the course of family change in many respects. They have removed the concept of illegitimacy from the law, changed the constitutional definition of the family by passing a referendum to permit divorce, and supported financial aid for unmarried parents and the abolition of allowances for children in the tax code. The immediate origin of these and other changes – both those that affected the distribution of resources available to families, and those that influenced the rules within which families operate – have been of three main types. There have been those that grew out of the initiatives of the government, frequently with a large amount of popular support, e.g. the Land Acts, or of individual ministers or civil servants, e.g. the *Succession Act*. Also in this category are those that grew from the suggestion of a single parliamentarian or from a Private Member's Bill, e.g. Deputy James Dillon in the case of children's allowances, and Deputy Alan Shatter in the case of Judicial Separation. Secondly, there have been those changes that came about as the result of a recommendation of a Commission of Enquiry or of a specialist Commission, as with the introduction of the Unmarried Mother's Allowance which was recommended by the Commission on the Status of Women, or the *Status of Children Act*, 1987, which changed the law on illegitimacy, and which came from a recommendation of the Law Reform Commission. Finally, there have been those changes that emanated from individuals or groups within the community, who campaigned and challenged the status quo, sometimes via resort to the Courts, as in the McGee case and in the campaign to repeal the constitutional ban on divorce.

It seems that with some notable exceptions, for example the *Succession Act*, governments of all complexions have been slow to take the initiative to change existing law, e.g. regarding contraception or divorce, until stimulated to do so by some element of public demand, or left with no option due to a decision of the Courts. Of crucial importance, not only in regard to the last mentioned category of change, but also in regard to certain initiatives that emanated from government and Commissions of Enquiry, have been the behavioural changes of the Irish people. As more children were born outside marriage, as more family planning was practised, as more marriages broke down, pragmatism, not ideology, dictated change.

10

Three Arches:
Economy – Policy – Values

Central to this study is the idea that changes in family patterns have been driven by economic factors which, when they gained sufficient strength, tended to outweigh those of tradition and religion. Policy and institutional changes were frequently introduced to accommodate choices already made by the people.

At the start of the twentieth century marriage between a man and a woman – ''til death us do part' – was the cornerstone of the family and of society. Lower expectation of life at the time of marriage, combined with a higher average age at marriage, resulted in a shorter average length of marriage. Due to the increased expectation of life over the course of the century, and the earlier age at marriage, marriages today may be longer on average. The introduction of divorce means that marriage may be terminated by law as well as by death. At the dawn of the twenty-first century, life-long marriage is an option among other lifestyle choices. In the opening days of 1999, the results of an opinion poll carried out by *Irish Marketing Surveys* were published, based on a sample of over one thousand adults at one hundred locations throughout the country. Bearing in mind the caveats attached to such polls, it emerged that among those aged 25 years and under, 89 per cent thought living with a partner before marriage was acceptable, while 86 per cent thought having sex before marriage was acceptable. Unmarried parents were acceptable to 80 per cent of the under 25s. For all adults, 18 years and over, 64 per cent accepted living with a partner before marriage, 59 per cent accepted sex before marriage, while 53 per cent found unmarried parents acceptable (Devlin, 1999).

One hundred years ago a majority lived on the land and the realities of survival helped to bind families together. Relatively few persons lived alone: only one in twelve of the population in 1926 compared with more than one in five in 1996. Less than one in twenty elderly persons lived alone compared with more than one in four today. The threat of poverty was real for many, if not most, families. For those who emigrated the needs of family and relatives remained insistent. In the 1950s adult children who had emigrated were still expected to send 'the slate money' home to their parents, so that the old thatch could be replaced (Healy, 1978). As late as 1961 over 50 per cent of the population lived in rural areas, and until the mid-1960s there were more people employed in agriculture than in industry (Kennedy, Giblin and McHugh, 1988:

143). By 2000 less than 8 per cent of the workforce were engaged in agriculture and Ireland no longer defines herself as an agricultural country. As jobs outside agriculture gradually expanded from the 1920s to the 1960s, priority was accorded to male employment, or jobs for breadwinners. To this end a marriage bar was introduced in the civil service and teaching professions together with restrictions on female employment in industry. The references to the family and to the woman in the home in the Constitution reflected widely held values. One can only guess at de Valera's private thoughts, but economic exigencies may have formed the base of that particular constitutional triangle, with traditional gender roles and Catholic Church teaching forming the other two sides.

Following the lean decades of the 1930s, 1940s and 1950s when the economic opportunities for marriage were restricted, growth in the 1960s ushered in the 'Golden Age of Marriage' in Ireland. For the majority of European countries, the post-war years until the mid-1960s represent the 'Golden Age of Marriage' (Van de Kaa, 1987), followed from the mid-1970s by a sharp decline in first marriage rates, with some stabilisation in the 1980s. Just as marriage was falling out of favour in much of the rest of Europe, in Ireland the 'Golden Age' was dawning. It persisted until the early 1970s and has since faded rapidly, with a glimmer of recovery in the past year or so. Most other European countries were experiencing the 'Dawn of Cohabitation' in the 1960s, a time when marriage was taking place in increasing numbers and at a rising rate in Ireland. In the words of Dutch social scientist Anton Kuijsten, on the menu of life choices, formal marriage shifted from an obligatory main course to optional dessert (Kuijsten, 1994:3). For twenty years from 1974 to 1993 the number of marriages in Ireland fell steadily, and the marriage rate fell by over 40 per cent from 7.4 to 4.4. An intriguing question is whether the upturn recorded since 1996 indicates a change in trend.

A comparable pattern occurred in relation to births, with a decline in births in Ireland following that in the rest of Europe. For most European countries, except Ireland, where the decline came some years later, there was a free-fall in fertility from the second half of the 1960s, a fall described by one demographer as 'la tempête dans le ciel d'azur' (a bolt from the blue) (Calot, 1990). The result of the fall in births has been below replacement fertility from the early 1970s until the present. Nowhere was the fall in births more dramatic than in the former German Democratic Republic. Following a brief initial rise, nine months after the fall of the Berlin Wall on 10 October 1989, births in East Germany plummeted from 216, 000 in 1988 to 80,000 in 1993. The fall in births has been accompanied by a fall in fertility. At the foundation of the Irish State completed fertility of married women was close to six children and very large families were commonplace. The decline in large families has been marked over the past thirty years. In 1965 there were 9,000 families with eight or more eligible children in receipt of children's allowances. Thirty years later in 1995, despite the extension of allowances to children up to 18 years, or including 18 years if in full-time education, the number of recipient families with eight or more eligible children had fallen to 974.

In 1921 the maternal mortality rate was 4.8 per 1,000 births, equivalent to the death of a mother for every 200 births. In the 1920s infant mortality was between 70 and 80 per 1,000 births. By the closing years of the century maternal and infant mortality rates reached record lows. Between 1980 and 1995 fewer children were born each year but their years of dependency were extended as more went on to third level education. Early in the century the majority of the population left school after primary level. In 1929 only 38 per cent of 14 and 15 year olds were at school. Educational participation has soared with 95 per cent of those aged 14-16 years at school, 61 per cent of 18-year-olds and 35 per cent of 20-year-olds in full-time education.

Ireland has also followed the general European trend with regard to the rise in births outside marriage. With a majority of births occurring outside marriage in a number of European countries and one-third of births so occurring in Ireland, marriage is clearly no longer the near universal framework for reproduction that it was in 1900. In the EU as a whole there are nearly seven million lone parents, 84 per cent of whom are women with dependent children, comprising 14 per cent of all families with dependent children. The UK has the highest proportion – 23 per cent of all its families with dependent children; Greece has the lowest share with 7 per cent, while Ireland occupies a middle position with 13 per cent (Eurostat, 1998). In 1996 only half of all families had a single breadwinner. In two-parent families with at least one child under fifteen, more than one in three were dual earner families, while one in eight of these families had no earner. Two-thirds of one-parent families had only one earner. These data 'highlight the emergence of "work rich" and "work poor" families which has been observed in other EU countries' (McKeown, Ferguson and Rooney, 1998: 22-3). The growth in dual earner households on the one hand and welfare dependent households on the other has been associated with the increase in the labour force participation of married women, both at work and out of work, which rose from only 5 per cent in 1966, to nearly 40 per cent in 1998.

The rise in living standards, combined with a reduction in child-bearing, and increased educational and employment opportunities, has vastly increased the options for women. The life chances of children, girls and boys, born in the early 1900s, varied widely; there were those born into privilege, there were those born with great ability who would succeed against the odds, there were those born into great poverty, and there were those born close to the average living standard. A majority of the population were born and died in their own homes. Half-way through the century one in three births and two in three deaths occurred at home. At the end of the century only 4 in 1,000 births were domiciliary while one in five persons died at home (Heanue, 2000: 33-5). A typical girl born in a rural cottage in the 1900s worked on the family homestead from childhood and left school at twelve years of age or earlier. In time she either married and lived out her life as mother and grandmother, and very likely also as a widow; or she remained single and worked as a 'relative assisting', or she emigrated. Those of her daughters who were born at home in the 1930s, and who survived, experienced a pattern of life closer to that of their mother than to that of their own daughters who would be born towards the end of the 1950s and in the early 1960s and who would benefit from post-primary education and the growth in the economy. By the time the first cohort of free post-primary beneficiaries was leaving school, methods of contraception were becoming available and women were choosing greater labour force involvement and the freedom of the wage packet. As more mothers entered employment, more small children were cared for in crèches.

A comparison of the life stories of four grandmothers born in the early decades of the twentieth century on the fringes of the EU in Finland, Greece, Ireland and Portugal show many common experiences. Before globalisation, these women had seen, and some had been involved in, two world wars, the Great Depression, and the oil crises. At the same time they had cared for their families and did the work of building the new generations. The conclusion of Julia, the Irishwoman in the study who was born in 1910, was:

> While the opportunities for my mother's generation and for my own when growing up were the same – if you got a man with a farm and a few acres you were alright – young girls in the 1990s have far more opportunities open to them. They are much better educated. However, old people are much better off now than in former times (Kangas, 1997: 173).

Economy

There is a strong current of continuity flowing throughout the century; the culmination of quantitative changes in the early years are such that qualitative change clearly emerges in the later years, but from the perspective of family change, entry into the EEC in 1973 represents a defining point of change. Until then Ireland was widely viewed as an agricultural society in which the family farm still provided the basis of livelihood, despite the fact that the long-term shift away from agriculture was already well under way as more and more breadwinners obtained jobs in the towns and cities. The agricultural policy of the EEC essentially encouraged the development of larger farms and hastened the demise of the traditional smaller family farm. The growth in the economy increased employment opportunities for women; in addition, the expansion of social welfare provision in the 1970s created the option for solo motherhood.

The conventional wisdom among economists and historians (Kennedy, Giblin and McHugh, 1988; Lee, 1989; Ó Gráda, 1997) is that from Independence through to the late 1980s, the Irish economy underperformed. In analysing the growth record, Kennedy argues that the record was 'mediocre' at best. He suggests the possibility that Ireland may have pursued other goals, for example, a quiet life, or large families (Kennedy, Giblin and McHugh, 1988: 15). He quotes Lee as the 'only other author to address this issue' and says that Lee dismisses the suggestion scornfully, saying that the Irish did not lack concern for material gain, though they may have been 'inefficient materialists'. Of course the Irish do not, and did not, 'lack concern for material gain', and it is clear from this study that economic factors have had a crucial influence on behaviour; but it is equally true to say that, at certain times in Irish history, economic growth was most emphatically *not* top of the political agenda, or the over-riding national goal. In the early years of the State, convulsed by civil war, the Cosgrave government had to ensure that the State itself survived. 'A quiet life' was an unimagined luxury: 'The major problem faced by Cosgrave and his colleagues was the damage done to the country's infrastructure wrought by the Civil War. In its determination to prove that Ireland was capable of self-government the Cosgrave government ran a tight fiscal policy as it re-built the country' (Collins, 1996: 44).

In uniquely difficult circumstances the economic achievements of those years were remarkable notwithstanding the fact that the primary goal was more urgent than economic growth. The allocation of tens of thousands of acres of land under the *Land Act* of 1923 provided the practical basis for the livelihood of thousands of families. The decision to build the hydro-electric plant on the river Shannon and its successful completion resulted in the most remarkable piece of infrastructure ever provided by the State. The integrity of the currency and of the banking system was maintained while the efficiency and effectiveness of the postal services were legendary in those days, matters of the greatest importance for the development of industry and commerce.

Fianna Fáil, in turn, when it came into Office in 1932, placed other goals ahead of economic growth. Although Industry and Commerce Minister, Seán Lemass, was developing his plan for industrialisation behind protective tariff barriers, de Valera was concerned with ending Partition and the creation of a self-sufficient rural society populated by small farm families, a type of society that was in opposition to growth. Economic growth was sacrificed in 1932 as Fianna Fáil held to its pre-election promise of refusing to repay £3 million annually to Britain in the form of land annuities due in return for a loan that helped to turn tenants into proprietors, and thus the devastating Economic War was started. There was an immense short-term appeal to farmers in the non-payment of the annuities, but the British struck back; harder than de Valera had calculated. British markets were closed to Irish exports. The hardship suffered by families as a result of the pursuit of the Economic War and the associated decline in farm exports was extreme. Only its eventual resolution which involved a once-off payment in 1938, and the subsequent outbreak of World War II, staved off serious collapse. Many Irish who might otherwise have joined the unemployed, joined the British Army, while British markets reopened to Irish foodstuffs.

Lemass realised that de Valera's dream of a closed society was becoming a nightmare (O'Sullivan, 1994: 82). He realised that little material progress could be achieved as long as the economic war with Britain raged. But 'De Valera's vision was bolstered by certain aspects of the economic war and Lemass went along with endorsing De Valera's economic fiction' (O'Sullivan, *ibid*: 83-4). When the destructive Economic War was ended by the Anglo-Irish Agreement in April 1938, the damage had been done. The Great Depression now added to the problems of the Irish economy; the 1930 volume of merchandise exports was not reached again until 1960, the year following de Valera's move from the Dáil to Áras an Uachtaráin. Even more remarkably the 1930 ratio of exports to GNP was not surpassed until 1968. While the volume of industrial production increased in the 1930s, the growth was almost entirely directed into a heavily protected home market (Kennedy, Giblin and McHugh, 1988: 47). But de Valera's thoughts were elsewhere; in his oft-quoted St Patrick's Day address in 1943, he spoke of Ireland as 'the home of a people who valued material wealth only as the basis of right living, of a people who were satisfied with frugal comfort and devoted their leisure to things of the spirit'.

A firm indicator of emphasis on economic growth was signalled by the establishment of the Industrial Development Authority (IDA) by the first Inter-Party government in 1949. Its initial role was to review the operation of tariffs and quotas and to develop industry. It was soon given 'the role of attracting foreign industry as well as encouraging the establishment of new indigenous industry' (Kennedy, Giblin and McHugh, 1988:62). It was not until de Valera's twilight years as an active politician – in the late 1950s – that Lemass could redirect the national effort and energies towards material progress. As Charles Haughey put it: Lemass 'had no objection to the idea of comely maidens dancing at the crossroads but he preferred to see them working in factories' (O'Sullivan, *ibid*: 139).

The soaring emigration of the mid-1950s provided unequivocal evidence of the failure of the land to provide an acceptable livelihood for hundreds of thousands of men and women and their families. According to Dr Lucey, the era of 'the vanishing Irish' had arrived: 'The rural population is vanishing and with it is vanishing the Irish race itself. Rural Ireland is stricken and dying and the will to marry on the land is almost gone' (Lucey, 1954). The lifeboat was about to be launched from the Department of Finance. While Lemass was working out his own ideas on how to increase employment and encourage industry, T.K. Whitaker, Secretary of the Department of Finance, together with departmental colleagues, was drafting the seminal *Economic Development*, the impact of which has been well documented. One point not always emphasised concerns the way in which it provided an opportunity for Fianna Fáil to move on from some of the rhetoric of its past to a practical programme geared towards improving living standards. From the 1960s onwards, economic growth became the explicit and predominant national objective, as set forth in the Programmes for Economic Expansion.

The 1960s was a decade of recovery and growth; hopes were high for continued growth when Ireland entered the EEC in 1973. However, it is worth considering the extent to which, even in the 1960s, the Irish and their political leaders chose to pursue goals other than the *maximisation* of economic growth. Partly because the UK welfare system was forging ahead and benefits were much higher in Northern Ireland than in the Republic, the government began to develop an elaborate welfare state that would necessitate high levels of taxation. Over the period of the *First Programme*, 1958-1963, the shares of public spending on education, health and social welfare as a proportion of GNP all grew. The 1970s was a critical decade with regard to the expansion of social welfare services (Kennedy, 1997). Of particular interest is the fact that in the two decades between the end of the 1960s and the end of the 1980s, when the share of social welfare in total public spending rose by nearly five percentage points from 16.4 to 21.3 per cent, the share of spending on the economic services – mining, manufacturing, construction, transport and communications and other economic services – *declined* by nearly six percentage points from 15.2 to 9.3 per cent of public expenditure. The relative emphasis placed on economic spending by Lemass was thus reduced by governments led by Jack Lynch and by the Cosgrave-Corish Coalition. This emphasis on goals other than the purely economic may have a bearing on the observation of Kennedy that among the less well-off European states, Finland, Greece, Italy, Portugal, and Spain all grew more rapidly than Ireland in the period 1960-73 (Kennedy *et al*, 1988: 122), but with the possible exception of Finland, these were countries where the welfare state did not expand so rapidly in those years. Since the late 1980s the Irish economy has turned around from one with slow growth, burdened with debt and unemployment, to the fastest growing economy in Europe. During the 1990s living standards in Ireland converged with average living standards in the EU, and the Irish economy has earned the title of 'The Celtic Tiger' (MacSharry and White, 2000).

Policy landmarks

If economic goals were not always the paramount national goals, in regard to pragmatic policies of financial support for the family, economic factors often outweighed ideological ones. In the 1920s, despite Church teaching on the family wage, the wages on the Shannon Scheme were kept low because economic reality insisted that it should be so. In the 1940s, when Dr Dignan produced his plan for social welfare, known popularly as 'Éire's Beveridge Plan', he got short shrift from Seán MacEntee who dismissed it on cost grounds as impractical (Kelly, 1998:15-16). From the 1920s to the 1960s, the importance of *financial,* as distinct from *religious,* conservatism, cannot be overestimated. If the first government of the Free State aimed to keep taxation to a minimum, so too did *Economic Development*. By contrast in the 1970s when funds were more freely available following entry to the EEC, there were no ideological brakes applied to the growth in state expenditure on a wide range of social payments, including those to unmarried mothers. The dominance of economic factors over ideological ones in policy is one which former Taoiseach Liam Cosgrave believes to have been the case.[1] Indeed there was even a case of a member of the hierarchy calling into question the relevance of papal encyclicals in the context of practical measures to confront poverty and the necessity to spend money on housing. Speaking of the poor housing conditions of families, Bishop MacNeely [2] of Raphoe said: 'We may discuss encyclicals as long as we like and the various remedies suggested, but until we get suitable housing for our people it will be impossible to make any decent progress whatever in solving our social problems' (Quoted in Kelly, 1998:12).

The development of an extensive network of social welfare services from pensions to lone parent allowances altered the financial framework for marriage. Guinnane has argued in relation to the nineteenth and early twentieth centuries that 'The Poor Law, and much later the Old Age Pensions Act, was another form of marriage substitute' (Guinnane, 1997: 232). His reasoning follows the line that the Poor Law provided some very minimal safety net for those without family members to support them, while the Old Age Pension Act likewise gave the elderly some degree of independence from their children. As the welfare state developed, services sometimes previously provided through the extended family or voluntary bodies were gradually provided for, or supplemented, by the State.

Reviewing statistical trends is one way of summarising the changes that have occurred in the family during the past one hundred years. Another way is to ask what were the really significant legislative landmarks, the key initiatives of government that made the difference. The *Status of Children Act*, 1987 which removed the distinction between children born inside and outside of marriage, and the introduction of divorce which redefined the nature of marriage, were two of the most significant. Other initiatives that may be counted as defining were the *Irish Land Act* in 1903, consolidated by the *Birrell Act* in 1911, and extended by the introduction of compulsory acquisition under the *Land Law (Commission Act),* 1923 (the *Hogan Act*), the *Old Age Pension Act* in 1908, the 1937 Constitution, the *Succession Act* in 1965, and the *Family Planning Act* in 1979.

The *Irish Land Act* marked the end of the Land Struggle and paved the way for tenant ownership. It provided more security and improved economic opportunities for the farming community, and these were to provide the backbone of Irish life and the framework of Irish family life for a long time. The *Old Age Pension Act* reduced the economic dependence of old people on their children. It broke the absolute economic link between the generations. It is scarcely necessary to comment in this concluding chapter on the significance of the 1937 Constitution for family life. It insisted that the family was exclusively the family based on marriage and it proscribed divorce. Much political and public energy has been expended over the past two decades in amending and reviewing the Constitution. Yet despite its rhetoric regarding the protection of mothers from being compelled into the workforce by economic necessity, practical policies to ensure that this did not occur were somewhat absent. The *Succession Act* fundamentally constrained the right of an individual, generally a man, to ignore his wife and children in his will. It was bitterly opposed, but, significantly, not by the hierarchy of the Catholic Church. The *Family Planning Act,* and subsequent amending Acts, contributed to breaking the link between sexual intercourse and procreation, facilitating major behavioural change.

Following Irish entry into the EEC in 1973 a plethora of Equality legislation ensued. During the first two years of the Coalition Government from 1973-75, equal pay legislation was passed, the marriage bar in the civil service was removed, an allowance for unmarried mothers was introduced and the pre-marriage social insurance contributions of married women were allowed for various benefits. Until then a woman had to start a fresh count of contributions following marriage, partly because many women would have been paid a marriage gratuity when leaving employment at the time of marriage. The 1980s were marked by major referendums on abortion in 1983 and divorce in 1986; the latter as part of Garret FitzGerald's 'constitutional crusade'. A decade later in 1995, a second referendum on divorce would be carried, although by a slender majority. The advent of divorce brought the curtain down on the presumption that, subsequent to marriage, a couple 'lived happily ever afterwards'. The introduction of divorce, while it will solve some problems, will undoubtedly spawn others. According to Dr Hillery, it was a strong belief of Lemass, that when you rectify one thing it creates a new situation. A policy change does not always create what you set out to create, but rather a new situation which itself may call for fresh measures. That is why there must be constant examination and ongoing review of all policies and their consequences. 'A policy maker should always be thinking.'[3] This interdependence of every area of society and social and economic policy was also emphasised by Charles Haughey who remarked that … 'a change in any one area can lead to an entirely new equilibrium.'[4]

Changing values

Values are a powerful influence on behaviour both of the individual and the group. An instructive definition of values is that of 'emotionally toned convictions

> … whether these convictions be objectively verifiable or purely subjective; whether they be intuitive or reasoned on common sense, scientific or philosophic grounds, or accepted by faith in divine or human authority; whether they exist on the conscious level or the level of the unconscious (Thomas, 1954, quoted in Humphreys, 1966: 225-6, fn.).

Church teaching on the nature of the family and the role of men and women fitted well into the agrarian context and into the domain of the traditional breadwinner-father family. When the people supported what the hierarchy and the clergy prescribed, it often coincided with economic imperatives. In a clear insight, the historian K.H. Connell, writing on the strict sexual code in the century following the Famine, says:

> But, for all the power of Church and State, so formalized a code would hardly have been adopted so generally if it were at variance with social and economic needs: indeed, the peasant's respect for the Catholic code as transmitted to him has sprung, not least, from its compatibility with his patriarchal and material ambition (Connell, 1968: 158).

As the economic structure evolved, church teaching, as presented by bishops and clergy, was popularly judged to be incongruent with the needs of the people. For at least the first half of the century, the emphasis in church social teaching was on independent, self-reliant families, free from state intervention. Changes in emphasis in Church teaching coincided with changes in Church leadership; none more so than the advent of Pope John XXIII, following the death of Pope Pius XII in 1958. The effects of the Second Vatican Council continue to reverberate, as individual Catholics have been challenged to think more for themselves and as the blanket condemnation of state intervention in family life has withered. In Ireland the old world was finally eclipsed with the departure in 1972 from the See of Dublin of John Charles McQuaid who had been Archbishop since 1940. Public opinion led by the media moved in a more liberal direction, reflecting the growing liberalism of ordinary Catholics whose behaviour drifted steadily away from strict observance of Catholic tenets, especially in regard to patterns of sexual behaviour. A radio advertisement in 1998, aimed to boost sales of the *News of the World*, a newspaper that was censored in the 1930s, suggests extreme change. The advertisement proclaims, '*The News of the World*, it's what Sunday is all about.' As in an earlier era when men joined secret revolutionary societies and took up arms in violation of the Church's teaching, women began to exercise their new-found choices in the family domain by reducing their child bearing within marriage and increasing it outside of marriage. Second wave feminism, which developed in the 1960s and 1970s, was a significant influence in this regard. Liam Ryan identifies three ways in which Vatican II was a major influence on the values and attitudes of Irish Catholics:

> … it revealed to many Catholics the possibility of a private world of conscience and behaviour; it stressed that the Church was not merely the pope and bishops but the entire people of God whose common convictions carry an inner truth of their own; and it transformed religious thinking from being introverted and pessimistic to be outward-looking and optimistic (Ryan, 1984: 104).

Ryan contends that while there is nothing new in secularisation, there is a new concept in Ireland of what it means to be a Catholic. He describes this new concept of a Catholic as

> ... one who seeks sacramental ministry from the Church but is free to ignore the rules when they seem impractical, i.e. when they conflict with one's own interests. In short there are many Catholics, who wish to remain within the Church, who may be weekly church-goers, but who question the Church's authority over their private lives (Ryan, *ibid*: 104).

Ryan's definition helps to make sense of the high, but declining, recorded levels of Mass attendances, combined with the decline in the acceptance of church teaching in family matters. Since Ryan wrote there has been a further decline in Mass attendance while attendance at Confession is negligible, and Registry Office marriages are rising rapidly. In 1970 less than 1 per cent of marriages were civil ceremonies. This had risen to 6 per cent in 1995 (Heanue, 2000:53). All of this highlights what Joe Lee has called the 'Say/Do Dichotomy' in Irish life (Lee, 1984:109).

The advent of Teilifís Éireann in 1961 brought a new dimension to family life as the television set became the focal point in homes. Without leaving their homes, women, in particular those who were at home minding children, could savour a whole new world of opportunity and experience. Few, if any, would question the unique influence of Gay Byrne in both his radio show, in which he gave a voice to women, and his *Late Late Show* on television. On the *Late Late Show* a whole series of taboos were broken, from the famous 'Bishop and the nightie' episode, to the sagas of Annie Murphy and Bishop Eamon Casey. It was on the *Late Late Show* that an unmarried mother was first enabled to tell her story to the Irish people. Television entered Irish life and culture at a time when Ireland was crossing the Rubicon between a rural and urban society. Alongside economic modernisation, the removal of tariffs and the opening to free trade, a parallel cultural modernisation was in train with an opening to fresh ideas. The analogy has been drawn between this point in Irish social change and a similar point in British society – the 1850s, one hundred years earlier (McLoone, 1984: 60). The cultural upheaval experienced in British society at the time is located in nineteenth-century English literature, especially in the novel, as Raymond Williams argued in *The Country and the City*. But '... because this fundamental shift occurs in Ireland more than a century later, the cultural medium best placed to mediate the ramifications involved was not primarily the novel, but television, itself a product of industrial and technological progress' (McLoone and MacMahon, 1984: 60)

Symbolically, the Gay Byrne radio show which continued for twenty-five years, ending on Christmas Eve 1998, began just as the era of Archbishop John Charles McQuaid ended. According to a farewell tribute by John Caden who produced the Show for several years, 'Gay's real achievement has been to change the face of this country by creating a forum for real, open, democratic debate' (Caden, 1998). Many of the social constraints on behaviour associated with the past have vanished; the alternate grip which is most apparent in society as a replacement for past values of Church and State seems to be a materialist one. The preferred values of the Celtic Tiger are economic growth, efficiency and competition. But that could be about to change if a new generation, reared in prosperity, fail to find satisfaction in that very prosperity, or if the alienated minority neglected by the Tiger begin to growl, or if those who argue on their behalf are listened to with greater attention.

The closing years of the century were a period when the mythology of 'happy families' was shattered in a dramatic manner. The dark side of family life, portrayed, for example, in the banned novels of Paul Smith (1959, 1975), emerged into the broad daylight in a number of cases, including those of Joanne Hayes and the 'Kerry Babies' in 1984 (McCafferty, 1985), the death of Longford schoolgirl Ann Lovett, the death of Kelly FitzGerald as a result of abuse within her own family, the Kilkenny incest case, and the McColgan case in which an entire family was abused by their father (McKay, 1998). The case of Ann Lovett was shrouded in poignant symbolism. A young girl died alone in a grotto dedicated to the Blessed Virgin in her home town of Granard which was also the home town of Kitty Kiernan, fiancée of the murdered hero of the War of Independence, Michael Collins. Her infant son died shortly afterwards. Very little ever became public knowledge regarding the deaths of Ann Lovett and her son, despite considerable coverage in the media. The opening up to the public gaze of the dark side of family life was both made possible by, and contributed to, the cultural shift from secrecy and concealment. For much of the century a culture of confidentiality was the norm. In an editorial entitled 'The Church in Retreat', in *The Irish Times* on 1 December 1994, the writer states:

> … the Catholic Church in Ireland is being buffeted as never before by a wave of child sex abuse allegations. The fact that individual priests exploited the privileged access they enjoy to young children for their own sexual gratification has provoked a sense of outrage throughout the state.

The writer suggests that the failure of those in authority in the Church to deal speedily and effectively with instances of abuse may be due to a failure to differentiate between abuse which is a crime, and 'sin' which is a personal failing. Furthermore the writer states that, 'the deep-seated culture of secrecy within the hierarchy has also helped to make the Church's difficulties even more acute'. It might be argued that a mirror-image of the culture of secrecy within the hierarchy can be located in the culture of secrecy in government. For example, during the course of the Beef Tribunal Enquiry, which cost millions of pounds of taxpayers' money, the then Attorney General went to the Courts to seek and obtain a judgment in favour of cabinet confidentiality, thus effectively precluding the public from ever knowing the full story, in pursuit of which their funds had been so generously expended.

Until the late twentieth century it was accepted practice, even regarded desirable by those in authority, that neither the citizenry of the state, nor the laity in the Church, had any business knowing about the inner workings of Church and State. Indeed it was regarded better that they should remain in the dark. The Mother and Child crisis of 1951 represents an early turning point towards greater openness. Until this episode, 'Church-State relations were little discussed in Ireland, and there was a widespread feeling that it was somehow disedifying for the role of the Church to be examined in public' (Whyte, 1980: 230). At the time, the Taoiseach, John A. Costello, was quite taken aback by Dr Browne's public disclosures of what he, Mr Costello, clearly regarded as private business. Speaking in the Dáil in the debate on Dr Browne's resignation, Mr Costello said: 'All this matter was intended to be private and to be adjusted behind closed doors and was never intended to be the subject of public controversy, as it has been made by the former Minister for Health.' Later in the same speech, Mr Costello said: 'All these matters could have been, and ought to have been, dealt with calmly, in quiet and in council, without the public becoming aware of the matter. The public never ought to have become aware of the matter' (Quoted in Whyte, *ibid*: 231).

In these days of openness, accountability and transparency, Mr Costello's words almost shock, and will shock the politically correct, but the fact that Costello should speak in such a manner in the Dáil indicates that he was sure that he was backed by public opinion. Times change and hidden Ireland gradually began to emerge, aided by the arrival of television and the subjection of authority figures to intensive scrutiny in ordinary living rooms and households, as a result of much more investigative journalism. The media handling of events has been crucial to raising the curtain on both politicians and churchmen, and indeed on a host of other groups, including gardaí, sportsmen, teachers and parents. The balance of authority within families was placed under scrutiny as second wave feminism focused on a woman's right to individual fulfilment and to equality in the workforce. Second wave feminism contributed to the establishment of the Commission on the Status of Women, chaired by Thekla Beere, which in turn laid the foundations for many changes in family life, notably through its recommendation of a payment to an unmarried mother who kept her child.

When Mary Robinson was elected President of Ireland, she called on the women of Ireland who 'rocked the cradle' to 'rock the system'. In many respects, it has been women who have changed most. Women who tended to focus their interest and energy mainly on the home and who were long assumed to be the strongest allies of the priest, began to question the implications of church teaching for their personal lives. The changes in the role of women have been marked by their full entry into public life. However, it remains as surely the central reality of their lives as it did one hundred years ago that women bear children. It is the 'housewife', not the mother, who is a vanishing species. In a symbolic manner the Calor-Kosangas 'Housewife of the Year' was replaced in 1994 by the Centra 'Homemaker' of the Year. Men are now eligible to compete for the prize.

The changing role of women does not, however, fit neatly into the slogan 'vanishing housewife', nor can the role of women be captured as a simple linear progression, but rather within overlapping and evolving cycles. The Revolutionary women were egalitarians in many respects. Kathleen Clarke, wife of the first signatory to the 1916 Proclamation, ran the family business when Tom Clarke was in jail, and following his execution, continued to do so. She later became a Senator and was the first woman elected as Lord Mayor of Dublin in 1939. She fitted in with Máire Mhac an tSaoi's description of Republican women as breadwinners. The cohort of women who were born into the Free State in the 1920s and 1930s and who married in the 1940s and 1950s were closely identified with the role of housewife. In turn their children, born in the 1940s and 1950s, included the second wave feminists of the 1970s while those born in the 1970s are currently embracing the challenge of combining work and family responsibilities, not necessarily in the context of life-long marriage.

In the context of the small family farm, family members worked together as producers; the fulfilment of the individual was necessarily subject to the survival of the family as a unit. With the growth of towns and the development of industries the role of the 'breadwinner' grew in importance. With the growth of off-farm employment and the emergence of the so-called 'working classes', the role of the man as breadwinner became central. Men who married were destined to become 'providers' for their wives and children. There was scant recognition of any other socially acceptable role for men; rights for men who fathered children outside of marriage were ignored; and men have been discriminated against in the Social Welfare Code. As the century drew to a close mothers were increasingly engaged in the workforce. At present almost 40 per cent of married women are in the workforce and half of all families with children under 15 years are dual earner families *(Labour Force Survey, 1997)*. At the same time there is a gathering movement among men to ensure that they have the opportunity not only to contribute to the financial, but also to the emotional, development of their children. In the dawn of a new century reflection and action are called for as to how the institutions of society can facilitate active fatherhood and support men who wish to play a full role as fathers (McKeown *et al*, 1998). Psychiatrist Anthony Clare argues that not only are fathers important to children, but that active fatherhood is a key civilising influence on men (Clare, 2000). The tendency for men to find their identity in the world of work and to have their roles as fathers measured in breadwinner terms, has been challenged. Many men are no longer the sole breadwinner in the household; many men face unemployment and cannot act as breadwinners, whilst others become invisible fathers either because they opt out or are pushed out of their role. If more and more women are finding fulfilment outside the home, the question arises as to how to provide more opportunities for men who seek fulfilment within the home.

The role and status of children has also changed. For the early part of the century children were often viewed as 'investments' by their parents. They added to farm labour and contributed to the support of parents in old age as they had to wait on the death of the parents to inherit the farm and establish a family of their own. The change in the economic position of children has been linked closely with the shift away from agriculture and the extension of the years of education. Now parents invest heavily *in* their children. The shift away from agriculture has also been linked with the decline in family size, although large families were commonplace in urban and rural life until the 1960s.

The level of religious practice among Catholics, as measured by attendance at Mass, although declining, remains high relative to other Catholic countries in Europe such as France or Italy. However, all indicators of behaviour in the most intimate and vital areas of life, including contraception, cohabitation, births outside marriage, abortion and so on, indicate the detachment of behaviour or practice from Church teaching. The rate at which these behavioural changes occurred – between the Pope's visit in 1979 and the passing of the divorce referendum in 1995 – has been very striking. People are deciding for themselves in these matters in Ireland, as they have already done in many other European countries. The fact that Church members have apparently rejected Church teaching in these areas and on a wide scale must give pause for thought. In every area of life Church members fail to live up to Church teaching for that is the essence of a Church composed of a pilgrim people, but in some areas the failure or the rejection of the teaching is more transparent than in others. In Gospel terms adultery committed 'in the heart' is invisible adultery. To focus on sexual teaching and its rejection, while clearly relevant to this study, represents a very narrow focus in terms of the Gospel which stresses service of neighbour as its overriding social message. In the name of that imperative much good has been done by Church leaders and Church members across the century, a great deal in private and out of the glare of the media.

The family in the twenty-first century

Writing in the middle of the twentieth century, Sean O'Faolain remarked: 'In the black forties of the nineteenth century we were hungry because we were so many. In the black forties of the next century will we be hungry because we are too few?' (O'Faolain, 1954:106-7). He was writing in the 1950s at a time of low marriage rates and high emigration. He could not have foreseen the huge fall in births that took place from the 1980 peak. There are signs in the last couple of years of a reversal of the decline in births, and population is at its highest level for one hundred years. Ireland at present is a country favoured by immigrants.

Will economic growth continue? Certain things are known. Ireland has thrown in its lot firmly with Europe and this is evident not only in the economic sphere, but in the social sphere also. If the European Union is ultimately a political endeavour, the fates of the people of Europe have deliberately been linked together in a common destiny. Odile Quentin of the European Commission has written:

> European society is changing. Couples, children, marriage, families, no longer occupy the same place in society that they used to. A declining birth-rate in almost all Member States of the Union, fewer marriages, more couples living together and children born out of wedlock and a rising divorce rate, this is the patchwork of features which today influence the family unit, and indeed, society as a whole (Quentin, 1999:2).

Europe-wide policies and Europe-wide trends interact. The European Community has no direct competence for family policy, but within its framework on equal opportunities for men and women, it has undertaken a number of initiatives aimed at reconciling work and family life. The Maternity Directive, the Parental Leave Directive, the Part-Time Work Directive and the Recommendation on Childcare are examples of this. Following the baby boom has come the birth dearth. Fewer babies were born in Europe in 1999 than in any year since World War II. Ireland still has the highest birth rate, ahead of Norway, the Netherlands and France, while Italy has the lowest, followed by Germany. Deaths outnumbered births in Germany, Italy and Sweden in 1999. Throughout Europe, the population is ageing. The population of the European Union ages by 2.5 months each year or by two years each decade. The proportion of the population below age 20 will further decrease as the proportion of those above 60 years is predicted to increase from 21 per cent to 34 per cent by 2030. By then the mean age of the European population, which is at present approximately 39 years, may reach 45 years (Lutz, 1999:8). Ageing will happen in Ireland slowly up to 2006 but rapidly after 2026. By 2020, 25 per cent of the population will be over 65 years.

The increase in the number and share of births taking place outside marriage is leading to a whole new vista in family life. Until the 1970s when a steep decline in births within marriage took place, family poverty was most closely associated with large families; now the problem of family poverty tends to be most closely associated with lone parents. The importance of individuals, especially children, within families, is seeping into the national consciousness, and with the increased concern for children has come an awareness of the importance of parenting. The unwritten assumption that because the ability to procreate is common to the human and animal worlds, anyone could be a parent, more or less, has been challenged by incidents of abuse, neglect and parental inadequacy.

'Modernisation' sometimes suggests movement from a backwater, shaking off the limiting constraints of the past. To interpret all change in such beneficial light is as naïve as to idealise the past. It is acknowledged that there was much that was undesirable in family life in the past including economic hardship, forced emigration and the subjugation of the individual to the group, but there were many elements, the value of which may only be fully appreciated when they have been lost. For all the criticism, and challenging of the motives behind the Articles in the Constitution regarding the role of women in the home, if a simple non-judgemental statement were made today, that a woman should not be forced out of her home on the basis of economic necessity, should she wish to remain in the home to care for her children, it might well receive widespread approval. It is possible that many couples with young children as well as single parents, struggling to keep a roof over their heads and food on the table, and to hold down jobs, might hanker after a world in which one parent could earn a livelihood for the family, while the other could take care of the child or children. Dr Mary Leader, Professor at the Royal College of Surgeons in Dublin, has claimed that many women doctors find it impossible to juggle a career and home life, and a significant number of female doctors are quitting the medical profession because of these pressures. 'Women between the ages of 25 and 35 – peak child bearing age – are working up to 70 hours a week' (*Irish Independent*, 15 January, 2000).

Financial and social recognition for work in both the private economy and the public sector are higher than those for family-related work (Kernthaler *et al*, 1999:6). Kernthaler concludes that '... the family is seriously disadvantaged when it comes to competing with public institutions and private companies' (Kernthaler *et al, ibid*). It may be asked whether the focus on the growth of GDP as the overriding measure of progress has blinded as well as illuminated. The introduction of the Human Development Index is a recognition of the limitations of the GDP measure (Chapter 3). Micklewright and Stewart, in an examination of the convergence of child-welfare in the European Union, have argued that national performance is being judged excessively on the basis of macroeconomic indicators (Micklewright and Stewart, 1999). They use four indicators of a 'good life'. These are, in addition to economic well-being, health and survival, education and personal development and social inclusion/participation. Their findings in regard to child mortality and educational enrolment among 16-year-olds exhibit clear trends towards convergence over the past 25 years and indicate rising levels of well-being. The indicator of teenagers' own assessment of life satisfaction also shows convergence:

> However, three indicators show countries to be diverging – child poverty, household worklessness, and youth unemployment; and the remaining two show stagnating disparities – young male suicides and teenage fertility. (The period concerned differs from indicator to indicator.) *And with the exception of teenage fertility, the average level of well-being in the EU measured by these indicators has fallen over time* (Micklewright and Stewart, *ibid*: F712, emphasis added).

With the achievement of 'the liberal agenda', of contraception and divorce, will an awareness of the needs of children lead to a revival in marriage or what other form of relationship will emerge to ensure that children get proper parenting? How will the nature of work change? Will it change in more family-friendly ways, as Dr Angela Russell hoped 50 years ago, when she asked, 'If the importance of the family was admitted, why were its wants so neglected? ... Why could not wages and hours and seasons of work be arranged to fit the needs of the family?' (Russell Scrapbooks, press cutting, 19 August 1946). A contemporary example of this general question might be whether trading on Sundays and holidays such as Christmas and Easter implies priority for profit above family time? Will a secular equivalent of the Sabbath emerge because of the demands of families to have time together? Will the revolution in information technology lead to an increase in the home as the centre of economic activity? Will concern for the environment and the increase in organic farming echo back to the small family farms of yesteryear? Will there be a reining in of State involvement in the family? Will the expectation of life continue to grow? What will happen in the field of reproductive technology? What values will inform policy and behaviour?

In the final analysis what happens in the future will depend on individuals. Significant changes in the social framework resulted from legal challenges mounted by individuals, including Mrs McGee and Senator Norris. Change is caused by the cumulative decisions and actions of individuals – 'the invisible mind' operating the 'invisible hand'. Influencing these decisions are a variety of factors. The family has been shaped primarily by changes in the economy, in public policy and in values. State policy towards the family has, in turn, been influenced by changing economic conditions and by changing values. For example, while economic growth helped many families to raise their living standards, other families became casualties of growth through structural changes and unemployment, and the State was called upon to intervene. Catholic thought and teaching have influenced both State policies and individual and family behaviour up to the point where individuals opted to ignore certain parts of the teaching, but economic change and government policies have also caused reaction and change in the Church, with economic factors often winning out. The observation of Guinnane regarding an earlier period that, 'The Irish Catholic Church was influential, but Catholics were not above ignoring it when they felt like it' (Guinnane, 1997: 77), would appear true of a later period also. In the course of this study it has been shown how family patterns and behaviour altered as the economic basis of families altered. It has also been shown how state policies contributed to changing family patterns. In many cases the changes that occurred ran counter to the predominant ideology of the Catholic Church. Yet they occurred as ordinary Catholics followed what they identified as their own interests, regardless of official Church teaching. The evidence of this study supports a general hypothesis that change in family patterns has been 'people driven'. The changes in the law regarding contraception, for example, were introduced by public representatives, because they were perceived to be in line with what the people wanted, and had been judged so by the Courts.

Any of the key indicators of change in family life may be taken – the long run decline in marital fertility throughout the twentieth century; the low marriage rate in the first half of the century, the boom in marriages in the 1960s and 1970s and the decline in the 1980s; the rise in total births to a peak in 1980 and the uninterrupted decline until 1995; the sharp rise in the births outside marriage – and the question may be posed 'Why?' Economic and policy factors will give part of the answer; but a critical part depends on why, in light of economic and policy factors, people chose as they did. Why did values change? Commenting on the decline in the marriage rate from the late 1970s, Garret FitzGerald says:

> One does not have to undertake research to discover that a crucial factor in the drop in the marriage rate has been a marked unwillingness of this generation of young people to commit themselves to the permanent relationship that marriage, despite the introduction of divorce, still implies (*The Irish Times*, 22 November, 1997).

This raises the question why there is an unwillingness among young people to make a permanent commitment. In the older generation economic and policy elements *demanded* commitment, and in so far as was feasible, enforced commitment. In rural Ireland, everything was dictated by the blood line. Arensberg and Kimball argued that everything a man did or was in rural Ireland in the 1930s could be referred to his blood (Arensberg and Kimball, 1940), or what was colourfully called, in the words of a rural TD, the 'the stud book'. Sexual activity outside marriage carried a risk of social exclusion. But this pattern was buttressed by a value system based on Catholic Church teaching. Behaviour patterns developed in clear contradiction of Church teaching, and so it appears that economic factors supported by policy measures provide the most important clues to changing patterns. A shift has taken place from a situation in which the interest of the individual was subordinate to the interests of the family, to one in which the interests of the individual family member takes precedence.

The demands of employment and income-earning frequently conflict with the demands of child bearing by women and the demands of child rearing by both men and women. They may also conflict with the demands of caring for elderly parents or other dependent family members. Moving into the twenty-first century a key issue for society is the reconciliation of income earning and family responsibilities. Calls for greater flexibility in the labour market are coming from two different sources. They are coming from employers who wish to increase productivity and they are coming from within the workforce itself where men and women work on the same terms, but frequently wish to exercise greater choice over their lives outside of the workforce. There has been relatively little debate in Ireland regarding the balance between, on the one hand, the freedom and fulfilment of individual men and women and, on the other, social responsibility.

There was much that was wrong in the past in the manner in which the interests of the individual family member were subordinated to that of the group. The past of the Irish family was not an unqualified Lost Paradise. What matters at this point is the clear recognition that the functioning of society depends on co-operation between individuals – men and women – and between generations. The young depend upon the old and in turn the old depend upon the young. If a measure of a civilised society is the protection and support that society provides for minorities, and ultimately for individuals, there are limits to which individual fulfilment can become the uniquely dominant objective, without a high social cost. The care of children, of the elderly and of other dependent family members needs to be placed centre stage. In September 1992 Ireland ratified the United Nations Convention on the Rights of the Child (1989). Article 7 on the Convention states, 'The child shall be registered immediately after birth and shall have the right from birth to a name, the right to acquire nationality and, as far as possible, the right to know and be cared for by his or her parents.' In Europe, the Childhood Policy Project 1992-96 of the Council of Europe and the European Strategy for Children 1996, indicate the growing focus on children.

Two big questions need to be addressed on the threshold of the twenty-first century. They are perennial questions, but the possible answers are changing, as this study has shown. What form of social control will there be for sexual reproductive activity? And, who will care for the children and for the elderly? It may be that the appropriate point of departure for family debate at the end of the twentieth century is the child. Helmut Wintersberger, of the Austrian Institute of Family Studies, and Co-ordinator of the European Observatory on Family Matters, remarks that it might be assumed that the whole issue of reconciling work and family responsibilities was predominantly about children, but that in fact the children's perspective is generally missing from the debate (Wintersberger, 1999: 18). It is, therefore, of considerable interest that in November 2000, the government announced a 'Children's Strategy', including the appointment of an Ombudsman for children and the establishment of Dáil na nÓg, or The Children's Parliament. In reviewing a century of family life it is possible to lose sight of this essential question for individuals and society: Who will rear the children? The issue to be addressed reflects the relative priority that society attaches to paid work and to family life in its widest sense. What is the relative respect that society really accords to the largely voluntary work within the family, as distinct from paid employment? With more children born outside marriage, how can a child best have access to both parents? How can a father best fulfil his role? At the other end of the age spectrum the number and proportion of elderly people in the population is set to grow rapidly, creating a major issue for policy in the coming years.

Finally, sexual reproductive activity requires social control if chaos is to be avoided. Throughout much of the twentieth century control was exercised by a combination of strict laws and social ostracism, together with economic hardship for those found to have broken the rules. It is easy to be critical with hindsight, but it was a system that kept society together and at times brought out the best, as well as the worst, in people. If it is accepted that Catholic moral values no longer inform the law, and if the bishops say that they have never insisted that they should, the question remains as to which values prevail. The law of the land was supported by, and to a marked degree, incorporated, the instructions of the Catholic Church which in turn represented the vast majority of the people. The desire to avoid scandal and to uphold a pleasant façade led to concealment and secrecy. By and large the Press obliged and for years maintained the façade of respectability, but then relentlessly stripped away that façade. The myth of the Irish family persisted alongside the myth of the Island of Saints and Scholars at least until the 1960s and like all myths, these myths contained elements of truth.

Chapter Notes

Notes to Chapter 1

1   The marriage and birth rates referred to are the crude rates per 1,000 population.

2   In Dinneen's Irish Dictionary, *Teaghlach* is translated as 'a family or household, familia or monastic family, an ethnic family or group, followers, escort; a house'.

3   A child is defined as any person with no partner and no child who has usual residence in the household of at least one of the parents. The term 'children' also includes stepchildren and adopted children, but not foster children. The term 'couple' includes married couples and couples who report that they are living in consensual unions.

4   Meeting with Aidan Punch who represented the Central Statistics Office in the discussions, 24 January 2000.

5   In 1980 NESC published a study, written by economist Eithne FitzGerald, entitled *Alternative Strategies for Family Income Support* (NESC, 1980). In 1982 the ESRI published a *Study in Social Class and Family-Cycle Inequalities* (Rottman *et al*, 1982) as well as a study on the elderly, *The Economic and Social Circumstances of the Elderly in Ireland* (Whelan and Vaughan, 1982). In 1989 the ESRI published *Family, Economy and Government in Ireland* (Kennedy, 1989), while a major *Survey of Income Distribution, Poverty and Usage of State Services* by the staff of the ESRI was published in 1987 and yielded data which were subsequently used in a number of studies of family and child poverty. In 1985 the Family Studies Unit in University College Dublin published a collection of papers, based on a conference held in 1984, entitled *The Changing Family*. Three further volumes of papers published by the Unit were *Family Policy: European Perspectives* (Kiely and Richardson, eds, 1991), *In and Out of Marriage*: *Irish and European Experience* (Kiely, ed., 1992) and *Irish Family Studies: Selected Papers* (McCarthy, ed., 1995). In 1986 the Jesuit Quarterly, *Studies,* devoted an issue to the Family, while in 1988, CORI published the proceedings of a conference, *Poverty and Family Income Policy* (Reynolds and Healy, eds, 1988).

6   In the area of *family formation and fission,* studies have dealt, for example, with demographic trends (Clancy, 1984 and 1991; Kennedy, 1989), single mothers (Flanagan and Richardson, 1992; McCashin, 1993) and the elderly (Whelan and Vaughan, 1982; National Council for the Aged, 1988). The increase in family and marital breakdown is reflected in the appearance of a White Paper (1992) as well as studies by Ward (1993), and Fahey and Lyons (1995). In the *family policy* area

261

fundamental work on family law has been carried out by Binchy (1984) and Shatter (1997). Aspects of taxation, social welfare and child care policies have been researched by Kennedy (1989), Gilligan (1991), McKenna (1988) and Buckley *et al,* (1997). Child poverty has been researched by Nolan and Farrell (1990), and the cost of rearing a child by Carney *et al* (1994). There has been a marked growth in interest in family life and family policy in the European Union during the past decade, an interest reflected in the establishment of the European Observatory on Family Matters. A major study of family life and family policies in Europe in the 1980s, edited by Kaufmann *et al,* was published in 1997 (Kaufmann *et al,* 1997). In the area of *women and work,* the focus has been twofold. A number of studies have dealt with women in the paid labour force: Blackwell (1986, 1989), Callan and Farrell (1991), Larson Pyle (1990) and Walsh (1993). Another approach has centred on the household sector, identifying two main components of unpaid work – on the family farm and within the household itself (Fahey, 1990). Varying methodologies have been employed. For example the study by Callan and Farrell is based on a neo-classical labour supply theory, while the work of Larson Pyle uses a more eclectic methodology, embracing both economic theory and the institutional framework, which includes legislative arrangements and state policies governing women's labour force participation within patriarchal structures. A fourth area of research concerns *dysfunction within families* and enters the realms of psychology and psychotherapy as well as domestic violence and abuse. Studies on these topics include McCarthy and Byrne (1988).

Notes to Chapter 3

1   There appears to be an error in the reference to 1901 in the above quotation, as the census data given later in Table 1.1 on p.27 of Bourke's book, show that 549,900 women were in designated occupations in 1901 and 430,100 in 1911.

Notes to Chapter 4

1   Article 41.2.1° and 41.2.2° provide examples of divergences between the English and Irish texts of the Constitution (Ó Cearúil, 1999:595-6). The words 'cannot be achieved' are expressed in the Irish text as 'nach bhféadfaí a ghnóthú', which translates literally as '*could not* be achieved'. The words 'economic necessity' are expressed in Irish as 'do dheasca uireasa', literally 'because of want'. 'Uireasa' is translated by Dinneen as 'deficiency, need, want, poverty' (Ó Cearúil, *ibid*).

2   Interview with Máire Mhac an tSaoi, 4 March, 1998.

3   Interview with Dr Hillery, 14 December 1998.

4   *Meath County Council, Housing Applicants by Status, 10 October 2000*

Status	Applicants Number	Applicants Per cent
Lone Parent	421	33.4
Married	245	19.5
Common law husband-wife	175	13.9
Single	172	13.7
Divorced, Separated	156	12.4
Elderly, Widowed	80	6.4
Not specified	10	0.8
Total	1259	100

Notes to Chapter 5

1   Hilda Tweedy was the daughter of a Church minister. She shared this background with two other women who were key figures in improving social conditions of twentieth-century Ireland – Kathleen Lynn and Thekla Beere. In 2000, Catherine McGuinness, daughter of a Church of Ireland minister, and with a record of social concern, was appointed to the Supreme Court.
2   Interview with Mr Haughey, 26 January 1999.
3   Interview with Dr Hillery, 14 December 1998.
4   Interview with Dr Hillery 14 December 1998.

Notes to Chapter 6

1   Conversation with Ita Healy, March 1998.
2   Communication from Seán Cromien to author, February 1999.
3   Conversation with Eoin O'Sullivan, 16 January 1998.
4   Interview with Dr Hillery, 14 December 1998.
5   Interview with Dr FitzGerald, 16 January 1999.

Notes to Chapter 7

1   Interview with Máire Mhac an tSaoi, 4 March 1998.
2   According to Dineen's dictionary, a *seanascal* is a high steward/major domo. It was the term employed by de Valera in lieu of Governor General, just as Taoiseach was used in lieu of Prime Minister.
3   Interview with Dr FitzGerald, 16 January 1999.
4   Interview with Dr FitzGerald, 16 January 1999.
5   Communication with author, 5 May 1999.

Notes to Chapter 8

1   The Manchester School was the name given by Disraeli to those who campaigned for the Repeal of the Corn Laws. The name came to be associated with arch advocacy of *laissez-faire*.

2   In 1926 Cahill founded *An Ríoghacht*, the League of the Kingship of Christ. The objectives of *An Ríoghacht* were '(a) To propagate among Irish Catholics a better knowledge of Catholic social principles, (b) To strive for the effective recognition of these principles in Irish public life, (c) To promote Catholic social action' (Jesuit archives, Cahill papers). In the summary document setting out the origin, objects and character of *An Ríoghacht*, it is stated that 'The country has lost touch with the traditional Catholic culture of Europe. The English literature upon which the mind of the people is largely formed is predominantly Protestant'. At the time, organisations with aims similar to *An Ríoghacht* were the *Volksverein* in Germany and *Action Populaire* in France. The *Catholic Social Guild* in England was also similar. The attendance at the first general meeting of *An Ríoghacht* included prominent civil servants and members of the Irish Bar: Maurice Moynihan, J. Garvin, L.M. Fitzgerald, George Gavan Duffy, Arthur Cleary, and Eoin O'Keeffe. Regular weekly meetings were held at which Cahill delivered a series of lectures, much of which would form the basis for his text, *The Framework of A Christian State*, 1932 (Waldron, 1950).

3   Interview with Mr Cosgrave, 12 November 1998.

4   Interview with James McPolin, SJ, 22 August 2000. In his biography of Noël Browne, John Horgan reports how in 1949 Bishop Browne of Galway wrote to Archbishop McQuaid of Dublin to tell him that the Bishop of Limerick had been in touch with him to express concern about the government's proposals (Horgan, 2000: 105).

5   In an article on family privacy (Fahey, 1995), Fahey looks at the Health Service reforms, 1945-54.

6   Conversation with Dr Whitaker, 6 May 1998.

7   Interview with Dr Nevin, 4 February 1999.

8   Interview with Dr Nevin, 4 February 1999.

9   Conversation with Fr Seán Healy, 31 March 1998.

10 Interview with Mr Cosgrave, 12 November 1998.

Notes to Chapter 9

1   Interview with Dr FitzGerald, 16 January 1999.

2   Interview with Dr Nevin, 4 February 1999.

3   Interview with Mr Haughey, 26 January 1999.

4   Interview with Mr Haughey, 26 January 1999.

5   Interview with Dr Nevin, 4 February 1999.

6   The Group was chaired by Ms Deirdre Carroll, Assistant Secretary, Department of Social, Community and Family Affairs. A majority of the Group members were from that Department and from the Department of Finance and the Department of Enterprise, Trade and Employment. The Group also included representatives from the Combat Poverty Agency and the National Social Services Board.

7   Interview with Dr Hillery, 14 December 1998.

8   Interview with Mr Haughey, 26 January 1999.

9   Interview with Mr Haughey, 26 January 1999.

10 This explanation was suggested by the former Senior Legal Assistant, now known as Director General, in the Attorney General's Office, Matthew Russell; conversation 13 November 1998.

11 Interview with Dr FitzGerald, 16 January 1999.

12   Interview with Dr FitzGerald, 16 January 1999.

13 Interview with Mr Cosgrave, 12 November 1998.

14 Interview with Mr Cosgrave, 12 November 1998.

15 Interview with Mr Haughey, 26 January 1999.

16 Interview with Dr FitzGerald, 16 January 1999.

Notes to Chapter 10

1   Interview with Mr Cosgrave, 12 November 1998.

2   Dr MacNeely was a member of the Commission of Inquiry into Banking, Currency and Credit 1938. With Professor George O'Brien, he wrote an Appendix to the Commission entitled, 'A Note on Some Aspects of Papal Encyclicals in Relation to the Terms of Reference of the Commission'.

3   Interview with Dr Hillery, 14 December 1998.

4   Interview with Mr Haughey, 26 January 1999.

References

All-Party Oireachtas Committee on the Constitution, The (2000), *Fifth Progress Report, Abortion*, Stationery Office, Dublin.

Archbishops and Bishops of Ireland (1951), *A Catechism of Catholic Doctrine*, M.H. Gill and Son Ltd, Dublin.

Addis, W.E. and Arnold, T. (eds) (1928), *A Catholic Dictionary*, Routledge and Kegan Paul, London.

Akerlof, G.A. (1998), 'Men Without Children', *Economic Journal*, 108: 287-309.

Ardagh, J. (1995), *Ireland and the Irish. Portrait of a Changing Society*, Penguin, London.

Arensberg, C.M. and Kimball, S. (1940, 1968 2nd edn), *Family and Community in Ireland*, Harvard University Press, Cambridge, Mass.

Baker, T.J. and O'Brien, L.M. (1979), *The Irish Housing System: A Critical Overview*, ESRI, Dublin.

Barrett, C.J. (1955), 'The Dependent Child', *Studies*, 44: 419-28.

Barrington, R. (1987), *Health, Medicine and Politics in Ireland, 1900-1970*, Institute of Public Administration, Dublin.

Becker, G.S. (1988), 'Family Economics and Macro Behaviour', *American Economic Review*, 78:1-13.

--- (1989), Introduction to Kennedy (1989).

Behan, B. (1967), 'The Confirmation Suit', in A. Martin (ed.), *Exploring English* 1, Gill & Macmillan Ltd and The Educational Co., Dublin: 244-50.

Beveridge, W. (1942), *Social Insurance and Allied Services*, HMSO (Cmnd. 6409).

Biever, B.F. (1976), *Religion, Culture, and Values. A Cross-Cultural Analysis of Motivational Factors in Native Irish and Native American Irish Catholicism*, Arno Press, New York.

Binchy, W. (1984), *A Casebook of Irish Family Law*, Professional Books, Abingdon, Oxon.

Birch, P. (1973), 'The Irish Family in Modern Conditions', *Social Studies,* 2: 485-97.

Blackwell, J. (1986), *Women in the Labour Force: a Statistical Digest*, Employment Equality Agency, Dublin.

--- (1989), *Women in the Labour Force*, 2nd edn, Employment Equality Agency, Dublin.

Bohan, H. (1996), Letter to *The Irish Times*, 23 December.

Bourke, J. (1993), *Husbandry to Housewifery: Women and Economic Change and Housework in Ireland 1890-1914*, Clarendon Press, Oxford.

Bradley, A. and Valiulis, M.G. (eds) (1997), *Gender and Sexuality in Modern Ireland*, University of Massachusetts Press, Amherst.

Buckley, H., Skehill, C. and O'Sullivan, E. (1997), *Child Protection Practices in Ireland. A Case Study*, Oak Tree Press, Dublin.

Burrowes, W. (1977), *The Riordans. A Personal History*, Gilbert Dalton, Dublin.

Caden, J. (1998), 'The man who always found room on his horse for two', *The Irish Times*, 24 December.

Cahill, E.J. (1930), 'The Catholic Social Movement', *Irish Ecclesiastical Record*, 36: 572-87.

--- (1932), *The Framework of a Christian State*, M.H. Gill and Son Ltd, Dublin.

--- (1934), Letter to President de Valera from West End Hotel, Kilkee, 7/7/34, de Valera papers, item 1095.

Callan, T. and Farrell, B. (1991), *Women's Participation in the Paid Labour Market*, National Economic and Social Council (NESC), Dublin.

Callan, T., Nolan, B., Walsh, J., and Nestor, R. (1999), 'Income Tax and Social Welfare Policies', Budget Perspectives, Proceedings of a Conference held on 27 September 1999, ESRI, Dublin: 18-45.

Calot, G. (1990), 'La Fécondité en Europe: Évolutions passés et Perspectives d'avenir', Bevolking en Gezin, 19:3:56-82.

Canavan, J.E. (1926), 'Family Endowment, in J.F. Leibell (ed.) (1926): 699-703.

Carbery, M. (1937), *The Farm by Lough Gur*, Longmans Green and Co., London.

Carney, C. (1985), 'A Case Study in Social Policy – The Non-Contributory Old Age Pension', *Administration*, 33: 483-529.

Carney, C., FitzGerald, E., Kiely, G., and Quinn, P. (1994), *The Cost of a Child: A report on the financial cost of child-rearing in Ireland*, Combat Poverty Agency, Dublin.

Carrigan, W. (1931), *Report of the Committee on the Criminal Law Amendment Acts (1880-1885), and Juvenile Prostitution*, Stationery Office, Dublin. The Report, known as the Carrigan Committee Report after the Chairman, was not made available to the public.

Carr-Saunders, A. (1936), *World Population*, Clarendon Press, Oxford.

Castles, F. (1998), 'The Fertility of Nations or Why Europe Will Soon Be Only Half The Place It Was', Paper read to the Policy Institute, Trinity College, Dublin.

Catholic Church (1994), *Catechism of the Catholic Church* (CCC), Veritas, Dublin.

Census of Population (1871), *General Report*, HMSO.

Census of Population (1881), *General* Report, HMSO.

Census of Population (1891), *General Report*, HMSO.

Census of Population (1901), *General Report*, HMSO.

Census of Population (1926), *General Report*, Stationery Office, Dublin.

Census of Population (1996), Vol. 7, *Occupations*, Stationery Office, Dublin.

Chadeau, A. (1992), 'What is Households' Non-market Production Worth?', *OECD Economic Studies*, 18.

Clancy, M. (1989), 'Aspects of Women's Contribution to the Oireachtas Debate in the Irish Free State, 1922-1937', in M. Luddy and C. Murphy (eds) (1989): 206-32.

Clancy, P. (1984), 'Demographic Changes and the Irish Family', *The Changing Family*, Family Studies Unit, University College Dublin: 1-38.

--- (1991), 'Irish Nuptuality and Fertility Patterns in Transition', in G. Kiely, and V. Richardson (eds), *Family Policy: European Perspectives*, University College Dublin: 9-29.

Clancy, P., Drudy, S., Lynch, K., and O'Dowd, L. (eds) (1995), *Sociological Perspectives*, Institute of Public Administration in association with the Sociological Association of Ireland, Dublin.

Clare, A. (2000), *On Men: Masculinity in Crisis*, Chatto & Windus, UK.

Clear, C. (1995), '"The Women Can Not be Blamed": The Commission on Vocational Organisation, Feminism and "Home-makers" in Independent Ireland in the 1930s and '40s' in M. O'Dowd and S. Wichert (eds), *Chattel, Servant or Citizen. Women's Status in Church, State and Society*, The Institute of Irish Studies, Belfast: 179-186.

Coleman, D.A. (1992), 'The Demographic Transition in Ireland in International Context', in J.H. Goldthorpe and C.T. Whelan (eds), *The Development of Industrial Society in Ireland*, Oxford University Press, Oxford: 53-78.

Collins, L. (1986), *The Irish Housewife – A Portrait*, Irish Consumer Research, Dublin.

Collins, S. (1996), *The Cosgrave Legacy*, Blackwater Press, Dublin.

Commission on Emigration (1954), *Reports of the Commission on Emigration and other Population Problems 1948-1954*, Stationery Office, Dublin.

Commission on the Family (1998), *Strengthening Families for Life*, Stationery Office, Dublin.

Commission on the Relief of the Sick and Destitute Poor including the Insane Poor (Commission on Poor Relief) (1927), *Report of the Commission on Poor Relief*, Stationery Office, Dublin.

Commission on the Status of Women (1972), *Report of the Commission on the Status of Women*, Stationery Office, Dublin.

Commission on Vocational Organisation (1939), *Report of the Commission on Vocational Organisation*, Stationery Office, Dublin.

Commission on Youth Unemployment (CYU) (1951), *Report of the Commission on Youth Unemployment*, Stationery Office, Dublin.

Conference of Religious of Ireland (CORI) (1994), *Towards an Adequate Income for All*, CORI, Dublin.

Connell, K.H. (1950), *The Population of Ireland, 1750-1845*, Clarendon Press, Oxford.

--- (1968), 'Illegitimacy Before the Famine', in K.H. Connell, *Irish Peasant Society*, Clarendon Press, Oxford: 51-86.

--- (1968a), 'Catholicism and Marriage in the Century after the Famine', in K.H. Connell, *Irish Peasant Society*, Clarendon Press, Oxford: 113-61.

Connolly, J. (1910), *Labour, Nationality and Religion*, Dublin.

Connolly, J. (1935), Letter to Edward Cahill SJ, 14 May, Cahill Papers, Jesuit Archives, Dublin.

Connolly, S.J., (1985), 'Marriage in pre-famine Ireland', in A. Cosgrove (ed.), *Marriage in Ireland*, College Press, Dublin: 78-98.

Constitution of Ireland (Bunreacht na hÉireann), 1937, Stationery Office, Dublin.

Constitution Review Group (CRG) (1996), *Report of the Constitution Review Group*, Stationery Office, Dublin.

Convention on the Rights of the Child. Treaty Series, 1994, No. 3, The Stationery Office.

Conway, C. (1997), Paper on Women's Magazines in the 1930s delivered to *1930s History Seminar*, University College Dublin.

Conway, W. (1946), 'Marriage in Ireland: Church and State', *Irish Ecclesiastical Record*, 68: 361-6.

Cooney, J. (1996), 'Adopted child's religion McQuaid's main concern', *The Irish Times*, 18 March.

Cosgrove, A. (ed.) (1985), *Marriage in Ireland*, College Press, Dublin.

Costello, D. (1988), 'The Family and the Constitution', paper read to International Conference, *Progress Through the Family*, Carysfort College Dublin, unpublished.

Coughlan, A. (1988), 'The Constitution and Social Policy', in F. Litton (ed.), *The Constitution of Ireland 1937-1987*, Institute of Public Administration, Dublin: 143-61.

Coulter, C. (1997), '"Hello Divorce, Goodbye Daddy": Women, Gender, and the Divorce Debate', in A. Bradley and M. G. Valiulis (eds), *Gender and Sexuality in Modern Ireland*, University of Massachusetts Press, Amherst: 275-98.

--- (1998), 'Deserted husband looks to UN after defeat in Court' and 'Man is convinced forces denied him equal treatment, *The Irish Times*, 25 August, 1998.

Council for Social Welfare (1972), *A Statement on Social Policy*, Spiral binding.

Coyne, E. (1942/43), 'The Ethical Aspect', Contribution to 'Irish Social Services: A Symposium', *Journal of the Statistical and Social Inquiry Society of Ireland*, 17: 107-10

--- (1948), Letter to Fr David, 16 September, Coyne papers, Jesuit Archives, Dublin.

Crafts, N.F.R. (1997), 'The Human Development Index and Changes in Standards of Living: Some Historical Comparisons', *European Review of Social History*, 1: 299-322.

Crawford, V.M. (1925), 'A New Method of Wage Distribution', *Studies*, 14: 218-30.

Creighton, C. (1996), 'The Rise of the Male Breadwinner Family: A Reappraisal', Comparative Studies in Society and History, 38, 2: 310-37.

Daly, C.B. (1951), 'Family Life: The Principles', *Christus Rex*, 5: 1-19.

Daly, M.E. (1986), *The Famine in Ireland*, Dundalgan Press, Dundalk.

--- (1997), '"Oh, Kathleen Ní Houlihan, Your Way's a Thorny Way!", The Condition of Women in Twentieth-Century Ireland', in A. Bradley and M.G. Valiulis (eds) (1997): 102-26.

--- (1997a), *Women and Work in Ireland*, Dundalgen Press (W. Tempest) Ltd, Dundalk.

--- (1997b), *The Spirit of Earnest Inquiry. The Statistical and Social Inquiry of Ireland 1847-1997*, Institute of Public Administration, Dublin.

Davidoff, L. (1992), 'The family in Britain', in F.M.L. Thompson (ed.), *Cambridge Social History of Britain, 1750-1950*, Cambridge University Press, Cambridge: 71-129.

de Valera, É. (1935), Vote of Thanks to the Auditor of the Literary and Historical Society, University College Dublin, reported as 'Are We Planning Right'? *Mayo News*, 30 March, Westport.

Deeny, J. (1995), 'The Campaign Against Peri-natal Mortality', in J. Deeny, *The End of an Epidemic – Essays in Irish Public Health* (Selected and edited by Tony Farmar), A and A Farmar, Dublin: 113-35.

Dennis, N. and Erdos, G. (1993), *Families Without Fatherhood,* Institute of Economic Affairs, London.

Department of Education (1936), *Report of Commission of Inquiry into the Reformatory and Industrial School System*, Stationery Office, Dublin (Cussen Report).

Department of Finance (1958), *Economic Development*, Stationery Office, Dublin.

Department of Health, *Health Statistics*, various, Stationery Office, Dublin.

--- *Reports*, various, Stationery Office, Dublin.

Department of Justice, Equality and Law Reform (1999), *Partnership 2000 Expert Working Group on Childcare*, Stationery Office, Dublin.

Department of Local Government and Public Health (LGD). *Reports*, various, Stationery Office, Dublin.

Department of Social Welfare (1949), *White Paper on Social Security*, Stationery Office, Dublin.

--- (1950), *First Report of the Department of Social Welfare 1947-49*, Stationery Office, Dublin.

--- (1996), *Report of Expert Working Group on the Integration of the Tax and Social Welfare Systems*, Stationery Office, Dublin.

Devane, R.S. (1928), 'The Unmarried Mother and the Poor Law Commission', *Irish Ecclesiastical Record*, Fifth Series, Vol. 31: 561-82.

--- (1931), 'The Legal Protection of Girls', *Irish Ecclesiastical Record*, Fifth Series, Vol. 37: 20-40.

Devlin Committee (1969), see Public Services Organisation Review Group.

Devlin, M. (1999), 'Marriage? That's more or less irrelevant', *Irish Independent,* 2 January.

Dewar, J. (1992), *Law and the Family*, Butterworths, London.

Dignan, J. (1945), *Social Security: Outlines of a Scheme of National Health Insurance*, Champion Publications, Sligo.

Duff, F. (1961, 3rd Printing, 1989), *Miracles On Tap*, Montfort Publications, Bay Shore New York.

Dun Laoghaire College of Art & Design (DLCAD) 1997, IFC Showcase, Programme, Dublin.

Durkan, T. (1997), *Goldenbridge. A View from Valparaiso*, Veritas, Dublin.

Economic and Social Research Institute (ESRI) (1987), *Survey of Income Distribution,*

Poverty and Usage of State Services, ESRI, Dublin.

Earner, L. (1999), Paper to Irish History Society, at Trinity College, Dublin, unpublished.

Expert Working Group on the Integration of the Tax and Social Welfare Systems (1996), *Report of the Expert Working Group*, Stationery Office, Dublin.

Fahey, T. (1990), 'Measuring the Female Labour Supply: Conceptual and Procedural Problems in Irish Official Statistics', *Economic and Social Review*, 21: 163-91.

--- (1992), 'State, Family and Compulsory Schooling in Ireland', *The Economic and Social Review*, 23: 369-95.

--- (1995), 'Privacy and the Family: Conceptual and Empirical Reflections', *Sociology*, 29, 4: 687-702.

--- (1998), 'The Catholic Church and Social Policy' in S. Healy and B. Reynolds (eds), *Social Policy in Ireland. Principles, Practices and Problems*, Oak Tree Press, Dublin.

--- (1998a), 'The Agrarian Dimension in the History of the Irish Welfare State', Seminar Paper, 28 May, ESRI, Dublin.

--- (1998b), 'Childcare Policy Options', in *Budget Perspectives*, Proceedings of a Conference, 27 October, ESRI, Dublin.

Fahey, T. and FitzGerald, J. (1997), *Welfare Implications of Demographic Trends*, Oak Tree Press in association with Combat Poverty Agency, Dublin.

Fahey, T., FitzGerald, J. and Maître, B. (1997/8), 'The Economic and Social Implications of Population Change', *Journal of the Statistical and Social Inquiry Society of Ireland*, Vol. 27 (1997/1998): 182-222.

Fahey, T. and Lyons, M. (1995), *Marital Breakdown and Family Law in Ireland*, Oak Tree Press in association with ESRI, Dublin.

Family Studies Unit (1984), *The Changing Family*, University College, Dublin.

Fanning, R. (1983), *Independent Ireland*, Helicon, Dublin.

Farmar, T. (1991, reprinted 1995), *Ordinary Lives*, A and A Farmar, Dublin.

Farragher, S. P. (1984), *Dev and his Alma Mater – Éamon de Valera's Lifelong Association with Blackrock College 1898-1975*, Paraclete Press, Dublin.

Ferguson, H. (1998), Analysis of the McColgan case, *The Irish Times,* 26 January.

Ferriter, D. (1995), *Mothers, Maidens and Myths. A History of the ICA*, FÁS/Irish Countrywomen's Association, Dublin.

Ffrench, Hon. Miss (1932), Address to the Annual Assembly of the Laurel Hill Past Pupils' Union, Limerick, *Mother and Maid*, 1,1, 20 February.

Fine Gael (1965), *The Just Society*, Fine Gael, Dorset Press, Dublin.

FitzGerald, G. (1964), 'Seeking a National Purpose', *Studies*, 50:337-51.

--- (1969), 'Towards an Equitable Society, *The Irish Times*, Supplement to commemorate 50th anniversary of the First Dáil, 21 January.

--- (1991), *All in a Life,* Gill & Macmillan, Dublin and London.

--- (1998), 'The Irish Constitution in Its Historical Context', in T. Murphy and P. Twomey (eds), *Ireland's Evolving Constitution, 1937-97: Collected Essays*, Hart Publishing, Oxford: 29-40.

--- (2001), 'Women in their 30s are pushing up the birth rate', *The Irish Times,* 3 March.

Fitzpatrick, D. (1990), 'Was Ireland Special? Recent Writing on the Irish Economy and Society in the Nineteenth Century', *Historical Journal* 33(1): 169-76.

Flanagan, N. and Richardson, V. (1992), *Unmarried Mothers: a Social Profile,* University College, Dublin.

Flynn, L. (1998), 'To Be an Irishman – Constructions of Masculinity within the Constitution', in T. Murphy and P. Twomey (eds) (1998), Oxford: 135-45.

Fogarty, M., Ryan, L., Lee, J.J. (1984), *Irish Values and Attitudes. The Irish Report of the European Value Systems Study,* Dominican Publications, Dublin.

Fox Harding, L. (1996), *Family, State and Social Policy,* Macmillan, Hampshire and London.

Fox, R.M. (1935), *Rebel Irishwomen,* Talbot Press, Dublin and Cork.

--- (1957), *Louie Bennett, Her Life and Times,* Talbot Press, Dublin.

Gauthier, A-H. (1996), *The State and the Family,* Clarendon Press, Oxford.

Geary, R.C. (1954), 'Some Reflections on Irish Population Questions', *Studies,* 43: 168-77.

--- (1954/55), 'The Family in Irish Census of Population Statistics', *Journal of the Statistical and Social Inquiry Society of Ireland,* Vol. 19: 1-30.

Gibbons, L. (1984), 'From Kitchen Sink to Soap: Drama and the Serial Form on Irish Television', in M. McLoone and J. MacMahon (eds), *Television and Irish Society: 21 Years of Irish Television,* RTÉ and Irish Film Institute, Dublin.

Gilligan, R. (1991), *Irish Child Care Services,* Institute of Public Administration, Dublin.

Government of Ireland (1970), Coiste Fiosrúcháin Choras Scoileanna Ceartúcháin agus Saothair, *Tuarascáil,* 1970. Reformatory and Industrial Schools Systems, *Report* 1970, Stationery Office, Dublin (Kennedy Report).

Gray, A. (1927), *Family Endowment: A Critical Analysis,* Ernest Benn, London.

Greeley, A. and Ward, C. (2000), 'How "secularised" is the Ireland we live in?', *Doctrine and Life,* Vol. 50, No.10: 581-617.

Guinnane, T. (1997), *The Vanishing Irish. Households, Migration and the Rural Economy in Ireland, 1850-1914,* Princeton University Press, Princeton.

Hanagan, M. (1998), 'Family, Work and Wages: The Stéphanois Region of France, 1840-1914', in A. Janssens (ed.), *The Rise and Decline of the Male Breadwinner Family?* Cambridge University Press, Cambridge: 129-51.

Hannan, D. and Katsiaouni, L. (1977), *Traditional Families? From Culturally Prescribed to Negotiated Roles in Farm Families,* ESRI, Dublin.

Hantrais, L. and Letablier, M-T. (1996), *Families and Family Policy in Europe,* Addison Wesley Longman Ltd, Harlow, Essex.

Harriss, J. (1992), *The Family. A Social History of the Twentieth Century,* Harrap, London.

Healy, J. (1978), *Nineteen Acres,* Kennys, Galway.

Healy, S. and Reynolds, B. (eds) (1988), *Poverty and Family Income Policy,* CORI, Dublin.

Heanue, M. (2000), 'Matters of Life and Death', in A. Redmond (ed.), *That was then, This is now. Change in Ireland, 1949-1999*, Central Statistics Office, Dublin: 29-39.

Hearn, M. (1993), *Below Stairs. Domestic Service Remembered*, Lilliput Press, Dublin.

Heron, M. (1993), *Sheila Conroy, Fighting Spirit*, Attic Press, Dublin.

Hierarchy of the Catholic Church (1977), *The Work of Justice*, Veritas Publications, Dublin.

Hinkson, P. (1991, reprinted 1995), *Seventy Years Young. Memories of Elizabeth, Countess of Fingall*, Told to Pamela Hinkson, Lilliput Press, Dublin.

Hogan, G. (1988), 'A fresh look at Tilson's case', *Irish Jurist*, 33: 311-32.

Horgan, J. (2000), *Noël Browne, Passionate Outsider*, Gill & Macmillan, Dublin.

Hourihane, A-M. (1997), 'Mags for swinging moderns', *Sunday Tribune*, 30 November.

Humphreys, A. J. (1966), *New Dubliners. Urbanization and the Irish Family*, Routledge and Kegan Paul, London.

Inglis, T. (1987), *Moral Monopoly. The Catholic Church in Modern Irish Society*, Gill & Macmillan, Dublin.

Inter-Departmental Committee on Raising the School Leaving Age (IDCRA) (1935), *Report of the Inter-Departmental Committee on Raising the School Leaving Age*, Stationery Office, Dublin.

ICTU (1982), *Twenty-Fourth Annual Report*, ICTU, Dublin.

--- (1983), *Twenty-Fifth Annual Report*, ICTU, Dublin.

--- (1984), *Submission to the Oireachtas Joint Committee on Marriage Breakdown*, typescript, January.

--- (1985), *Report of Proceedings at Annual Delegate Conference*, ICTU, Dublin.

--- (1986), *Twenty-Eight Annual Report*, ICTU, Dublin.

Irish Medical Association (IMA) (1958), 'Ten Fruitful Years', anon., *Journal of the Irish Medical Association*, XL, 250.

Irish Vocational Education Association (IVEA) (1947), *Forty-Third Congress Report*, IVEA, Dublin.

Janssens, A. (ed.) (1998), *The Rise and Decline of the Male Breadwinner Family?*, Cambridge University Press, Cambridge.

Kaim-Caudle, P.R. (1964), *Social Security in Ireland and Western Europe*, ERI, Dublin.

Kane, R. SJ (1910), *The Plain Gold Ring. Lectures on Home*, Longmans Green & Co., London.

Kane Papers, Jesuit Archives, Dublin.

Kangas, I. (1997), *SEW – Situation of Elderly Women. Four life stories of grandmothers on the fringes of the European Union*, STAKES, Helsinki.

Kaufmann, F-X., Kuijsten A., Schulze H-J., and Strohmeier, K-P. (eds) (1997), *Family Life and Family Policies in Europe, Volume 1, Structures and Trends in the 1980s*, Clarendon Press, Oxford.

Kavanagh, P. (1971 edn), *The Green Fool*, Penguin Books.

Kearns, K. C. (1994), *Dublin Tenement Life – An Oral History*, Gill & Macmillan, Dublin.

Kelly, A. (1998), 'Catholic Action and the Development of the Irish Welfare State in the 1930s and 1940s', Paper to the Irish Catholic Historical Committee Conference, All Hallows, Drumcondra, Dublin: 1-25.

Kelly, J. (1980), *The Irish Constitution*, Jurist Publishing Company, Dublin.

Kennedy, F. (1989, reprinted 1991), *Family, Economy and Government in Ireland*, ESRI, Dublin.

--- (1997), 'The Course of the Irish Welfare State', in F. Ó Muircheartaigh (ed.), *Ireland in the Coming Times. Essays to Celebrate T.K. Whitaker's 80 Years,* Institute of Public Administration, Dublin.

--- (1998), 'Two Priests, the Family and the Irish Constitution', *Studies*, Vol. 87: 353-64.

--- (2000), 'The Suppression of the Carrigan Report', *Studies*, Vol. 89: 354-63.

Kennedy, F. and McCormack, K. (1997), 'Marriage Loses Popularity', in Kaufmann *et al* (eds) (1997), Clarendon Press, Oxford: 195-224.

Kennedy, K., Giblin, T. and McHugh, D. (1988), *The Economic Development of Ireland in the Twentieth Century*, Routledge, London and New York.

Kennedy, R.E. (1973), *The Irish – Emigration, Marriage and Fertility*, University of California Press, San Francisco.

Keogh, D. (1995), *Ireland and the Vatican: the policy and diplomacy of Church-State relations 1922-1960*, Cork University Press, Cork.

Kernthaler, I., Trnka, S. and Wintersberger, H. (1999), '10th Anniversary of the European Observatory on Family Matters', *Family Observer*, Commission of the European Communities, Luxembourg: 4-6.

Kerrigan, G. (1998), *Another Country. Growing Up in '50s Ireland*, Gill & Macmillan, Dublin.

Kiely, G. (1986), 'Church, State and Family Policy', *Studies*, 75: 150-56.

--- (ed.) (1992), *In and Out of Marriage: Irish and European Experience*, University College, Dublin.

Kiely, G. and Richardson, V. (eds) 1991, *Family Policy: European Perspectives*, University College, Dublin.

Kiernan, K.E. (1992), 'The Respective Roles of Men and Women in Tomorrow's Europe', *Human Resources in Europe at the Dawn of the 21st Century*, Eurostat, Luxembourg.

Killanin (1918-19), *Report of the Vice-Regal Committee of Enquiry into Primary Education (Ireland) 1918-1919* (Killanin Committee).

Kirwin, B. (1989), 'The Social Policy of *The Bell*', *Administration*, 37: 99-118.

Kuijsten, A. (1994), 'Variation and Change in Family Forms in the 1980s', Paper presented to Working Group on the Family, Bielefeld: 1-44.

Labour Force Surveys, (1986, 1996), Stationery Office, Dublin.

Larson Pyle, J. (1990), *The State and Women in the Economy: Lessons from Sex Discrimination in the Republic of Ireland*, State University of New York Press, Albany.

Law Reform Commission, The (1994), *Consultation Paper on Family Courts*, Law Reform Commission, Ireland.

--- (1996), *Report on Family Courts*, Law Reform Commission, Ireland.

Lee, J.J. (1984), 'Reflections on the Study of Irish Values', in M. Fogarty *et al* (1984): 107-24.

--- (1989), *Ireland 1912-1985: Politics and Society*, Cambridge University Press, Cambridge.

Legion of Mary (1993), *The Official Handbook of the Legion of Mary*, Concilium Legionis Mariae, Dublin.

Leibell, J.F. (ed.) (1926), *Readings In Ethics*, Loyola University Press, Chicago.

Leslie, S. (1937), Introduction to Mary Carbery, *The Farm by Lough Gur,* Longmans, Green and Co., London.

Levine, J. (1982), *Sisters*, Ward River Press, Dublin.

Lewis, J. (1984), *Women in England 1870-1950*, Wheatsheaf Books, Sussex.

LGD, various. Department of Local Government and Public Health, *Reports*, Stationery Office, Dublin.

Longfield, M. (1871-76), 'The Limits of State Interference with the Distribution of Wealth in Applying Taxation to the Assistance of the Public', *Journal of the Statistical and Social Inquiry Society of Ireland*, 6: 107-8.

Luce, A.A. (1954), Reservation no. 6 to Commission on Emigration, 1948-54: 230-31.

Lucey, C. (1954), in J.A. O'Brien (ed.), *The Vanishing Irish*, W.H. Allen, London, foreword.

--- (1954a), *Minority Report of Most Rev Dr C. Lucey*, Commission on Emigration, 1948-54: 335-63.

Luddy, M. and Murphy, C. (eds) (1989), *Women Surviving. Studies in Irish Women's History in the 19th and 20th Centuries*, Poolbeg, Dublin.

Lutz, W. (1999), 'Will Europe be Short of Children?', *Family Observer*, 10th Anniversary Issue: 8-16, Commission of the European Communities, Luxembourg.

Lynch, P. (nom de plûme, Brian O'Kennedy) (1945), 'À propos of Dr Dignan', *The Bell,* 10: 384-94.

--- (1953), 'The Economist and Public Policy', *Studies,* 42: 241-60.

--- (1966), 'The Social Revolution that Never Was', D. Williams (ed.), *The Irish Struggle, 1916-1926,* Routledge and Kegan Paul, London:

--- (1998), Communication with author, 6 March.

Lyons, F.S.L. (1977), *Charles Stewart Parnell*, Collins, London.

Lyons, M. (2000), 'Retiring Microsoft executive broke management mould', *The Irish Times*, Business This Week, 31 March.

Lysaght, C. (1998), 'Crime and Punishment', in K.A. Kennedy (ed.), *From Famine to Feast. Economic and Social Change in Ireland 1847-1997*, Institute of Public Administration, Dublin.

McCafferty, N. (1985), *A Woman to Blame*, Attic Press, Dublin.

--- (1998), 'Back on the train – this time for childcare', *Sunday Tribune*, 18 October.

McCarthy, I.C. (ed.) (1995), *Irish Family Studies: Selected Papers*, University College Dublin.

McCarthy, I.C. and Byrne, N. O'R. (1988), 'Mis-Taken Love: Conversations on the Problem of Incest in an Irish Context', *Family Process*, 27: 181-99.

McCarthy, M. (1990), *Early Days,* Kildanore Press, Dublin.

McCashin, A. (1993), *Lone Parents in the Republic of Ireland*, ESRI, Dublin.

McCormack, I. (1983), 'National Statutory Minimum Wage', in ICTU, *Report of Proceedings at Annual Delegate Conference 1983*, ICTU, Dublin.

McCourt, F. (1996), *Angela's Ashes*, Harper Collins, London.

McCullagh, C. (1991), 'A Tie That Blinds: Family and Ideology in Ireland', *Economic and Social Review,* 22: 199-211.

MacCurtain, M. (1989), 'Fullness of Life: Defining Female Spirituality in Twentieth Century Ireland, in M. Luddy and C. Murphy (eds) (1989).

MacDonagh, O. (1991), *O'Connell. The Life of Daniel O'Connell 1775-1847,* Weidenfeld and Nicolson, London.

MacGill, P. (1983), *Glenmoran*, Brandon, Dingle. First published by Herbert Jenkins.

McKay, S. (1996), Interview with Catriona Crowe, *Sunday Tribune*, 10 March.

--- (1998), *Sophia's Story,* Gill & Macmillan, Dublin.

McKenna, A. (1988), *Childcare and Equal Opportunities*, Employment Equality Agency, Dublin.

McKeown, K., Ferguson, H. and Rooney, D. (1998), *Changing Fathers? Fatherhood and Family Life in Modern Ireland*, Collins Press, Cork.

McKevitt, P. (1943), 'The Beveridge Plan Reviewed', *Irish Ecclesiastical Record,* 61: 145-50.

McLaughlin, B. (1999), 'GPs want clear guidelines on sex advice for under-age girls', *The Irish Times*, 17 May 1999.

McLoone, M. and MacMahon, J. (eds) (1984), *Television and Irish Society: 21 Years of Irish Television*, RTÉ and Irish Film Institute, Dublin.

MacMahon, B. (1967), 'The Holy Kiss, in A. Martin (ed.) (1967):139-48.

McNabb, P. (1964), 'Social Structure', in J. Newman (ed.) *The Limerick Rural Survey*, 1958-64, Muintir na Tíre, Tipperary: 193-247.

MacNeely, L. and O'Brien, G. (1938), 'A Note on Some Aspects of Papal Encyclicals in Relation to the Terms of Reference of the Commission', in *Reports of the Commission of Inquiry into Banking, Currency and Credit 1938,* Stationery Office, Dublin: 502-10.

McPolin, J. (1947), 'Public Health Bill', *Christus Rex*, 1: 3-16.

MacSharry, R. and White, P. (2000), *The Making of the Celtic Tiger*, Mercier Press, Cork.

Manning, M. (1999), *James Dillon. A Biography*, Wolfhound, Dublin.

Manning, M. and McDowell, M. (1985), *Electricity Supply In Ireland. The History of the ESB*, Gill & Macmillan, Dublin.

Manning Robertson, O. (1945), 'Court Circular', *The Bell*, 10: 395-401.

Martin, A. (ed.) (1967), *Exploring English 1*, Gill & Macmillan Ltd and Educational Co., Dublin.

Marshall, A. (1920), 8th edn, *Principles of Economics*, Macmillan, London.

Meehan, I. (1959), 'Woman's Place in the Community', *Christus Rex,* 13: 90-102.

Meenan, J. (1933), 'Some Causes and Consequences of the Low Irish Marriage Rate', *Journal of the Statistical and Social Inquiry Society of Ireland*:19-27.

--- (1962), 'Studies 1912-1962', *Studies*, 51: 1-8.

--- (1970), *The Irish Economy since 1922*, Liverpool University Press, Liverpool.

Micklewright, J. and Stewart, K. (1999), 'Is the well-being of children converging in the European Union?', *The Economic Journal*, 109 (November), F692-F714.

Minister for Education (1963), Statement of the Minister for Education in regard to Post-Primary Education.

Model Housekeeping (1934), Picture and Commentary on 'Mr Frank Aiken's Wedding Cake', 7:1.

Mokyr, J. (1985), *Why Ireland Starved: A Quantitative and Analytical History of the Irish Economy, 1800-1850*, Allen and Unwin, London.

Moloney, H. and Curtayne, A. (1935), 'Women's Status in Ireland', *Model Housekeeping,* 7: 10, August.

Morgan, E. (1999), 'House Prices this Century, *The Irish Times*, 2 December, Property 3.

MRBI (1983), *The People of Ireland, How They See Themselves*, 21st Anniversary Survey, Marketing Bureau of Ireland, Dublin.

--- (1987), *Éire Inníu*, 25th Anniversary Survey, Marketing Bureau of Ireland, Dublin.

--- (1992), *Mná na hÉireann, An MRBI Perspective on Women in Irish Society Today*, 30th Anniversary Survey, Marketing Bureau of Ireland.

Murphy, H. (1952), 'The Rural Family: The Principles', *Christus Rex,* 6: 3-20.

Murphy, W. and Rouse, P. (1999), 'Tillage versus mixed farming', *Irish Farmers' Journal*, 25 December, 1999: 13.

Murray, E.J. (1954), 'The Key to the Problem', in J.A. O'Brien (ed.), *The Vanishing Irish*, W.H. Allen, London: 65-77.

National Council for the Aged (1988), *Caring for the Elderly, Part 1: A Study of Carers at Home and in the Community*, Stationery Office, Dublin.

National Economic and Social Council (NESC) (1980), *Alternative Strategies for Family Income Support*, Stationery Office, Dublin.

National Women's Council of Ireland (1998), *Caring for All Our Futures*, National Women's Council of Ireland, Dublin.

Nic Ghiolla Phádraigh, M. (1995), 'The Power of the Catholic Church in the Republic of Ireland', in P. Clancy *et al* (eds) (1995), IPA, Dublin: 593-619.

Nolan, B. and Callan, T. (eds) (1994), *Poverty and Policy in Ireland*, Gill & Macmillan, Dublin.

Nolan, B. and Farrell, B. (eds) (1990), *Child Poverty in Ireland*, Combat Poverty Agency, Dublin.

Norris, D. (1998), *The Development of the Gay Movement in Ireland. A Personal and Political Memoir.* Chapter for a book published in Holland sent to the author, 3 March, 1998.

O'Brien, G. (1936), 'Patrick Hogan. Minister for Agriculture 1922-1932', *Studies*, 25: 353-68.

O'Brien, G. (1962), 'The Economic Progress of Ireland', *Studies*, 51: 9-26.

O'Brien, J. A. (ed.) (1954), *The Vanishing Irish*, W.H. Allen, London.

O'Brien, M. (ed.) (1995), *Divorce? Facing the Issues of Marital Breakdown*, Basement Press, Dublin.

Ó Broin, L. (1982), *Frank Duff. An Autobiography*, Gill & Macmillan, Dublin.

Ó Cearúil, M. (1999), *Bunreacht na hÉireann. A study of the Irish text*, Stationery Office, Dublin.

Ó Cinnéide, S. (1969), 'The Development of the Home Assistance Service', *Administration*, 17: 284-308.

--- (1994), 'Family Income Support over 50 Years', paper read to Conference on the Family, Dublin Castle, September, unpublished.

O'Connor, F. (1967), 'First Confession', in A. Martin (ed.) (1967): 65-73.

O'Connor, K. (1994), 'The Cruel End of Honour Bright in K. O'Connor, I. Craigie, F. Daly, C. O'Shannon and T. Reddy, *Thou Shalt Not Kill,* Gill & Macmillan, Dublin: 107-12.

O'Connor, P. (1998), *Emerging Voices. Women in Contemporary Irish Society*, Institute of Public Administration, Dublin.

O'Connor, R. (nd.), *My Life and Times*, unpublished.

O'Daly, N. and Ó Cinnéide, S. (1980), *Supplementary Report* to Task Force on Child Care Services. *Final Report to the Minister for Health*, Stationery Office, Dublin: 279-407.

Ó Danachair, C. (1962), 'The Family in Irish Tradition', *Christus Rex, XVI*, 3:185-196, July.

--- (1985), 'Marriage in Irish folk tradition' in A. Cosgrove (ed.) (1985): 99-115.

O'Donnell, L. (1997), *The Days of the Servant Boy*, Mercier Press, Cork and Dublin.

O'Dowd, M. and Wichert, S. (eds) (1995), *Chattel, Servant or Citizen. Women's Status in Church, State and Society*, Institute of Irish Studies, Queen's University, Belfast.

O'Faolain, S. (1940), 'This is Your Magazine', *The Bell*, 1: 5-9.

--- (1951), 'The Dáil and the Bishops', *The Bell*, 17, 3:5-13.

--- (1954), 'Love among the Irish', in J.A. O'Brien (ed.) (1954): 105-16.

Ó Fiaich, T. (1991), Letter to Doctor FitzGerald, in FitzGerald (1991): 648-50.

Ó Gráda, C. (1994), *Ireland: A New Economic History, 1780-1939*, Oxford University Press, New York.

--- (1997), *A Rocky Road: The Irish Economy since the 1920s,* Manchester University Press, Manchester.

--- (1998), 'The Rise in Living Standards', in Kieran A. Kennedy (ed.), *From Famine to Feast. Economic and Social Change in Ireland 1847-1997*, Institute of Public Administration, Dublin: 12-22.

Ó hÓgartaigh, M. (1997), Ph.D. thesis, NUI, unpublished.

O'Leary, E. (1987), 'The Irish National Teachers' Organisation and the Marriage Bar for Women National Teachers 1933-58', *Saothar*, 12: 47-52.

O'Mahony, (1996), *Criminal Chaos. Seven Crises in Irish Criminal Justice*, Round Hall Sweet & Maxwell, Dublin.

O'Malley, T. (1996), *Sexual Offences: Law Policy and Punishment*, Round Hall Sweet & Maxwell, Dublin.

Ó Muircheartaigh, F.S. (1976/77), 'The Changing Burden of Personal Income Tax in Ireland and the Social Valuation of Income 1946-76', *Journal of the Statistical and Social Inquiry Society of Ireland*, Vol. 23, Part 4.

O'Rahilly, A. (1948), *Social Principles*, Cork University Press, Cork.

O'Rahilly, A. (1948), *Moral Principles*, Cork University Press, Cork.

O'Sullivan, M. (1994), *Seán Lemass. A Biography*, Blackwater Press.

O'Toole, A. (1995), Interview with Margaret Hayes, *Sunday Business Post*, 23 July.

Ó Tuathaigh, G. (1998), 'Land and Society', in K.A. Kennedy (ed.), *From Famine to Feast. Economic and Social Change in Ireland 1847-1997*, Institute of Public Administration, Dublin: 38-49.

OECD Survey Team on Education (1965), Report of the Survey Team Appointed by the Minister for Education in 1962, *Investment in Education*, Stationery Office, Dublin.

Office of Population Censuses and Surveys (1994), *Report*, HMSO, London.

Office of the Minister for Justice (1992), *Marital Breakdown: a Review and Proposed Changes*, White Paper, Stationery Office, Dublin.

Oireachtas Committee (1967), *Report of the Informal Committee on the Constitution*, Stationery Office, Dublin.

Papal Encyclicals – *Casti Connubii, Rerum Novarum, Quadragesimo Anno*.

Parliamentary Debates Dáil Éireann (PDDE), various.

Parliamentary Debates Seanad Éireann (PDSE), various.

Pearse, P. (1912), 'The Murder Machine', *The Complete Works of P. H. Pearse. Political Writings and Speeches*, The Phoenix Publishing Co. Ltd, Dublin, Cork, Belfast: 5-50.

Pedersen, S. (1995), *Family, Dependence and the Origins of the Welfare State: Britain and France, 1914-1945*, Cambridge University Press, Cambridge.

Philbin, W. (1957), 'A City on a Hill', *Studies*, 46: 259-70.

Pihl, L. (1999), '"A Muzzle Made in Ireland": Irish Censorship and Signe Toksvig', *Studies, 88*, 352: 448-57.

Public Services Organisation Review Group (1969), *Report of Public Services Organisation Review Group 1966-69*. Presented to the Minister for Finance (Devlin Committee Report), Stationery Office, Dublin.

Punch, A. (1999), 'Irish Demographic Trends. Impact on the Family', Paper to UCD Family Conference, 13 November.

Punch, A. and Finneran, C. (2000), 'Changing Population Structure', in A. Redmond (ed.), *That was then, This is now. Change in Ireland, 1949-1999*, Central Statistics Office, Dublin: 13-23.

Quarterly National Household Survey (2000), Central Statistics Office, Dublin.

Quentin, O. (1999), Editorial, *Family Observer*, European Communities, Luxembourg.

Quinn, B. (1999), 'Journalism and Child Abuse', Letter to the Editor, *The Irish Times*, 11 May.

Raftery, M. and O'Sullivan, E. (1999), *Suffer the Little Children*, New Island, Dublin.

Rathbone, E. (1924), *The Disinherited Family*, Edward Arnold, London.

Redmond, A. and Heanue, M. (2000), 'Aspects of Society', in A. Redmond (ed.), *That was then, This is now. Change in Ireland, 1949-1999*: 45-66.

Reid, G. (1901), 'Infant Mortality and the Employment of Married Women in Factories', *British Medical Journal*: 410-12.

Reynolds, B. and Healy, S. (eds) (1988), *Poverty and Family Income Policy*, Conference of Major Religious Superiors (Ireland), Dublin.

Riordan, P. (1995), 'Creating Space for Debate: The Catholic Church's Contribution', in M. O'Brien (ed.), *Divorce? Facing the Issues of Marital Breakdown*, Basement Press, Dublin: 123-30.

Rohan, D. (1969), *Marriage Irish Style*, Mercier Press, Cork.

Rottman, D.B., Hannan, D., Hardiman, N. and Wiley, M. (1982), *The Distribution of Income in the Republic of Ireland: A Study in Social Class and Family-cycle Inequalities*, ESRI, Dublin.

Rowthorn, R. (1999), 'Marriage and trust: some lessons from economics', *Cambridge Journal of Economics,* 23, 5: 661-91.

Russell, E. (1997), Paper to '1930s History Symposium', University College Dublin.

Russell Scrapbooks (nd), Scrapbooks of Dr Angela Russell.

Ryan, J.A. (1926), 'A Living Wage', in Leibell (ed.) (1926): 687-98.

Ryan, L. (1979), 'Church and Politics. The Last Twenty-five Years', *The Furrow*, 30, 1: 3-18.

--- (1984), 'The Changing Face of Irish Values', in M. Fogarty *et al* (1984): 95-106.

Ryan, M. (1993) (ed.), *The Church and the Nation. The Vision of Peter Birch Bishop of Ossory 1964-1981*, Columba Press, Dublin.

Sammon, P.J. (1997), *In The Land Commission. A Memoir 1933-1978*, Ashfield Press, Dublin.

Second Commission on the Status of Women (1993), *Report,* Stationery Office, Dublin.

Second Programme for Economic Expansion (*SPEE*) (1963, Part 1), (1964, Part 2), Stationery Office, Dublin.

Shatter, A. J. (1997, 4th edn), *Family Law in the Republic of Ireland*, Butterworths, Dublin.

--- (1998), Analysis of the McColgan Case, *The Irish Times*, 5 February.

Sheridan, J.D. (1954), 'We're Not Dead Yet', in J.A. O'Brien (ed.) (1954): 177-92.

Smith, A. (1969 edn), *The Theory of Moral Sentiments*, Liberty Fund, Indianapolis.

Smith, P. (1959), *Esther's Altar*, Abelard-Schumann, London, New York.

--- (1975), *The Countrywoman*, Quartet Books, London. First published Heinemann, 1962.

Soffe, E. (1997), *The Need For Widow's Pensions In Ireland*, a thesis submitted in partial fulfilment of the B A in Public Management, Institute of Public Administration, Dublin, unpublished.

Sullivan, A. M. (1952), *The Last Serjeant. The Memoirs of Serjeant A. M. Sullivan Q.C.*, Macdonald, London.

Sweeney, G. (1990), *In Public Service*, Institute of Public Administration, Dublin.

Swift, J.P. (1991), *John Swift. An Irish Dissident*, Gill & Macmillan, Dublin.

Task Force on Child Care Services (1980), *Final Report to the Minister for Health*, Stationery Office, Dublin.

Thomas, J. (1954), 'The Catholic Family in a Complex Society', *Social Order*, 4, 10: 451-7.

Travers, P. (1995), 'Emigration and Gender: the Case of Ireland 1922-1960', in M. O'Dowd and S. Wichert (eds) (1995):187-99.

Treacy, J. and O'Connell, N. (2000), 'Labour Market', in A. Redmond (ed.), *That was then, This is now. Change in Ireland 1949-1999*, Central Statistics Office, Dublin: 105-113.

Tweedy, H. (1992), *A Link in the Chain. The Story of the Irish Housewives' Association 1942-1992,* Attic Press, Dublin.

United Nations (1998), *Recommendations for the 2000 Censuses of Population and Housing in the ECE Region*, United Nations, Statistical Standards and Studies, No. 49.

Valiulis, M. (1995), 'Neither Feminist or Flapper: the Ecclesiastical Construction of the Ideal Irish Woman', in M. O'Dowd and S. Wichert (eds) (1995): 168-78.

Van de Kaa, D.J. (1987), 'Europe's Second Demographic Transition', *Population Bulletin*, 42, 1, Population Reference Bureau, Washington DC.

von Ketteler, W. (1926), 'Social Reform', in Leibell (ed.) (1926): 631-9.

Waldron, J. (1950), 'An Ríoghacht – a retrospect', *Irish Monthly*, 78, 924: 274-80.

Walsh, B. (1988), 'The Constitution and Constitutional Rights', in F. Litton (ed.), *The Constitution of Ireland 1937-1987*, Institute of Public Administration, Dublin.

Walsh, B.M. (1970), 'Marriage rates and population pressure, Ireland 1871 and 1911,' in *Economic History Review*, 23:148-62.

---- (1970a), 'A Study of Irish County Marriage Rates, 1961-1966', *Population Studies*, Vol. 24, No. 2: 205-16.

--- (1972), 'Trends in Age at Marriage in Post-war Ireland', Demography, Vol. 9, No. 2:187-202.

--- (1986), 'The Growth of Government', in K.A. Kennedy (ed.), *Ireland in Transition*, The Mercier Press in Association with Radio Telefís Éireann, Cork and Dublin: 62-70.

--- (1993), 'Labour Force Participation and the Growth of Women's Employment, Ireland 1971-1991', *Economic and Social Review*, 24:369-400.

--- (1995), 'Marriage and Fertility in Ireland', Paper read to the Merriman Summer School, Co. Clare, unpublished.

Ward, P. (1993), *Divorce in Ireland: Who Should Bear the Cost?*, Cork University Press, Cork.

Waring, M. (1990), *If Women Counted: A New Feminist Economics*, Harper and Collins, San Francisco.

Weigel, G. (1992), 'Catholicism and Democracy: The "Other Twentieth-Century

Revolution"', in G.L. Anderson and M.A. Kaplan (eds), *Morality and Religion* in Liberal Democratic Societies, Paragon House, New York: 223-50.

Whelan, B.J. and Vaughan, R.N. (1982), *The Economic Circumstances of the Elderly in Ireland*, ESRI, Dublin.

Whyte, J. (1980), 2nd edn, *Church and State in Modern Ireland*, Gill & Macmillan, Dublin and Barnes and Noble, New Jersey.

Wintersberger, H. (1999), 'Work viewed from a Childhood Perspective', *Family Observer*, Commission of the European Communities, Luxembourg: 18-24.

Wood, K. and O'Shea, P. (1997), *Divorce in Ireland*, O'Brien Press, Dublin.

Working Group (1999), *Report of the Working Group Examining the Treatment of Married, Cohabiting and One-Parent Families under the Tax and Social Welfare Codes*, Stationery Office, Dublin.

Wylie, J.C.W. (1975), *Irish Land Law,* Professional Books, London.

Index